PENGUIN

PENGUIN SELECT[
GENERAL EDITOR: CHRISTOPHER RICKS

SELECTED POEMS OF ROBERT HENRYSON
AND WILLIAM DUNBAR

ROBERT HENRYSON (*c*.1420–*c*.1505) is the outstanding poet of the flourishing literary culture of late medieval Scotland. Almost nothing is known of his life except that he was a university graduate and schoolmaster at Dunfermline. His works, however, reveal a sophisticated, humane writer delighting in irony and combining grave and earnest morality with witty comedy and satire. His *Fables* make the simple animal fable into a work of art and *The Testament of Cresseid* offers a powerful and sombre account of the fate of the heroine of Chaucer's *Troilus and Criseyde*. His death is recorded by Dunbar in his 'Lament for the Makars' (1505–6).

WILLIAM DUNBAR (*c*.1460–*c*.1513) was Henryson's younger contemporary, and was also a graduate (perhaps of St Andrews). He was a priest and a member of the royal household where he may have served as a chaplain, a secetary or an envoy. Dunbar writes on public and private events both great and small and his poems range from the ecstatically religious to the frankly bawdy. Formal allegorical dream-visions like *The Goldyn Targe* or *The Thrissill and the Rois* (1503) stand alongside the exuberant *Twa Mariit Wemen and the Wedo*, a lively descendant of Chaucer's Wife of Bath's Prologue in the *Canterbury Tales*. His poetry is marked by a dynamic energy of language and a dazzling display of stylistic skills.

DOUGLAS GRAY was born in 1930 and educated at Wellington College, Wellington, New Zealand, and at the Victoria University of Wellington. He continued his studies at Merton College, Oxford, and taught medieval literature at Oxford for many years, firstly at Pembroke College and then from 1980 to 1997 as the J. R. R. Tolkien Professor of English Literature and Language at Lady Margaret Hall. He is the author of many articles and books, including *Themes and Images in the Medieval English Religious Lyric*, *Robert Henryson*, and *The Oxford Book of Late Medieval Verse and Prose*. He is a member of the council of the Early English Text Society and a Fellow of the British Academy.

SELECTED POEMS OF ROBERT HENRYSON AND WILLIAM DUNBAR

Edited by DOUGLAS GRAY

PENGUIN BOOKS

PENGUIN BOOKS

Published by the Penguin Group
Penguin Books Ltd, 27 Wrights Lane, London w8 5TZ, England
Penguin Putnam Inc., 375 Hudson Street, New York, New York 10014, USA
Penguin Books Australia Ltd, Ringwood, Victoria, Australia
Penguin Books Canada Ltd, 10 Alcorn Avenue, Toronto, Ontario, Canada M4V 3B2
Penguin Books (NZ) Ltd, Private Bag 102902, NSMC, Auckland, New Zealand

Penguin Books Ltd, Registered Offices: Harmondsworth, Middlesex, England

First published in Penguin Classics 1998
10 9 8 7 6 5 4 3 2 1

Set in 10/11.5 pt PostScript Monotype Ehrhardt
Typeset by Rowland Phototypesetting Ltd, Bury St Edmunds, Suffolk
Printed in England by Clays Ltd, St Ives plc

CONTENTS

PREFACE   vii
ACKNOWLEDGEMENTS   x
TABLE OF DATES   xi
NOTE ON LANGUAGE   xiii
FURTHER READING   xiv
THE TEXTS   xv

ROBERT HENRYSON

Robene and Makyne   3
The Testament of Cresseid   10
Orpheus and Eurydice (extract)   41

The Fables   50
The Prologue   50
The Cock and the Jasp   53
The Two Mice   58
The Cock and the Fox   70
The Fox and the Wolf   81
The Trial of the Fox   91
The Sheep and the Dog   110
The Lion and the Mouse   119
The Preaching of the Swallow   134
The Fox, the Wolf, and the Cadger   151
The Fox, the Wolf, and the Husbandman   166
The Wolf and the Wether   178
The Wolf and the Lamb   187
The Paddock and the Mouse   196

The Ressoning betuix Deth and Man   208
The Annunciation   211

WILLIAM DUNBAR

Rorate Celi Desuper   217

Done is a battell on the dragon blak   220

Hale, sterne superne   223

My heid did yak yester nicht   227

Sir Jhon Sinclair begowthe to dance   228

The wardraipper of Venus boure   231

O gracious Princes, guid and fair   233

This waverand warldis wretchidnes   235

Schir, lat it never in toune be tald   241

Schir, ye have mony servitouris   245

The Flyting of Dunbar and Kennedy (extract)   249

We that ar heir in hevynnis glorie   258

Now lythis off ane gentill knycht   264

As yung Awrora with cristall haile (*The Abbot of Tungland*)   267

This hyndir nycht in Dumfermling   274

In secreit place this hyndir nycht   281

Apon the midsummer evin, mirriest of nichtis (*The Tretis of
    the Twa Mariit Wemen and the Wedo*)   282

Quhy will ye, merchantis of renoun   310

Sweit rois of vertew and of gentilnes   314

Ryght as the stern of day begouth to schyne (*The Goldyn
    Targe*)   315

Quhen Merche wes with variand windis past (*The Thrissill and
    the Rois*)   330

Illuster Lodovick, of France most Cristin king (*Lament for
    Lord Bernard Stewart*)   340

Quhat is this lyfe bot ane straucht way to deid?   342

Quhom to sall I compleine my wo   343

Into thir dirk and drublie dayis   348

I that in heill wes and gladnes (*The Lament for the
    Makars*)   351

Full oft I mus and hes in thocht   357

TEXTUAL SOURCES AND ABBREVIATIONS   361

NOTES   363

LIST OF SOME COMMON WORDS AND FORMS   402

FIRST LINES AND TITLES   407

In the fifteenth and early sixteenth centuries Scottish poetry enjoyed a period of great creativity of which two excellent poets, Robert Henryson and William Dunbar, represent the high point. They are not isolated figures, but part of a company that includes Gavin Douglas the translator of Virgil, Richard Holland and Hary, and the other poets listed in Dunbar's *Lament for the Makars*, and many whose names are lost. They inherited and developed a tradition of considerable variety – heroic narrative in John Barbour's fourteenth-century *Bruce*, Chaucerian allegorical dream-poetry in the earlier fifteenth-century *Kingis Quair* attributed to King James I, romances, alliterative poetry, religious and didactic poetry, and lyrics. Perhaps Henryson and Dunbar might have been surprised to find themselves in a series devoted to *English* poets but, since they were citizens of what was then a proudly independent kingdom, they might not have felt the need to protest in the way some modern Scottish poets would. Indeed, they are aware that the Lowland Scots in which they write is a distinctive northern version of the English language, 'oure Inglisch' as Dunbar calls it in *The Goldyn Targe*. Furthermore, they both express their admiration of and devotion to their great predecessor Chaucer, who was, Dunbar says, 'of oure Inglisch all the lycht' – although it should be said clearly that the crude old label of 'Scottish Chaucerian' which used to be attached to them in no way does justice to their independence or to the intelligent ways in which they respond to the English poet.

Very little is known of their lives. Robert Henryson was dead by 1505, the date of Dunbar's *Lament for the Makars*. There he is also called 'Maister', i.e. a university graduate, and associated with Dunfermline (confirmed by the early printed texts which often refer to him as 'schoolmaster of Dunfermline'). The other references are less certain. He is often identified with a 'Magister Robertus Henrisone' who was incorporated as a graduate member of the University of Glasgow in 1462 (if so, the adjective used of this man, 'venerabilis', might suggest that he was not then very young, and may have been born in the 1420s) and also with a notary public of the same name who witnessed deeds for the Abbot of Dunfermline in 1477-8 (the first three recorded schoolmasters of Dunfermline were notaries, and the poet Henryson shows a good knowledge of legal procedures and terminology).

William Dunbar appears more frequently in records, but we still have only scraps. It is quite likely that he is the William Dunbar who graduated from St Andrews as a Master in 1479 (if so, it would suggest that he was born c.1460). Then we hear nothing of him until 1501, when a note of the payment of his salary for 1500-1501 remarks that it was paid to him 'after he came out of England', where he may have been part of the embassy negotiating the betrothal of James IV and Margaret Tudor. From 1501 to 1513 the accounts of the Lord High Treasurer record regular payments of a salary to him as a member of the royal household. He had become a priest by March 1503-4, but does not seem to have received a benefice or ecclesiastical preferment (a fact which he mentions several times in his poems with a good deal of feeling). It is not clear what his duties as one of the king's 'servitouris' were: perhaps he acted as secretary, envoy, or chaplain. The last reference to him is on 14 May 1513; he was probably dead by 1515 at the latest (the accounts from August 1513 to June 1515 have been lost).

Fortunately these half-anonymous poets have lived on in their poetry. The 'voices' that we hear there are in many ways strikingly dissimilar. That of Henryson is more consistent: there is a coherence about his works from which a distinct poetic individuality emerges. His voice is often grave and serious (especially when he is faced with examples of oppression and injustice or of violent death) but capable of delicate comedy and irony. His characteristic combination of detachment and compassion produces some of the most impressive scenes of pathos in late medieval literature. It is narrative poetry which shows his skills at their best. His two masterpieces, *The Testament of Cresseid* and *The Fables*, are here given in full, together with an extract from *Orpheus and Eurydice*. Twelve shorter poems can be attributed to him with some degree of certainty. Of these three are included, because of their intrinsic interest and because they afford points of comparison with Dunbar – a witty pastoral wooing, a poem on death, and another religious poem on the Annunciation.

Dunbar (who in general prefers the shorter poem) speaks with many different voices, in many different genres, on many different topics. He moves easily from high religious devotion to parody, to bawdy, and to courtly allegory. He tells us much about himself – his adventures at court, his health, his lack of preferment, etc. – and yet somehow seems elusive, or to have a number of poetic 'selves'. Some of his poems are highly local and particular in a way that Henryson's are not, naming real people at court, celebrating or satirizing court or public events, recording the streets and smells of Edinburgh. Very often he loves to demonstrate his linguistic virtuosity in what Edwin Morgan called 'the display of poetic energy'. No two or three poems can catch the 'essential Dunbar'. Out of the eighty-three poems usually attributed to him I have chosen twenty-seven, which I think give a good idea of the range and the variety of his poetic achievement.

Although the differences between the poets are so obvious, the careful reader will find some similarities and – for all the difference in treatment – a number of topics in common. Like other medieval poets they are working with an inherited tradition – of genres, forms and subjects – and they handle this with marked individuality. They both show interest in the fragility (and the absurdity) of man's life on earth, of sin and folly and the Christian hope of heaven, of love and passion and the relationship of men and women, and – often with specific reference to the Scotland of their day – of man's behaviour in society, the good commonwealth, and the duties of a king. They are both highly skilled in the art of rhetoric, and in their different ways show what Scottish medieval poets were able to do with 'oure Inglisch'.

ACKNOWLEDGEMENTS

In the preparation of this edition I have made extensive use of the work of previous scholars. I am much indebted to the edition of Henryson by Denton Fox, and to the editions of Dunbar by James Kinsley and by Priscilla Bawcutt (1996). I am grateful to Anne Wenzel, who tested my early attempts at glossing, and especially to Dr Sally Mapstone, who read the whole edition and provided a stream of thoughtful and learned comments. My thanks are also due to Paul Keegan, the Penguin Classics Editor, and to Christopher Ricks, the general editor of this series, for valuable suggestions and help.

TABLE OF DATES

1412 University of St Andrews founded

1420s ?Henryson born

1423 James I released from English captivity

c.1423 ?*The Kingis Quair* (attributed to James I)

1425 death of Andrew Wyntoun, author of the verse *Oryginalle Chronykill of Scotland*

1437 James I murdered; James II succeeds as a minor

1448 ?Holland's *Buke of the Howlat*

1449 death of Lydgate

1451 Glasgow University founded

1460 James II dies at Roxburgh; James III succeeds as a minor

c.1460 ?Dunbar born

1462 a 'Magister Robertus Henrisone' incorporated as a graduate of Glasgow University

c.1475–8 Hary's *Wallace*

1475 ?Gavin Douglas born

1476 Caxton establishes printing press at Westminster

1477–8 a 'Magister Robertus Henrison', notary public, witnesses deeds for the Abbot of Dunfermline

1477–9 ?Dunbar at St Andrews

1485 in England, Richard III defeated and killed at Bosworth; accession of Henry VII

1488 Battle of Sauchieburn. Death of James III; accession of James IV

1490 John of Ireland's *Meroure of Wysdome*

1494 Gavin Douglas licentiate at St Andrews; King's College, Aberdeen founded

1500 first record of Dunbar's salary

1501 Gavin Douglas, *The Palice of Honour*

1503 Marriage of James IV and Margaret Tudor

1504 (17 March) Dunbar celebrates his first Mass

1505 (after July or early 1506) Dunbar writes the *Lament for the Makars* (which records Henryson's death)

1507 James IV grants patent to Walter Chepman and Andrew Myllar, the first Scottish printers

1509 in England, death of Henry VII; accession of Henry VIII

1513 (14 May) last mention of a payment to Dunbar
(22 July) Douglas completes the *Eneados*
(9 September) James IV defeated and killed at Flodden; accession of James V

NOTE ON LANGUAGE

Middle Scots is not at first easy to read, but soon becomes more familiar. Readers will quickly learn to recognize some characteristic spellings and forms: *quh-* for Modern English *wh-* (*quhat* 'what'); *sch-* for *sh-* (*scheip* 'sheep'); *-u-* for *-oo-* (*gude* 'good'); *-a-* for *-o-* (*stane* 'stone'); *-cht* for *-ght* (*nicht* 'night'); or the present participle ending *-and* for *-ing* (*havand* 'having').

Nouns very often form their plural and possessive forms in *-is* (*thir birdis* 'these birds', *the doggis skyn* 'the dog's skin'). Some older plural forms survive, like *ene* ('eyes') or *brether* ('brothers').

Distinctive pronouns include *scho* 'she'; *thay* 'those'; *thir* 'these'; *quhilk, the quhilk, quhilkis* 'which', 'who'.

Verb endings in *-is* do not present difficulty for modern readers when they are our third person singular present forms (*God sendis* 'God sends'), but they are also found in the second singular (*thow reivis* 'thou robbest'), and in the plural (*clerkis sayis* 'scholars say'), and even in the first person singular, especially when the pronoun does not stand next to it (*nathing of lufe I knaw, / Bot keipis my scheip* 'nothing of love I know, but [I] keep my sheep'). The Scottish equivalent of the *-ed* ending of verbs in the past tense and past participle is *-it* (*lukit* 'looked', *vexit* 'vexed').

Periphrastic forms of the past tense will be unfamiliar. *Can*, *culd*, and *couth* (or *cowth*) are all used (alongside the English *did* or *gan*) to form simple past tenses: *can rin* 'ran', *culd heir* 'heard', *cowth weip* 'wept'.

As in fifteenth- and early sixteenth-century English, spelling is not consistent: the most obvious example is the alternation of i/y (*bricht* or *brycht* 'bright'). And Scottish writers will often use English grammatical forms alongside those of their own language (*quhisling* as well as *quhisland* 'whistling').

FURTHER READING

Fuller bibliographies can be found in D. Gray, *Robert Henryson* and *William Dunbar* (Authors of the Middle Ages 9 and 10, Aldershot, 1996)

Editions

Priscilla Bawcutt, *William Dunbar Selected Poems* (London, New York, 1996)
Priscilla Bawcutt and Felicity Riddy, *Selected Poems of Henryson and Dunbar* (Edinburgh, 1992)
John Burrow, *English Verse 1300–1500* (London, 1977)
Denton Fox, *The Poems of Robert Henryson* (Oxford, 1981, 1987)
James Kinsley, *The Poems of William Dunbar* (Oxford, 1979)

Critical and Historical Works

Priscilla Bawcutt, *Dunbar the Makar* (Oxford, 1992)
J. W. Baxter, *William Dunbar: A Biographical Study* (Edinburgh, 1952)
Douglas Gray, *Robert Henryson* (Leiden, 1979)
R. D. S Jack (ed.), *The History of Scottish Literature* I (Aberdeen, 1988)
Michael Lynch, *Scotland: A New History* (London, 1992)
Matthew P. McDiarmid, *Robert Henryson* (Edinburgh, 1981)
John MacQueen, *Robert Henryson: A Study of the Major Narrative Poems* (Oxford, 1967)
Ian Ross, *William Dunbar* (Leiden, 1981)
Jennifer Wormald, *Court, Kirk and Community: Scotland 1470–1625* (London, 1981)

THE TEXTS

In this edition the spelling has been slightly modernized: ʒ appears as y; the use of i/j has been standardized according to modern practice, as has that of u/v; the occasional use of w in words like *wpon* or *wnto* has been modernized. The punctuation is editorial. Because of the difficulty of many of the texts the glossing on the page has been generous, but a word has not normally been glossed after its first or second appearance. While there is general agreement about the titles of Henryson's poems and individual fables, the titles given by modern editors to Dunbar's poems vary considerably. To avoid confusion I have followed Bawcutt in using the first lines as titles.

ROBERT HENRYSON

ROBENE AND MAKYNE

Robene sat on gud grene hill
Kepand a flok of fe;
Mirry Makyne said him till;
'Robene, thow rew on me!
5   I haif the lovit lowd and still
Thir yeiris two or thre;
My dule in dern bot gif thow dill,
Dowtles but dreid I de!'

Robene ansuerit; 'Be the rude!
10   Nathing of lufe I knaw,
Bot keipis my scheip undir yone wud –
Lo, quhair thay raik on raw!
Quhat hes marrit the in thy mude,
Makyne, to me thow schaw;
15   Or quhat is lufe, or to be lude?
Fane wald I leir that law.'

'At luvis lair gife thow will leir,
Tak thair ane A B C:
Be heynd, courtas, and fair of feir,
20   Wyse, hardy, and fre,

---

1 gud grene *good green*   2 Kepand *looking after* fe *livestock, sheep*
3 him till *to him*   4 rew *have pity*   5 haif the lovit *have loved you*
lowd and still *(= loudly and silently) in every way, constantly*
6 Thir yeiris *these years*   7 *unless you assuage my sorrow in secrecy*
8 *doubtless I will die for certain*

9 ansuerit *answered* Be the rude *by the cross*   10 *I know nothing of love*
11 keipis *mind* scheip undir yone wud *sheep in yonder wood*
12 quhair *where* raik *go* on raw *in a line, together*
13 *what has disturbed you in your mood, disposition*
14 to me thow schaw *reveal it to me*   15 lude *loved*
16 Fane wald I leir *gladly I would learn*

17 *if you wish to learn of love's doctrine*   18 thair *there*   19 heynd *gracious*
courtas *courteous* feir *bearing, manner*   20 hardy *bold* fre *generous*

So that no denger do the deir,
Quhat dule in dern thow dre;
Preis the with pane at all poweir, –
Be patient and previe.'

25   Robene ansuerit hir agane;
'I wait nocht quhat is luve,
Bot I haif mervell in certane
Quhat makis the this wanrufe.
The weddir is fair and I am fane,
30   My scheip gois haill aboif;
And we wald play us in this plane,
Thay wald us bayth reproif.'

'Robene, tak tent unto my taill,
And wirk all as I reid,
35   And thow sall haif my hairt all haill,
Eik and my madinheid.
Sen God sendis bute for baill
And for murning remeid,
In dern with the bot gif I daill,
40   Dowtles I am bot deid.'

21 no denger do the deir *no disdain does you harm*
22 *whatever grief you may suffer in secret*
23 *urge your case with vehemence, as strongly as you can*   24 previe *discreet*

25 agane *in return*   26 wait nocht *know not*   27 mervell *wonder*
in certane *in truth*   28 makis the this wanrufe *causes you this distress*
29 weddir *weather* fane *happy*   30 gois haill aboif *go safely up there*
31 *if we were to enjoy ourselves in this field*
32 wald us bayth reproif *would reprove us both*

33 tak tent unto my taill *pay heed to my words*
34 wirk all as I reid *do exactly as I advise*
35 sall haif my hairt all haill *shall have my heart entirely*
36 *and also my maidenhead*   37 Sen *since*
sendis bute for baill *sends relief for suffering*   38 *and remedy for grief*
39 *unless I make love with you in secret*   40 *in truth I am good as dead*

'Makyne, to morne this ilk a tyde,
And ye will meit me heir,
Peraventure my scheip ma gang besyd
Quhill we haif liggit full neir –
45 Bot mawgré haif I and I byd,
Fra thay begin to steir;
Quhat lyis on hairt I will nocht hyd,
Makyn, than mak gud cheir.'

'Robene, thow reivis me roif and rest –
50 I luve bot the allone.'
'Makyne, adew, the sone gois west,
The day is neir-hand gone.'
'Robene, in dule I am so drest
That lufe wil be my bone.'
55 'Ga lufe, Makyne, quhairever thow list,
For lemman I bid none.'

'Robene, I stand in sic a styll;
I sicht, and that full sair.'
'Makyne, I haif bene heir this quhyle –
60 At hame God gif I wair!'

---

41 to morne this ilk a tyde *tomorrow at this same time* **42** And *if*
meit me heir *meet me here* **43** Peraventure *perhaps*
ma gang besyd *may stay nearby* **44** *until we have lain closely together*
45 mawgré haif I and I byd *I shall be blamed if I stay*
46 Fra *once* steir *move* **47** on hairt *in (my) heart* nocht hyd *not hide*
48 mak gud cheir *cheer up*

49 reivis me *take from me* roif *peace* **51** sone gois *sun goes*
52 neir-hand *almost* **53** dule *grief* so drest *beset, placed* **54** bone *slayer*
55 Ga *go* quhairever thow list *wherever you please* **56** *I do not seek any lover*

57 sic *such* styll *state* **58** sicht *sigh* full sair *grievously*
59 I haif bene heir *have been here* quhyle *while, time*
60 *God grant that I were at home*

'My huny Robene, talk ane quhyll,
Gif thow will do na mair.'
'Makyne, sum uthir man begyle,
For hamewart I will fair.'

65 Robene on his wayis went,
Als licht as leif of tre;
Mawkin murnit in hir intent,
And trowd him nevir to se.
Robene brayd attour the bent;
70 Than Mawkyne cryit on hie:
'Now ma thow sing, for I am schent!
Quhat alis lufe at me?'

Mawkyne went hame withowttin faill;
Full wery eftir cowth weip.
75 Than Robene in a ful fair daill
Assemblit all his scheip.
Be that, sum pairte of Mawkynis aill
Outthrow his hairt cowd creip.
He fallowit hir fast thair till assaill,
80 And till hir tuke gude keip.

61 huny *honey, sweet* quhyll *while*   62 Gif *if* na mair *no more*
63 sum uthir man begyle *beguile some other man*
64 hamewart *homewards* fair *go*

66 Als licht *as light (of heart)* leif of tre *leaf of tree*   67 murnit *mourned*
intent *mind*   68 trowd *believed*   69 brayd attour the bent *hurried over the field*
70 on hie *loudly*   71 ma *may* schent *destroyed*
72 *what does love hold against me?*

73 withowttin faill *indeed*   74 eftir *afterwards* cowth weip *wept*
75 daill *dale, valley*   77 Be that *by that time* aill *ailment*
78 Outthrow *throughout* cowd creip *crept*   79 fallowit *followed* till *to*
assaill *make advances to*   80 tuke gude keip *paid good heed*

'Abyd, abyd, thow fair Makyne!
A word for ony thing!
For all my luve it sal be thyne,
Withowttin depairting.
85 All haill thy harte for till haif myne
Is all my cuvating;
My scheip tomorne quhill houris nyne
Will neid of no keping.'

'Robene, thow hes hard soung and say
90 In gestis and storeis auld;
The man that will nocht quhen he may
Sall haif nocht quhen he wald.
I pray to Jesu every day,
Mot eik thair cairis cauld
95 That first preisis with the to play,
Be firth, forrest or fawld.'

'Makyne, the nicht is soft and dry,
The wedder is warme and fair,
And the grene woid rycht neir us by
100 To walk attour allquhair;

81 abyd *stay*   82 *just one word at any price*   84 *without separation, totally*
85 *to have your heart wholly as mine*   86 cuvating *desire*
87 tomorne quhill houris nyne *until nine o'clock tomorrow*
88 *will need no looking after*

89 hes hard soung *have heard sung*   90 gestis *tales* auld *old*
91 will *will (not)* quhen he may *when he can (have it)*
92 Sall haif *shall have* nocht *nothing, not*
quhen he wald *when he would (have it)*
94 *(that he) may increase their bitter sorrows*
95 *who first tries to make love with you*   96 Be firth *in woodland*
fawld *fold, enclosed field*

97 nicht *night*   98 wedder *weather*
99 woid rycht neir us by *wood (is) very close to us*   100 allquhair *everywhere*

Thair ma na janglour us espy,
That is to lufe contrair;
Thairin, Makyne, bath ye and I,
Unsene we ma repair.'

105   'Robene, that warld is all away
And quyt brocht till ane end,
And nevir agane thairto perfay
Sall it be as thow wend,
For of my pane thow maid it play,
110   And all in vane I spend;
As thow hes done, sa sall I say;
Murne on! I think to mend.'

'Mawkyne, the howp of all my heill,
My hairt on the is sett,
115   And evirmair to the be leill
Quhill I may leif but lett;
Nevir to faill as uthiris feill,
Quhat grace that evir I gett.'
'Robene, with the I will nocht deill;
120   Adew! for thus we mett.'

101 janglour *gossip, backbiter*   102 contrair *opposed*
103 Thairin *therein* bath *both*   104 *can go without being seen*

105 warld *world, state of affairs*   106 quyt *quite, entirely*   107 thairto *in that*
perfay *indeed*   108 wend *supposed, believed*   109 pane *suffering*
play *a game, jest*   110 spend *spent (my time, effort)*   111 sa *so*
112 mend *recover*

113 howp *hope* heill *well-being*   115 leill *faithful to you*   116 Quhill *while*
leif *live* but lett *(?)without ceasing, (?)without delay, indeed*
117 faill *fail, be wanting* uthiris feill *like many others*
118 *whatever favour I receive*   119 nocht deill *not have to do*

Malkyne went hame blyth annewche,
Attour the holttis hair.
Robene murnit and Malkyne lewche;
Scho sang, he sichit sair –
125 And so left him bayth wo and wewche,
In dolour and in cair,
Kepand his hird under a huche,
Amangis the holtis hair.

121 hame *home* blyth *happy* annewche *enough*   122 Attour *over, through*
holttis hair *grey woods*   123 murnit *mourned* lewche *laughed*
124 Scho *she* sichit sair *sighed bitterly*
125 bayth wo and wewche *both sad and miserable*
126 *in grief and sorrow*   127 *guarding his flock under a cliff*
128 *amongst the frosty woods*

THE TESTAMENT OF CRESSEID

Ane doolie sessoun to ane cairfull dyte
Suld correspond and be equivalent:
Richt sa it wes quhen I began to wryte
This tragedie – the wedder richt fervent,
5   Quhen Aries, in middis of the lent,
Schouris of haill gart fra the north discend,
That scant me fra the cauld I micht defend.

Yit nevertheles within myne oratur
I stude, quhen Titan had his bemis bricht
10   Withdrawin doun and sylit under cure,
And fair Venus, the bewtie of the nicht,
Uprais and set unto the west full richt
Hir goldin face, in oppositioun
Of god Phebus, direct discending doun.

15   Throwout the glas hir bemis brast sa fair
That I micht se on everie syde me by;
The northin wind had purifyit the air
And sched the mistie cloudis fra the sky;

1 doolie sessoun *a dismal season* cairfull dyte *sorrowful poem*
2 Suld correspond *should conform*
3 Richt sa it wes quhen *just so it was when* 4 wedder *weather*
richt fervent *(?)eerily intense* 5 Aries *the Ram (in the Zodiac)*
middis *middle* lent *spring* 6 *caused showers of hail to descend from the north*
7 *so that I could scarcely ward off the cold*

8 oratur *oratory, room for private study and devotion* 9 stude *stood*
Titan *Titan, the sun* bemis bricht *bright beams* 10 sylit *concealed* cure *cover*
11 bewtie *beauty* nicht *night* 12 Uprais *rose up* richt *straight*
13 oppositioun *(astronomical) opposition* 14 Phebus *Phoebus, the sun*
direct *directly*

15 Throwout *through* glas *window* brast *burst* 16 micht se *could see*
me by *around me* 17 northin *northern* purifyit *purified, cleared*
18 sched *scattered*

The froist freisit, the blastis bitterly
20 Fra Pole Artick come quhisling loud and schill,
And causit me remufe aganis my will.

For I traistit that Venus, luifis quene,
To quhome sum tyme I hecht obedience,
My faidit hart of lufe scho wald mak grene,
25 And therupon with humbill reverence
I thocht to pray hir hie magnificence;
Bot for greit cald as than I lattit was,
And in my chalmer to the fyre can pas.

Thocht lufe be hait, yit in ane man of age
30 It kendillis nocht sa sone as in youtheid,
Of quhome the blude is flowing in ane rage;
And in the auld the curage doif and deid,
Of quhilk the fyre outward is best remeid:
To help be phisike quhair that nature faillit
35 I am expert, for baith I have assaillit.

19 froist freisit *frost became icy*
20 *from the North Pole came whistling loudly and shrilly*
21 remufe *move away, withdraw* aganis *against*

22 traistit *trusted* luifis quene *love's queen*   23 *to whom I once vowed obedience*
24 faidit *faded, withered* hart *heart* lufe *love*
scho wald mak grene *she would make green, flourishing*   25 humbill *humble*
26 thocht *thought* hie magnificence *high majesty*
27 Bot for greit cald *because of the great cold* as than *at that time*
lattit *prevented*   28 chalmer *chamber, private room* can pas *went*

29 Thocht *though* hait *hot* yit *yet*   30 kendillis *kindles, is aroused*
nocht sa sone *not so soon* youtheid *youth*   31 blude *blood* rage *passion*
32 auld *old* curage doif and deid *desire (is) dull and dead*
33 quhilk *which* outward *outer* remeid *remedy*   34 be phisike *by medicine*
quhair that nature faillit *where nature has failed*   35 expert *experienced*
baith I have assaillit *I have made trial of both*

I mend the fyre and beikit me about,
Than tuik ane drink, my spreitis to comfort,
And armit me weill fra the cauld thairout.
To cut the winter nicht and mak it schort
40   I tuik ane quair – and left all uther sport –
Writtin be worthie Chaucer glorious,
Of fair Creisseid and worthie Troylus.

And thair I fand, efter that Diomeid
Ressavit had that lady bricht of hew,
45   How Troilus neir out of wit abraid
And weipit soir with visage paill of hew;
For quhilk wanhope his teiris can renew,
Quhill esperance rejoisit him agane:
Thus quhyle in joy he levit, quhyle in pane.

50   Of hir behest he had greit comforting,
Traisting to Troy that scho suld mak retour,
Quhilk he desyrit maist of eirdly thing,
Forquhy scho was his only paramour.
Bot quhen he saw passit baith day and hour
55   Of hir ganecome, than sorrow can oppres
His wofull hart in cair and hevines.

36 mend *improved, added fuel to* beikit me *warmed myself*   37 tuik *took*
spreitis *spirits, vital faculties*
38 weill fra the cauld thairout *well against the cold outside*   39 cut *cut short*
40 quair *(small) book* uther *other* sport *diversion*

43 fand *found* efter *after*   44 Ressavit *received, taken in* bricht *bright, fair*
hew *colour, complexion*   45 neir *almost* wit *mind* abraid *burst, went*
46 weipit soir *wept bitterly*   47 wanhope *despair*
teiris can renew *tears burst out again*   48 *until hope gladdened him again*
49 quhyle ... quhyle *now ... now* levit *lived* pane *distress*

50 behest *promise*   51 Traisting *trusting* mak retour *should return*
52 desyrit *desired* maist of cirdly thing *most of any earthly thing*
53 Forquhy *because* paramour *beloved*   54 quhen *when* passit *(had) passed*
55 ganecome *return* can oppres *oppressed*
56 *his grieving heart in misery and melancholy*

Of his distres me neidis nocht reheirs,
For worthie Chauceir in the samin buik,
In gudelie termis and in joly veirs,
60   Compylit hes his cairis, quha will luik.
To brek my sleip ane uther quair I tuik,
In quhilk I fand the fatall destenie
Of fair Cresseid, that endit wretchitlie.

Quha wait gif all that Chauceir wrait was trew?
65   Nor I wait nocht gif this narratioun
Be authoreist, or fenyeit of the new
Be sum poeit, throw his inventioun
Maid to report the lamentatioun
And wofull end of this lustie Creisseid,
70   And quhat distres scho thoillit, and quhat deid.

Quhen Diomeid had all his appetyte,
And mair, fulfillit of this fair ladie,
Upon ane uther he set his haill delyte,
And send to hir ane lybell of repudie,
75   And hir excludit fra his companie.
Than desolait scho walkit up and doun,
And sum men sayis, into the court, commoun.

57 me neidis nocht *I need not* reheirs *recount, repeat*   58 samin buik *same book*
59 gudelie *goodly, excellent* termis *words* joly *fine, pleasant* veirs *verse*
60 *has described his sorrows, if anyone wishes to look*   61 brek *break, interrupt*
sleip *sleep* ane uther quair I tuik *I took another (small) book*   62 fand *found*
fatall destenie *fated destiny*

64 Quha wait gif *who knows if* wrait *wrote* trew *true*
66 Be authoreist *has authority* fenyeit of the new *is newly imagined*
67 inventioun *poetic invention*   68 report *relate*   69 lustie *beautiful, passionate*
70 quhat *what* thoillit *suffered* deid *death*

72 mair *more* fulfillit *satisfied*   73 haill delyte *whole desire*   74 send *sent*
lybell *bill, formal document* repudie *rejection, divorce*   75 excludit *banished*
76 desolait *desolate, abandoned*
77 *and some men say, in the court, (?)as a promiscuous woman*

O fair Creisseid, the flour and A per se
Of Troy and Grece, how was thow fortunait
80   To change in filth all thy feminitie,
And be with fleschelie lust sa maculait,
And go amang the Greikis air and lait,
Sa giglotlike takand thy foull plesance!
I have pietie thow suld fall sic mischance!

85   Yit nevertheless, quhat ever men deme or say
In scornefull langage of thy brukkilnes,
I sall excuse als far furth as I may
Thy womanheid, thy wisdome and fairnes,
The quhilk fortoun hes put to sic distres
90   As hir pleisit, and nathing throw the gilt
Of the, throw wickit langage to be spilt!

This fair lady, in this wyse destitute
Of all comfort and consolatioun,
Richt privelie, but fellowschip or refute,
95   Disagysit passit far out of the toun
Ane myle or twa, unto ane mansioun
Beildit full gay, quhair hir father Calchas
Quhilk than amang the Greikis dwelland was.

78 flour *flower* A per se *paragon*   79 fortunait *destined by Fortune*
80 feminitie *womanliness*   81 fleschelie *fleshly* maculait *defiled*
82 Greikis *Greeks* air and lait *(early and late =) continually*
83 giglotlike *like a wanton woman* takand *taking* plesance *pleasure*
84 pietie *pity* fall *(befall =) experience* sic mischance *such misfortune*

85 deme *judge*   86 brukkilnes *frailty*
87 *I shall exempt from blame as far as I may*
88 womanheid *womanly nature* fairnes *beauty*   89 fortoun *fortune*
90 hir pleisit *pleased her* nathing *not at all* gilt *guilt*   91 the *thee*
wickit *wicked* spilt *injured*

92 wyse *manner*   94 privelie *secretly*
but fellowschip or refute *without companions or protector*
95 Disagysit *disguised* passit *went* toun *town*   96 twa *two*
97 Beildit *constructed* full gay *handsomely* quhair *where (was)*
98 dwelland *dwelling*

Quhen he hir saw, the caus he can inquyre
100   Of hir cumming; scho said, siching full soir,
'Fra Diomeid had gottin his desyre
He wox werie and wald of me no moir.'
Quod Calchas, 'Douchter, weip thow not thairfoir;
Peraventure all cummis for the best.
105   Welcum to me; thow art full deir ane gest!'

This auld Calchas, efter the law was tho,
Wes keiper of the tempill as ane preist
In quhilk Venus and hir sone Cupido
War honourit, and his chalmer was thame neist;
110   To quhilk Cresseid, with baill aneuch in breist,
Usit to pas, hir prayeris for to say,
Quhill at the last, upon ane solempne day,

As custome was, the pepill far and neir
Befoir the none unto the tempill went
115   With sacrifice, devoit in thair maneir;
Bot still Cresseid, hevie in hir intent,
Into the kirk wald not hir self present,
For giving of the pepill ony deming
Of hir expuls fra Diomeid the king;

99 can inquyre *inquired*   100 siching *sighing* full soir *bitterly*
101 Fra *after, when*   102 wox werie *grew weary* wald *would* moir *more*
103 Quod *said* Douchter *daughter* weip *weep*   104 Peraventure *perhaps*
105 deir ane gest *beloved guest*

106 efter *in accordance with* tho *in those days*   107 preist *priest*
108 sone Cupido *son Cupid*   109 chalmer *private room*
thame neist *next, closest to them (the images of the gods?)*   110 baill *misery*
aneuch *enough* breist *breast*   111 Usit to pas *was accustomed to go*
112 Quhill *until* solempne *solemn, of religious significance*

113 pepill *people* neir *near*   114 Befoir *before* none *noon*   115 devoit *devout*
maneir *manner, behaviour*   116 hevie *sorrowful* intent *mind*   117 kirk *church*
118 For *for fear of* deming *suspicion*   119 expuls *expulsion*

120   Bot past into ane secreit orature,
       Quhair scho micht weip hir wofull desteny.
       Behind hir bak scho cloisit fast the dure
       And on hir kneis bair fell doun in hy;
       Upon Venus and Cupide angerly
125   Scho cryit out, and said on this same wyse:
       'Allace, that ever I maid yow sacrifice!

       'Ye gave me anis ane devine responsaill
       That I suld be the flour of luif in Troy;
       Now am I maid ane unworthie outwaill,
130   And all in cair translatit is my joy.
       Quha sall me gyde? Quha sall me now convoy,
       Sen I fra Diomeid and nobill Troylus
       Am clene excludit, as abject odious?

       'O fals Cupide, is nane to wyte bot thow
135   And thy mother, of lufe the blind goddes!
       Ye causit me alwayis understand and trow
       The seid of lufe was sawin in my face,
       And ay grew grene throw your supplie and grace.
       Bot now, allace, that seid with froist is slane,
140   And I fra luifferis left, and all forlane.'

120 past *went* orature *oratory, room for private study and devotion*
122 cloisit fast the dure *closed the door firmly*   123 kneis bair *bare knees*
hy *haste*   124 angerly *angrily, resentfully*   125 cryit out *cried out, exclaimed*
same wyse *very manner*

127 anis *once* responsaill *response, reply (by oracle)*
128 flour of luif *flower of love*   129 unworthie outwaill *worthless outcast*
130 all *utterly* cair *sorrow* translatit *changed, transformed*   131 Quha *who*
gyde *guide, direct* convoy *protect*   132 Sen *since*
133 *completely banished, like a hateful outcast?*

134 nane *none* wyte *blame*   135 lufe *love*   136 trow *believe*   137 seid *seed*
sawin *sown*   138 ay *ever* supplie and grace *help and favour*   139 froist *frost*
slane *slain, destroyed*   140 fra *from, by* luifferis *lovers*
all forlane *abandoned, worthless*

Quhen this was said, doun in ane extasie,
Ravischit in spreit, intill ane dreame scho fell,
And be apperance hard, quhair scho did ly,
Cupide the king ringand ane silver bell,
145   Quhilk men micht heir fra hevin unto hell;
At quhais sound befoir Cupide appeiris
The sevin planetis, discending fra thair spheiris;

Quhilk hes power of all thing generabill,
To reull and steir be thair greit influence
150   Wedder and wind, and coursis variabill.
And first of all Saturne gave his sentence,
Quhilk gave to Cupide litill reverence,
Bot as ane busteous churle on his maneir
Come crabitlie with auster luik and cheir.

155   His face fronsit, his lyre was lyke the leid,
His teith chatterit and cheverit with the chin,
His ene drowpit, how sonkin in his heid,
Out of his nois the meldrop fast can rin,

141 extasie *trance*   142 Ravischit *ravished, carried away* spreit *spirit* intill *into*
143 apperance *seemingly* hard *heard*   144 ringand *ringing*   145 heir *hear*
146 quhais *whose* appeiris *appear*   147 planetis *planets* spheiris *spheres*

148 hes *have* generabill *capable of being generated, generating*
149 reull *rule* steir *govern* greit *great*
influence *(planetary) influence (streams of ethereal fluid which affect earthly
things and persons)*   150 Wedder *weather* coursis *movements*
variabill *changeable*   151 sentence *judgement*   152 reverence *respect*
153 busteous *rough* churle *churl, rustic*   154 Come *came*
crabitlie *ill-naturedly, in a bad-tempered way* auster *austere, stern*
luik and cheir *look and expression*

155 fronsit *wrinkled* lyre *face, complexion* leid *lead*   156 teith *teeth*
cheverit *shivered*   157 ene *eyes* drowpit *drooped* sonkin *hollow(ly) sunken*
heid *head*   158 nois *nose* meldrop *drop of mucus* fast can rin *continually ran*

With lippis bla and cheikis leine and thin;
160   The ice-schoklis that fra his hair doun hang
Was wonder greit, and as ane speir als lang.

Atovir his belt his lyart lokkis lay
Felterit unfair, ovirfret with froistis hoir,
His garmound and his gyte full gay of gray,
165   His widderit weid fra him the wind out woir,
Ane busteous bow within his hand he boir,
Under his girdill ane flasche of felloun flanis
Fedderit with ice and heidit with hailstanis.

Than Juppiter, richt fair and amiabill,
170   God of the starnis in the firmament
And nureis to all thing generabill;
Fra his father Saturne far different,
With burelie face and browis bricht and brent;
Upon his heid ane garland wonder gay
175   Of flouris fair, as it had bene in May.

159 lippis *lips* bla *livid, bluish* cheikis *cheeks* leine *lean*
160 ice-schoklis *icicles* hang *hung*
161 *were wondrously large and as long as a spear*

162 Atovir *down over* lyart *grey, streaked with grey* lokkis *locks*
163 Felterit unfair *matted in an ugly way*
ovirfret *covered (as with embroidery or ornaments)* froistis hoir *white frosts*
164 garmound *garments* gyte *mantle*
full gay of gray *handsomely made of grey cloth*
165 widderit weid *withered garments* out woir *(?)carried out, caused to flutter*
166 busteous *cruel* boir *bore*   167 girdill *girdle*
flasche of felloun flanis *sheaf of deadly arrows*
168 Fedderit *feathered* heidit *headed* hailstanis *hailstones*

169 richt fair *very beautiful* amiabill *friendly*   170 starnis *stars*
171 nureis *nurse, nourisher*   173 burelie *handsome, imposing*
browis *eyebrows, forehead* bricht *fair* brent *(?)smooth, (?)lofty*
175 flouris *flowers* as it had bene *as if it had been*

His voice was cleir, as cristall wer his ene,
As goldin wyre sa glitterand was his hair,
His garmound and his gyte full gay of grene
With goldin listis gilt on everie gair;
180 Ane burelie brand about his middill bair,
In his richt hand he had ane groundin speir,
Of his father the wraith fra us to weir.

Nixt efter him come Mars the god of ire,
Of strife, debait, and all dissensioun,
185 To chide and fecht, als feirs as ony fyre,
In hard harnes, hewmound, and habirgeoun,
And on his hanche ane roustie fell fachioun,
And in his hand he had ane roustie sword,
Wrything his face with mony angrie word.

190 Schaikand his sword, befoir Cupide he come,
With reid visage and grislie glowrand ene,
And at his mouth ane bullar stude of fome,
Lyke to ane bair quhetting his tuskis kene;

176 cleir *clear* cristall *crystal* ene *eyes*   177 glitterand *glittering*
178 gyte *mantle, cloak*   179 listis *edgings*
gilt on everie gair *gilded on every gore (triangular piece of cloth in a garment)*
180 burelie brand *strong sword* bair *bore*   181 richt *right*
groundin *ground sharp* speir *spear*   182 wraith *wrath* weir *ward off*

183 come *came*   184 debait *contention*   185 chide *dispute* fecht *fight*
als feirs as ony fyre *as fierce as any fire*   186 harnes *armour*
hewmound *helmet* habirgeoun *habergeon (sleeveless jacket of mail or armour)*
187 hanche *haunch*
roustie fell fachioun *rusty cruel falchion (sword with a curved blade)*
189 Wrything *twisting, distorting*

190 Schaikand *shaking* befoir *before*   191 reid *red*
grislie glowrand ene *terrible staring eyes*   192 bullar *bubble* stude *stood*
fome *foam*   193 bair *boar* quhetting *whetting* kene *sharp*

Richt tuilyeour lyke, but temperance in tene,
195 Ane horne he blew with mony bosteous brag,
Quhilk all this warld with weir hes maid to wag.

Than fair Phebus, lanterne and lamp of licht,
Of man and beist, baith frute and flourisching,
Tender nureis, and banischer of nicht,
200 And of the warld causing, be his moving
And influence, lyfe in all eirdlie thing,
Without comfort of quhome, of force, to nocht
Must all ga die that in this warld is wrocht.

As king royall he raid upon his chair,
205 The quhilk Phaeton gydit sum tyme unricht;
The brichtnes of his face quhen it was bair
Nane micht behald for peirsing of his sicht;
This goldin cart with fyrie bemis bricht
Four yokkit steidis full different of hew
210 But bait or tyring throw the spheiris drew.

194 *just like a brawler, without moderation in anger*
195 bosteous brag *violent blast*   196 warld *world* weir *war* wag *shake*

197 licht *light*   198 beist *beast*
baith frute and flourisching *of both fruit and blossom*
199 nureis *nurse, nourisher*   201 eirdlie *earthly*
202–3 *without whose comfort, all that is created in this world must of necessity die and turn to nought*

204 raid *rode* chair *chariot*
205 Phaeton *Phaeton, son of Phoebus, and his charioteer* gydit *guided, drove*
sum tyme *on one occasion* unricht *astray, wrongly*   206 brichtnes *brightness*
bair *uncovered*   207 Nane micht behald *no one could look upon*
for peirsing *for fear of wounding* sicht *sight*   208 cart *chariot* bemis *beams*
209 yokkit steidis *yoked steeds* hew *colour*
210 *without halt or wearying drew through the spheres*

The first was soyr, with mane als reid as rois,
Callit Eoye, into the orient;
The secund steid to name hecht Ethios,
Quhitlie and paill, and sum deill ascendent;
215 The thrid Peros, richt hait and richt fervent;
The feird was blak, and callit Philogie,
Quhilk rollis Phebus doun into the sey.

Venus was thair present, that goddes gay,
Hir sonnis querrell for to defend, and mak
220 Hir awin complaint, cled in ane nyce array,
The ane half grene, the uther half sabill blak,
Quhyte hair as gold, kemmit and sched abak;
Bot in hir face semit greit variance,
Quhyles perfyte treuth and quhyles inconstance.

225 Under smyling scho was dissimulait,
Provocative with blenkis amorous,
And suddanely changit and alterait,
Angrie as ony serpent vennemous,
Richt pungitive with wordis odious;
230 Thus variant scho was, quha list tak keip:
With ane eye lauch, and with the uther weip,

211 soyr *sorrel* mane als reid as rois *mane as red as rose*   212 Eoye *Eous*
into the orient *in the east*   213 to name hecht *was called*
Ethios *Ethous (or Aethon)*   214 Quhitlie and paill *whitish and pale*
sum deill ascendent *rising up somewhat*   215 thrid *third* Peros *Pyrois*
richt hait *very hot* richt fervent *burning*   216 feird *fourth*
Philogie *Philogeus (or Phlegon)*   217 sey *sea*

219 sonnis querrell *son's cause, accusation*   220 awin *own* cled *clad*
nyce *strange*   221 ane *one* uther *other* sabill *sable*   222 Quhyte *shining*
kemmit *combed* sched abak *parted backwards*   223 semit *seemed, appeared*
224 Quhyles *now, sometimes* perfyte treuth *perfect faithfulness*
inconstance *inconstancy*

225 dissimulait *deceitful*   226 Provocative *alluring* blenkis *glances*
227 alterait *altered*   229 Richt pungitive *stinging* odious *hateful*
230 variant *changeable* quha *whoever, if anyone* list tak keip *wished to take heed*
231 lauch *laughed* weip *wept*

In taikning that all fleschelie paramour,
Quhilk Venus hes in reull and governance,
I sum tyme sweit, sum tyme bitter and sour,
235   Richt unstabill and full of variance,
Mingit with cairfull joy and fals plesance,
Now hait, now cauld, now blyith, now full of wo,
Now grene as leif, now widderit and ago.

With buik in hand than come Mercurius,
240   Richt eloquent and full of rethorie,
With polite termis and delicious,
With pen and ink to report all reddie,
Setting sangis and singand merilie;
His hude was reid, heklit atovir his croun,
245   Lyke to ane poeit of the auld fassoun.

Boxis he bair with fyne electuairis,
And sugerit syropis for digestioun,
Spycis belangand to the pothecairis,
With mony hailsum sweit confectioun;
250   Doctour in phisick, cled in ane skarlot goun,
And furrit weill – as sic ane aucht to be –
Honest and gude, and not ane word culd lie.

232 taikning *token, sign*   233 reull *rule, control*   234 sweit *sweet*
235 Richt unstabill *very unstable*   236 Mingit *mingled*
cairfull joy *sorrowful pleasure*   237 hait *hot* cauld *cold* blyith *happy*
238 widderit *withered* ago *gone, passed*

239 buik *book* Mercurius *Mercury*   240 rethorie *rhetoric*
241 *with polished and delightful words*
242 to report all reddie *ready to make a report*
243 Setting sangis *composing songs* singand *singing*   244 hude *hood*
heklit *fringed (like a cock's hackle?)* atovir his croun *over the top of his head*
245 fassoun *manner*

246 electuairis *electuaries (medicines compounded with syrup into a paste)*
247 sugerit syropis *syrups sweetened with sugar*   248 Spycis *spices*
belangand *pertaining* pothecairis *apothecaries*   249 hailsum *health-giving*
confectioun *preparation*   250 phisick *medical science* skarlot *rich red cloth*
251 furrit weill *with plenty of fur* as sic ane *such a one* aucht *ought*

Nixt efter him come lady Cynthia,
The last of all and swiftest in hir spheir;
255 Of colour blak, buskit with hornis twa,
And in the nicht scho listis best appeir;
Haw as the leid, of colour nathing cleir,
For all hir licht scho borrowis at hir brother
Titan, for of hirself scho hes nane uther.

260 Hir gyte was gray and full of spottis blak,
And on hir breist ane churle paintit full evin
Beirand ane bunche of thornis on his bak,
Quhilk for his thift micht clim na nar the hevin.
Thus quhen thay gadderit war, thir goddes sevin,
265 Mercurius thay cheisit with ane assent
To be foirspeikar in the parliament.

Quha had bene thair and liken for to heir
His facound toung and termis exquisite,
Of rethorick the prettick he micht leir,
270 In breif sermone ane pregnant sentence wryte.
Befoir Cupide veiling his cap a-lyte,
Speiris the caus of that vocatioun,
And he anone schew his intentioun.

255 buskit *arrayed, adorned* hornis twa *two horns*   256 listis *likes*
257 Haw *pale, bluish-grey* leid *lead* nathing *not at all*   258 at *from*
259 Titan *Titan, the sun*

260 gyte *mantle*   261 breist *breast* churle *peasant* full evin *exactly*
262 Beirand *carrying* bunche *bundle*   263 thift *theft*
micht clim na nar *could climb no nearer*   264 gadderit war *were assembled*
thir *these*   265 cheisit *chose*   266 foirspeikar *spokesman, speaker*

267 Quha *if anyone* liken *desirous*   268 *his eloquent tongue and choice diction*
269 *he could learn the practice of rhetoric*   270 breif sermone *brief discourse*
pregnant sentence *weighty meaning, significance*   271 veiling *doffing*
a-lyte *a little*   272 Speiris *inquires* vocatioun *summoning*   273 anone *quickly*
schew *revealed* intentioun *charge, accusation*

'Lo,' quod Cupide, 'quha will blaspheme the name
275   Of his awin god, outher in word or deid,
To all goddis he dois baith lak and schame,
And suld have bitter panis to his meid;
I say this by yone wretchit Cresseid,
The quhilk throw me was sum tyme flour of lufe,
280   Me and my mother starklie can reprufe,

'Saying of hir greit infelicitie
I was the caus, and my mother Venus,
Ane blind goddes hir cald, that micht not se,
With sclander and defame injurious.
285   Thus hir leving unclene and lecherous
Scho wald retorte in me and my mother,
To quhome I schew my grace abone all uther.

'And sen ye ar all sevin deificait,
Participant of devyne sapience,
290   This greit injure done to our hie estait
Me think with pane we suld mak recompence;
Was never to goddes done sic violence.
As weill for yow as for myself I say:
Thairfoir ga help to revenge, I yow pray!'

275 outher *either* deid *deed*   276 lak *insult*   277 panis *punishments*
meid *recompense*   279 the quhilk *who* throw *through* sum tyme *once*
flour of lufe *flower of love*   280 starklie can reprufe *harshly reproved*

281 infelicitie *ill-fortune*   283 cald *called* se *see*
284 *with slander and offensive defamation*   285 leving *living* unclene *impure*
286 retorte in *throw back on*   287 schew *showed, granted* abone *above*

288 deificait *deified, having divine powers*   289 *sharing divine wisdom*
290 injure *injury, insult* hie estait *high rank*   291 Me think *it seems to me*
(that)
pane *punishment*   292 violence *violence, insult*
293 As weill for yow as *as well for you (other gods) as* say *speak*
294 ga help *go and help*

295   Mercurius to Cupide gave answeir
      And said, 'Schir King, my counsall is that ye
      Refer yow to the hiest planeit heir
      And tak to him the lawest of degré,
      The pane of Cresseid for to modifie –
300   As God Saturne, with him tak Cynthia.'
      'I am content', quod he, 'to tak thay twa.'

      Than thus proceidit Saturne and the Mone
      Quhen thay the mater rypelie had degest:
      For the dispyte to Cupide scho had done
305   And to Venus, oppin and manifest,
      In all hir lyfe with pane to be opprest,
      And torment sair with seiknes incurabill,
      And to all lovers be abhominabill.

      This duleful sentence Saturne tuik on hand,
310   And passit doun quhair cairfull Cresseid lay,
      And on hir heid he laid ane frostie wand.
      Than lawfullie on this wyse can he say:
      'Thy greit fairnes and all thy bewtie gay,
      Thy wantoun blude, and eik thy goldin hair,
315   Heir I exclude fra the for evermair.

---

295 answeir *answer*   296 counsall *counsel*   297 Refer yow *commit yourself*
hiest *highest* heir *here*   298 tak *add* lawest *lowest* degré *rank*
299 modifie *assess, determine*   301 thay *those*

302 proceidit *proceeded* Mone *Moon*   303 rypelie *with deliberation*
degest *considered*   304 dispyte *injury*   305 oppin *open*
306 with pane to be opprest *to be burdened with suffering*
307 torment sair *tormented grievously* seiknes incurabill *incurable sickness*
308 abhominabill *abominable*

309 duleful *fraught with grief* tuik on hand *took charge of*
310 passit doun quhair *passed down (to) where* cairfull *sorrowful*
311 heid *head* wand *rod*   312 lawfullie *in accordance with legal procedure*
on this wyse can he say *spoke in this manner*   313 greit fairnes *great fairness*
bewtie gay *fine beauty*   314 wantoun blude *unruly, passionate blood* eik *also*
315 exclude *banish*

'I change thy mirth into melancholy,
Quhilk is the mother of all pensivenes;
Thy moisture and thy heit in cald and dry;
Thyne insolence, thy play and wantones
320   To greit diseis; thy pomp and thy riches
In mortall neid; and greit penuritie
Thow suffer sall, and as ane beggar die.'

O cruell Saturne, fraward and angrie,
Hard is thy dome and to malitious!
325   On fair Cresseid quhy hes thow na mercie,
Quhilk was sa sweit, gentill and amorous?
Withdraw thy sentence and be gracious –
As thow was never; sa schawis throw thy deid,
Ane wraikfull sentence gevin on fair Cresseid.

330   Than Cynthia, quhen Saturne past away,
Out of hir sait discendit doun belyve,
And red ane bill on Cresseid quhair scho lay,
Contening this sentence diffinityve:
'Fra heit of bodie I the now depryve,
335   And to thy seiknes sall be na recure
Bot in dolour thy dayis to indure.

317 pensivenes *sadness*   318 heit *(vital) heat* in cald *into cold*
319 insolence *arrogance* play *pleasure, wantonness*   320 diseis *distress*
321 mortall neid *deadly poverty* penuritie *penury*

323 fraward *perverse, ill-humoured*   324 dome *judgement*
to malitious *too malicious*
325 quhy hes thow na mercie *why have you no mercy*
326 amorous *loving*   328 sa schawis *is evident* deid *deed*
329 wraikfull *vindictive* gevin *given, passed*

331 sait *seat* belyve *swiftly*   332 red ane bill *read a formal document*
333 *containing this final sentence*   334 Fra heit of bodie *of bodily heat*
335 sall be na recure *(there) shall be no cure*   336 dolour *misery*
indure *endure*

'Thy cristall ene minglit with blude I mak,
Thy voice sa cleir, unplesand, hoir and hace,
Thy lustie lyre ovirspred with spottis blak,
340 And lumpis haw appeirand in thy face:
Quhair thow cummis, ilk man sall fle the place.
This sall thow go begging fra hous to hous
With cop and clapper lyke ane lazarous.'

This doolie dreame, this uglye visioun
345 Brocht to ane end, Cresseid fra it awoik,
And all that court and convocatioun
Vanischit away. Than rais scho up and tuik
Ane poleist glas, and hir schaddow culd luik;
And quhen scho saw hir face sa deformait,
350 Gif scho in hart was wa aneuch, God wait!

Weiping full sair, 'Lo, quhat it is', quod sche,
'With fraward langage for to mufe and steir
Our craibit goddis; and sa is sene on me!
My blaspheming now have I bocht full deir;
355 All eirdlie joy and mirth I set areir.
Allace, this day! allace, this wofull tyde
Quhen I began with my goddis for to chyde!'

337 cristall *crystal, clear* minglit *mingled*   338 unplesand *unpleasing*
hoir and hace *rough and hoarse*   339 lustie lyre *beautiful skin* ovirspred *covered*
340 lumpis haw *livid lumps* appeirand *appearing*   341 ilk *each, every* fle *flee*
342 This *thus*   343 cop *bowl, cup* clapper *rattle* lazarous *leper*

344 doolie *woeful* uglye *fearsome*   345 Brocht *brought* awoik *awoke*
346 convocatioun *assembly*   347 Vanischit *vanished* rais *rose* tuik *took*
348 poleist glas *mirror* hir schaddow culd luik *looked at her reflection*
350 *if she was deeply sorrowful in heart, God knows!*

351 full sair *bitterly*   352 fraward *perverse*
mufe and steir *provoke and stir (to anger)*   353 craibit *ill-tempered*
sa is sene on me *so is evident in me*   354 bocht full deir *paid for most dearly*
355 eirdlie *earthly* areir *behind*   356 tyde *time*   357 chyde *dispute, quarrel*

Be this was said, ane chyld come fra the hall
To warne Cresseid the supper was reddy;
360 First knokkit at the dure, and syne culd call,
'Madame, your father biddis yow cum in hy:
He hes merwell sa lang on grouf ye ly,
And sayis your beedes bene to lang sum deill;
The goddis wait all your intent full weill.'

365 Quod scho, 'Fair chyld, ga to my father deir,
And pray him cum to speik with me anone.'
And sa he did, and said, 'Douchter, quhat cheir?'
'Allace!' quod scho, 'Father, my mirth is gone!'
'How sa?' quod he; and scho can all expone,
370 As I have tauld, the vengeance and the wraik
For hir trespas Cupide on hir culd tak.

He luikit on hir uglye lipper face,
The quhylk befor was quhite as lillie flour;
Wringand his handis, oftymes he said, allace
375 That he had levit to se that wofull hour!
For he knew weill that thair was na succour
To hir seiknes, and that dowblit his pane;
Thus was thair cair aneuch betuix thame twane.

358 Be *when* come *came*   359 warne *warn, tell*   360 dure *door*
syne culd call *then called out*   361 hy *haste*
362 *he marvels (that) you lie prostrate so long*
363 beedes bene to lang sum deill *prayers are somewhat too long*
364 wait *know*

365 deir *dear*   366 speik *speak* anone *quickly*   367 quhat cheir? *how are you?*
369 can all expone *described everything*   370 tauld *told* wraik *revenge*
371 *that Cupid took on her for her transgression*

372 luikit *looked* lipper *leprous*   373 *which before was white as the lily-flower*
375 levit *lived*   376 succour *help, aid*   377 dowblit *doubled*
378 cair aneuch *great sorrow* thame twane *the two of them*

Quhen thay togidder murnit had full lang,
380   Quod Cresseid: 'Father, I wald not be kend;
Thairfoir in secreit wyse ye let me gang
Unto yone spitall at the tounis end,
And thidder sum meit for cheritie me send
To leif upon, for all mirth in this eird
385   Is fra me gane – sic is my wickit weird!'

Than in ane mantill and ane baver hat,
With cop and clapper, wonder prively,
He opnit ane secreit yet, and out thairat
Convoyit hir, that na man suld espy,
390   Unto ane village half ane myle thairby;
Delyverit hir in at the spittaill hous,
And daylie sent hir part of his almous.

Sum knew hir weill, and sum had na knawledge
Of hir becaus scho was sa deformait,
395   With bylis blak ovirspred in hir visage,
And hir fair colour faidit and alterait.
Yit thay presumit, for hir hie regrait
And still murning, scho was of nobill kin;
With better will thairfoir they tuik hir in.

379 murnit *lamented*   380 kend *recognized*   381 secreit wyse *secretly*
let me gang *let me go*   382 *unto that leper-house at the end of the town*
383 thidder *thither* meit *food* cheritie *charity*   384 leif *live* mirth *joy*
eird *earth*   385 Is fra me gane *has gone from me* wickit weird *evil fate*

386 mantill *cloak* baver *beaver-skin*   387 cop and clapper *cup and rattle*
prively *secretly*   388 opnit *opened* yet *gate* thairat *there*
389 Convoyit *escorted* that *so that*   390 thairby *near there, from there*
391 Delyverit *delivered* spittaill hous *leper-house*   392 almous *alms*

393 knawledge *recognition*   394 deformait *deformed*
395 bylis blak *black boils* ovirspred *covered*   396 faidit *faded* alterait *altered*
397 *Yet they assumed because of her great lamentation*
398 still *(?)quiet, (?)constant* murning *mourning*

400 The day passit and Phebus went to rest,
The cloudis blak overheled all the sky.
God wait gif Cresseid was ane sorrowfull gest,
Seing that uncouth fair and harbery!
But meit or drink scho dressit hir to ly
405 In ane dark corner of the hous allone,
And on this wyse, weiping, scho maid hir mone:

'O sop of sorrow, sonkin into cair!
O cative Creisseid! For now and ever mair
Gane is thy joy and all thy mirth in eird;
410 Of all blyithnes now art thou blaiknit bair;
Thair is na salve may saif or sound thy sair!
Fell is thy fortoun, wickit is thy weird,
Thy blys is baneist, and thy baill on breird!
Under the eirth, God gif I gravin wer,
415 Quhair nane of Grece nor yit of Troy micht heird!

'Quhair is thy chalmer wantounlie besene,
With burely bed and bankouris browderit bene?
Spycis and wyne to thy collatioun,
The cowpis all of gold and silver schene,

---

401 overheled *covered over*   403 Seing *seeing* uncouth *unaccustomed* fair *food*
harbery *lodging*   404 But meit *without food* dressit hir *prepared herself*
406 mone *lament*

407 sop *sop (piece of bread steeped in liquid)* sonkin *sunk*
408 cative *wretched*   409 Gane *gone* eird *earth*   410 blyithnes *joy*
blaiknit bair *made pale and bare*   411 salve *salve, remedy* saif *heal*
sound *make sound, cure* sair *suffering*   412 Fell *cruel* fortoun *fortune*
wickit *evil* weird *fate*   413 blys *joy* baneist *banished* baill *misery*
on breird *spreading wide*   414 gif gravin wer *grant I were buried*
415 micht heird *could hear it*

416 wantounlie *luxuriously* besene *furnished*   417 burely *handsome*
bankouris *covers for seats* browderit *embroidered finely*   418 to *for*
collatioun *collation (a light meal, often taken late at night)*
419 cowpis *goblets* schene *shining*

420   The sweitmeitis servit in plaittis clene
       With saipheron sals of ane gude sessoun?
       Thy gay garmentis with mony gudely goun,
       Thy plesand lawn pinnit with goldin prene?
       All is areir, thy greit royall renoun!

425   'Quhair is thy garding with thir greissis gay
       And fresche flowris, quhilk the quene Floray
       Had paintit plesandly in everie pane,
       Quhair thou was wont full merilye in May
       To walk and tak the dew be it was day,
430   And heir the merle and mawis mony ane,
       With ladyis fair in carrolling to gane,
       And se the royall rinkis in thair ray,
       In garmentis gay garnischit on everie grane?

       'Thy greit triumphand fame and hie honour,
435   Quhair thou was callit of eirdlye wichtis flour,
       All is decayit, thy weird is welterit so;
       Thy hie estait is turnit in darknes dour;

420 *the dainties served on elegant dishes*   421 saipheron sals *saffron sauce*
gude sessoun *good seasoning*   423 plesand lawn *delightful fine linen*
pinnit *pinned* prene *pin, brooch*   424 areir *past, gone*

425 garding *garden* thir greissis gay *these fine plants, herbs*
426 fresche flowris *fresh flowers* Floray *Flora, goddess of flowers*
427 pane *(?)part, (?)side* 429 tak the dew *gather the (May-)dew*
be it was day *as soon as*
430 heir the merle and mawis *hear the blackbird and thrush*
431 carrolling *singing and dancing carols* gane *go*   432 rinkis *knights* ray *array*
433 garnischit *decorated* grane *(?)particular, (?)hue*

434 triumphand *triumphant, splendid* hie *high*
435 of eirdlye wichtis flour *the flower of earthly creatures*
436 weird *destiny* welterit *overturned*   437 dour *stern, harsh*

This lipper ludge tak for thy burelie bour,
And for thy bed tak now ane bunche of stro,
440   For waillit wyne and meitis thou had tho
Tak mowlit breid, peirrie and ceder sour:
Bot cop and clapper now is all ago.

'My cleir voice and courtlie carrolling,
Quhair I was wont with ladyis for to sing,
445   Is rawk as ruik, full hiddeous, hoir and hace;
My plesand port, all utheris precelling,
Of lustines I was hald maist conding
Now is deformit the figour of my face;
To luik on it na leid now lyking hes.
450   Sowpit in syte, I say with sair siching,
Ludgeit amang the lipper leid, "Allace!"

'O ladyis fair of Troy and Grece, attend
My miserie, quhilk nane may comprehend,
My frivoll fortoun, my infelicitie,
455   My greit mischeif, quhilk na man can amend.

---

438 lipper ludge *lepers' hut* tak *take* for *instead of*
burelie bour *handsome bower*   **439** bunche *bundle* stro *straw*   **440** waillit *choice*
meitis *dishes* tho *then, in former days*   **441** mowlit breid *mouldy bread*
peirrie *perry (a drink made from pears)* ceder *cider*   **442** Bot *except for*
ago *gone*

445 rawk as ruik *raucous as a rook* hoir *grating* hace *hoarse*   **446** port *bearing*
all utheris precelling *excelling all others*
447 in beauty I was considered most worthy   **448** figour *appearance*
449 na leid now lyking hes *no person now has pleasure*   **450** Sowpit *sunk*
syte *sorrow* siching *sighing*
451 Ludgeit amang the lipper leid *lodged among the leper folk*

452 attend *consider*   **454** frivoll *fickle* infelicitie *misery*   **455** mischeif *distress*

Be war in tyme, approchis neir the end,
And in your mynd ane mirrour mak of me:
As I am now, peradventure that ye
For all your micht may cum to that same end,
460 Or ellis war, gif ony war may be.

'Nocht is your fairnes bot ane faiding flour,
Nocht is your famous laud and hie honour
Bot wind inflat in uther mennis eiris;
Your roising reid to rotting sall retour;
465 Exempill mak of me in your memour,
Quhilk of sic thingis wofull witnes beiris.
All welth in eird, away as wind it weiris;
Be war thairfoir, approchis neir the hour:
Fortoun is fikkill quhen scho beginnis and steiris!'

470 Thus chydand with hir drerie destenye,
Weiping scho woik the nicht fra end to end;
Bot all in vane – hir dule, hir cairfull cry,
Micht not remeid nor yit hir murning mend.
Ane lipper lady rais and till hir wend,
475 And said: 'Quhy spurnis thow aganis the wall
To sla thyself and mend nathing at all?

---

456 war *prepared* approchis neir *approaches near*   458 peradventure *perchance*
459 micht *strength*   460 ellis war *else worse*
gif ony war may be *if anything worse can be*

462 laud *glory*   463 inflat *puffed* uther mennis eiris *other men's ears*
464 *your rosy red (complexion) shall change to rottenness*
465 Exempill *example* memour *memory*
466 *who gives a lamentable proof of such things*
467 away as wind it weiris *passes away like wind*   469 steiris *moves*

470 drerie *miserable*   471 woik *stayed awake*   472 dule *grief*
473 remeid *provide a remedy* mend *amend, lessen*
474 rais *rose* till hir wend *went to her*   475 spurnis *kick, beat*
aganis *against*   476 sla *slay*

'Sen thy weiping dowbillis bot thy wo,
I counsall the mak vertew of ane neid;
Go leir to clap thy clapper to and fro,
480   And leif efter the law of lipper leid.'
Thair was na buit, bot furth with thame scho yeid
Fra place to place, quhill cauld and hounger sair
Compellit hir to be ane rank beggair.

That samin tyme, of Troy the garnisoun,
485   Quhilk had to chiftane worthie Troylus,
Throw jeopardie of weir had strikken doun
Knichtis of Grece in number mervellous;
With greit tryumphe and laude victorious
Agane to Troy richt royallie thay raid
490   The way quhair Cresseid with the lipper baid.

Seing that companie, all with ane stevin
Thay gaif ane cry, and schuik coppis gude speid;
Said: 'Worthie lordis, for Goddis lufe of hevin,
To us lipper part of your almous deid!'
495   Than to thair cry nobill Troylus tuik heid,
Having pietie, neir by the place can pas
Quhair Cresseid sat, not witting quhat scho was.

477 dowbillis bot *only doubles*   478 counsall *counsel*
mak vertew of ane neid *make virtue of a necessity*   479 Go leir *go and learn*
480 leif efter *live according to* leid *people*   481 buit *help, remedy* yeid *went*
482 quhill cauld and hounger sair *until cold and grievous hunger*
483 rank *absolute*

484 samin *same* garnisoun *garrison*   485 chiftane *as leader*
486 Throw *through* jeopardie *(?)daring exploit, (?)chance* weir *war*
487 Knichtis of Grece *knights of Greece* mervellous *wondrous*   488 laude *glory*
489 Agane *back* richt royallie *in regal splendour* raid *rode*   490 lipper *lepers*
baid *waited, dwelt*

491 ane stevin *one voice*
492 gaif *gave* schuik coppis gude speid *shook (their) bowls quickly*
493 Goddis lufe of hevin *love of God in heaven*   494 part *give a share*
almous deid *alms*   495 tuik heid *took heed*   496 pietie *pity* can pas *passed*
497 witting *knowing* quhat *who*

Than upon him scho kest up baith hir ene –
And with ane blenk it come into his thocht
500 That he sumtime hir face befoir had sene.
Bot scho was in sic plye he knew hir nocht;
Yit than hir luik into his mynd it brocht
The sweit visage and amorous blenking
Of fair Cresseid, sumtyme his awin darling.

505 Na wonder was, suppois in mynd that he
Tuik hir figure sa sone – and lo, now quhy:
The idole of ane thing in cace may be
Sa deip imprentit in the fantasy
That it deludis the wittis outwardly,
510 And sa appeiris in forme and lyke estait
Within the mynd as it was figurait.

Ane spark of lufe than till his hart culd spring
And kendlit all his bodie in ane fyre:
With hait fewir, ane sweit and trimbling
515 Him tuik, quhill he was reddie to expyre;
To beir his scheild his breist began to tyre;
Within ane quhyle he changit mony hew,
And nevertheles not ane ane uther knew.

---

498 kest *cast* baith hir ene *both her eyes*   **499** blenk *glance, look* come *came*
thocht *mind*   **501** sic plye *such plight, condition*   **502** luik *look*
503 blenking *glancing*   **504** sumtyme *once* awin *own*

505 suppois *if*   **506** Tuik *received, apprehended* figure *image* sa sone *so quickly*
507 idole *image* in cace *by chance*   **508** Sa deip imprentit *so deeply imprinted*
fantasy *imagination, memory*   **509** wittis *senses* outwardly *externally*
510 appeiris *appears* lyke estait *similar state*
511 *as it was shaped within the mind*

512 till his hart culd spring *sprang to his heart*   **513** kendlit *kindled*
514 hait fewir *hot fever* sweit *sweat* trimbling *trembling*
515 Him tuik, quhill *seized him until* reddie *likely*   **516** beir *bear*
scheild *shield*   **517** quhyle *short time*
he changit mony hew *his colour kept on changing*
518 not ane *neither* ane uther knew *recognized the other*

For knichtlie pietie and memoriall
520 Of fair Cresseid, ane gyrdill can he tak,
Ane purs of gold, and mony gay jowall,
And in the skirt of Cresseid doun can swak;
Than raid away and not ane word he spak,
Pensive in hart, quhill he come to the toun,
525 And for greit cair oftsyis almaist fell doun.

The lipper folk to Cresseid than can draw
To se the equall distributioun
Of the almous, bot quhen the gold thay saw,
Ilkane to uther prevelie can roun,
530 And said; 'Yone lord hes mair affectioun,
However it be, unto yone lazarous
Than to us all; we knaw be his almous.'

'Quhat lord is yone,' quod scho, 'have ye na feill,
Hes done to us so greit humanitie?'
535 'Yes,' quod a lipper man, 'I knaw him weill;
Schir Troylus it is, gentill and fre.'
Quhen Cresseid understude that it was he,
Stiffer than steill thair stert ane bitter stound
Throwout hir hart, and fell doun to the ground.

519 memoriall *remembrance*   520 ane gyrdill can he tak *he took a girdle*
521 gay jowall *fine jewel*   522 can swak *flung*   523 raid *rode* spak *spoke*
524 Pensive *brooding* quhill he come *until he came*   525 oftsyis *often*
almaist *almost*

526 can draw *approached*   528 almous *alms*
529 *each one to the other whispered secretly*   530 Yone *that*
mair affectioun *more fondness*   531 However it be *however it is* lazarous *leper*
532 knaw *know, recognize*

533 feill *knowledge, idea*   534 Hes *(who) has* humanitie *kindness*
536 gentill *noble* fre *generous*   538 Stiffer *stronger* steill *steel*
thair stert ane bitter stound *there sprang a bitter pain*
539 fell doun *(she) fell down*

540   Quhen scho ovircome, with siching sair and sad,
       With mony cairfull cry and cald ochane:
       'Now is my breist with stormie stoundis stad,
       Wrappit in wo, ane wretch full will of wane!'
       Than swounit scho oft or scho culd refrane,
545   And ever in hir swouning cryit scho thus;
       'O fals Cresseid and trew knicht Troylus!

       'Thy lufe, thy lawtie, and thy gentilnes
       I countit small in my prosperitie,
       Sa elevait I was in wantones,
550   And clam upon the fickill quheill sa hie.
       All faith and lufe I promissit to the
       Was in the self fickill and frivolous:
       O fals Cresseid and trew knicht Troilus!

       'For lufe of me thow keipt gude continence,
555   Honest and chaist in conversatioun;
       Of all wemen protectour and defence
       Thou was, and helpit thair opinioun;
       My mynd in fleschelie foull affectioun
       Was inclynit to lustis lecherous:
560   Fy, fals Cresseid! O trew knicht Troylus!

540 ovircome *came to, revived*
siching sair and sad *grievous and sorrowful sighing*   541 cald *cold, mournful*
ochane *'alas!' (cry of lamentation)*
542 with stormie stoundis stad *beset with tempestuous onslaughts of grief*
543 Wrappit *totally enclosed* full will of wane *destitute, hopeless*
544 *then she often swooned before she ceased*

547 lawtie *loyalty, fidelity* gentilnes *nobility*
548 countit small *reckoned as little* prosperitie *happy days*
549 elevait *raised high*   550 clam *climbed*
fickill quheill *unstable wheel (of Fortune)*
551 I promissit to the *(which) I promised to you*   552 the self *itself*
fickill and frivolous *false and worthless*

554 keipt *maintained* gude continence *self-restraint*
555 *honourable and pure in conduct*   557 opinioun *reputation*
558 affectioun *passion*

'Lovers be war and tak gude heid about
Quhome that ye lufe, for quhome ye suffer paine.
I lat yow wit, thair is richt few thairout
Quhome ye may traist to have trew lufe agane;
565   Preif quhen ye will, your labour is in vaine.
Thairfoir I reid ye tak thame as ye find,
For thay ar sad as widdercok in wind.

'Becaus I knaw the greit unstabilnes,
Brukkill as glas, into my self, I say,
570   Traisting in uther als greit unfaithfulnes,
Als unconstant, and als untrew of fay —
Thocht sum be trew, I wait richt few ar thay;
Quha findis treuth, lat him his lady ruse!
Nane but myself as now I will accuse.'

575   Quhen this was said, with paper scho sat doun,
And on this maneir maid hir testament:
'Heir I beteiche my corps and carioun
With wormis and with taidis to be rent;
My cop and clapper, and myne ornament,
580   And all my gold the lipper folk sall have
Quhen I am deid, to burie me in grave.

561 about *concerning*
563 *I would have you know there are very few in the world*
564 traist to have trew lufe agane *trust to have true love in return*
565 Preif *test*   566 reid *advise*   567 sad *steadfast* widdercok *weathercock*

569 Brukkill *fragile* into *in* say *speak*
570 *expecting (to find) in others as great unfaithfulness*
571 *(to find them) as inconstant and as untrue of faith*
572 Thocht *though*   573 Quha findis treuth *whoever finds fidelity* ruse *praise*
574 as now *now, at this time*

576 maneir *manner*   577 beteiche *commit* corps *corpse* carioun *dead body*
578 taidis *toads* rent *devoured*

'This royall ring set with this rubie reid,
Quhilk Troylus in drowrie to me send,
To him agane I leif it quhen I am deid,
585   To mak my cairfull deid unto him kend.
Thus I conclude schortlie, and mak ane end:
My spreit I leif to Diane, quhair scho dwellis,
To walk with hir in waist woddis and wellis.

'O Diomeid, thou hes baith broche and belt
590   Quhilk Troylus gave me in takning
Of his trew lufe!' and with that word scho swelt.
And sone ane lipper man tuik of the ring,
Syne buryt hir withouttin tarying;
To Troylus furthwith the ring he bair,
595   And of Cresseid the deith he can declair.

Quhen he had hard hir greit infirmitie,
Hir legacie and lamentatioun,
And how scho endit in sic povertie,
He swelt for wo and fell doun in ane swoun;
600   For greit sorrow his hart to brist was boun;
Siching full sadlie, said, 'I can no moir –
Scho was untrew and wo is me thairfoir.'

583 in drowrie *(?)as a love-token, (?)out of love* send *sent* 584 leif *leave*
deid *dead* 585 deid *death* kend *known* 587 spreit *spirit*
Diane *Diana, virgin goddess associated with the hunt and the moon, and in the
Middle Ages sometimes with fairies* 588 waist woddis *wild woods* wellis *springs*

589 broche *brooch* 590 takning *sign* 591 swelt *died* 592 sone *quickly*
tuik of *took off* 593 *then buried her without delay* 594 bair *bore*
595 can declair *told of*

599 swelt *fainted* 600 to brist was boun *was ready to break*

Sum said he maid ane tomb of merbell gray,
And wrait hir name and superscriptioun,
605   And laid it on hir grave quhair that scho lay,
In goldin letteris, conteining this ressoun:
'Lo, fair ladyis! Cresseid of Troyis toun,
Sumtyme countit the flour of womanheid,
Under this stane, lait lipper, lyis deid.'

610   Now, worthie wemen, in this ballet schort,
Maid for your worschip and instructioun,
Of cheritie, I monische and exhort,
Ming not your lufe with fals deceptioun.
Beir in your mynd this schort conclusioun
615   Of fair Cresseid, as I have said befoir.
Sen scho is deid, I speik of hir no moir.

---

603 merbell *marble*   604 wrait *wrote* superscriptioun *inscription*

606 ressoun *statement*   608 *once reckoned the flower of womankind*
609 stane *stone* lait *formerly* lyis deid *lies dead*

610 ballet *poem*   611 worschip *honour*   612 cheritie *charity*
monische *admonish*   613 Ming *mingle*   616 Sen scho is deid *since she is dead*

ORPHEUS AND EURYDICE (extract)

Orpheus goes to the Underworld

. . . I will tell how Orpheus tuke the way
To seke his wyf atour the gravis gray,
Hungry and cald, our mony wilsum wane,
Wythoutyn gyde, he and his harp allane.

5   He passit furth the space of twenty dayis,
Fer and full fer and ferther than I can tell,
And ay he fand stretis and redy wayis,
Tyll at the last unto the yett of hell
He come, and thare he fand a portar fell
10   With thre hedis, was callit Cerberus,
A hund of hell, a monster mervailus.

Than Orpheus began to be agast
Quhen he beheld that ugly hellis hund.
He tuke his harp, and on it playit fast,
15   Till at the last, throu suetenes of the sound,
The dog slepit and fell unto the ground,
And Orpheus atour his wame in stall,
And nethir-mare he went, as ye here sall.

1 tuke *took*   2 atour the gravis gray *over the grey groves*   3 cald *cold*
our mony wilsum wane *over many a wild and lonely place*
4 Wythoutyn gyde *without a guide* allane *alone*

5 passit furth *went on*   6 Fer and full fer *far and very far* ferther *further*
7 ay he fand stretis *always found roads* redy *likely*   8 yett *gate*   9 come *came*
portar *porter, gate-keeper* fell *cruel, grim*   10 thre hedis *three heads*
Cerberus *(on Cerberus, and the following persons, see n.)*
11 hund *hound, dog* mervailus *marvellous, wondrous*

12 agast *filled with horror*   13 Quhen *when* ugly *fearsome*   14 fast *firmly*
15 throu suetenes *through sweetness*   16 slepit *slept*
17 atour his wame in stall *stole in over his belly*
18 nethir-mare *further downwards* here sall *shall hear*

Than come he till ane rywir wonder depe,
20   Our it a brig, and on it sisteris thre,
Quhilk had the entree of the brig to kepe:
Alecto, Megera, and Thesiphonee,
Turnand a quhele, was ugly for to see,
And on it spred a man hecht Ixione,
25   Rowit about rycht wonder wobegone.

Than Orpheus playit a joly spryng;
The thre sistirs full fast thay fell on slepe;
The ugly quhele sessit of hir quhirlyng;
Thus left was none the entree for to kepe.
30   Than Ixion out of the quhele can crepe
And stall away; than Orpheus anone,
Without stoping, atour the brig is gone.

Syne come he till a wonder grisely flude,
Droubly and depe, that rathly doun can ryn,
35   Quhare Tantalus nakit full thristy stude,
And yit the water yede abone his chyn;
Thouch he gapit, thare wald na drop cum in –
Quhen he dulkit, the water wald descend;
Thus gat he noucht his thrist to slake no mend.

19 come *came* till ane rywir wonder depe *to a wondrously deep river*
20 Our *over* brig *bridge*   **21** *whose task it was to guard the entrance of the bridge*
23 Turnand a quhele, was *turning a wheel, which was*   **24** hecht *called*
25 *(who) rolled (it) around in the most wondrous torment*

26 joly spryng *lively tune*   **27** on slepe *asleep*   **28** sessit of *ceased from*
quhirlyng *whirling*   **30** can crepe *crept*   **31** stall *stole* anone *immediately*
32 atour *over*

33 Syne *then* grisely *grisly, terrible* flude *river*   **34** Droubly *turbulent*
rathly doun can ryn *swiftly ran down*   **35** Quhare *where* thristy *thirsty*
stude *stood*   **36** yit *yet* yede abone *went above*
37 Thouch he gapit *though he gaped* wald *would*   **38** dulkit *ducked (his head)*
39 gat he noucht *he got nothing* thrist *thirst* assuage *no nor*

40 Before his face ane apill hang also,
    Fast at his mouth, apon a tolter threde;
    Quhen he gapit, it rokkit to and fro,
    And fled as it refusit hym to fede.
    Than Orpheus had reuth of his grete nede,
45 Tuke out his harp and fast on it can clink:
    The water stude, and Tantalus gat drink.

    Syne our a mure wyth thornis thik and scharp,
    Weping allone, a wilsum way he went,
    And had noucht bene throu suffrage of his harp,
50 Wyth scharp pikis he had bene schorne and schent;
    And as he blent besyde hym on the bent
    He saw speldit a wonder wofull wicht,
    Nailit full fast, and Ticius he hicht.

    And on his breste thare sat a grisely gripe
55 Quhilk wyth his bill his bally throu can bore,
    Bath maw, mydred, hert, lyvir, and trype
    He ruggit out – his paynis war the more.
    Quhen Orpheus saw hym this suffer sore,
    Has tane his harp and maid suete melody;
60 The grype is fled; Ticius left his cry.

40 apill *apple* hang *hung*   **41** Fast at *close to*
apon a tolter threde *upon an unsteady thread*   **42** rokkit *swayed*   **43** as *as if*
fede *feed*   **44** reuth *pity* grete nede *great hardship*
45 fast on it can clink *plucked so that it rang*   **46** stude *stood still*

47 *then over a moor with thick and sharp thorns*   **48** wilsum *wild*
49 And had noucht bene throu suffrage *and if it had not been for the help*
50 pikis *thorns*
he had bene schorne and schent *he would have been torn and destroyed*
51 blent *looked* bent *field*   **52** speldit *stretched out*
a wonder wofull wicht *a wondrously miserable creature*
53 Nailit *nailed* Ticius he hicht *he was called Tityus*

54 gripe *vulture*   **55** Quhilk *which* bally *belly* can bore *pierced*
56 *both stomach, midriff, heart, liver and guts*   **57** ruggit *tore*
paynis war the more *pains were the greater*   **58** this *(?)thus, (?)this (torment)*
59 tane *taken* suete *sweet*

Beyond this more he fand a ferefull strete,
Myrk as the nycht, to pas rycht dangerus –
For slydernes scant mycht he hald his fete –
In quhilk thare was a stynk rycht odiouse

65   That gydit hym to hydouse hellis house,
Quhare Rodomantus and Proserpina
Were king and quene; Orpheus in coud ga.

O dolly place and grondles depe dungeon!
Furnes of fyre wyth stynk intollerable,

70   Pit of dispair, wythout remission!
Thy mete venym, thy drink is poysonable,
Thy grete paynis to compt unnowmerabil;
Quhat creature cummys to duell in the
Is ay deyand and newirmore may dee!

75   Thare fand he mony carefull king and quene,
Wyth croun on hede of brasse full hate birnand,
Quhilk in thair lyf rycht maisterfull had bene,
Conquerouris of gold, richesse and land:
Ector of Troy and Priam thare he fand,

80   And Alexander for his wrang conquest;
Anthiocus thare for his foule incest,

61 more *moor* fand *found* ferefull *fearsome*
62 Myrk as the nycht *dark as the night*   63 slydernes *slipperiness*
scant mycht he hald his fete *he could scarcely keep his feet*
65 *that guided him to the hideous house of hell*   66 Rodomantus *Rhadamanthus*
67 in coud ga *went in*

68 dolly *dismal* grondles *bottomless*   69 Furnes *furnace*   70 dispair *despair*
71 mete *food* venym *venom* poysonable *poisonous*   72 paynis *torments*
to compt unnowmerabil *innumerable to count*   73 Quhat *whatever*
cummys *comes*   74 ay deyand *ever dying* newirmore may dee *nevermore may die*

75 carefull *sorrowful*   76 croun *crown* hate *hot* birnand *burning*   77 lyf *life*
rycht maisterfull *exulting in their power*   78 richesse *wealth*
79 Ector *Hector*   80 wrang *wrongful*

Thare fand he Julius Cesar for his crueltee,
And Herode wyth his brotheris wyf he sawe;
And Nero for his grete iniquitee,
85   And Pilot for his breking of the lawe;
Syne under that he lukit and coud knawe
Cresus the king, none michtiar on mold,
For covatise, yett full of byrnand gold.

Thare fand he Pharo, for oppression
90   Off Goddis folk, on quhilk the plagis fell;
And Saul eke for the grete abusion
Off justice to the folk of Israell;
Thare fand he Acab and quene Jesabell,
Quhilk sely Nabot was a prophet trewe,
95   For his wyne-yarde wythoutyn pitee sleue.

Thare fand he mony pape and cardinall
In haly kirk quhilk dois abusion;
And bischopis in thair pontificall
Be symony and wrang intrusioun;
100   Abbotis and men of all religion,
For evill disponyng of thair placis rent
In flambe of fyre were bitterly turment.

83 brotheris wyf *brother's wife*   85 Pilot *Pilate* breking *breaking*
86 Syne *then* lukit *looked* knawe *recognized*
87 Cresus *Crassus (see n.)* michtiar on mold *mightier on earth*
88 covatise *covetousness* yett *poured* byrnand *burning*

89 Pharo *Pharaoh*   90 plagis *plagues*   91 eke *also* abusion *abuse*
93 Acab *Ahab*   94 sely *innocent* Nabot *Naboth (who)*
95 wythoutyn pitee sleue *slew without pity*

96 pape *pope*   97 haly kirk *holy church* dois abusion *do wrong*
98 pontificall *vestments*
99 Be symony *by simony (trading in church benefits)* wrang intrusioun *(?)unjust
seizure of benefices*   100 religion *religious orders*
101 disponyng *disposition* placis rent *income from their foundations*
102 flambe *flame* turment *tormented*

Syne nethir-mare he went quhare Pluto was
And Proserpine, and thiderward he drewe,
105   Ay playand on his harp as he coud pas;
Till at the last Erudices he knewe,
Lene and dedelike, pitouse and pale of hewe,
Rycht warsch and wan, and walowit as a wede,
Hir lily lyre was lyke unto the lede.

110   Quod he: 'My lady lele and my delyte,
Full wa is me to se yow changit thus.
Quhare is thy rude as rose, wyth chekis quhite?
Thy cristall eyne with blenkis amorouse?
Thi lippis rede to kis diliciouse?'
115   Quod scho, 'As now, I dar noucht tell, perfay,
Bot ye sall wit the cause ane othir day.'

Quod Pluto, 'Sir, thouch scho be like ane elf,
Thare is na cause to plenye, and forquhy?
Scho fure als wele dayly as did myself,
120   Or king Herode for all his chevalry.

103 Syne nethir-mare *further downwards* quhare *where*   104 drewe *went*
105 Ay playand *always playing* coud pas *moved on*   106 Erudices *Eurydice*
knewe *recognized*   107 Lene *thin* dedelike *deathly* pitouse *pitiful* hewe *colour*
108 Rycht warsch and wan *very sickly and pale*
walowit as a wede *withered like a weed*   109 lily lyre *lily-white complexion*
lede *lead*

110 Quod *said* lele *true* delyte *delight*   111 wa *woe* se *see*
112 rude *complexion* as *like a* chekis quhite *white cheeks*
113 cristall eyne *crystal clear eyes* blenkis amorouse *loving glances*
114 rede *red* to kis diliciouse *delightful to kiss*   115 scho *she*
As now *at this time* noucht *not* perfay *in truth*   116 wit *know*

117 thouch *though* elf *elf, otherworldly creature*   118 plenye *complain*
forquhy *why*   119 fure als wele *has fared as well*
120 chevalry *knights, knighthood*

It is langour that puttis hir in sik ply;
Were scho at hame in hir contree of Trace,
Scho wald refete full sone in fax and face.'

Than Orpheus before Pluto sat doun,
125 And in his handis quhite his harp can ta,
And playit mony suete proporcion,
With base tonys in ypodorica,
With gemilling in yperlydica;
Till at the last, for reuth and grete pitee
130 Thay wepit sore that coud hym here and see.

Than Proserpyne and Pluto bad hym as
His warison, and he wald ask rycht noucht
Bot licence wyth his wyf away to pas
Till his contree, that he so fer had soucht.
135 Quod Proserpyne: 'Sen I hir hidir broucht,
We sall noucht part bot wyth condicion.'
Quod he: 'Thareto I mak promission.'

121 langour *grief, longing* sik ply *such plight*
122 Were scho at hame *if she were at home* contree *country* Trace *Thrace*
123 Scho wald refete full sone *would recover very quickly* fax *hair*

125 handis quhite *white hands* can ta *took*
126 suete proporcion *sweet harmony*
127 base tonys in ypodorica *low notes in the hypodorian mode*
128 gemilling in yperlydica *doubling in the hyperlydian mode*
129 reuth *compassion*

131 as *ask*   132 warison *reward* rycht noucht *nothing at all*
133–4 *except permission to go away to his country with his wife, for whom he had
searched for so long*   135 Sen *since* hir hidir broucht *brought her hither*
136 bot wyth condicion *except with a stipulation*   137 Thareto *to that*
promission *promise*

'Erudices than be the hand thou tak,
And pas thy way, bot underneth this payne:
140 Gyf thou turnis, or blenkis behind thy bak,
We sall hir have forevir till hell agayn.'
Thouch this was hard, yit Orpheus was fayn,
And on thai went, talkand of play and sport,
Quhill thay almaist come to the utter port.

145 Thus Orpheus, wyth inwart lufe replete,
So blyndit was in grete affection,
Pensif apon his wyf and lady suete,
Remembrit noucht his hard condicion.
Quhat will ye more? In schort conclusion,
150 He blent bakward and Pluto come anone,
And unto hell agayn with hir is gone.

Allace, it was rycht grete hertsare for to here
Of Orpheus the weping and the wo,
Quhen that his wyf, quhilk he had bocht so dere,
155 Bot for a luke sa sone was hynt hym fro.
Flatlyngis he fell and mycht no forthir go,
And lay a quhile in suoun and extasy;
Quhen he ourcome, thus out on lufe can cry:

139 underneth this payne *under this penalty*   140 Gyf *if* blenkis *look*
141 *we shall have her back in hell forever*   142 fayn *glad, willing*
143 talkand *talking* play *amusement*
144 *until they came almost to the outer gate*

145 Thus *and so* wyth inwart lufe replete *filled with inner love*
146 affection *desire*   147 Pensif *musing anxiously*   150 blent *looked*
anone *at once*

152 rycht grete hertsare *cause of profound sorrow* here *hear*
154 bocht *redeemed* so dere *dearly, at such high cost*
155 *merely for a look was so quickly torn from him*   156 Flatlyngis *prostrate*
forthir *further*   157 quhile *while* suoun and extasy *a swoon and trance*
158 ourcome *recovered* can cry *cried*

'Quhat art thou lufe? How sall I the dyffyne?
160 Bitter and suete, cruel and merciable;
Plesand to sum, til othir playnt and pyne;
To sum constant, till othir variabil.
Hard is thy law, thi bandis unbrekable;
Quha servis the, thouch he be newir sa trewe,
165 Perchance sum tyme he sall have cause to rewe!

'Now fynd I wele this proverbe trew,' quod he,
' "Hert is on the hurd, and hand is on the sore;
Quhare lufe gois, on forse turnis the ee."
I am expert, and wo is me tharfore;
170 Bot for a luke my lady is forlore.'
Thus chydand on with lufe, our burn and bent,
A wofull wedow hamewart is he went . . .

159 dyffyne *describe*   160 merciable *merciful*   161 Plesand *pleasing*
playnt *(a cause of) lamentation* pyne *suffering*   163 bandis *bonds*
164 Quha servis *whoever serves* newir *never*   165 rewe *rue*

167 *heart is on the treasure and hand is on the sore*
168 *where love goes of necessity the eye must turn*
169 expert *experienced* wo is me tharfore *I am in grief because of it*
170 forlore *lost*   171 chydand *complaining*
our burn and bent *over stream and field*   172 wedow *widower*
hamewart *homewards*

THE FABLES

The Prologue

Thocht feinyeit fabils of ald poetré
Be not al grunded upon truth, yit than,
Thair polite termes of sweit rhetoré
Richt plesand ar unto the eir of man;
5 And als the cause that thay first began
Wes to repreif the haill misleving
Of man, be figure of ane uther thing.

In lyke maner as throw a bustious eird,
Swa it be laubourit with grit diligence,
10 Springis the flouris and the corne abreird,
Hailsum and gude to mannis sustenence;
Sa dois spring ane morall sweit sentence
Oute of the subtell dyte of poetry,
To gude purpois, quha culd it weill apply.

1 Thocht *though* feinyeit fabils *fictitious tales* ald *old*
2 grunded *grounded* yit than *nevertheless* 3 polite termes *polished words*
sweit rhetoré *sweet rhetoric* 4 Richt plesand *pleasing* eir *ear* 5 als *also*
6 repreif *reprove* haill misleving *whole wicked life* 7 be *by, through*
figure *symbol* ane uther *an other*

8 In lyke maner *in a similar way* throw *through* bustious eird *rough earth*
9 Swa it be laubourit *as long as it is tilled* grit *great* 10 Springis *spring up*
flouris *flowers* abreird *in first shoots* 11 Hailsum *health-giving*
gude *good* mannis *man's* 12 Sa dois *so does* sentence *meaning*
13 subtell dyte *subtle texture, style* 14 purpois *purpose*
quha culd *whoever knew how to* weill *well* apply *apply, interpret*

15   The nuttis schell, thocht it be hard and teuch,
      Haldis the kirnell, and is delectabill;
      Sa lyis thair ane doctrine wyse aneuch
      And full of frute, under ane fenyeit fabill;
      And clerkis sayis, it is richt profitabill
20   Amangis ernist to ming ane merie sport,
      To light the spreit and gar the tyme be schort.

      Forthermair, ane bow that ay is bent
      Worthis unsmart and dullis on the string;
      Sa dois the mynd that is ay diligent
25   In ernistfull thochtis and in studying.
      With sad materis sum merines to ming
      Accordis weill; thus Esope said, iwis,
      Dulcius arrident seria picta iocis.

      Of this authour, my maisteris, with your leif,
30   Submitting me to your correctioun,
      In mother toung, of Latyng, I wald preif
      To mak ane maner of translatioun –
      Nocht of myself, for vane presumptioun,
      Bot be requeist and precept of ane lord,
35   Of quhome the name it neidis not record.

15 nuttis schell *nut's shell* teuch *tough*   16 Haldis *holds* kirnell *kernel*
delectabill *delightful*   17 lyis *lies* thair *there* wyse aneuch *very wise*
18 frute *fruit*   19 clerkis *scholars, wise men* sayis *say* richt *very*
20 Amangis ernist *amongst seriousness* ming *mix* merie sport *merry playfulness*
21 light *lighten* spreit *spirit* gar *cause, make*

22 Forthermair *furthermore* ay *always*   23 Worthis unsmart *becomes weak*
dullis *loses force, slackens*   25 ernistfull thochtis *serious thoughts*
26 sad *solemn, serious* materis *matters* sum merines to ming *mix some merriness*
27 Accordis weill *is very appropriate* Esope *Aesop* iwis *indeed*
28 *serious things arrayed with jests smile more sweetly*

29 leif *leave*   31 toung *tongue* of Latyng *from Latin*
wald preif *would like to try*   32 *to make a kind of translation*
33 Nocht of myself *not from my own wish* vane *out of, for fear of*
34 Bot be requeist and precept *but according to the request and command*
35 quhome *whom* it neidis not *it is not necessary to*

In hamelie language and in termes rude
Me neidis wryte, forquhy of eloquence
Nor rethorike, I never understude.
Thairfoir meiklie I pray your reverence,
40 Gif ye find ocht that throw my negligence
Be deminute, or yit superfluous,
Correct it at your willis gratious.

My author in his fabillis tellis how
That brutal beistis spak and understude,
45 Into gude purpois dispute and argow,
Ane sillogisme propone, and eik conclude;
Putting exempill and similitude
How mony men in operatioun
Ar like to beistis in conditioun.

50 Na mervell is, ane man be lyke ane beist,
Quhilk lufis ay carnall and foull delyte,
That schame can not him renye nor arreist,
Bot takis all the lust and appetyte,
Quhilk throw custum and the daylie ryte
55 Syne in the mynd sa fast is radicate
That he in brutal beist is transformate.

36 hamelie *homely, plain* termes rude *rough words*   37 Me neidis *I must*
forquhy *because*   39 Thairfoir meiklie *therefore humbly*
40 Gif *if* ocht *anything*   41 deminute *incomplete, abbreviated*
superfluous *long-winded*   42 at *according to* willis gratious *gracious will*

44 brutal beistis *irrational animals* spak *spoke*
45 purpois *purpose* argow *argue*   46 propone *propound* eik *also*
47 exempill *example* similitude *likeness*   48 mony *many*
operatioun *behaviour, conduct*   49 conditioun *nature*

50 Na mervell is *no wonder is it that*   51 Quhilk lufis *who loves* delyte *pleasure*
52 That *so that* renye *(?)check, (?)arraign* arreist *stop*
53 takis *(he) takes, seizes*   54 Quhilk *which* daylie ryte *habit*
55 Syne *then* radicate *rooted*   56 in *into* transformate *transformed*

This nobill clerk, Esope, as I haif tauld,
In gay metir, facound and purperat,
Be figure wrait his buke, for he nocht wald
60   Tak the disdane off hie nor low estate;
And to begin, first of ane cok he wrate,
Seikand his meit, quhilk fand ane jolie stone,
Of quhome the fabill ye sall heir anone.

The Cock and the Jasp

Ane cok sum tyme with feddram fresch and gay,
65   Richt cant and crous, albeit he was bot pure,
Fleu furth upon ane dunghill sone be day;
To get his dennar set was al his cure.
Scraipand amang the as, be aventure
He fand ane jolie jasp, richt precious,
70   Wes castin furth in sweping of the hous.

57 haif tauld *have told*   58 gay metir *fine verse*
facound and purperat *eloquent and magnificent*
59 Be figure wrait his buke *wrote his book in a figurative way, symbolically*
nocht wald *did not wish*   60 Tak *to receive* hie *high*
62 Seikand his meit *seeking his food* fand *found* jolie *pretty, bright*
63 quhome *whom* heir anone *hear immediately*

64 sum tyme *once upon a time* feddram *feathers*
65 Richt cant and crous *very jaunty and bold* albeit *although* pure *poor*
66 Fleu furth *flew out* sone *early*   67 dennar *dinner* set *directed*
cure *care, effort*   68 Scraipand *scraping* as *ash* be aventure *by chance*
69 fand *found* jolie *pretty, bright* jasp *jasper (a precious stone)*
70 Wes castin furth *which had been thrown out* sweping *sweeping*

As damisellis wantoun and insolent
That fane wald play and on the streit be sene,
To swoping of the hous thay tak na tent
Quhat be thairin, swa that the flure be clene;
75 Jowellis ar tint, as oftymis hes bene sene,
Upon the flure, and swopit furth anone.
Peradventure, sa wes the samin stone.

Sa mervelland upon the stane, quod he,
'O gentill Jasp, O riche and nobill thing,
80 Thocht I the find, thow ganis not for me;
Thow art ane jouell for ane lord or king.
Pietie it wer thow suld ly in this mydding,
Be buryit thus amang this muke and mold,
And thow so fair and worth sa mekill gold.

85 'It is pietie I suld the find, forquhy
Thy grit vertew, nor yit thy cullour cleir,
I may nouther extoll nor magnify,
And thow to me may mak bot lyttill cheir;

71 damisellis *servant girls* wantoun and insolent *careless and arrogant*
72 fane wald play *dearly want to enjoy themselves* streit *street* sene *seen*
73 swoping *sweepings, refuse* tak na tent *pay no heed*
74 Quhat be thairin *what is in it*
swa that the flure be clene *so long as the floor is clean* 75 Jowellis *jewels*
tint *lost* oftymis *often* 76 swopit furth anone *swept out immediately*
77 Peradventure *perhaps* samin *same*

78 mervelland *marvelling* stane *stone* quod *said* 79 gentill *noble, fine*
80 Thocht *though* thow ganis not for me *you are not fitting for me*
82 Pietie *pity* suld ly *should lie* mydding *midden, dunghill*
83 buryit *buried* muke *muck* mold *earth* 84 mekill *much*

85 forquhy *because* 86 grit vertew *great excellence, power*
cullour cleir *beautiful colour* 87 nouther *neither* magnify *glorify*
88 may mak bot lyttill cheir *can provide only small enjoyment*

To grit lordis thocht thow be leif and deir,
90   I lufe fer better thing of les availl,
As draf or corne to fill my tume intraill.

'I had lever ga skraip heir with my naillis
Amangis this mow, and luke my lifys fude,
As draf or corne, small wormis, or snaillis,
95   Or ony meit wald do my stomok gude,
Than of jaspis ane mekill multitude;
And thow agane, upon the samin wyis
For les availl may me as now dispyis.

'Thow hes na corne, and thairof haif I neid;
100   Thy cullour dois bot confort to the sicht,
And that is not aneuch my wame to feid,
For wyfis sayis lukand werkis ar licht.
I wald sum meit have, get it geve I micht,
For houngrie men may not weill leve on lukis:
105   Had I dry breid, I compt not for na cukis.

89 be leif *beloved* deir *precious*   90 lufe *love* fer *far* les availl *less value*
91 draf *draff (the residue of husks left over after brewing)*
tume intraill *empty stomach*

92 I had lever ga *I would rather go (and)* naillis *nails, claws*
93 Amangis *amongst* mow *rubbish, dust*
luke my lifys fude *look for my sustenance*   95 ony meit *any food* gude *good*
96 mekill *great*   97 thow agane *in return* upon the samin wyis *in the same way*
98 *may now despise me as of less use*

99 hes *have* thairof haif I neid *I have need of it*
100 dois bot confort *only brings comfort* sicht *sight*
101 aneuch my wame to feid *enough to feed my belly*
102 wyfis sayis *women say*
lukand werkis ar licht *(?)deeds which only consist of looking are easy, (?)things
that look well are insubstantial*   103 get it geve I micht *if I could get it*
104 houngrie *hungry* leve *live* lukis *looks*   105 breid *bread*
compt not for na cukis *I do not care about cooks*

'Quhar suld thow mak thy habitatioun?
Quhar suld thow duell, bot in ane royall tour?
Quhar suld thow sit, bot on ane kingis croun,
Exaltit in worschip and in grit honour?
110 Rise, gentill Jasp, of all stanis the flour,
Out of this fen, and pas quhar thow suld be:
Thow ganis not for me, nor I for the.'

Levand this jowell law upon the ground,
To seik his meit this cok his wayis went.
115 Bot quhen, or how, or quhome be it wes found,
As now I set to hald na argument.
Bot of the inward sentence and intent
Of this fabill, as myne author dois write,
I sall reheirs in rude and hamelie dite.

Moralitas

120 This jolie jasp had properteis sevin:
The first, of cullour it was mervelous,
Part lyke the fyre and part lyke to the hevin;
It makis ane man stark and victorious,
Preservis als fra cacis perrillous;
125 Quha hes this stane sall have gude hap to speid,
Of fyre nor fallis him neidis not to dreid.

---

106 Quhar *where*   107 bot *except* tour *tower*   108 croun *crown*
109 worschip *esteem, dignity*   110 stanis *stones* flour *flower, perfection*
111 fen *filth* pas *go*

113 Levand *leaving* law *low*   114 seik *seek*
115 quhen *when* quhome be *by whom*   116 set *intend* hald *hold, carry on*
117 sentence *meaning*   119 sall reheirs *shall relate*
in rude and hamelie dite *rough and homely style*

120 properteis sevin *seven qualities*   122 hevin *heaven, sky*   123 stark *strong*
124 als *also* cacis *happenings*   125 Quha *whoever* gude hap *good fortune*
speid *prosper*   126 fallis *falls* him neidis not *he does not need* dreid *fear*

This gentill jasp, richt different of hew,
Betakinnis perfite prudence and cunning,
Ornate with mony deidis of vertew,
130 Mair excellent than ony eirthly thing,
Quhilk makis men in honour ay to ring,
Happie, and stark to wyn the victorie
Of all vicis and spirituall enemie.

Quha may be hardie, riche, and gratious?
135 Quha can eschew perrell and aventure?
Quha can governe ane realme, cietie, or hous
Without science? No man, I yow assure.
It is riches that ever sall indure,
Quhilk maith, nor moist, nor uther rust can freit:
140 To mannis saull it is eternall meit.

This cok, desyrand mair the sempill corne
Than ony jasp, may till ane fule be peir,
Quhilk at science makis bot ane moik and scorne,
And na gude can; als lytill will he leir –
145 His hart wammillis wyse argumentis to heir,
As dois ane sow to quhome men for the nanis
In hir draf-troich wald saw the precious stanis.

127 richt different *differing*, *(?)excellent* hew *colour*   128 Betakinnis *signifies*
perfite *perfect* cunning *knowledge*   129 Ornate *adorned* deidis *deeds*
130 Mair *more* eirthly *earthly*   131 Quhilk *which* ay to ring *ever to reign*
132 Happie *fortunate*   133 Of all vicis *over all vices*

134 hardie *bold* gratious *fortunate*   135 eschew *overcome*
perrell and aventure *danger and chance*   136 cietie *city*   137 science *wisdom*
138 riches *wealth* indure *endure*
139 *which neither worm, nor dampness, nor other rust can devour*   140 saull *soul*

141 desyrand *desiring* sempill *simple*   142 till ane fule *to a fool* peir *equal*
143 moik *mockery*   144 na gude can *has no knowledge of good*
als lytill will he leir *and wishes to learn just as little*
145 hart wammillis *heart turns sick* heir *hear*   146 the nanis *deliberately*
147 draf-troich *draff-trough* saw *scatter*

Quha is enemie to science and cunning
Bot ignorants, that understandis nocht
150   Quhilk is sa nobill, sa precious, and sa ding,
That it may not with eirdlie thing be bocht?
Weill wer that man, over all uther, that mocht
All his lyfe-dayis in perfite studie wair
To get science, for him neidis na mair.

155   Bot now, allace, this jasp is tynt and hid.
We seik it nocht, nor preis it for to find;
Haif we richis, na better lyfe we bid,
Of science thocht the saull be bair and blind.
Of this mater to speik, it wer bot wind,
160   Thairfore I ceis and will na forther say.
Ga seik the jasp, quha will, for thair it lay.

The Two Mice

Esope, myne authour, makis mentioun
Of twa myis, and thay wer sisteris deir,
Of quham the eldest duelt in ane borous toun;
165   The uther wynnit uponland weill neir,
Soliter, quhyle under busk, quhyle under breir,
Quhilis in the corne, in uther mennis skaith,
As owtlawis dois, and levit on hir waith.

149 ignorants *ignorant people*   150 ding *worthy*   151 eirdlie *earthly*
bocht *bought*   152 Weill wer *well would it be for*   mocht *might, could*
153 wair *spend*   154 get *acquire*   for him neidis na mair *he needs no more*

155 tynt *lost, destroyed*   156 preis *strive*   157 Haif we *if we have*   bid *ask for*
158 thocht *though*   159 bot *only*   160 ceis *cease*   161 Ga *go*

162 Esope *Aesop*   163 twa myis *two mice*   deir *loving*   164 quham *whom*
duelt *dwelt*   borous toun *burgh (town incorporated with a charter, and enjoying a
degree of self-government)*   165 *the other dwelt in the country close by*
166 Soliter *solitary*   quhyle *sometimes*   busk *bush*   breir *briar*
167 Quhilis *sometimes*   in uther mennis skaith *to the harm of other men*
168 owtlawis dois *outlaws do*   levit on hir waith *lived on her plunder*

This rurall mous into the wynter tyde
170   Had hunger, cauld, and tholit grit distres;
The uther mous, that in the burgh can byde,
Was gild brother and made ane fre burges,
Toll-fre als, but custum mair or les,
And fredome had to ga quhairever scho list
175   Amang the cheis in ark, and meill in kist.

Ane tyme quhen scho wes full and unfutesair,
Scho tuke in mynd hir sister uponland,
And langit sair to heir of hir weilfair,
To se quhat lyfe scho led under the wand.
180   Bairfute, allone, with pykestaf in hir hand,
As pure pylgryme scho passit owt off town
To seik hir sister, baith oure daill and down.

Furth mony wilsum wayis can scho walk,
Throw mosse and mure, throw bankis, busk, and breir,
185   Fra fur to fur, cryand fra balk to balk,
'Cum furth to me, my awin sister deir!

169 into *in* tyde *time*   170 cauld *cold* tholit grit distres *suffered great distress*
171 can byde *dwelt*   172 gild brother *member of a guild*
burges *citizen of the burgh*   173 Tax-free also exempt from dues *large and small*
174 ga quhairever scho list *go wherever she desired*   175 cheis *cheese*
ark *container* meill *meal, flour* kist *chest*

176 Ane *one* quhen *when* unfutesair *not footsore*
177 tuke in mynd *remembered, thought of* uponland *in the country*
178 langit *longed* heir *hear*   179 se quhat lyfe *see what kind of life*
under the wand *(under the branch =) in the forest*
180 pykestaf *pikestaff, spiked stick*   181 pure *poor*
182 baith oure daill and down *over both dale and hill*

183 *forth over many wild and lonely ways she walked*
184 Throw mosse and mure *through bog and moor*
bankis, busk, and breir *hillsides, bush and briar*
185 Fra fur to fur *from furrow to furrow* cryand *crying*
balk *ridge (in a ploughed field)*   186 Cum furth *come out* awin *own*

Cry peip anis!' With that the mous culd heir
And knew hir voce, as kinnisman will do
Be verray kynd, and furth scho come hir to.

190   The hartlie joy, Lord God, geve ye had sene
Beis kithit quhen that thir sisteris met,
And grit kyndnes wes schawin thame betuene,
For quhylis thay leuch, and quhylis for joy thay gret,
Quhyle kissit sweit, quhylis in armis plet;
195   Ane thus thay fure quhill soberit wes their mude;
Syne fute for fute unto the chalmer yude.

As I hard say, it was ane sober wane,
Off fog and farne full misterlyk wes maid,
Ane sillie scheill under ane erdfast stane,
200   Off quhilk the entres wes not hie nor braid;
And in the samin thay went, but mair abaid,
Withoutin fyre or candill birnand bricht,
For comonly sic pykeris luffis not lycht.

187 peip *'peep'* anis *once* culd heir *heard*   188 knew *recognized*
voce *voice* kinnisman *kinsfolk*
189 Be verray kynd *naturally, through nature itself* come *came*

190 hartlie *heartfelt* geve *if*   191 Beis kithit *(that) is shown* thir *these*
192 grit kyndnes *great affection* schawin *shown*   193 quhylis *sometimes*
leuch *laugh* gret *wept*   194 sweit *sweetly* armis plet *embraced*
195 fure *behaved* quhill *until* mude *mood*
196 Syne fute for fute *then keeping pace together* chalmer *chamber* yude *went*

197 hard *heard* sober wane *humble dwelling*   198 fog and farne *moss and fern*
full misterlyk *poorly, in a way which revealed poverty*
199 sillie *simple, wretched* scheill *hovel* erdfast stane *stone fixed in the earth*
200 quhilk *which* entres *entrance* hie nor braid *high or wide*   201 samin *same*
but mair abaid *without more delay*   202 birnand bricht *burning brightly*
203 sic pykeris luffis not lycht *such thieves do not love light*

Quhen thay wer lugit thus, thir sely myse,
205 The youngest sister into hir butterie hyid,
And brocht furth nuttis and peis, insteid off spyce;
Giff this wes gude fair, I do it on thame besyde.
This burges mous prompit forth in pryde,
And said, 'Sister, is this your dayly fude?'
210 'Quhy not,' quod scho, 'is not this meit richt gude?'

'Na, be my saull, I think it bot ane scorne.'
'Madame,' quod scho, 'ye be the mair to blame.
My mother sayd, sister, quhen we wer borne,
That I and ye lay baith within ane wame;
215 I keip the rate and custome off my dame,
And off my syre, levand in povertie,
For landis have we nane in propertie.'

'My fair sister,' quod scho, 'have me excusit –
This rude dyat and I can not accord.
220 To tender meit my stomok is ay usit,
Forquhy I fair als weill as ony lord.
Thir wydderit peis and nuttis, or thay be bord,
Will brek my teith and mak my wame full sklender,
Quhilk usit wes before to meitis tender.'

204 lugit *lodged, installed* sely *simple, poor* 205 butterie *larder* hyid *hastened*
206 brocht furth *brought out* peis *peas* 207 Giff *if* gude fair *good fare*
do it on thame besyde *I leave it to those here* 208 burges *burgess, town*
prompit *(?)(was) pressed on, (?)burst out* 209 fude *food* 210 Quhy *why*
quod *said* meit *food*

211 saull *soul* scorne *insult* 214 baith *both* ane wame *one womb*
215 rate *standard* dame *mother* 216 syre *father* levand *living*
217 propertie *possession, ownership*

219 rude dyat *rough diet* 220 tender meit *delicate food* usit *used, accustomed*
221 Forquhy *because* fair *fare* als weill as *as well as* 222 wydderit *withered*
or *before* bord *pierced* 223 brek *break* teith *teeth* wame *stomach*
sklender *thin*

225 'Weil, weil, sister,' quod the rurall mous,
    'Geve it pleis yow, sic thing as ye se heir,
    Baith meit and dreink, harberie and hous,
    Sal be your awin, will ye remane al yeir.
    Ye sall it have wyth blyith and hartlie cheir,
230 And that suld mak the maissis that ar rude,
    Amang freindis, richt tender, and wonder gude.

    'Quhat plesure is in the feistis delicate,
    The quhilkis ar gevin with ane glowmand brow?
    Ane gentill hart is better recreate
235 With blyith visage, than seith to him ane kow.
    Ane modicum is mair for till allow,
    Swa that gude will be kerver at the dais,
    Than thrawin vult and mony spycit mais.'

    For all hir mery exhortatioun,
240 This burges mous had littill will to sing,
    Bot hevilie scho kest hir browis doun
    For all the daynteis that scho culd hir bring;
    Yit at the last scho said, halff in hething,
    'Sister, this victuall and your royall feist
245 May weill suffice unto ane rurall beist.

---

226 Geve *if* pleis *please* sic *such* heir *here*   227 harberie *lodging*
228 *shall be your own even if you wish to remain all year*
229 blyith *happy* hartlie *heartfelt, sincere* cheir *attitude, expression*
230 maissis *dishes* rude *rustic, simple*   231 wonder *extremely, wondrously*

232 feistis delicate *dainty feasts*   233 quhilkis ar gevin *which are given*
glowmand *frowning*   234 gentill *noble, gracious* recreate *refreshed*
235 than seith to him ane kow *than if a whole cow were cooked for him*
236 modicum *small portion* till allow *to praise*   237 Swa that *provided that*
kerver *carver* dais *high table*   238 thrawin *twisted, frowning* vult *face*
mony spycit mais *many highly seasoned dishes*

241 hevilie *sorrowfully* kest *cast, lowered* browis *eyebrows*
242 scho culd hir bring *she (the country mouse) brought her*   243 hething *scorn*
244 victuall *food*

'Lat be this hole and cum into my place:
I sall to yow schaw, be experience,
My Gude Friday is better nor your Pace,
My dische likingis is worth your haill expence.
250 I have housis anew off grit defence;
Off cat nor fall-trap I have na dreid.'
'I grant,' quod scho, and on togidder thay yeid.

In skugry ay, throw rankest gers and corne,
And under cowert prevelie couth thay creip;
255 The eldest wes the gyde and went beforne,
The younger to hir wayis tuke gude keip.
On nicht thay ran and on the day can sleip,
Quhill in the morning, or the laverok sang,
Thay fand the town, and in blythlie couth gang.

260 Not fer fra thyne unto ane worthie wane,
This burges brocht thame sone quhare thay suld be.
Withowt 'God speid' thair herberie wes tane
Into ane spence with vittell grit plentie:

246 Lat be *leave*   247 be *by*
248 *my Good Friday (with its penitential fare) is better than your Easter (feast)*
249 likingis *leavings* haill expence *whole expenditure*   250 anew *in plenty*
defence *security*   251 fall-trap *(?)mouse-trap with a falling door* dreid *fear*
252 yeid *went*

253 skugry *secrecy* rankest *thickest* gers *grass*   254 cowert *cover*
prevelie couth thay creip *stealthily they crept*
256 tuke gude keip *paid close attention*   257 nicht *night* can sleip *slept*
258 Quhill *until* or *before* laverok *lark*   259 fand *found, came to*
in blythlie couth gang *merrily went in*

260 fer fra thyne *far from thence* wane *dwelling*   261 sone *quickly*
262 Withowt 'God speed' *(a greeting, i.e. without ceremony) their lodging was
taken*   263 spence *pantry* vittell grit plentie *food in abundance*

Baith cheis and butter upon thair skelfis hie,
265 And flesche and fische aneuch, baith fresche and salt,
And sekkis full off grotis, meill, and malt.

Efter, quhen thay disposit wer to dyne,
Withowtin grace, thay wesche and went to meit,
With all coursis that cukis culd devyne,
270 Muttoun and beif, strikin in tailyeis greit.
Ane lordis fair thus couth thay counterfeit
Except ane thing: thay drank the watter cleir
Insteid off wyne; bot yit thay maid gude cheir.

With blyith upcast and merie countenance,
275 The eldest sister sperit at hir gest
Giff that scho be ressone fand difference
Betuix that chalmer and hir sarie nest.
'Ye, dame,' quod scho, 'how lang will this lest?'
'For evermair, I wait, and langer to.'
280 'Giff it be swa, ye ar at eis,' quod scho.

264 skelfis hie *high shelves*   265 flesche *meat* aneuch *in plenty*
266 sekkis *sacks* grotis *groats (oat kernels)* meill *meal, flour*

268 Withowtin grace *without saying grace* wesche *washed* to meit *to their food*
269 cukis *cooks* devyne *devise*   270 strikin in tailyeis greit *carved in big slices*
271 fair *fare, style of eating* couth thay counterfeit *they imitated*
273 maid gude cheir *enjoyed themselves*

274 blyith upcast *pleasant taunting*   275 sperit *asked* gest *guest*
276 be ressone *according to reason, with good reason*   277 sarie *sorry, wretched*
278 Ye, dame *yes, lady* lang *long* lest *last*   279 wait *expect, know*
langer to *longer too*   280 swa *so* at eis *at ease, in comfort*

Till eik thair cheir ane subcharge furth scho brocht –
Ane plait off grottis, and ane disch full off meill;
Thraf-caikkis als I trow scho spairit nocht
Aboundantlie about hir for to deill,
285 And mane full fyne scho brocht insteid off geill,
And ane quhyte candill owt off ane coffer stall
Insteid off spyce, to gust thair mouth withall.

This maid thay merie, quhill thay micht na mair,
And 'Haill, Yule, haill!' cryit upon hie.
290 Yit efter joy oftymes cummis cair,
And troubill efter grit prosperitie.
Thus as thay sat in all thair jolitie,
The spenser come with keyis in his hand,
Oppinnit the dure, and thame at denner fand.

295 Thay taryit not to wesche, as I suppose,
Bot on to ga, quha micht formest win.
The burges had ane hole, and in scho gois;
Hir sister had na hole to hyde hir in.
To se that selie mous, it wes grit sin;
300 So desolate and will off ane gude reid;
For verray dreid scho fell in swoun neir deid.

281 *to increase their entertainment she brought out an extra course*
282 plait off grottis *plate of groats*
283 Thraf-caikkis *flat unleavened cakes of oatmeal* als *also* trow *believe*
spairit nocht *did not spare*   284 deill *serve, hand out*
285 mane *white bread* geill *jelly*   286 quhyte *white* coffer *chest* stall *stole*
287 to gust *add relish to*

288 This *thus* quhill thay micht na mair *until they could (eat) no more*
289 upon hie *loudly*   290 oftymes cummis cair *often comes sorrow*
293 spenser come *steward came*   294 Oppinnit the dure *opened the door*
denner *dinner*

295 taryit not to wesche *did not wait to wash*   296 on to ga *off they went*
quha micht formest win *(to see) who might be the first*   299 selie *wretched*
sin *pity*   300 will *at a loss, bewildered* reid *plan*   301 verray *sheer*
neir deid *almost dead*

Bot, as God wald, it fell ane happie cace:
The spenser had na laser for to byde,
Nowther to seik nor serche, to sker nor chace,
305   Bot on he went, and left the dure up wyde.
The bald burges his passage weill hes spyde;
Out off hir hole scho come and cryit on hie,
'How fair ye, sister? Cry peip, quhairever ye be!'

This rurall mous lay flatling on the ground,
310   And for the deith scho wes full sair dredand,
For till hir hart straik mony wofull stound;
As in ane fever scho trimbillit, fute and hand.
And quhan hir sister in sic ply hir fand,
For verray pietie scho began to greit,
315   Syne confort hir with wordis hunny-sweit.

'Quhy ly ye thus? Ryse up, my sister deir!
Cum to your meit; this perrell is overpast.'
The uther answerit with hevie cheir,
'I may not eit, sa sair I am agast!
320   I had lever thir fourty dayis fast
With watter-caill, and to gnaw benis or peis,
Than all your feist in this dreid and diseis.'

302 wald *willed*   it fell ane happie cace *there befell a fortunate chance*
303 laser *leisure* byde *stay*   304 Nowther *neither*
seik nor serche *seek or search* sker nor chace *frighten away or chase*
305 up wyde *open*   306 bald *bold*

309 flatling *flat*   310 deith scho wes full sair dredand *was sorely fearing death*
311 till hir hart straik *to her heart struck* stound *pang*   312 trimbillit *trembled*
fute *foot*   313 quhan *when* sic ply *such plight*   314 pietie *pity, compassion*
greit *weep*   315 Syne *then* confort *comforted* hunny-sweit *sweet as honey*

318 hevie *sorrowful, gloomy* cheir *expression, demeanour*   319 eit *eat*
sair *grievously* agast *terrified*   320 lever *rather* thir *these*
321 watter-caill *cabbage broth* benis *beans*   322 diseis *distress*

With fair tretie yit scho gart hir upryse,
And to the burde thay went and togidder sat.
325 And scantlie had thay drunkin anis or twyse,
Quhen in come Gib Hunter, our jolie cat,
And bad 'God speid.' The burges up with that,
And till hir hole scho fled as fyre of flint;
Bawdronis the uther be the bak hes hint.

330 Fra fute to fute he kest hir to and fra,
Quhylis up, quhylis down, als cant as ony kid.
Quhylis wald he lat hir rin under the stra;
Quhylis wald he wink, and play with hir buk-heid;
Thus to the selie mous grit pane he did;
335 Quhill at the last throw fortune and gude hap,
Betwix ane dosor and the wall scho crap.

And up in haist behind the parraling
Scho clam so hie that Gilbert micht not get hir,
Syne be the cluke thair craftelie can hing
340 Till he wes gane; hir cheir wes all the better.
Syne doun scho lap quhen thair wes nane to let hir,
And to the burges mous loud can scho cry,
'Fairweill, sister, thy feist heir I defy!

323 tretie *entreaty* gart *caused* upryse *get up*   324 burde *table*
togidder *together*   325 scantlie *scarcely* anis *once*
326 Gib *Gib, Gilbert (common name for a tomcat)*
327 'God speid' *may God help you (a greeting, cf. line 262)* up *(leapt) up*
328 fyre of flint *fire (sparked) from flint*
329 Bawdronis *a Scottish name for a cat* hint *seized*

330 kest *tossed* to and fra *to and fro*   331 Quhylis *sometimes* cant *brisk*
kid *kid, young goat*   332 rin *run* stra *straw*   333 wink *close his eyes*
buk-heid *blindman's buff*   334 selie *wretched*   335 gude hap *good luck*
336 dosor *wall-hanging* crap *crept*

337 parraling *(?)tapestry, hanging*   338 clam *climbed*   339 cluke *claw*
thair craftelie can hing *cleverly hung there*   340 gane *gone* cheir *mood, spirit*
341 lap *leapt* let *hinder, prevent*   342 can *did*   343 defy *defy, renounce*

'Thy mangerie is mingit all with cair;
345   Thy guse is gude, thy gansell sour as gall;
The subcharge off thy service is bot sair;
Sa sall thow find heir-efterwart ma fall.
I thank yone courtyne and yone perpall wall
Off my defence now fra yone crewell beist.
350   Almichtie God keip me fra sic ane feist.

'Wer I into the kith that I come fra,
For weill nor wo I suld never cum agane.'
With that scho tuke hir leif and furth can ga,
Quhylis throw the corne, and quhylis throw the plane.
355   Quhen scho wes furth and fre scho wes full fane,
And merilie markit unto the mure;
I can not tell how eftirwart scho fure,

Bot I hard say scho passit to hir den,
Als warme as woll, suppose it wes not greit,
360   Full beinly stuffit, baith but and ben,
Off beinis and nuttis, peis, ry, and quheit;
Quhenever scho list scho had aneuch to eit,
In quyet and eis withoutin ony dreid,
Bot to hir sisteris feist na mair scho yeid.

344 mangerie *banquet* mingit *mingled* cair *anxiety, distress*   345 guse *goose*
gansell *garlic sauce (for the goose)* gall *gall, bile*   346 subcharge *extra course*
service *serving of food* sair *sorrow, suffering*   347 heir-efterwart *hereafterwards*
ma fall *may turn out, befall*   348 courtyne *curtain* perpall wall *partition*
349 crewell beist *cruel beast*   350 keip *keep, preserve*

351 *if I were in the land I came from*
352 weill nor wo *(weal nor woe =) anything in the world*
cum agane *return here*   353 leif *leave* furth can ga *went off*
354 plane *plain, open fields*   355 furth and fre *away and free* fane *glad*
356 markit *went* mure *moor*   357 fure *fared*

358 hard *heard*   359 woll *wool* suppose *even though* greit *big*
360 *very cosily furnished both in the outer and inner parts*   361 ry *rye*
quheit *wheat*   362 Quhenever *whenever* list *wished, desired* aneuch *enough*
364 yeid *went*

Moralitas

365 Freindis, heir may ye find, and ye will tak heid,
     Into this fabill ane gude moralitie:
     As fitchis myngit ar with nobill seid,
     Swa intermellit is adversitie
     With eirdlie joy, swa that na estate is frie
370 Without trubill and sum vexatioun,
     And namelie thay quhilk clymmis up maist hie,
     That ar not content with small possessioun.

     Blissed be sempill lyfe withoutin dreid;
     Blissed be sober feist in quietie.
375 Quha hes aneuch, of na mair hes he neid,
     Thocht it be littill into quantatie.
     Grit aboundance and blind prosperitie
     Oftymes makis ane evill conclusioun;
     The sweitest lyfe, thairfoir, in this cuntrie,
380 Is sickernes with small possessioun.

     O wantoun man, that usis for to feid
     Thy wambe, and makis it a god to be;
     Luke to thyself, I warne the weill, but dreid.
     The cat cummis, and to the mous hes ee;

365 and *if*   367 fitchis *vetches (plants thought to be worthless)*
myngit *mingled* seid *seed*   368 intermellit *intermixed*   369 eirdlie *earthly*
estate *rank, condition* frie *free*   370 trubill *trouble*   371 namelie *especially*
quhilk *who* clymmis *climb* maist *most*   372 possessioun *possessions*

373 Blissed *blessed*   374 sober *moderate* quietie *quietness*   375 Quha *whoever*
376 Thocht *though*   380 sickernes *security*

381 wantoun *wanton, unruly* usis *is accustomed*   382 wambe *belly*
383 but dreid *without doubt*   384 ee *eye*

385 Quhat vaillis than thy feist and royaltie,
With dreidfull hart and tribulatioun?
Best thing in eird, thairfor, I say for me,
Is blyithnes in hart, with small possessioun.

Thy awin fyre, freind, thocht it be bot ane gleid,
390 It warmis weill, and is worth gold to the;
And Solomon sayis, gif that thow will reid,
'Under the hevin I can not better be
Than ay be blyith and leif in honestie.'
Quhairfoir I may conclude be this ressoun:
395 Of eirthly joy it beiris maist degré,
Blyithnes in hart, with small possessioun.

The Cock and the Fox

Thocht brutall beistis be irrationall,
That is to say, wantand discretioun,
Yyt ilk ane in thair kyndis naturall
400 Hes mony divers inclinatioun:
The bair busteous, the wolff, the wylde lyoun,
The fox fenyeit, craftie and cawtelows,
The dog to bark on nicht and keip the hows.

385 vaillis *avails*   386 dreidfull *fearful*   387 eird *earth*
I say for me *for my part, as far as I am concerned*   388 blyithnes *happiness*

389 awin *own* thocht *even if* gleid *ember*   390 the *thee*   391 reid *read*
393 ay *ever, always* blyith *happy* leif in honestie *live in virtue*
394 Quhairfoir *wherefore* ressoun *proposition, statement*
395 beiris maist degré *holds the highest place*

397 Thocht *though* brutall beistis *unreasoning animals*
398 wantand discretioun *lacking judgement, discrimination*
399 Yyt ilk ane *yet each one* kyndis *species*
400 divers inclinatioun *different dispositions*   401 bair *boar* busteous *violent*
402 fenyeit *deceitful* cawtelows *cunning*   403 keip *guard*

Sa different thay ar in properteis
405   Unknawin unto man, and sa infinite,
In kynd havand sa fell diversiteis,
My cunning it excedis for to dyte.
Forthy as now I purpose for to wryte
Ane cais I fand quhilk fell this ather yeir
410   Betwix ane foxe and ane gentill chantecleir.

Ane wedow dwelt intill ane drop thay dayis
Quhilk wan hir fude off spinning on hir rok,
And na mair had, forsuth, as the fabill sayis,
Except off hennis scho had ane lyttill flok,
415   And thame to keip scho had ane jolie cok,
Richt curageous, that to this wedow ay
Devydit nicht and crew befoir the day.

Ane lyttill fra this foirsaid wedowis hows,
Ane thornie schaw thair wes off grit defence,
420   Quhairin ane foxe, craftie and cautelous,
Maid his repair and daylie residence,

404 properteis *characteristics*   405 Unknawin *unknown*
406 kynd *nature, species* havand sa fell diversiteis *having so many differences*
407 cunning *knowledge, ability* excedis *exceeds, is beyond the limit of*
dyte *write, describe*   408 Forthy *therefore* as now *for the present*
409 cais *event* fand *found*
quhilk fell this ather yeir *which occurred a year or two ago*
410 gentill chantecleir *noble cock*

411 wedow *widow* intill ane drop thay dayis *in a hamlet in those days*
412 wan *earned* fude *food, sustenance* rok *distaff*   413 na mair *no more*
forsuth *in truth*   414 scho *she* lyttill *little*   415 thame to keip *to protect them*
jolie *handsome*   416 curageous *lusty* ay *always*
417 Devydit nicht *marked the divisions of night* crew *crowed*

418 fra *from* foirsaid *foresaid*   419 schaw *thicket* grit *great, strong*
defence *security*   420 Quhairin *wherein* cautelous *cunning*   421 repair *haunt*

Quhilk to this wedow did grit violence
In pyking off pultrie baith day and nicht,
And na way be revengit on him scho micht.

425   This wylie tod, quhen that the lark couth sing,
Full sair hungrie unto the toun him drest,
Quhair Chantecleir, into the gray dawing,
Werie for nicht, wes flowen fra his nest.
Lowrence this saw and in his mynd he kest
430   The jeperdie, the wayis, and the wyle,
Be quhat menis he micht this cok begyle.

Dissimuland into countenance and cheir,
On kneis fell and simuland thus he said,
'Gude morne, my maister, gentill Chantecleir!'
435   With that the cok start bakwart in ane braid:
'Schir, be my saull, ye neid not be effraid,
Nor yit for me to start nor fle abak;
I come bot heir service to yow to mak.

422 violence *injury*   423 pyking off pultrie *stealing poultry* baith *both*
424 *and no way could she be revenged on him*

425 tod *fox* quhen *when* couth *did*
426 Full sair hungrie *grievously hungry* toun *(enclosed) farmyard*
him drest *made his way*   427 Quhair *where* into *in* dawing *dawn*
428 Werie for nicht *weary because of the night* wes flowen *had flown*
429 Lowrence *Laurence (a name for a fox)* kest *considered*
430 jeperdie *enterprise* wayis *ways, devices* wyle *deceit*
431 quhat menis *what means* begyle *beguile*

432 into countenance and cheir *in look and demeanour*   433 kneis *knees*
simuland *pretending*   434 gentill *noble*   435 start bakwart *started backwards*
braid *sudden movement*   436 Schir, be my saull *sir, by my soul* effraid *alarmed*
437 fle abak *run away*   438 *I only came here to offer service to you*

'Wald I not serve to yow, it wer bot blame,
440   As I have done to yowr progenitouris.
Your father full oft fillit hes my wame,
And send me meit fra midding to the muris:
And at his end, I did my besie curis
To hald his heid and gif him drinkis warme;
445   Syne at the last, the sweit swelt in my arme.'

'Knew ye my father?' quod the cok, and leuch.
'Yea, my fair sone, forsuth I held his heid
Quhen that he deit under ane birkin beuch;
Syne said the dirigie quhen that he wes deid.
450   Betuix us twa how suld thair be ane feid?
Quhame suld ye traist bot me, your servitour,
That to your father did sa grit honour?

'Quhen I behald your fedderis fair and gent,
Your beik, your breist, your hekill, and your kame –
455   Schir, be my saull, and the blissit sacrament,
My hart is warme, me think I am at hame.
To mak yow blyith, I wald creip on my wame
In froist and snaw, in wedder wan and weit,
And lay my lyart loikkis under your feit.'

439 *if I would not serve you it would be nothing but a disgrace*
440 progenitouris *forefathers*   441 fillit *filled* wame *belly*   442 send *sent*
meit *food* midding *midden* muris *moors*   443 besie curis *(made) diligent efforts*
444 hald his heid *hold his head* gif *give*
445 Syne *then* sweit *sweet fellow* swelt *died*

446 leuch *laughed*   447 forsuth *in truth*   448 deit *died*
birkin beuch *birch bough*   449 dirigie *Office for the Dead* deid *dead*
450 twa *two* suld *should* feid *feud, quarrel*   451 Quhame *whom* traist *trust*
servitour *servant*

453 behald *behold* fedderis *feathers* gent *fine*   454 beik *beak* breist *breast*
hekill *hackle (long feathers on the neck)* kame *comb*
455 blissit sacrament *blessed sacrament, the Eucharist*
456 me think *it seems to me* hame *home*   457 blyith *happy* creip *creep*
458 froist and snaw *frost and snow* wedder wan and weit *weather dark and wet*
459 lyart loikkis *grey locks* feit *feet*

460 This fenyeit foxe, fals and dissimulate,
  Maid to this cok ane cavillatioun:
  'Ye ar, me think, changit and degenerate
  Fra your father and his conditoun.
  Off craftie crawing he micht beir the croun,
465 For he wald on his tais stand and craw –
  This is na le; I stude beside and saw.'

  With that the cok, upon his tais hie,
  Kest up his beik, and sang with all his micht.
  Quod schir Lowrence, 'Weill said, sa mot I the.
470 Ye ar your fatheris sone and air upricht,
  Bot off his cunning yit ye want ane slicht.'
  'For', quod the tod, 'he wald, and haif na dout,
  Baith wink, and craw, and turne him thryis about.'

  The cok, inflate with wind and fals vanegloir,
475 That mony puttis unto confusioun,
  Traisting to win ane grit worschip thairfoir,
  Unwarlie winkand, walkit up and doun,
  And syne to chant and craw he maid him boun –
  And suddandlie, be he had crawin ane note,
480 The foxe wes war, and hint him be the throte.

460 fenyeit *deceitful* dissimulate *dissimulating*   **461** cavillatioun *quibble*
463 conditioun *character, nature*   **464** craftie crawing *skilful crowing*
beir the croun *take the prize*   **465** tais *toes*   **466** le *lie* stude *stood*

468 Kest up his beik *raised up his beak* micht *strength*
469 sa mot I the *so may I prosper*   **470** air *heir* upricht *rightful, legitimate*
471 want ane slicht *lack one trick*   **472** haif na dout *have no doubt*
473 wink *shut his eyes* thryis *thrice*

474 inflate *inflated* vanegloir *vainglory*   **476** Traisting *trusting*
worschip *honour*   **477** Unwarlie *without taking heed* winkand *closing his eyes*
478 syne *then* chant *sing* boun *ready*   **479** be *by the time* crawin *crowed*
480 war *alert* hint *seized*

Syne to the woid but tarie with him hyit,
Off that cryme haifand bot lytill dout.
With that Pertok, Sprutok and Coppok cryit;
The wedow hard, and with ane cry come out.
485   Seand the cace scho sichit and gaif ane schout,
'How, murther, reylok!' with ane hiddeous beir,
'Allace, now lost is gentill Chantecleir!'

As scho wer woid, with mony yell and cry,
Ryvand hir hair, upon hir breist can beit;
490   Syne paill off hew, half in ane extasy,
Fell doun for cair in swoning and in sweit.
With that the selie hennis left thair meit,
And quhill this wyfe wes lyand thus in swoun,
Fell of that cace in disputatioun.

495   'Allace', quod Pertok, makand sair murning,
With teiris grit attour hir cheikis fell,
Yone wes our drowrie and our dayis darling,
Our nichtingall, and als our orlege bell,
Our walkryfe watche, us for to warne and tell
500   Quhen that Aurora with hir curcheis gray
Put up hir heid betuix the nicht and day.

481 woid *wood* tarie *without delay* hyit *hastened*   482 haifand *having*
dout *fear*   483 Pertok *Pertok, etc. (names of the hens, see n.)*
484 hard *heard* come *came*   485 Seand *seeing* the cace *what had happened*
sichit *sighed*   486 How, murther, reylok! *Ho! murder, robbery!* beir *noise*

488 woid *mad*   489 Ryvand *tearing* can beit *beat*   490 extasy *frenzy*
491 cair *grief* swoning *swooning* sweit *sweat*   492 selie *poor*   493 lyand *lying*
494 *fell to debating the situation*

495 quod *said* makand sair murning *making sorrowful lamentation*
496 teiris *tears* attour *(which) over* cheikis *cheeks*   497 drowrie *beloved*
our dayis darling *darling of our lives*   498 nichtingall *nightingale* als *also*
orlege *clock*   499 walkryfe watche *vigilant watchman*
500 Aurora *Aurora, the dawn* curcheis *kerchiefs*

'Quha sall our lemman be? Quha sall us leid?
Quhen we ar sad quha sall unto us sing?
With his sweit bill he wald brek us the breid;
505   In all this warld wes thair ane kynder thing?
In paramouris he wald do us plesing,
At his power, as nature did him geif.
Now efter him, allace, how sall we leif?'

Quod Sprutok than, 'Ceis, sister, off your sorrow.
510   Ye be to mad, for him sic murning mais.
We sall fair weill, I find Sanct Johne to borrow;
The proverb sayis, "Als gude lufe cummis as gais."
I will put on my halydayis clais
And mak me fresch agane this jolie May,
515   Syne chant this sang, "Wes never wedow sa gay!"

'He wes angry and held us ay in aw,
And woundit with the speir off jelowsy.
Off chalmerglew, Pertok, full weill ye knaw
Waistit he wes, off nature cauld and dry.
520   Sen he is gone, thairfoir, sister, say I,
Be blyith in baill, for that is best remeid.
Let quik to quik, and deid ga to the deid.'

502 Quha *who* lemman *lover* leid *lead, guide*   504 brek us *break for us*
506 paramouris *love-making* plesing *pleasure*   507 At *according to*
geif *give, endow*   508 leif *live*

510 to mad *too distraught*
for him sic murning mais *(that) make such mourning for him*
511 I find Sanct Johne to borrow *St John be my security (a phrase used at
parting)*   512 Als *as* gais *goes*   513 halydayis clais *holiday, best clothes*
514 agane *ready for*   515 sang *song*

516 held *kept* aw *fear*   517 speir *spear*   518 chalmerglew *sport in bed*
knaw *know*   519 Waistit *worn out* cauld *cold*   520 Sen *since*
521 baill *distress* remeid *remedy*   522 quik *living* deid *dead*

Than Pertok spak, that feinyeit faith befoir,
'In lust but lufe he set all his delyte,
525   Sister, ye wait, off sic as him ane scoir
Wald not suffice to slaik our appetyte.
I hecht yow be my hand, sen he is quyte,
Within ane oulk, for schame and I durst speik,
To get ane berne suld better claw oure breik.'

530   Than Coppok lyke ane curate spak full crous:
'Yone wes ane verray vengeance from the hevin.
He wes sa lous and sa lecherous.
He had,' quod scho, 'kittokis ma than sevin,
Bot rychteous God, haldand the balandis evin,
535   Smytis rycht sair, thocht he be patient,
Adulteraris that will thame not repent.

'Prydefull he wes, and joyit off his sin,
And comptit not for Goddis favour nor feid,
Bot traistit ay to rax and sa to rin,
540   Quhill at the last his sinnis can him leid
To schamefull end and to yone suddand deid.
Thairfoir it is the verray hand off God
That causit him be werryit with the tod.'

523 feinyeit *feigned, pretended*   524 In lust but lufe *in lust without love*
525 wait *know* off sic as him ane scoir *a score of such as him*
527 hecht *promise* sen he is quyte *has got what he deserved*   528 oulk *week*
for schame and I durst speik *if I dared say it for modesty*   529 berne *man*
suld *who should* breik *rump*

530 curate *priest* full crous *confidently, boldly*   531 Yone *that* verray *true*
532 lous *dissolute*   533 kittokis *wenches* ma *more*   534 haldand *holding*
balandis *balance*   535 sair *grievously*

537 joyit off *rejoiced in*   538 comptit *cared* feid *wrath*   539 traistit *trusted*
rax *extend his power* rin *(?)run, continue (?)reign*
540 Quhill *until* can him leid *brought him*   541 suddand *sudden*
543 werryit *torn to death* with the tod *by the fox*

Quhen this wes said, this wedow fra hir swoun
545   Start up on fute, and on hir kennettis cryde,
'How! Birkye, Berrie, Bell, Bawsie Broun,
Rype-Schaw, Rin-Weil, Curtes, Nuttieclyde!
Togidder all but grunching furth ye glyde!
Reskew my nobill cok or he be slane,
550   Or ellis to me se ye cum never agane!'

With that, but baid, thay braidet over the bent;
As fyre off flint thay over the feildis flaw;
Full wichtlie thay throw wood and wateris went,
And ceissit not, schir Lourence quhill thay saw.
555   Bot quhen he saw the Kennettis cum on raw,
Unto the cok in mynd he said, 'God sen
That I and thow wer fairlie in my den.'

Then spak the cok, with sum gude spirit inspyrit,
'Do my counsall and I sall warrand the:
560   Hungrie thow art, and for grit travell tyrit,
Richt faint off force and may not ferther fle.
Swyith turne agane and say that I and ye
Freindis ar maid and fellowis for ane yeir.
Than will thay stint – I stand for it – and not steir.'

545 on fute *on her feet* kennettis *(small) hounds*   546 How! *ho!*
Birkye *(on the names, see n.)*   548 Togidder *together*
all but grunching *without any grumbling* furth ye glyde *off you go*
549 Reskew *rescue* or *before*   550 *or else see that you never come back to me*

551 but baid *without delay* braidet over the bent *sprang over the field*
552 off *from* feildis *fields* flaw *flew*   553 Full wichtlie *strongly, swiftly*
554 ceissit not *did not stop*   555 on raw *in a line*   556 in mynd *in his mind*
sen *grant*

558 spak *said* inspyrit *inspired*   559 Do my counsall *follow my advice*
warrand *protect*   560 travell *toil, effort* tyrit *tired*   561 force *strength* fle *flee*
562 Swyith *quickly* agane *back*   563 fellowis *comrades* yeir *year*
564 stint *stop* stand for it *guarantee it* steir *move*

565   This tod, thocht he wes fals and frivolus,
       And had frawdis his querrell to defend,
       Desavit wes be menis richt mervelous,
       For falset failyeis ay at the latter end.
       He start about, and cryit as he wes kend –
570   With that the cok he braid unto a bewch.
       Now juge ye all quhairat schir Lowrence lewch.

       Begylit thus, the tod under the tre
       On kneis fell, and said, 'Gude Chantecleir,
       Cum doun agane, and I but meit or fe
575   Sal be your man and servand for ane yeir.'
       'Na, fals theif, and revar, stand not me neir.
       My bludy hekill and my nek sa bla
       Hes partit freindschip for ever betwene us twa.

       'I wes unwyse that winkit at thy will,
580   Quhairthrow almaist I loissit had my heid.'
       'I wes mair fule,' quod he, 'coud nocht be still,
       Bot spake to put my pray into pleid.'
       'Fair on, fals theif, God keip me fra thy feid.'
       With that the cok over the feildis tuke his flicht,
585   And in at the wedowis lewer couth he licht.

       565 thocht *though* frivolus *wanton*
       566 frawdis his querrell to defend *tricks to maintain his cause*
       567 Desavit *deceived* menis *means* richt mervelous *wonderful*
       568 falset failyeis ay *falsehood always fails*   569 start *started, jumped*
       about *around* kend *instructed*   570 braid *leapt* bewch *bough, branch*
       571 juge *judge* quhairat *at what* lewch *laughed*

       572 Begylit *tricked*   574 but meit or fe *without board or wages*
       575 man *retainer* servand *servant*   576 revar *robber* neir *near*
       577 bludy hekill *bloody hackle* bla *livid*

       580 *through which I almost lost my head*   581 mair fule *more foolish*
       coud nocht be still *(who) could not keep silent*   582 pray *prey*
       into pleid *in doubt*   583 Fair *fare, go* feid *hostility*   584 flicht *flight*
       585 lewer *louver (turret on the roof with openings)* couth he licht *he alighted*

Moralitas

Now worthie folk, suppose this be ane fabill,
And overheillit wyth typis figurall,
Yit may ye find ane sentence richt agreabill
Under thir fenyeit termis textuall.
590   To our purpose this cok weill may we call
Nyse proud men, woid and vaneglorious,
Of kin and blude, quhilk is presumpteous.

Fy, puft up pryde, thow is full poysonabill!
Quha favoris the on force man haif ane fall;
595   Thy strenth is nocht, thy stule standis unstabill.
Tak witnes of the feyndis infernall,
Quhilk houndit doun wes fra that hevinlie hall
To hellis hole and to that hiddeous hous,
Because in pryde thay wer presumpteous.

600   This fenyeit foxe may weill be figurate
To flatteraris with plesand wordis quhyte,
With fals mening and mynd maist toxicate,
To loif and le that settis thair haill delyte.

---

586 suppose *even if*   587 overheillit *covered over*
typis figurall *figurative symbols*   588 sentence *meaning*
agreabill *(?)fitting, suitable, (?)pleasing*
589 *Under these literal words of the fictional tale*   591 Nyse *foolish*
woid *mad, reckless*   592 Of *concerning* presumpteous *arrogant*

593 full poysonabill *poisonous*   594 Quha *whoever*
on force man haif *of necessity must have*   595 nocht *nothing* stule *seat*
596 feyndis infernall *fiends of hell*   597 houndit *hounded, hunted*
598 hellis hole *pit of hell*

600 figurate *taken to symbolize*   601 quhyte *(white =) fair*
602 toxicate *venomous*   603 loif *praise, flatter* le *lie* haill *whole*

All worthie folk at sic suld haif despyte,
605 For quhair is thair mair perrellous pestilence
Nor gif to learis haistelie credence?

The wickit mynd and adullatioun,
Of sucker sweit haifand similitude,
Bitter as gall and full of fell poysoun
610 To taist it is, quha cleirlie understude.
Forthy as now schortlie to conclude,
Thir twa sinnis, flatterie and vaneglore,
Ar vennomous: gude folk, fle thame thairfoir!

The Fox and the Wolf

Leif we this wedow glaid, I yow assure,
615 Off Chantecleir, mair blyith than I can tell,
And speik we off the subtell aventure
And destinie that to this foxe befell,
Quhilk durst na mair with miching intermell
Als lang as leme or licht wes off the day,
620 Bot bydand nicht full styll lurkand he lay

604 at sic *such (people)* haif despyte *have contempt for*
606 *than hastily to give credence to liars*

607 mynd *intention* adullatioun *flattery* 608 *of sweet sugar having the likeness*
609 fell *cruel* 610 taist *taste*
quha cleirlie understude *if anyone understood it clearly*
611 Forthy as now *therefore for now* 612 Thir *these*

614 Leif *leave* 616 subtell *subtle, strange* aventure *adventure*
618 *who dared no more meddle with pilfering* 619 leme *gleam* licht *light*
620 *but awaiting night he lay silently lurking*

Quhill that Thetes the goddes off the flude
Phebus had callit to the harbery,
And Hesperous put up his cluddie hude,
Schawand his lustie visage in the sky.
625 Than Lourence luikit up, quhair he couth ly,
And kest his hand upon his ee on hicht,
Merie and glade that cummit wes the nicht.

Out off the wod unto ane hill he went,
Quhair he micht se the tuinkling sternis cleir,
630 And all the planetis off the firmament,
Thair cours and eik thair moving in thair spheir,
Sum retrograde and sum stationeir,
And off the Zodiak in quhat degré
Thay wer ilkane, as Lowrence leirnit me.

635 Than Saturne auld wes enterit in Capricorne,
And Juppiter movit in Sagittarie,
And Mars up in the Rammis heid wes borne,
And Phebus in the Lyoun furth can carie;

621 Quhill *until* Thetes *Thetis, a Nereid or sea-maiden*
goddes off the flude *goddess of the sea*
622 *had called Phoebus (the sun) to her dwelling-place*
623 Hesperous *Hesperus, the evening star* cluddie hude *cloudy hood*
624 Schawand *showing* lustie *handsome*   625 Lourence *Laurence (the fox)*
luikit *looked* quhair he couth ly *where he lay*
626 *and put up his hand (?)to shade his eye*   627 that cummit *had come*

628 wod *wood*   629 Quhair *where* tuinkling sternis *twinkling stars*
cleir *clear, bright*   631 cours *course, path* eik *also*
moving in thair spheir *movement in their (individual) sphere*
632 retrograde *moving from east to west* stationeir *stationary*
633 quhat degré *what (astronomical) degree*   634 ilkane *each one*
leirnit *taught, told*

635 auld *old* enterit in Capricorne *entered into Capricorn (sign of the Zodiac)*
636 Sagittarie *Sagittarius*
637 *and Mars was carried up into the head of Aries (the sign of the Ram)*
638 in the Lyoun furth can carie *moved on into Leo*

Venus the Crab, the Mone wes in Aquarie;
640   Mercurius, the god off eloquence,
Into the Virgyn maid his residence.

But astrolab, quadrant, or almanak,
Teichit off nature be instructioun,
The moving off the hevin this tod can tak,
645   Quhat influence and constellatioun
Wes lyke to fall upon the eirth adoun;
And to himself he said, withoutin mair,
'Weill worth my father, that send me to the lair.

'My destenie and eik my weird I watt;
650   My aventure is cleirlie to me kend,
With mischeif myngit is my mortall fait
My misleving the soner bot gif I mend;
Deid is reward off sin and schamefull end.
Thairfoir I will ga seik sum confessour,
655   And schryiff me clene off my sinnis to this hour.

639 Mone *Moon* Aquarie *Aquarius*   641 Into the Virgyn *in Virgo*

642 But astrolab *without astrolabe*
quadrant *quadrant (instrument for determining the position of heavenly bodies)*
almanak *almanac (book of astronomical tables)*
643 *taught by the instruction of nature*   644 tak *ascertain*
645 *the position of the planets and what influence (the ethereal fluid which streamed down from them and acted on the characters and destiny of men)*
646 lyke *likely* eirth *earth* adoun *down*
647 withoutin mair *without more ado, at once*   648 Weill worth *blessed be*
lair *to school*

649 eik *also* weird *fate* watt *know*   650 aventure *fortune* cleirlie *clearly*
kend *made known*   651 mischeif *disaster* myngit *mixed* mortall fait *deadly fate*
652 *unless I end my wicked living the sooner*   653 Deid *death*
654 Thairfoir *therefore* ga seik *go and seek out* confessour *confessor*
655 schryiff *confess and be absolved*

'Allace,' quod he, 'richt waryit ar we thevis!
Our lyifis set ilk nicht in aventure,
Our cursit craft full mony man mischevis,
For ever we steill and ever ar lyke pure;
In dreid and schame our dayis we indure;
Syne "Widdi-nek" and "Crak-raip" callit als,
And till our hyre ar hangit be the hals.'

Accusand thus his cankerit conscience,
Into ane craig he kest about his ee;
So saw he cummand, ane lyttill than frome hence,
Ane worthie doctour in divinitie,
Freir Wolff Waitskaith, in science wonder sle,
To preiche and pray wes new cummit fra the closter,
With beidis in hand, sayand his Pater Noster.

Seand this wolff, this wylie tratour tod
On kneis fell, with hude into his nek:
'Welcome, my gostlie father under God!'
Quod he with mony binge and mony bek.

656 richt waryit *most cursed* thevis *thieves*
657 *Our lives placed every night in jeopardy*
658 full mony man mischevis *injures many a man*   659 steill *steal*
lyke *likewise* pure *poor*   660 dreid *fear* indure *endure*   661 Syne *then*
'Widdi-nek' and 'Crak-raip' *'withy-throat' and 'crack-rope' (i.e. gallows-birds)*
callit *called* als *also*   662 till our hyre *for our reward*
hangit be the hals *hanged by the neck*

663 Accusand *accusing, revealing* cankerit *corrupt*   664 craig *crag*
kest about his ee *looked about*   665 cummand *coming* than *then*
667 Freir *friar* Waitskaith *Waitskaith (probably = 'Do-Harm')*
science *learning* wonder sle *wondrously subtle*
668 new cummit fra the closter *newly come from the cloister*
669 beidis *rosary beads* sayand *saying* Pater Noster *'Our Father'*

670 Seand *seeing* wylie tratour tod *wily treacherous fox*   671 kneis *knees*
hude into his nek *hood (thrown back) on his neck*   672 gostlie *ghostly, spiritual*
673 mony binge and mony bek *many a bob and many a bow*

'Ha,' quod the wolff, 'schir Tod, for quhat effek
675 Mak ye sic feir? Ryse up! Put on your hude!'
'Father,' quod he, 'I haif grit cause to dude.

'Ye ar mirrour, lanterne, and sicker way
Suld gyde sic sempill folk as me to grace;
Your bair feit and your russet coull off gray,
680 Your lene cheik, your paill pietious face,
Schawis to me your perfite halines;
For weill wer him that anis in his lyve
Had hap to yow his sinnis for to schryve.'

'Na, selie Lowrence,' quod the wolf, and leuch,
685 'It plesis me that ye ar penitent.'
'Off reif and stouth, schir, I can tell aneuch,
That causis me full sair for to repent.
Bot father, byde still heir upon the bent,
I yow beseik, and heir me to declair
690 My conscience, that prikkis me sa sair.'

674 effek *purpose*   675 sic feir *such demeanour*
676 haif grit cause to dude *have great cause to do it*

677 mirrour *mirror* lanterne *lantern* sicker *trusty, certain*
678 Suld gyde *(that) should guide* sempill *simple*   679 bair feit *bare feet*
russet coull *cowl made of russet (a coarse homespun cloth)*
680 lene cheik *lean cheek* paill *pale* pietious *piteous/full of pity/full of piety*
681 Schawis *show* perfite *perfect* halines *holiness*
682 weill wer him *well would it be for him* anis *once* lyve *life*
683 hap *the good fortune* schryve *confess*

684 Na *well* selie *poor* leuch *laughed*   685 plesis *pleases*   686 reif *robbery*
stouth *thieving* aneuch *plenty*   687 full sair *grievously*   688 byde *wait*
bent *field*   689 beseik *beseech* declair *make clear, make known*
690 prikkis *pains* sair *bitterly*

'Weill,' quod the wolff, 'sit doun upon thy kne.'
And he doun bair-heid sat full humilly,
And syne began with 'Benedicitie!'
Quhen I this saw, I drew ane lytill by,
695 For it effeiris nouther to heir nor spy
Nor to reveill thing said under that seill.
Bot to the tod this-gait the wolf couth mele:

'Art thow contrite and sorie in thy spreit
For thy trespas?' 'Na, schir, I can not duid.
700 Me think that hennis ar sa honie-sweit,
And lambes flesche that new ar lettin bluid;
For to repent my mynd can not concluid,
Bot off this thing – that I haif slane sa few.'
'Weill,' quod the wolf, 'in faith thow art ane schrew.

705 'Sen thow can not forthink thy wickitnes,
Will thow forbeir in tyme to cum, and mend?'
'And I forbeir, how sall I leif, allace,
Haifand nane uther craft me to defend?
Neid causis me to steill quhairever I wend:
710 I eschame to thig; I can not wirk, ye wait,
Yit wald I fane pretend to gentill stait.'

691 sit doun upon thy kne *kneel down*
692 *and bare headed he knelt down very humbly*
693 'Benedicitie!' *'God's blessing on you!' (a prayer before confession)*
694 lytill by *aside*   695 *for it is fitting neither to hear nor look on*
696 reveill *reveal* seill *seal (of confession)*   697 this-gait *in this manner*
couth mele *spoke*

698 sorie *sorrowful* spreit *spirit*   699 duid *do it*   700 Me think *it seems to me*
hennis ar sa honie-sweit *hens are sweet as honey*
701 *and the flesh of lambs that are newly bled*   702 concluid *decide*
703 slane *killed*   704 schrew *rogue*

705 Sen *since* forthink *repent of*   706 forbeir *refrain* mend *amend*
707 And *if* leif *live*   708 Haifand *having*   709 Neid *need* steill *steal*
quhairever I wend *wherever I go*   710 I eschame to thig *I am ashamed to beg*
wirk *work* wait *know*
711 fane pretend to gentill stait *gladly aspire to noble rank*

'Weill,' quod the wolf, 'thow wantis pointis twa
Belangand to perfyte confessioun;
To the thrid part off pennance let us ga:
715   Will thow tak pane for thy transgressioun?'
'Na, schir, considder my complexioun,
Selie and waik, and off my nature tender;
Lo, will ye se, I am baith lene and sklender.

'Yit nevertheles I wald, swa it wer licht,
720   Schort and not grevand to my tendernes,
Tak part off pane – fulfill it gif I micht –
To set my selie saull in way off grace.'
'Thow sall', quod he, 'forbeir flesch untill Pasche,
To tame this corps, that cursit carioun,
725   And heir I reik the full remissioun.'

'I grant thairto, swa ye will giff me leif
To eit puddingis, or laip ane lyttill blude,
Or heid, or feit, or paynchis let me preif
In cace I falt of flesch into my fude.'
730   'For grit mister I gif the leif to dude
Twyse in the oulk, for neid may haif na law.'
'God yeild yow, schir, for that text weill I knaw.'

712 thow wantis pointis twa *are wanting in two points (contrition and confession)*
713 Belangand *belonging* perfyte *perfect*   714 thrid *third (satisfaction)* ga *go*
715 pane *penance*   716 complexioun *constitution*   717 Selie *wretched*
waik *weak*   718 se *see* lene *thin* sklender *slender*

719 wald *would* swa it wer licht *provided it were easy*   720 grevand *harmful*
721 *undertake some penance if I could carry it out*   722 selie saull *poor soul*
723 flesch *meat* Pasche *Easter*   724 tame *subdue* corps *body*
cursit carioun *cursed flesh*   725 reik *grant* remissioun *pardon*

726 swa *provided* giff me leif *give me leave*   727 eit puddingis *eat sausages*
laip *drink* blude *blood*   728 heid *head* feit *feet* paynchis *entrails* preif *try*
729 cace *case* falt *lack* flesch into my fude *meat in my food*
730 grit mister *great need* dude *do it*   731 Twyse in the oulk *twice in the week*
732 yeild *repay*

Quhen this wes said, the wolf his wayis went;
The foxe on fute he fure unto the flude –
735   To fang him fisch haillelie wes his intent;
Bot quhen he saw the watter and wallis woude,
Astonist all still into ane stair he stude
And said, 'Better that I had biddin at hame
Nor bene ane fischar, in the devillis name.

740   'Now man I scraip my meit out off the sand,
For I haif nouther boittis, net, nor bait.'
As he wes thus for falt off meit murnand,
Lukand about his leving for to lait,
Under ane tre he saw ane trip off gait;
745   Than wes he blyith, and in ane hewch him hid,
And fra the gait he stall ane lytill kid.

Syne over the heuch unto the see he hyis,
And tuke the kid be the hornis twane,
And in the watter outher twyis or thryis
750   He dowkit him, and till him can he sayne,
'Ga doun schir Kid, cum up schir Salmond, agane!' –
Quhill he wes deid, syne to the land him drewch,
And off that new-maid salmond eit anewch.

734 fute *foot* fure *went* flude *water*
735 fang him fisch *catch fish for himself* haillelie *entirely*
736 wallis woude *violent waves*
737 *astounded and very silent he stood staring in bewilderment*
738 biddin at hame *stayed at home*   739 Nor *than* fischar *fisher* devillis *devil's*

740 man *must* scraip *scrape* meit *food*   741 nouther *neither* boittis *boots*
742 falt *lack* murnand *lamenting*   743 Lukand *looking*
his leving for to lait *in order to search for sustenance*   744 tre *tree*
trip off gait *flock of goats*   745 hewch *craggy cliff, steep ravine*
him hid *hid himself*   746 stall *stole*

747 heuch *cliff* see *sea, lake* hyis *hurries*   748 tuke *took* twane *two*
749 outher twyis or thryis *either twice or thrice*   750 dowkit *plunged* till *to*
can he sayne *said*   751 Salmond *salmon*   752 Quhill *until* deid *dead*
drewch *dragged*   753 eit anewch *ate plenty*

Thus fynelie fillit with young tender meit,
755 Unto ane derne for dreid he him addrest;
Under ane busk, quhair that the sone can beit,
To beik his breist and bellie he thocht best;
And rekleslie he said, quhair he did rest,
Straikand his wame aganis the sonis heit;
760 'Upon this wame set wer ane bolt full meit.'

Quhen this wes said, the keipar off the gait,
Cairfull in hart his kid wes stollen away,
On everilk syde full warlie couth he wait;
Quhill at the last he saw quhair Lowrence lay:
765 Ane bow he bent, ane flane with fedderis gray
He haillit to the heid, and or he steird,
The foxe he prikkit fast unto the eird.

'Now,' quod the foxe, 'allace and wellaway!
Gorrit I am, and may na forther gane;
770 Me think na man may speik ane word in play,
Bot nowondayis in ernist it is tane.'
He harlit him, and out he drew his flane,
And for his kid, and uther violence,
He tuke his skyn and maid ane recompence.

754 fynelie *(?)finely, excellently, (?)completely* fillit *filled*
755 derne *secret place* dreid *fear* he him addrest *made his way*
756 busk *bush* quhair that the sone can beit *where the sun beat down*
757 beik *warm* breist *breast* thocht *thought*   758 rekleslie *carelessly*
759 *stroking his belly against the sun's heat*
760 set wer ane bolt full meit *(could be planted very suitably =) is a good target for an arrow/ I might justly be shot*

761 keipar *keeper*   762 Cairfull *grieving* hart *heart* stollen *stolen*
763 everilk *every* warlie *warily* couth he wait *did he look*   765 flane *arrow*
fedderis *feathers*   766 haillit to the heid *pulled to the head (of the arrow)*
or he steird *before he moved*   767 prikkit *impaled* eird *earth*

768 wellaway *woe*   769 Gorrit *pierced* may na forther gane *can go no further*
771 nowondayis *nowadays* in ernist it is tane *taken in earnest*
772 He harlit him *the keeper dragged him off*
773 uther violence *other acts of violence*   774 recompence *reparation*

Moralitas

775 This suddand deith and unprovysit end
Of this fals tod, without contritioun,
Exempill is exhortand folk to amend,
For dreid of sic ane lyke conclusioun;
For mony gois now to confessioun
780 Yit not repentis for thair sinnis greit,
Because thay think thair lustie lyfe sa sweit.

Sum bene also, throw consuetude and ryte,
Vincust with carnall sensualitie;
Suppose thay be as for the tyme contryte,
785 Can not forbeir, nor fra thair sinnis fle;
Use drawis nature swa in propertie
Of beist and man, that neidlingis thay man do
As thay of lang tyme hes bene hantit to.

Be war gude folke, and feir this suddand schoit,
790 Quhilk smytis sair withoutin resistence:
Attend wyislie, and in your hartis noit,
Aganis deith may na man mak defence;
Ceis of your sin, remord your conscience;
Do wilfull pennance here; and ye sall wend
795 Efter your deith to blis withouttin end.

---

775 suddand *sudden* unprovysit *unforeseen*
777 Exempill *example* exhortand *exhorting*   **778** dreid *fear*   **779** gois *go*
780 Yit not repentis *yet do not repent* greit *great*   **781** lustie *carefree*

782 consuetude *habit* ryte *custom*   **783** Vincust with *vanquished by*
784 Suppose *even though*   **785** fle *flee*
786 *(?)custom draws nature so in the character*   **787** neidlingis *of necessity*
man *must*   **788** hes bene hantit to *have been accustomed to*

789 feir *fear* schoit *shot*   **790** Quhilk smytis sair *which strikes grievously*
withoutin resistence *irresistibly*   **791** Attend wyislie *consider wisely*
in your hartis noit *take note*   **792** Aganis *against*
793 Ceis *cease* remord *fill with remorse*   **794** wilfull *voluntary, of your own will*

The Trial of the Fox

This foirsaid foxe that deit for his misdeid,
Had not ane barne wes gottin richteouslie,
That to his airschip micht of law succeid,
Except ane sone, quhilk in lemanrye
800   He gottin had in purches privelie,
And till his name wes callit Father-War,
That luifit weill with pultrie to tig and tar.

It followis weill be ressoun naturall,
And gré be gré off richt comparisoun,
805   Off evill cummis war, off war cummis werst of all;
Off wrangus get cummis wrang successioun.
This foxe, bastard of generatioun,
Off verray kynde behuifit to be fals;
Swa wes his father, and his grandschir als.

810   As nature will, seikand his meit be sent,
Off cace he fand his fatheris carioun,
Nakit, new-slane, and till him hes he went,
Tuke up his heid, and on his kne fell doun,

796 foirsaid *aforesaid* deit *died* misdeid *misdoing*
797 *had not a child that was begotten lawfully*   798 airschip *inheritance* of *by*
799 quhilk *which* lemanrye *illicit love*
800 purches privelie *concubinage secretly*   801 till *for* callit *called*
Father-War *'Worse than his Father'*   802 luifit weill *loved well* pultrie *poultry*
tig and tar *(?)tap and tease (i.e. play with)*

803 be *according to*   804 *and step by step in correct comparison*
805 Off evill cummis war *from bad comes worse* werst *worst*
806 wrangus get *wrongful begetting*
808 Off verray kynde behuifit *of very nature had to be*
809 grandschir *grandfather*

810 will *requires* seikand *seeking* meit *food* sent *scent*   811 Off cace *by chance*
fand *found* carioun *corpse*   812 Nakit *naked* new-slane *newly slain* till *to*
went *gone*   813 Tuke *took* heid *head* kne *knee*

Thankand grit God off that conclusioun,
815 And said, 'Now sall I bruke, sen I am air,
The boundis quhair thow wes wont for to repair.'

Fy, covetice, unkynd and venemous!
The sone wes fane he fand his father deid,
Be suddand schot for deidis odious,
820 That he micht ringe and raxe intill his steid,
Dreidand nathing the samin lyfe to leid
In thift and reif as did his father befoir,
Bot to the end attent he tuke no moir.

Yit nevertheles, throw naturall pietie,
825 The carioun upon his bak he tais.
'Now find I weill this proverb trew,' quod he,
' "Ay rinnis the foxe, als lang as he fute hais." '
Syne with the corps unto ane peit-poit gais
Off watter full, and kest him in the deip,
830 And to the devill he gaif his banis to keip.

814 Thankand grit *thanking great*
815 sall I bruke, sen I am air *shall I possess, since I am heir*
816 Boundis *bounds, lands* quhair *where* repair *resort*

817 covetice *covetousness* unkynd *unnatural, wicked*   818 fane *glad*
fand his father deid *found his father dead*
819 Be suddand schot *by sudden shot* deidis *deeds*
820 ringe *reign* raxe intill his steid *extend his power in his place*
821 Dreidand nathing *fearing not at all*
the samin lyfe to leid *to lead the same (kind of) life*
822 thift and reif *theft and robbery*   823 attent *heed* tuke *took*

824 pietie *piety, duty*   825 tais *takes*   826 weill *well* trew *true* quod *said*
827 Ay rinnis *always runs* als lang as he fute hais *as long as he has foot*
828 Syne *then* peit-poit *peat-hole* gais *goes*   829 kest *threw* deip *deep water*
830 gaif his banis to keip *gave his bones to keep*

O fulische man plungit in wardlynes
To conqueis wrangwis guidis, gold and rent,
To put thy saull in pane or hevines,
To riche thy air, quhilk efter thow art went,
835 Have he thy gude, he takis bot small tent
To sing or say for thy salvatioun.
Fra thow be dede, done is thy devotioun.

This tod to rest him he passit to ane craig,
And thair he hard ane buisteous bugill blaw,
840 Quhilk, as him thocht, maid all the warld to waig.
Than start he up quhen he this hard, and saw
Ane unicorne come lansand over ane law,
With horne in hand: ane buste in breist he bure;
Ane pursephant semelie, I yow assure.

845 Unto ane bank, quhair he micht se about
On everilk syde, in haist he culd him hy,
Schot out his voce full schyll, and gaif ane schout,
And 'Oyas! Oyas!' twyse or thryse did cry.

831 fulische *foolish* plungit in wardlynes *plunged in worldliness*
832 conqueis wrangwis guidis *acquire wrongful goods* rent *property, income*
833 saull *soul* pane *torment* hevines *grief*   834 riche *enrich*
quhilk *who* efter thow art went *after you are gone*   835 Have he *if he has*
gude *goods* takis *takes* tent *heed, care*   836 say *say offices, prayers*
837 Fra *from the time that* dede *dead* done *finished*
thy devotioun (?)*prayers for you,* (?)*your (previous) devotion to him*

838 rest him *take his rest* passit to ane craig *made his way to a crag*
839 thair *there* hard *heard* buisteous bugill *loud horn* blaw *blow*
840 as him thocht *seemed to him* warld *world* waig *shake*   841 start *started*
quhen *when*   842 lansand *bounding* law *hill*   843 buste *box* breist *breast*
bure *carried*   844 pursephant *pursuivant, herald, messenger* semelie *fair, proper*

845 se *see, look*   846 everilk *every* in haist he culd him hy *in haste he sped*
847 Schot out his voce full schyll *sent forth his voice shrilly*
848 'Oyas' *'oyez', hear (herald's call for attention)*
twyse or thryse *twice or thrice*

With that the beistis in the feild thairby,
850 All mervelland quhat sic ane thing suld mene,
Govand agast, thay gaderit on ane grene.

Out off his buste ane bill sone can he braid
And red the text withoutin tarying.
Commandand silence, sadlie thus he said,
855 'We, nobill Lyoun, off all beistis the king,
Greting to God, helth everlestyng
To brutall beistis and irrationall
I send, as to my subjectis grit and small.

'My celsitude and hie magnificence
860 Lattis yow to wit, that evin incontinent,
Thinkis the morne with royall deligence
Upon this hill to hald ane parliament:
Straitlie thairfoir I gif commandement
For to compeir befoir my tribunall,
865 Under all pane and perrell that may fall.'

849 beistis *animals* feild *field* thairby *thereby*
850 *all marvelling what such a thing should mean*
851 Govand agast *staring in fear* gaderit *gathered* grene *green, grassy space*

852 bill *document* sone can he braid *he quickly pulled out*   853 red *read*
tarying *delay*   854 sadlie *solemnly*   855 Lyoun *lion*
856 Greting to God *honour to God* helth everlestyng *lasting health*
858 grit *great*

859 celsitude *majesty* hie *high, noble*
860 Lattis yow to wit *makes known to you* evin incontinent *forthwith*
861 Thinkis the morne *(my majesty) is minded on the morrow*   862 hald *hold*
863 Straitlie *strictly* gif *give*   864 compeir *appear*   865 Under *subject to*
pane *penalty, punishment* perrell *danger* fall *befall*

The morrow come, and Phebus with his bemis
Consumit had the mistie cluddis gray;
The ground wes grene, and als as gold it glemis,
With gers growand gudelie, grit, and gay,
870 The spyce thay spred to spring on everilk spray;
The lark, the maveis, and the merll full hie
Sweitlie can sing, trippand fra tre to tre.

Thre leopardis come, a croun off massie gold
Beirand thay brocht unto that hillis hicht,
875 With jaspis jonit, and royall rubeis rold,
And mony diveris dyamontis dicht.
With pollis proud ane palyeoun doun thay picht,
And in that throne thair sat ane wild lyoun,
In rob royall, with sceptour, swerd, and croun.

880 Efter the tennour off the cry befoir,
That gais on fut, all beistis in the eird,
As thay commandit wer, withoutin moir,
Befoir thair lord the lyoun thay appeird:
And quhat thay wer, to me as Lowrence leird,
885 I sall reheirs ane part off everilk kynd,
Als fer as now occurris to my mynd.

866 come *came* Phebus *Phoebus, the sun* bemis *beams*   867 cluddis *clouds*
868 als *also* glemis *gleams*
869 gers growand gudelie *grass growing luxuriantly* grit, and gay *tall and fine*
870 *spices unfolded to spring up on every shoot*   871 maveis *song-thrush*
merll *blackbird*   872 Sweitlie *sweetly* trippand *skipping*

873 Thre leopardis come *three leopards came (see n.)* massie *solid*
874 Beirand *bearing* brocht unto that hillis hicht *brought to the top of that hill*
875 jaspis jonit *jaspers attached* royall rubeis *noble rubies*
rold *(?)arrayed, (?)polished*   876 diveris dyamontis *various diamonds*
dicht *(?)set in it, (?)adorned with*   877 pollis proud *fine poles*
palyeoun *pavilion* picht *pitched*   879 rob *robe* swerd *sword*

880 Efter the tennour *according to the purport* cry *proclamation*
881 That gais on fut *(those) that go on foot*   882 withoutin moir *at once*
883 appeird *appeared*   884 leird *taught, told*
885 sall reheirs *shall relate* kynd *species*   886 occurris *comes back*

The minotaur, ane monster mervelous,
Bellerophont, that beist of bastardrie,
The warwolff, and the Pegase perillous,
890   Transformit be assent of sorcerie,
The linx, the tiger full off tiranie,
The elephant, and eik the dromedarie,
The cameill with his cran-nek furth can carie.

The leopard, as I haif tauld beforne,
895   The anteloip, the sparth furth couth speid,
The peyntit pantheir, and the unicorne,
The rayndeir ran throw reveir, rone, and reid,
The jolie gillet, and the gentill steid,
The asse, the mule, the hors of everilk kynd,
900   The da, the ra, the hornit hart, the hynd.

The bull, the beir, the bugill, and the bair,
The tame cat, wild cat, and the wild wod-swyne,
The hard-bakkit hurcheoun, and the hirpland hair;
Baith otter, and aip, and pennit porcupyne;

887 The minotaur *the minotaur, a monster with a man's body and a bull's head*
888 Bellerophont *apparently the Chimaera, a hybrid monster, which was slain by
the hero Bellerophon* beist of bastardrie *hybrid beast*   889 warwolff *werewolf*
Pegase *Pegasus, Bellerophon's winged horse* perillous *fearsome*   890 assent *aid*
891 linx *lynx* tiranie *cruelty*   892 eik *also*   893 cameill *camel*
cran-nek *crane-like neck* furth can carie *came forth*

894 tauld beforne *told before*   895 sparth *(unknown)* furth couth speid *sped out*
896 peyntit *painted (with spots)*   897 rayndeir *reindeer* reveir *river*
rone *thicket* reid *reeds*   898 jolie gillet *lusty mare* gentill steid *noble steed*
900 da *doe (female of fallow deer)* ra *roe-deer* hornit *horned*
hynd *hind (female red deer)*

901 beir *bear* bugill *wild ox* bair *boar*   902 wod-swyne *forest pig*
903 hard-bakkit hurcheoun *hard-backed hedgehog* hirpland hair *limping hare*
904 Baith *both* aip *ape* pennit *quilled*

905   The gukit gait, the selie scheip, the swyne,
      The wylde once, the buk, the welterand brok;
      The fowmart with the fibert furth can flok.

      The gray grewhound with slewthound furth can slyde,
      With doggis all divers and different;
910   The rattoun ran, the globard furth can glyde,
      The quhrynand quhitret with the quhasill went;
      The feitho that hes furrit mony fent,
      The mertrik, with the cunning and the con,
      The bowranbane, and eik the lerion.

915   The marmisset the mowdewart couth leid,
      Because that nature denyit had hir sicht.
      Thus dressit thay all furth for dreid off deid;
      The musk, the lytill mous with all hir micht
      In haist haikit unto that hill off hicht,
920   And mony kynd off beistis I couth not knaw,
      Befoir thair lord the lyoun thay loutit law.

905 gukit gait *foolish goat* selie scheip *innocent sheep*
906 wylde once *ounce (lynx or wildcat)* buk *buck*
welterand *rolling (in the earth?), ungainly* brok *badger*   **907** fowmart *polecat*
fibert *beaver* furth can flok *trooped out*

908 gray grewhound *greyhound*
slewthound *(sleuth-hound, tracking dog like a bloodhound)*
furth can slyde *glided out*   **910** rattoun *rat* globard *dormouse*
911 quhrynand *whining* quhitret *stoat* quhasill *weasel*
912 feitho *(kind of) polecat* hes furrit *provided fur for*
fent *slit, opening (in a robe)*   **913** mertrik *marten* cunning *rabbit* con *squirrel*
914 bowranbane *(unknown)* lerion *(also obscure)*

915 marmisset *marmoset, small monkey* mowdewart *mole* couth leid *led out*
916 denyit *denied* sicht *sight*   **917** dressit *proceeded* dreid off deid *fear of death*
918 musk *(?)civet cat* micht *might, strength*   **919** haikit *trudged* hicht *height*
920 couth not knaw *did not know*   **921** loutit law *bowed low*

Seing thir beistis all at his bidding boun,
He gaif ane braid and luikit him about,
Than flatlingis to his feit thay fell all doun –
925   For dreid off deith, thay droupit all in dout.
He lukit quhen that he saw thame lout,
And bad thame, with ane countenance full sweit,
'Be not efferit, bot stand up on your feit.

'I lat yow wit, my micht is merciabill,
930   And steiris nane that ar to me prostrait;
Angrie, austerne, and als unamyabill
To all that standfray ar to myne estait.
I rug, I reif all beistys that makis debait
Aganis the micht off my magnyficence:
935   Se nane pretend to pryde in my presence.

'My celsitude and my hie majestie
With micht and mercie myngit sall be ay.
The lawest heir I can full sone up hie,
And mak him maister over yow all I may:
940   The dromedarie, giff he will mak deray,
The grit camell, thocht he wer never sa crous,
I can him law als lytill as ane mous.

922 Seing *seeing* thir *these* boun *ready*   923 braid *sudden start* luikit *looked*
924 flatlingis *flat on their faces, prostrate*   925 droupit *drooped, were downcast*
dout *fear*   926 lukit *looked*   927 full sweit *sweet, gentle*   928 efferit *afraid*

929 lat yow wit *would have you know* merciabill *merciful*
930 steiris nane *molests none* prostrait *prostrate, submissive*
931 austerne *stern* als *also* unamyabill *hostile*
932 standfray *refractory, rebellious* estait *estate, rank*   933 rug *rend apart*
reif *tear to pieces* debait *strife*   934 Aganis *against*
935 Se nane pretend to *see that no one aspire to*

937 myngit *mingled* ay *always*   938 lawest heir *lowest here*
full sone up hie *quickly raise up*   940 giff *if* deray *disturbance*
941 thocht *though* crous *bold*   942 law *bring low, humble*

'Se neir be twentie mylis quhair I am
The kid ga saiflie be the gaittis syde,
945   The tod Lowrie luke not to the lam,
Na revand beistis nouther ryn nor ryde.'
Thay couchit all efter that this wes cryde;
The justice bad the court for to gar fence,
The sutis call, and foirfalt all absence.

950   The panther, with his payntit coit-armour,
Fensit the court, as off the law effeird;
Than Tod Lowrie luikit quhair he couth lour,
And start on fute, all stonist and all steird,
Ryifand his hair, he cryit with ane reird,
955   Quaikand for dreid and sichand couth he say,
'Allace, this hour! allace, this dulefull day!

'I wait this suddand semblie that I se,
Haifand the pointis off ane parliament,
Is maid to mar sic misdoars as me.
960   Thairfoir geve I me schaw, I will be schent;

943 Se neir be *see that within* mylis *miles*   944 ga saiflie *go safely*
gaittis syde *goat's side*   945 lam *lamb*   946 revand *plundering, thieving*
nouther *neither* ryn *run*   947 couchit *cowered, lay down* cryde *proclaimed*
948 justice *justiciar, judge*
bad the court for to gar fence *caused the proceedings to be opened by the recitation
of a formula ('of defence') which forbade disruption or interruption*
949 *call the names of those bound to attend (and 'give suit') condemn all absentees
to the forfeiture of their estates*

950 coit-armour *surcoat*   951 Fensit *'fenced'*
as off the law effeird *as was proper by law*   952 couth lour *lurked*
953 start on fute *started to his feet*
all stonist and all steird *alarmed and disturbed*   954 Ryifand *tearing*
reird *loud cry*   955 Quaikand *quaking* sichand *sighing* couth he say *he said*
956 dulefull *sorrowful*

957 wait *know* suddand semblie *sudden assembly*
958 Haifand the pointis *having the marks*
959 mar sic misdoars *harm such misdoers*
960 geve I me schaw *if I show myself* schent *destroyed*

I will be socht, and I be red absent;
To byde or fle, it makis no remeid;
All is alyke – thair followis not bot deid!'

Perplexit thus in his hart can he mene
965   Throw falset how he micht himself defend.
His hude he drew laich attoure his ene,
And winkand with ane eye furth he wend.
Clinscheand he come, that he micht not be kend,
And for dreddour that he suld bene arreist,
970   He playit buk-hude behind, fra beist to beist.

O fylit spreit, and cankerit conscience!
Befoir ane roy renyeit with richteousnes,
Blakinnit cheikis and schamefull countenance!
Fairweill thy fame; now gone is all thy grace!
975   The phisnomie, the favour off thy face,
For thy defence is foull and disfigurate,
Brocht to the licht basit, blunt, and blait.

961 socht *searched for* red *declared*   **962** byde or fle *remain or flee*
remeid *remedy*   **963** All is alyke *it is all the same*
not bot deid *nothing but death*

964 can he mene *he planned*   **965** Throw falset *through deceit*
966 hude *hood* laich attoure his ene *low over his eyes*
967 winkand with *closing* furth he wend *off he went*
968 Clinscheand *limping* kend *recognized*   **969** dreddour *fear*
suld bene arreist *should be apprehended*
970 *he played blindman's buff behind, from animal to animal*

971 fylit *defiled* cankerit *corrupt*
972 Befoir ane roy renyeit *arraigned before a king* richteousnes *justice*
973 Blakinnit cheikis *cheeks made pale*   **974** fame *good name*
975 phisnomie *face, physiognomy* favour *appearance*
976 For thy defence *for your defence (?as a means of defence)*
foull and disfigurate *foul and disfigured*
977 *brought to the light (it is) downcast, dull and lacking spirit*

Be thow atteichit with thift, or with tressoun,
For thy misdeid wrangous, and wickit fay,
980 Thy cheir changis, Lowrence; thow man luke doun:
Thy worschip of this warld is went away.
Luke to this tod, how he wes in effray,
And fle the filth of falset, I the reid,
Quhairthrow thair fallowis syn and schamefull deid.

985 Compeirand thus befoir thair lord and king,
In ordour set, as to thair stait effeird,
Of everilk kynd he gart ane part furth bring,
And awfullie he spak, and at thame speird
Geve there wes ony kynd of beistis in eird
990 Absent, and thairto gart thame deiplie sweir,
And thay said nane, except ane gray stude meir.

'Ga, make ane message sone unto that stude.'
The court than cryit, 'My lord, quha sall it be?'
'Cum furth, Lowrie, lurkand under thy hude.'
995 'Aa, schir, mercie! Lo, I have bot ane ee,

978 Be thow atteichit *if you are accused and arrested* thift *theft* tressoun *treason*
979 wrangous *wrongful* fay *faithlessness* 980 cheir *demeanour* man *must*
981 worschip *honour* 982 effray *terror* 983 I the reid *I counsel thee*
984 Quhairthrow *through which* fallowis *ensues* deid *deed(s)*

985 Compeirand *appearing* 986 ordour *order* set *placed*
stait *estate, rank* effeird *was fitting* 987 everilk kynd *every species*
he gart ane part furth bring *he (the king) caused a part to be brought out*
988 awfullie he spak *sternly spoke* at thame speird *demanded of them*
989 Geve *if*
990 thairto gart thame deiplie sweir *to that made them solemnly swear*
991 nane *none* stude meir *mare for breeding*

992 *go, cause a messenger to go forthwith to that stud-mare* 993 quha *who*
994 furth *out* lurkand *lurking* hude *hood* 995 schir *sir* bot ane ee *only one eye*

Hurt in the hoche, and cruikit as ye may se.
The wolff is better in ambassatry
And mair cunning in clergie fer than I.'

Rampand he said, 'Ga furth, brybouris baith!'
1000 And thay to ga withowtin tarying;
Over ron and rute thay ran togidder raith,
And fand the meir at hir meit in the morning.
'Now,' quod the tod, 'madame, cum to the king;
The court is callit, and ye ar *contumax*.'
1005 'Let be, Lowrence,' quod scho, 'your cowrtlie knax.'

'Maistres,' quod he, 'cum to the court ye mon;
The lyoun hes commandit so indeid.'
'Schir Tod, tak ye the flyrdome and the fon;
I have respite ane yeir, and ye will reid.'
1010 'I can not spell,' quod he, 'sa God me speid.
Heir is the wolff, ane nobill clerk at all,
And of this message is maid principall.

996 hoche *hock (joint in hind leg)* cruikit *lamed*
997 ambassatry *the art of being an ambassador*
998 mair cunning in clergie fer *far more skilled in clerkly learning*

999 Rampand *rearing up in rage* brybouris *rascals*
1000 *and off they went without delay*   1001 ron and rute *thicket and root*
togidder raith *together quickly*   1002 fand *found* meir *mare* meit *food*
1004 callit *summoned* contumax *in contempt of court*   1005 Let be *leave*
scho *she* cowrtlie knax *courtly or legal tricks, turns of speech*

1006 Maistres *mistress* mon *must*   1007 indeid *in truth*
1008 tak ye the flyrdome and the fon *you take the mockery and the folly (i.e. the
joke is on you)*   1009 respite *respite, extension of time* ane yeir *for one year*
and *if* reid *read*   1010 spell *read, spell* sa God me speid *so God help me*
1011 at all *in all respects*   1012 message *mission* principall *leader*

'He is autentik, and ane man of age,
And hes grit practik of the chanceliary.
1015 Let him ga luke, and reid your privilage,
And I sall stand and beir witnes yow by.'
'Quhair is thy respite?' quod the wolff in hy.
'Schir, it is heir under my hufe, weill hid.'
'Hald up thy heill!' quod he, and so scho did.

1020 Thocht he wes blindit with pryde, yit he presumis
To luke doun law, quhair that hir letter lay.
With that the meir gird him upon the gumis
And straik the hattrell off his heid away;
Halff out off lyif thair lenand doun he lay.
1025 'Allace,' quod Lowrence, '*Lupus*, thow art loist.'
'His cunning', quod the meir, 'wes worth sum coist!'

'Lowrence,' quod scho, 'will thow luke on my letter,
Sen that the wolff nathing thairoff can wyn?'
'Na, be Sanct Bryde!' quod he. 'Me think it better
1030 To sleip in haill nor in ane hurt skyn.

1013 autentik *of authority, trustworthy*
1014 *and has great experience of the chancellery (i.e. with legal documents)*
1015 ga luke *go and look* reid *read* privilage *exemption*   1016 beir *bear*
by *beside*   1017 Quhair *where* in hy *loudly*   1018 hufe *hoof*
1019 Hald *hold* heill *heel*

1020 Thocht *though* blindit *blinded* presumis *undertakes, ventures*
1021 law *low* quhair that *where*   1022 gird *kicked* gumis *gums*
1023 straik the hattrell off his heid *struck the crown of his head*
1024 Halff out off lyif *half lifeless* lenand *sinking*   1025 Lupus *wolf*
loist *destroyed*
1026 wes worth sum coist *was worth some expense (i.e. he deserved to be paid for
his learning)*

1028 Sen that *since* nathing thairoff can wyn *can get nothing from it*
1029 Sanct Bryde *St Bridget (of Ireland; perhaps an appropriately rustic saint,
depicted with a cow at her feet; patron* inter alia *of blacksmiths)*
1030 *to sleep in a whole rather than in a hurt skin*

Ane skrow I fand, and this wes writtin in –
For fyve schillingis I wald not anis forfaut him –
Felix quem faciunt aliena pericula cautum.'

With brokin skap and bludie cheikis reid,
1035   This wretchit wolff weipand thus on he went,
Off his menye markand to get remeid;
To tell the king the cace wes his intent.
'Schir,' quod the tod, 'byde still upon this bent,
And fra your browis wesche away the blude,
1040   And tak ane drink, for it will do yow gude.'

To fetch watter this fraudfull foxe furth fure;
Sydelingis abak he socht unto ane syke.
On cace, he meittis, cummand fra the mure,
Ane trip off lambis dansand on ane dyke.
1045   This tratour tod, this tirrant, and this tyke,
The fattest off this flock he fellit hais,
And eit his fill; syne to the wolff he gais.

1031 skrow *scroll*   1032 fyve *five* schillingis *shillings* anis *once*
forfaut him *(?)break it (the dictum), (?)lose it (the scroll)*
1033 *happy is he whom another's perils make circumspect*

1034 brokin skap *broken scalp* bludie cheikis reid *red bloody cheeks*
1035 weipand *weeping*   1036 menye *wound* markand *intending*
remeid *remedy*   1037 the cace *of the happening*
1038 byde still *wait quietly* bent *field*   1039 browis *brows* wesche *wash*
1040 gude *good*

1041 fraudfull *deceitful* furth fure *went off*
1042 Sydelingis abak *sideways and to the rear*
socht unto ane syke *went to a small stream*
1043 On cace, he meittis *by chance he meets*
cummand fra the mure *coming from the moor*
1044 trip off lambis *little flock of lambs* dansand *dancing*
dyke *(?)embankment, (?)wall*   1045 tratour *traitor, treacherous*
tirrant *cruel villain* tyke *cur*   1046 fellit hais *has killed*
1047 eit *ate* syne *then* gais *goes*

Thay drank togidder, and syne thair journey takis
Befoir the king; syne kneillit on thair kne.
1050 'Quhair is yone meir, schir Tod, wes *contumax*?'
Than Lowrence said, 'My lord, speir not at me!
Speir at your doctour off divinitie,
With his reid cap can tell you weill aneuch.'
With that the lyoun and all the laif thay leuch.

1055 'Tell on the cais, now Lowrence, let us heir.'
'This wittie wolff,' quod he, 'this clerk off age,
On your behalff he bad the meir compeir,
And scho allegit to ane privilage –
"Cum neir, and se, and ye sall haiff your wage."
1060 Because he red hir rispite plane and weill,
Yone reid bonat scho raucht him with hir heill.'

The lyoun said, 'Be yone reid cap I ken
This taill is trew, quha tent unto it takis.
The greitest clerkis ar not the wysest men;
1065 The hurt off ane happie the uther makis.'
As thay wer carpand in this cais, with knakis,
And all the court in garray and in gam,
Swa come the yow, the mother off the lam.

1048 takis *take*   1049 kneillit on thair kne *knelt down on their knees*
1051 speir *ask* at *of*   1053 With his reid cap *(who) with his red cap*
weill aneuch *well enough, very well*   1054 laif *rest, others* leuch *laughed*

1055 cais *event* heir *hear*   1056 wittie *learned* clerk *scholar*
1057 compeir *appear*   1058 allegit to *claimed to have* privilage *exemption*
1059 wage *payment*   1060 red *read* rispite *document of extension* plane *clearly*
1061 Yone reid bonat *that red bonnet* raucht *gave*

1062 ken *perceive*   1063 *this saying is true, for anyone who pays attention to it*
1064 greitest clerkis *greatest scholars*
1065 *one man's hurt makes the other happy*   1066 carpand *talking*
cais *situation* knakis *(?)taunts, jests*
1067 garray and in gam *commotion and delight*   1068 Swa *so* come *came in*
yow *ewe* lam *lamb*

Befoir the justice on hir kneis fell,
1070 Put out hir playnt on this wyis wofully,
'This harlet huresone and this hound off hell,
Devorit hes my lamb full doggitly
Within ane myle, in contrair to your cry.
For Goddis lufe, my lord, gif me the law
1075 Off this lurker!' With that Lowrence let draw.

'Byde!' quod the lyoun. 'Lymmer, let us se
Giff it be suthe the selie yow hes said.'
'Aa, soverane lord, saif your mercie!' quod he.
'My purpois wes with him for to haif plaid.
1080 Causles he fled as he had bene effraid;
For dreid off deith, he duschit over ane dyke
And brak his nek.' 'Thow leis,' quod scho, 'fals tyke!

'His deith be practik may be previt eith:
Thy gorrie gumis and thy bludie snout;
1085 The woll, the flesche, yit stikkis on thy teith;
And that is evidence aneuch, but dout!'

1069 justice *judge* kneis *knees*
1070 Put out hir playnt *made her formal complaint* wyis *manner*
1071 harlet huresone *rascal son of a whore*   1072 Devorit hes *has devoured*
full doggitly *cruelly*   1073 ane myle *one mile*
contrair to your cry *in violation of your proclamation*   1074 lufe *love*
gif me the law *give me (the redress of) the law*
1075 Off this lurker *on this skulker* let draw *withdrew*

1076 Byde *stay* Lymmer *rogue*   1077 Giff it be suthe *if it be true (what)*
selie *poor*   1078 soverane *sovereign*
saif your mercie *(?)vouchsafe your pardon, (?)maintain your mercy*
1079 purpois *purpose* to haif plaid *to have played*
1080 Causles *without cause* as he had bene effraid *as if he had been frightened*
1081 dreid off deith *fear of death* duschit *rushed violently*
dyke *(?)ditch, (?)wall*   1082 brak *broke* Thow leis *you lie* tyke *cur*

1083 practik *practical evidence* previt eith *proved easily*
1084 gorrie *gory, bloodstained* gumis *gums*   1085 woll *wool* flesche *flesh*
yit *still* teith *teeth*   1086 aneuch *enough, sufficient* but dout *without doubt*

The justice bad ga cheis ane assyis about,
And so thay did, and fand that he wes fals
Off murther, thift, pyking, and tressoun als.

1090   Thay band him fast; the justice bad belyif
To gif the dome, and tak off all his clais.
The wolff, that new-maid doctour, couth him schrif;
Syne furth him led and to the gallous gais,
And at the ledder-fute his leif he tais.
1095   The aip wes basare and bad him sone ascend,
And hangit him, and thus he maid his end.

Moralitas

Richt as the mynour in his minorall
Fair gold with fyre may fra the leid weill wyn,
Richt so under ane fabill figurall
1100   Sad sentence men may seik, and efter fyne,
As daylie dois the doctouris of devyne,
That to our leving full weill can apply
And paynt thair mater furth be poetry.

1087 cheis *choose* assyis *jury*   1088 fals *(?)guilty (of)*   1089 thift *theft*
pyking *stealing* tressoun *treason* als *also*

1090 band *bound*   1091 gif *give* dome *judicial sentence* clais *clothes*
1092 couth him schrif *shrove, confessed and absolved him*
1093 Syne *then* gallous *gallows* gais *goes*   1094 ledder-fute *foot of the ladder*
leif he tais *takes his leave*   1095 aip *ape* basare *executioner* sone *quickly*
1096 hangit *hanged*

1097 Richt *just* mynour *miner* minorall *(?)metallurgical work, (?)ore*
1098 fra the leid *from the lead* wyn *get, extract*   1099 figurall *figurative*
1100 Sad sentence *serious meaning* seik *seek*
fyne *(?)refine, embellish, (?)find*   1101 dois *do* devyne *divinity*
1102 *can well apply (their interpretation) to our manner of living*
1103 *and express their matter vividly by poetry*

The lyoun is the warld be liknes,
1105   To quhome loutis baith empriour and king,
And thinkis of this warld to get incres,
Thinkand daylie to get mair leving;
Sum for to reull, and sum to raxe and ring,
Sum gadderis geir, sum gold, sum uther gude;
1110   To wyn this warld sum wirkis as thay wer wod.

The meir is men of contemplatioun,
Off pennance walkand in this wildernes,
As monkis and othir men of religioun
That presis God to pleis in everilk place,
1115   Abstractit from this warldis wretchitnes,
In wilfull povertee, fra pomp and pryde,
And fra this warld in mynd ar mortyfyde.

This wolf I likkin to sensualitie,
As quhen lyke brutall beistis we accord
1120   Our mynd all to this warldis vanitie,
Lyking to tak and loif him as our lord:
Fle fast thairfra, gif thow will richt remord.
Than sall ressoun ryse, rax, and ring,
And for thy saull thair is na better thing.

1104 warld *world* liknes *similitude*
1105 To quhome loutis *to whom bow down* empriour *emperor*
1106 incres *increase (in prosperity, glory, wealth, etc.)*
1107 Thinkand *thinking* leving *livelihood, income*   1108 Sum *some*
reull *rule* raxe *extend their power* ring *reign, hold sway*
1109 gadderis geir *gather possessions, attire* uther gude *other goods*
1110 wyn *gain* wirkis *work, strain* as *as if* wod *mad*

1111 meir *mare*   1112 walkand *walking*   1113 of religioun *in religious orders*
1114 presis *endeavour* pleis *please* everilk *every*   1116 wilfull *voluntary*

1118 likkin *liken*   1119 accord *bring into agreement*   1120 all *entirely*
1121 Lyking *choosing* loif *(?)praise, (?)love*   1122 thairfra *from that*
gif *if* richt remord *truly feel remorse*   1123 ressoun *reason*
ryse, rax, and ring *rise, spread and rule*

1125   Hir hufe I likkin to the thocht of deid:
         Will thow remember, man, that thow man de?
         Thow may brek sensualiteis heid;
         And fleschlie lust away fra the sall fle.
         Fra thow begin thy mynd to mortifie,
1130   Salomonis saying thow may persaif heirin,
         'Think on thy end; thow sall not glaidlie sin.'

         This tod I likkin to temptationis,
         Beirand to mynd mony thochtis vane,
         That daylie sagis men of religiounis,
1135   Cryand to thame, 'Cum to the warld agane!'
         Yit gif thay se sensualitie neir slane,
         And suddand deith with ithand panis sore,
         Thay go abak, and temptis thame no moir.

         O Mary myld, mediatour of mercy meik,
1140   Sitt doun before thy sone celestiall,
         For us synnaris his celsitude beseik
         Us to defend fra pane and perrellis all,
         And help us up unto that hevinlie hall,
         In gloir quhair we may se the face of God!
1145   And thus endis the talking of the tod.

1125 hufe *(the mare's) hoof* thocht of deid *thought of death*
1126 man *must* de *die*   1127 brek *break*   1128 fle *flee*
1129 Fra *from the time that*   1130 Salomonis *Solomon's*
persaif heirin *perceive in this*

1133 Beirand *bringing* thochtis *thoughts*   1134 sagis *besieges*
1136 neir slane *almost slain*   1137 *and sudden death with continual torments*
1138 abak *back* moir *more*

1139 meik *humble*   1140 Sitt *kneel* sone celestiall *heavenly son*
1141 celsitude *majesty* beseik *beseech*   1144 gloir *glory*   1145 talking *tale*

The Sheep and the Dog

Esope ane taill puttis in memorie
How that ane doig, because that he wes pure,
Callit ane scheip to the consistorie,
And certane breid fra him for to recure.
Ane fraudfull wolff wes juge that tyme, and bure
Authoritie and jurisdictioun,
Ane on the scheip send furth ane strait summoun.

For by the use and cours and commoun style,
On this maner maid his citatioun:
'I, maister Wolff, partles off fraud and gyle,
Under the panis off hie suspensioun,
Off grit cursing, and interdictioun,
Schir Scheip, I charge the straitly to compeir,
And answer to ane doig befoir me heir.'

1150

1155

1146 Esope *Aesop* memorie *records*   1147 doig *dog*
he wes pure *he (?the dog ?ironic; ?the sheep) was poor*
1148 Callit ane scheip *summoned a sheep*
consistorie *consistory (ecclesiastical) court*
1149 *to recover a certain loaf of bread from him*
1150 fraudfull *deceitful* juge *judge* that tyme *at that time* bure *bore, held*
1152 send furth *sent out* strait *rigorous, peremptory* summoun *summons*

1153 *according to the (legal) use and procedure and common style (of drawing up
a document)*   1154 maner *manner* citatioun *summons*
1155 partles off *free from*   1156 panis *pains, penalties*
hie suspensioun *total suspension*   1157 cursing *excommunication*
interdictioun *interdiction*   1158 Schir *sir* straitly *strictly* compeir *appear*
1159 befoir me heir *here before me*

1160 Schir Corbie Ravin wes maid apparitour,
Quha pykit had full mony scheipis ee;
The charge hes tane, and on the letteris bure;
Summonit the scheip befoir the wolff, that he
'Peremptourlie within the dayis thre,
1165 Compeir under the panis in this bill,
To heir quhat Perrie Doig will say the till.'

This summondis maid befoir witnes anew,
The ravin, as to his office weill effeird,
Indorsat hes the write, and on he flew.
1170 The selie scheip durst lay na mouth on eird
Till he befoir the awfull juge appeird.
The oure off cause quhilk that the juge usit than,
Quhen Hesperus to schaw his face began.

The foxe wes clerk and noter in the cause;
1175 The gled, the graip at the bar couth stand,
As advocatis expert into the lawis,
The doggis pley togidder tuke on hand,
Quhilk wer confidderit straitlie in ane band
Aganis the scheip to procure the sentence;
1180 Thocht it wes fals, thay had na conscience.

1160 Corbie Ravin *Raven* apparitour *summoner*   1161 Quha *who*
pykit *picked, pierced* mony scheipis ee *many sheep's eyes*
1162 charge *summons* tane *taken* letteris bure *carried, served the document*
1164 Peremptourlie *peremptorily, without option*   1165 Compeir *appear*
panis *penalties* bill *document*   1166 heir quhat *hear what* the till *to thee*

1167 maid *(having been) made* anew *sufficient*
1168 weill effeird *was very proper*   1169 Indorsat *endorsed* write *writ, summons*
1170 selie *poor* lay na mouth on eird *(lay no mouth on ground =) stop to eat*
1171 awfull *fearsome* appeird *appeared*
1172 oure off cause *hour appointed for the trial* usit than *used then (was)*
1173 Quhen *when* Hesperus *Hesperus, the evening star* schaw *show*

1174 noter *notary public*   1175 gled *kite* graip *vulture* couth *did*
1176 advocatis *advocates* into *in*   1177 *together undertook the dog's suit*
1178 *who were closely associated in a compact*   1179 Aganis *against*
1180 Thocht *though*

The clerk callit the scheip, and he wes thair;
The advocatis on this wyse couth propone:
'Ane certane breid, worth fyve schilling or mair,
Thow aw the doig, off quhilk the terme is gone.'
1185 Off his awin heid, but advocate, allone,
The scheip avysitlie gaif answer in the cace:
'Heir I declyne the juge, the tyme, the place.

'This is my cause, in motive and effect:
The law sayis it is richt perrillous
1190 Till enter in pley befoir ane juge suspect,
And ye, schir Wolff, hes bene richt odious
To me, for with your tuskis ravenous
Hes slane full mony kinnismen off myne;
Thairfoir as juge suspect I yow declyne.

1195 'And schortlie, of this court ye memberis all,
Baith assessouris, clerk, and advocate,
To me and myne ar ennemies mortall,
And ay hes bene, as mony scheipheird wate.
The place is fer, the tyme is feriate,
1200 Quhairfoir na juge suld sit in consistory
Sa lait at evin: I yow accuse forthy.'

1181 thair *there*   1182 wyse *manner* couth propone *stated the case*
1183 schilling *shillings* mair *more*   1184 aw *owe* terme *set date*
1185 Off his awin heid *on his own behalf, following his own counsel* but *without*
allone *alone*   1186 avysitlie *advisedly, with consideration* gaif *gave*
cace *case, matter*   1187 declyne *reject (the legal authority of)*

1188 cause *case* motive and effect *(?)purpose and effect (i.e. in its essentials)*
1189 perrillous *dangerous*   1190 Till *to* pley *litigation* suspect *biased*
1192 tuskis *fangs, teeth*   1193 Hes slane *(you) have slain* kinnismen *kinsmen*

1195 schortlie *shortly, in brief* memberis *members*   1196 Baith *both*
assessouris *assessors, advisers to the judge*
1198 *and always have been, as many a shepherd knows*
1199 fer *far (?outside the court's jurisdiction)* feriate *a holiday, in vacation*
1200 Quhairfoir *wherefore* suld *should*
1201 Sa lait at evin *so late in the evening* accuse forthy *challenge therefore*

Quhen that the juge in this wyse wes accusit,
He bad the parteis cheis with ane assent
Twa arbeteris, as in the law is usit,
1205 For to declair and gif arbitriment
Quhidder the scheip suld answer in jugement
Befoir the wolff; and so thay did, but weir,
Off quhome the namis efterwart ye sall heir.

The beir, the brok, the mater tuke on hand,
1210 For to discyde gif this exceptioun
Wes off na strenth nor lauchfully mycht stand;
And thairupon as jugis thay sat doun
And held ane lang quhyle disputatioun,
Seikand full mony decreitis off the law,
1215 And glosis als, the veritie to knaw.

Of civile mony volum thay revolve,
The codies and digestis new and ald,
Contra and *pro*, strait argumentis thay resolve,
Sum objecting and sum can hald;

1202 accusit *challenged*
1203 parties cheis with ane assent *parties choose unanimously*
1204 arbeteris *arbiters*   1205 declair *declare, settle*
gif arbitriment *give arbitration*   1206 Quhidder *whether*
suld answer in jugement *should answer the charge*   1207 but weir *without doubt*
1208 quhome *whom* efterwart *afterwards* sall heir *shall hear*

1209 beir *bear* brok *badger* the mater tuke on hand *undertook the matter*
1210 discyde *decide* exceptioun *defence*
1211 *was of no force nor could stand legally*   1213 quhyle *for a long time*
1214 Seikand full mony decreitis *searching out many decrees*
1215 glosis als *glosses also* veritie *truth* knaw *know, discover*

1216 civile *civil law* volum *volumes* revolve *search through*
1217 codies *(legal) codes* digestis *Digests (of Justinian)* ald *old*
1218 Contra *and* pro *against and in favour* strait *rigorous* resolve *analyse*
1219 can hald *upheld*

1220   For prayer or price, trow ye, thay wald fald?
       Bot held the glose and text of the decreis
       As trew jugis – I beschrew thame ay that leis.

       Schortlie to mak ane end off this debait,
       The arbiteris than sweirand plane
1225   The sentence gave, and proces fulminait:
       The scheip suld pas befoir the wolff agane
       And end his pley. Than wes he nathing fane,
       For fra thair sentence couth he not appeill.
       On clerkis I do it, gif this sentence wes leill.

1230   The scheip agane befoir the wolff derenyeit,
       But advocate, abasitlie couth stand.
       Up rais the doig, and on the scheip thus plenyeit:
       'Ane soume I payit have befoir the hand
       For certane breid.' Thairto ane borrow he fand,
1235   That wrangouslie the scheip did hald the breid;
       Quhilk he denyit, and thair began the pleid.

1220 prayer *petition* price *payment, bribe* trow ye *do you believe*
wald fald *would give away*   1221 held *kept to, abided by* glose *gloss*
1222 beschrew thame *curse them* leis *lie*

1223 debait *debate*   1224 sweirand plane *swearing clearly*
1225 sentence *judgement, decision* proces fulminait *formally issued the mandate*
1226 pas *go* agane *again*   1227 pley *suit* nathing fane *not at all happy*
1228 fra *from* couth he not appeill *he could not appeal*
1229 On clerkis I do it *I put it to the learned* gif *if* leill *just*

1230 derenyeit *arraigned*   1231 But *without* abasitlie *humbly, dejectedly*
couth stand *stood*   1232 rais *rose* plenyeit *complained*
1233 soume *sum of money* payit *paid* befoir the hand *in advance*
1234 borrow *pledge, surety* fand *found (to confirm that)*
1235 wrangouslie *wrongfully*   1236 Quhilk *which* denyit *denied* pleid *dispute*

And quhen the scheip this stryif had contestait,
The justice in the cause furth can proceid.
Lowrence the actis and the proces wrait,
1240 And thus the pley unto the end thay speid.
This cursit court, corruptit all for meid,
Aganis gude faith, law, and eik conscience,
For this fals doig pronuncit the sentence.

And it till put to executioun,
1245 The wolff chargit the scheip, without delay,
Under the panis off interdictioun,
The soume off silver or the breid to pay.
Off this sentence, allace, quhat sall I say,
Quhilk dampnit hes the selie innocent,
1250 And justifyit the wrangous jugement?

The scheip, dreidand mair the execution,
Obeyand to the sentence, he couth tak
His way unto ane merchand off the toun,
And sauld the woll that he bure on his bak,
1255 Syne bocht the breid, and to the doig couth mak
Reddie payment, as it commandit was;
Naikit and bair syne to the feild couth pas.

1237 this stryif had contestait *had entered into this suit*
1238 *The judge continued the proceedings*   1239 actis *records*
proces *proceedings* wrait *wrote*   1240 pley *suit* speid *hurry on*
1241 cursit *cursed* meid *bribery*   1242 Aganis *against* gude *good* eik *also*
1243 pronuncit *pronounced, delivered* sentence *judgement*

1244 till put to executioun *to execute it, impose the appropriate penalty*
1245 chargit *ordered*   1246 panis *penalties*   1248 quhat *what*
1249 Quhilk dampnit *which condemned* selie *poor*
1250 justifyit *maintained as true* wrangous *wrongful*

1251 dreidand mair *fearing more*   1252 Obeyand *obeying* couth tak *took*
1254 *and sold the wool that he bore on his back*   1255 Syne bocht *then bought*
couth mak *made*   1256 Reddie *prompt*   1257 Naikit *naked* bair *bare*
couth pas *went*

Moralitas

This selie scheip may present the figure
Of pure commounis, that daylie ar opprest
1260 Be tirrane men, quhilkis settis all thair cure
Be fals meinis to mak ane wrang conquest,
In hope this present lyfe suld ever lest.
Bot all begylit, thay will in schort tyme end,
And efter deith to lestand panis wend.

1265 This wolf I likkin to ane schiref stout
Quhilk byis ane forfalt at the kingis hand,
And hes with him ane cursit assyis about,
And dytis all the pure men uponland;
Fra the crownar haif laid on him his wand –
1270 Thocht he wer trew as ever wes Sanct Johne –
Slane sall he be, or with the juge compone.

1258 figure *figure, symbol*
1259 pure commounis *(the) poor commons, common people*
1260 tirrane *tyrannous*
quhilkis settis all thair cure *who devote all their attention*
1261 *by false means to make a wrongful acquisition*
1262 suld ever lest *should last forever*   1263 begylit *deceived*
1264 deith *death* lestand panis *lasting torments*

1265 likkin *liken* schiref *sheriff* stout *powerful*   1266 byis *buys*
forfalt *right to collect fines and to seize the property of offenders*
at the kingis hand *from the king's hand*   1267 assyis *jury*
1268 dytis *indicts* uponland *in the country*
1269 *as soon as the coroner (who had power to make arrests) has laid his rod (his sign of office) upon him (a poor man)*
1270 Thocht *though* trew *honest, true* Sanct Johne *St John*
1271 Slane sall he be *he shall be slain* compone *come to an agreement*

This ravin I likkin to ane fals crownair,
Quhilk hes ane porteous of the inditement,
And passis furth befoir the justice air,
1275   All misdoaris to bring to jugement;
Bot luke gif he wes of ane trew intent,
To scraip out Johne, and wryte in Will or Wat,
And swa ane bud at boith the parteis skat.

Of this fals tod, of quhilk I spak befoir,
1280   And of this gled, quhat thay micht signify,
Of thair nature, as now I speik no moir.
Bot of this scheip and of his cairfull cry
I sall reheirs, for as I passit by
Quhair that he lay, on cais I lukit doun,
1285   And hard him mak sair lamentatioun.

'Allace,' quod he, 'this cursit consistorie
In middis of the winter now is maid,
Quhen Boreas with blastis bitterlie
And hard froistes thir flouris doun can faid;
1290   On bankis bair now may I mak na baid.'
And with that word into ane coif he crap,
Fra sair wedder and froistis him to hap.

1272 ravin *raven* crownair *coroner*
1273 porteous of the inditement *roll of the indictment (with names of offenders on it)*   1274 justice air *circuit court*   1275 misdoaris *wrongdoers*
1276 luke gif *decide whether*
1277 scraip *scrape out (a name from the document)*
1278 *and thus exact a bribe from both parties*

1280 gled *kite*   1281 speik *speak*   1282 cairfull cry *sorrowful lament*
1283 reheirs *relate*   1284 Quhair that *where* on cais *by chance* lukit *looked*
1285 hard *heard* sair *grievous*

1287 middis *midst*   1288 Boreas *Boreas, the north wind*
1289 *and hard frosts cause these flowers to wither*   1290 bankis bair *bare banks*
baid *abode*   1291 coif *cave* crap *crept*
1292 sair wedder *bitter weather* froistis *frosts* hap *cover himself*

Quaikand for cauld, sair murnand ay amang,
Kest up his ee unto the hevinnis hicht,
1295   And said, 'Lord God, quhy sleipis thow sa lang?
Walk, and discerne my cause groundit on richt;
Se how I am be fraud, maistrie, and slicht
Peillit full bair, and so is mony one
Now in this warld richt wonder wo-begone.

1300   'Se how this cursit syn of covetice
Exylit hes baith lufe, lawtie, and law.
Now few or nane will execute justice,
In fault of quhome, the pure man is overthraw.
The veritie, suppois the juge it knaw,
1305   He is so blindit with affectioun,
But dreid, for meid, he lettis the richt go doun.

'Seis thow not, lord, this warld overturnit is,
As quha wald change gude gold in leid or tyn?
The pure is peillit, the lord may do na mis,
1310   And simonie is haldin for na syn.

1293 *trembling for cold, bitterly lamenting again and again*
1294 *(he) raised his eye to the highest part of the heavens*
1295 quhy sleipis thow sa lang? *why do you sleep so long?*   1296 Walk *wake*
discerne *perceive/judge* groundit on richt *based on justice*   1297 Se *see* be *by*
maistrie *force* slicht *trickery*   1298 Peillit *stripped*   1299 warld *world*
richt wonder wo-begone *wondrously beset with misery*

1300 covetice *covetousness*   1301 Exylit *exiled* lufe *love* lawtie *loyalty*
1303 In fault of quhome *in the absence of whom* overthraw *cast down, ruined*
1304 *even if the judge knows the truth*   1305 affectioun *passion, partiality*
1306 But dreid *in truth* meid *bribery* richt *right, justice*

1307 Seis thow not *do you not see*
1308 *as if someone were to change good gold to lead or tin*
1309 peillit *stripped* na mis *no wrong*
1310 simonie *simony (the buying or selling of spiritual benefits or preferments)*
haldin *held*

Now is he blyith with okker maist may wyn;
Gentrice is slane, and pietie is ago.
Allace, gude lord, quhy tholis thow it so?

'Thow tholis this evin for our grit offence;
1315   Thow sendis us troubill and plaigis soir,
As hunger, derth, grit weir, or pestilence;
Bot few amendis now thair lyfe thairfoir.
We pure pepill as now may do no moir
Bot pray to the: sen that we are opprest
1320   Into this eirth, grant us in hevin gude rest.'

The Lion and the Mouse

In middis of June, that sweit seasoun,
Quhen that fair Phebus with his bemis bricht
Had dryit up the dew fra daill and doun,
And all the land maid with his lemis licht,
1325   In ane mornyng betuix mid day and nicht
I rais and put all sleuth and sleip asyde,
And to ane wod I went allone but gyde.

1311 *now that man is happy who can gain most by usury*
1312 Gentrice *nobility, graciousness* pietie *pity, compassion*
1313 quhy tholis thow it so? *why do you suffer it (to be) thus?*

1314 evin *precisely* grit *great*   1315 plaigis *plagues, afflictions*
1316 As *such as* derth *famine* weir *war, strife*   1317 amendis *amend*
now *nowadays*   1318 pure pepill as now *poor people at this time*
1319 sen that *since*   1320 Into *in* eirth *earth, world*

1321 middis *(the) middle* sweit *sweet*   1322 Quhen *when*
Phebus *Phoebus, the sun* bemis bricht *bright beams*   1323 dryit *dried*
fra daill and doun *from dale and hill*
1324 maid with his lemis licht *made light with his rays*
1325 betuix *between* nicht *night*   1326 rais *arose* sleuth *sloth* sleip *sleep*
1327 wod *wood* allone *alone* but gyde *without a guide*

Sweit wes the smell off flouris quhyte and reid,
The noyes off birdis richt delitious,
1330   The bewis braid blomit abone my heid,
The ground growand with gers gratious;
Off all plesance that place wes plenteous,
With sweit odouris and birdis harmony;
The morning myld – my mirth wes mair forthy.

1335   The rosis reid arrayit on rone and ryce,
The prymeros and the purpour violat bla;
To heir it wes ane poynt off Paradice,
Sic mirth the mavis and the merle couth ma;
The blossummis blythe brak up on bank and bra;
1340   The smell off herbis and off fowlis cry,
Contending quha suld have the victory.

Me to conserve than fra the sonis heit,
Under the schaddow off ane hawthorne grene
I lenit doun amang the flouris sweit,
1345   Syne cled my heid and closit baith my ene.

1328 flouris *flowers* quhyte and reid *white and red*
1329 noyes off birdis *noise of birds* delitious *delightful*
1330 *the broad boughs were covered with flowers above my head*
1331 growand with gers gratious *growing with pleasant herbs*
1332 plesance *delight*
1334 mirth wes mair forthy *joy was the greater therefore*

1335 rosis *roses* arrayit on rone and ryce *arrayed on thicket and twig*
1336 prymeros *primrose* purpour violat bla *bluish-purple violet*
1337 heir *hear* poynt *part*   1338 Sic mirth *such joy*
mavis *thrush* merle *blackbird* couth ma *did make*   1339 blythe *pleasant*
brak up on bank and bra *broke open on bank and hillside*   1340 fowlis *birds'*
1341 quha suld *who should*

1342 *to protect myself from the sun's heat*
1343 hawthorne grene *green hawthorn*
1344 lenit doun amang *reclined among*
1345 *then covered my head and closed both my eyes*

On sleip I fell amang thir bewis bene,
And in my dreme, me thocht come throw the schaw
The fairest man that ever befoir I saw.

His gowne wes off ane claith als quhyte as milk,
1350 His chemeris wes off chambelate purpour broun,
His hude off scarlet, bordowrit weill with silk
On hekillit wyis untill his girdill doun,
His bonat round, and off the auld fassoun,
His beird wes quhyte, his ene wes grit and gray,
1355 With lokker hair quhilk over his schulderis lay.

Ane roll off paper in his hand he bair,
Ane swannis pen stikand under his eir,
Ane inkhorne, with ane prettie gilt pennair,
Ane bag off silk, all at his belt can beir.
1360 Thus wes he gudelie grathit in his geir,
Off stature large, and with ane feirfull face.
Evin quhair I lay he come ane sturdie pace,

1346 On sleip *asleep* thir bewis bene *those pleasant boughs*
1347 *And in my dream it seemed to me came through the wood there*
1348 befoir *before*

1349 claith *cloth* als *as*   1350 chemeris *(sleeveless) robe*
chambelate *camlet, a fine cloth* purpour broun *dark purple*   1351 hude *hood*
bordowrit *bordered*   1352 hekillit wyis *(?) fringed like a hackle*
untill his girdill doun *down to his girdle*   1353 bonat *cap* auld fassoun *old style*
1354 beird *beard* grit *large*   1355 lokker *curling* quhilk *which*
schulderis *shoulders*

1356 bair *bore*   1357 swannis pen *pen made from swan's quill* eir *ear*
1358 prettie gilt pennair *ingeniously made gilt pen-case*   1359 can beir *bore*
1360 gudelie grathit *finely arrayed* geir *attire*
1361 feirfull *awesome, inspiring reverence*   1362 Evin *just* quhair *where*
come ane sturdie pace *came vigorously*

And said, 'God speid, my sone', and I wes fane
Off that couth word, and off his cumpany.
1365 With reverence I salusit him agane,
'Welcome, father', and he sat doun me by.
'Displeis yow not, my gude maister, thocht I
Demand your birth, your facultye, and name;
Quhy ye come heir, or quhair ye dwell at hame.'

1370 'My sone,' said he, 'I am off gentill blude;
My native land is Rome, withoutin nay,
And in that towne first to the sculis I yude,
In civile law studyit full mony ane day,
And now my winning is in hevin for ay.
1375 Esope I hecht; my writing and my werk
Is couth and kend to mony cunning clerk.'

'O maister Esope, poet lawriate,
God wait ye ar full deir welcum to me!
Ar ye not he that all thir fabillis wrate,
1380 Quhilk in effect, suppois thay fenyeit be,
Ar full off prudence and moralitie?'
'Fair sone,' said he, 'I am the samin man.'
God wait gif that my hert wes merie than.

1363 speid *help (you)* sone *son* fane *glad*   1364 couth *known, familiar*
1365 salusit *greeted* agane *in return*   1366 me by *beside me*
1367 Displeis yow not *do not be displeased* gude maister *good master*
thocht *though, if*   1368 Demand *ask* facultye *profession, branch of learning*
1369 Quhy *why* hame *home*

1370 gentill blude *noble blood*   1371 withoutin nay *without doubt, for sure*
1372 sculis *schools, university* yude *went*   1373 studyit *studied*
1374 winning *dwelling* hevin for ay *heaven forever*
1375 Esope I hecht *Aesop I am called* werk *work*
1376 couth and kend *known and familiar*

1377 lawriate *laureate*   1378 wait *knows* full deir welcum *dearly welcome*
1379 all thir fabillis wrate *wrote all these fables*   1380 in effect *in fact*
suppois *though* fenyeit *fictitious*   1381 prudence *wisdom*   1382 samin *same*
1383 *God knows if my heart was joyful then*

I said, 'Esope, my maister venerabill,
1385   I yow beseik hartlie for cheritie,
Ye wald dedene to tell ane prettie fabill
Concludand with ane gude moralitie.'
Schaikand his heid, he said, 'My sone, lat be,
For quhat is it worth to tell ane fenyeit taill,
1390   Quhen haly preiching may nathing availl?

'Now in this warld me think richt few or nane
To Goddis word that hes devotioun;
The eir is deif, the hart is hard as stane;
Now oppin sin without correctioun,
1395   The hart inclynand to the eirth ay doun.
Sa roustit is the warld with canker blak
That now my taillis may lytill succour mak.'

'Yit, gentill schir,' said I, 'for my requeist,
Not to displeis your fatherheid, I pray,
1400   Under the figure off ane brutall beist,
Ane morall fabill ye wald denye to say.
Quha wait nor I may leir and beir away
Sum thing thairby heirefter may availl?'
'I grant,' quod he, and thus begouth ane taill:

1385 beseik hartlie *beseech sincerely* cheritie *charity*
1386 wald dedene *would deign* prettie *artful, skilfully made*
1387 Concludand *concluding*   1388 Schaikand *shaking*   1389 quhat *what*
taill *tale*   1390 *when holy preaching can be of no avail*

1391 warld *world* few or nane *(there are) few or none*
1393 eir is deif *ear is deaf* stane *stone*   1394 oppin *(there is) open, manifest*
1396 Sa roustit *so decayed, corrupted*
1397 may lytill succour mak *be of little help*

1398 gentill schir *gracious sir* for my requeist *as for my request*
1399 fatherheid *fatherhood*   1400 brutall *irrational*   1401 denye *deign*
1402 *who knows but I may learn and bear away*   1403 thairby *from it*
heirefter *(which) hereafter*   1404 quod *said* begouth *began*

1405   Ane lyoun, at his pray wery foirrun,
      To recreat his limmis and to rest,
      Beikand his breist and belly at the sun,
      Under ane tre lay in the fair forest;
      Swa come ane trip off myis out off thair nest,
1410   Richt tait and trig, all dansand in ane gyis,
      And over the lyoun lansit twyis or thryis.

      He lay so still, the myis wes not effeird,
      Bot to and fro out over him tuke thair trace;
      Sum tirlit at the campis off his beird,
1415   Sum spairit not to claw him on the face;
      Merie and glaid, thus dansit thay ane space,
      Till at the last the nobill lyoun woke,
      And with his pow the maister mous he tuke.

      Scho gave ane cry, and all the laif, agast,
1420   Thair dansing left and hid thame sone alquhair.
      Scho that wes tane cryit and weipit fast,
      And said allace oftymes that scho come thair:
      'Now am I tane ane wofull presonair,
      And for my gilt traistis incontinent
1425   Off lyfe and deith to thoill the jugement.'

1405 *a lion, exhausted by running in the hunt for his prey*
1406 recreat his limmis *refresh his limbs*   1407 Beikand *warming*
breist *breast*   1408 tre *tree*   1409 Swa come *then came*
trip off myis *company of mice*   1410 tait and trig *lively and nimble*
dansand *dancing* in ane gyis? *in a dance? in the same manner*
1411 lansit *bounded* twyis or thryis *twice or thrice*

1412 wes not effeird *were not frightened*   1413 out over *over*
tuke thair trace *took their way*   1414 *some plucked the whiskers of his beard*
1415 spairit not to claw *did not refrain from clawing*   1416 space *time*
1418 pow *paw* maister *chief, leading*

1419 Scho *she* laif *rest* agast *terrified*   1420 sone *at once*
alquhair *everywhere*   1421 tane *captured* weipit fast *wept loudly, copiously*
1422 oftymes *often*   1423 presonair *prisoner*   1424 gilt *offence*
traistis incontinent *expect immediately*
1425 thoill the jugement *suffer judgement, i.e. be tried for my life*

Than spak the lyoun to that cairfull mous:
'Thow cative wretche and vile unworthie thing,
Over-malapart and eik presumpteous
Thow wes, to mak out over me thy tripping.
1430   Knew thow not weill I wes baith lord and king
Off beistis all?' 'Yes,' quod the mous, 'I knaw,
Bot I misknew, because ye lay so law.

'Lord, I beseik thy kinglie royaltie,
Heir quhat I say, and tak in patience.
1435   Considder first my simple povertie,
And syne thy mychtie hie magnyfycence;
Se als how thingis done off neglygence,
Nouther off malice nor of presumptioun,
The rather suld have grace and remissioun.

1440   'We wer repleit, and had grit aboundance
Off alkin thingis, sic as to us effeird;
The sweit sesoun provokit us to dance
And mak sic mirth as nature to us leird;
Yet lay so still and law upon the eird
1445   That be my sawll we weind ye had bene deid –
Elles wald we not have dancit over your heid.'

1426 spak *spoke* cairfull *sorrowful*   1427 cative *miserable*
1428 Over-malapart *too impertinent* eik *also*   1429 tripping *dancing*
1432 misknew *was unaware, failed to recognize* law *low*

1433 beseik *beseech*   1434 *hear what I say, and attend (to it) patiently*
1436 syne *then* hie *high*   1437 Se als *consider also* off *by*
1438 Nouther *neither*   1439 The rather *the more quickly* remissioun *pardon*

1440 repleit *replete, filled* grit *great*
1441 *of all kinds of things, such as were fitting for us*   1443 leird *taught*
1444 eird *earth*   1445 be my sawll *by my soul* weind *thought* deid *dead*
1446 Elles *else, otherwise*

'Thy fals excuse', the lyoun said agane,
'Sall not availl ane myte, I underta.
I put the cace, I had bene deid or slane,
1450 And syne my skyn bene stoppit full off stra;
Thocht thow had found my figure lyand swa,
Because it bare the prent off my persoun,
Thow suld for feir on kneis have fallin doun.

'For thy trespas thow can mak na defence,
1455 My nobill persoun thus to vilipend;
Off thy feiris, nor thy awin negligence,
For to excuse thow can na cause pretend;
Thairfoir thow suffer sall ane schamefull end
And deith, sic as to tressoun is decreit –
1460 Onto the gallous harlit be the feit.'

'Na! mercie, lord, at thy gentrice I ase,
As thow art king off beistis coronate,
Sober thy wraith, and let thi yre overpas,
And mak thy mynd to mercy inclynate.
1465 I grant offence is done to thyne estate,
Quhairfoir I worthie am to suffer deid,
Bot gif thy kinglie mercie reik remeid.

1447 agane *in reply*   1448 availl ane myte *be worth a jot*
underta *undertake, promise*   1449 I put the cace *(let us) suppose*
1450 stoppit *stuffed* stra *straw*   1451 figure lyand swa *image lying thus*
1452 bare *bore* prent *impress, image* persoun *person*   1453 feir *fear*
kneis *knees*

1454 trespas *wrongdoing*   1455 vilipend *dishonour*
1456 *the negligence of your companions, nor your own*   1457 na cause *no reason*
pretend *put forward*   1459 decreit *decreed*   1460 gallous *gallows*
harlit be the feit *dragged by the feet*

1461 Na *no* gentrice *graciousness* ase *ask*   1462 coronate *crowned*
1463 Sober thy wraith *moderate your wrath* yre overpas *anger pass over*
1464 inclynate *inclined*   1465 estate *rank*   1466 Quhairfoir *wherefore*
deid *death*   1467 Bot gif *unless* reik remeid *grant relief*

'In everie juge mercy and reuth suld be
As assessouris and collaterall;
1470   Without mercie, justice is crueltie,
As said is in the lawis speciall:
Quhen rigour sittis in the tribunall,
The equitie off law quha may sustene?
Richt few or nane, but mercie gang betwene.

1475   'Alswa ye knaw the honour triumphall
Off all victour upon the strenth dependis
Off his conqueist, quhilk manlie in battell
Throw jeopardie of weir lang defendis.
Quhat pryce or loving, quhen the battell endis,
1480   Is said off him that overcummis ane man
Him to defend quhilk nouther may nor can?

'Ane thowsand myis to kill and eik devoir
Is lytill manheid to ane strang lyoun;
Full lytill worschip have ye wyn thairfoir,
1485   To qwhais strenth is na comparisoun.
It will degraid sum part off your renoun
To sla ane mous, quhilk may mak na defence
Bot askand mercie at your excellence.

1468 juge *judge* reuth *pity*   1469 *as advisers and colleagues*
1471 speciall *particularly, specially*   1472 rigour *severity, strictness*
tribunall *judgement seat*   1473 equitie *impartial justice* sustene *endure*
1474 but *unless* gang between *go between, intervene*

1475 Alswa *also* knaw *know*   1476 all *every* strenth *strength*
1477 conqueist *conquest, the one he has conquered*
quhilk *who* manlie in battell *manfully in battle*
1478 *through daring enterprise in war long defends himself*
1479 pryce or loving *honour or praise*
1481 *who neither may nor can defend himself*

1482 eik devoir *also devour*   1483 manheid *manliness, valiant deed*
strang *strong*   1484 worschip *honour* wyn thairfoir *won for that*
1485 qwhais *whose*   1486 degraid *diminish, lessen*   1487 sla *slay*
1488 Bot askand *except by asking*

'Also it semis not your celsitude,
1490 Quhilk usis daylie meittis delitious,
To fyle your teith or lippis with my blude,
Quhilk to your stomok is contagious.
Unhailsum meit is of ane sarie mous,
And that namelie untill ane strang lyoun,
1495 Wont till be fed with gentill vennesoun.

'My lyfe is lytill worth, my deith is les,
Yit and I leif, I may peradventure
Supplé your hienes beand in distres;
For oft is sene, ane man off small stature
1500 Reskewit hes ane lord off hie honour,
Keipit that wes, in poynt to be overthrawin;
Throw misfortoun sic cace may be your awin.'

Quhen this wes said, the lyoun his language
Paissit, and thocht according to ressoun,
1505 And gart mercie his cruell ire asswage,
And to the mous grantit remissioun,
Oppinnit his pow, and scho on kneis fell doun,
And baith hir handis unto the hevin upheild,
Cryand, 'Almichty God mot yow foryeild!'

1489 semis not *is not befitting (to)* celsitude *majesty*   1490 usis *uses, eats*
meittis delitious *refined, dishes*   1491 fyle *defile*
1492 is contagious *causes illness*   1493 Unhailsum *unhealthy* sarie *wretched*
1494 namelie untill *especially for*   1495 gentill vennesoun *noble venison*

1496 lytill worth *of little value* les *less*
1497 *yet if I live I may perchance*
1498 *help your majesty if you are in distress*   1499 sene *seen*
stature *size, condition*   1500 Reskewit has *has rescued*
1501 *who was held prisoner, in danger of being overthrown*
1502 cace *case, happening* awin *own*

1504 Paissit *moderated* thocht *considered* ressoun *reason*   1505 gart *caused*
asswage *assuage, moderate*   1507 Oppinnit his pow *opened his paw*
1508 upheild *held up*   1509 *Crying 'may Almighty God requite you.'*

1510 Quhen scho wes gone, the lyoun held to hunt,
For he had nocht, bot levit on his pray,
And slew baith tayme and wyld, as he wes wont,
And in the cuntrie maid ane grit deray;
Till at the last the pepill fand the way
1515 This cruell lyoun how that thay mycht tak:
Off hempyn cordis strang nettis couth thay mak,

And in ane rod, quhair he wes wont to ryn,
With raipis rude fra tre to tre it band;
Syne kest ane range on raw the wod within,
1520 With hornis blast and kennettis fast calland.
The lyoun fled, and throw the ron rynnand
Fell in the net and hankit fute and heid;
For all his strenth he couth mak na remeid,

Welterand about with hiddeous rummissing,
1525 Quhyle to, quhyle fra, quhill he mycht succour get.
Bot all in vane – it vailyeit him nathing –
The mair he flang, the faster wes the net.
The raipis rude wes sa about him plet
On everilk syde that succour saw he nane,
1530 Bot styll lyand and murnand maid his mane.

1510 held *proceeded*   1511 nocht *nothing* levit *lived*   1513 cuntrie *country*
deray *disturbance*   1514 pepill fand *people found*   1515 tak *capture*
1516 *they made strong nets of cords of hemp*

1517 rod *road* ryn *run*   1518 raipis rude *rough ropes* band *bound*
1519 *drew up a line of hunters inside the wood*   1520 kennettis *small hounds*
calland *calling out, giving voice*
1521 throw the ron rynnand *running through the undergrowth*
1522 hankit *entangled*
1523 couth mak na remeid *could not manage to free himself*

1524 Welterand *rolling, twisting* rummissing *roaring*
1525 Quhyle *sometimes* quhill *until*   1526 vailyeit *availed*
1527 flang *flung himself around* faster *more firm*   1528 plet *woven*
1529 everilk *every*   1530 lyand *lying* murnand *mourning* mane *lament*

'O lamit lyoun, liggand heir sa law,
Quhair is the mycht off thy magnyfycence,
Off quhome all brutall beist in eird stude aw,
And dred to luke upon thy excellence?
1535   But hoip or help, but succour or defence,
In bandis strang heir man I ly, allace,
Till I be slane; I se nane uther grace.

'Thair is na wy that will my harmis wreik
Nor creature do confort to my croun.
1540   Quha sall me bute? Quha sall my bandis breik?
Quha sall me put fra pane off this presoun?'
Be he had maid this lamentatioun,
Throw aventure, the lytill mous come neir,
And off the lyoun hard the pietuous beir;

1545   And suddanlie it come intill hir mynd
That it suld be the lyoun did hir grace,
And said, 'Now wer I fals and richt unkynd
Bot gif I quit sumpart thy gentrace
Thow did to me', and on this way scho gais
1550   To hir fellowis, and on thame fast can cry,
'Cum help! cum help!' and thay come all in hy.

1531 lamit *crippled* liggand heir sa law *lying here so low*   1532 Quhair *where*
1533 quhome *whom* eird *earth* stude aw *stood in awe*   1534 dred *feared*
1535 But hoip *without hope*   1536 bandis *bonds* man *must*

1538 wy *man* wreik *avenge*   1540 Quha *who* bute *help* breik *break*
1541 pane *(the) torment* presoun *prison*   1542 Be *as soon as*
1543 aventure *chance* neir *near*   1544 hard *heard*
pietuous beir *pitiful lament*

1545 intill *into*   1546 did hir grace *(who) showed mercy to her*
1547 richt unkynd *completely unnatural*
1548 *if I did not repay to some extent your gracious deed*
1549 on this way *thus* gais *goes*   1550 fast can cry *persistently cried*
1551 come *came* in hy *in haste*

'Lo,' quod the mous, 'this is the samin lyoun
That grantit grace to me quhen I wes tane,
And now is fast heir bundin in presoun,
1555 Brekand his hart with sair murning and mane;
Bot we him help, off souccour wait he nane.
Cum help to quyte ane gude turne for ane uther;
Go, lous him sone!' and thay said, 'Ye, gude brother.'

Thay tuke na knyfe – thair teith wes scharpe anewch;
1560 To se that sicht, forsuith, it wes grit wounder –
How that they ran amang the rapis tewch,
Befoir, behind, sum yeid abone, sum under,
And schuir the raipis off the net in-schunder;
Syne bad him ryse, and he start up anone,
1565 And thankit thame; syne on his way is gone.

Now is the lyoun fre off all danger,
Lows and delyverit to his libertie
Be lytill beistis off ane small power,
As ye have hard, because he had pietie.
1570 Quod I, 'Maister, is thair ane moralitie
In this fabill?' 'Yea, sone,' he said, 'richt gude.'
'I pray yow, schir,' quod I, 'ye wald conclude.'

1552 samin *same*   1554 bundin *bound*   1555 Brekand *breaking*
sair *grievous* mane *lamentation*   1556 Bot *unless* souccour *succour*
wait *expects*   1557 quyte *repay* ane *one* ane uther *another*   1558 lous *loose*
sone *quickly* brother *(?) comrade*

1559 their teith wes scharpe anewch *their teeth were sharp enough*
1560 forsuith *in truth*   1561 rapis tewch *tough ropes*
1562 yeid abone *went above*   1563 schuir *cut* in-schunder *asunder*
1564 start *sprang* anone *immediately*

1566 fre *free*   1567 Lows *released* delyverit *delivered, restored*   1568 Be *by*
1569 hard *heard* pietie *pity*

Moralitas

As I suppois, this mychtie gay lyoun
May signifie ane prince or empriour,
1575 Ane potestate, or yit ane king with croun –
Quhilk suld be walkrife gyde and governour
Of his pepill – that takis na labour
To reule and steir the land, and justice keip,
Bot lyis still in lustis, sleuth, and sleip.

1580 The fair forest with levis, lowne and le,
With foulis sang and flouris ferlie sweit,
Is bot the warld and his prosperitie,
As fals plesance, myngit with cair repleit.
Richt as the rois with froist and wynter weit
1585 Faidis, swa dois the warld, and thame desavis
Quhilk in thair lustis maist confidence havis.

Thir lytill myis ar bot the commountie,
Wantoun, unwyse, without correctioun;
Thair lordis and princis quhen that thay se
1590 Of justice mak nane executioun,

1574 empriour *emperor*   1575 potestate *potentate*
1576 walkrife gyde *vigilant guide*   1577 labour *pains*
1578 reule and steir *rule and govern*   keip *maintain*   1579 still *continually*
lustis *pleasures*   sleuth *sloth*

1580 levis *leaves*   lowne and le *calm and sheltered*
1581 foulis sang *song of birds*   flouris ferlie sweit *wondrously delightful flowers*
1582 bot *(nothing) but*   1583 myngit with cair *mingled with sorrow*
repleit *(?) complete, perfect, (?) abundant, pervading*   1584 rois *rose*
froist *frost*   weit *shower, storm*   1585 Faidis *withers*   swa dois *so does*
thame desavis *deceives them*   1586 maist confidence *greatest trust*

1587 Thir *these*   commountie *common people, commons*   1588 Wantoun *wilful*
1590 *do not enforce justice*

Thay dreid nathing to mak rebellioun
And disobey, for quhy thay stand nane aw,
That garris thame thair soveranis misknaw.

Be this fabill, ye lordis of prudence
1595 May considder the vertew of pietie,
And to remit sumtyme ane grit offence,
And mitigate with mercy crueltie.
Oftymis is sene ane man of small degré
Hes quit ane kinbute, baith of gude and ill,
1600 As lord hes done rigour or grace him till.

Quha wait how sone ane lord of grit renoun,
Rolland in wardlie lust and vane plesance,
May be overthrawin, destroyit, and put doun
Throw fals Fortoun, quhilk of all variance
1605 Is haill maistres, and leidar of the dance
Till injust men, and blindis thame so soir
That thay na perrell can provyde befoir?

1591 Thay dreid nathing *are not at all afraid*
1592 for quhy thay stand nane aw *because they have no fear*
1593 *this causes them to disregard their lords*

1595 vertew *virtue* pietie *pity*   1596 remit *pardon*
1598 small *little, low* degré *rank*
1599 quit ane kinbute *requited (a payment for kin=) a recompense*
1600 *(?) according as a lord has acted with severity or mercy towards him*

1601 Quha wait *who knows*   1602 Rolland *rolling, luxuriating* wardlie *worldly*
1603 overthrawin *overthrown*   1604 Fortoun *Fortune*
1605 haill maistres *complete mistress* leidar of the dance *leader of the dance*
1606 soir *grievously*   1607 perrell *peril*
provyde befoir *foresee, provide against beforehand*

Thir rurall men, that stentit hes the net
In quhilk the lyoun suddandlie wes tane,
1610 Waittit alway amendis for to get,
For hurt men wrytis in the marbill stane.
Mair till expound, as now, I lett allane,
Bot king and lord may weill wit quhat I mene:
Figure heirof oftymis hes bene sene.

1615 Quhen this wes said, quod Esope, 'My fair child,
I the beseik and all men for to pray
That tressoun of this cuntrie be exyld,
And justice regne, and lordis keip thair fay
Unto thair soverane lord baith nycht and day.'
1620 And with that word he vanist and I woke;
Syne throw the schaw my journey hamewart tuke.

The Preaching of the Swallow

The hie prudence and wirking mervelous,
The profound wit off God omnipotent;
Is sa perfyte and sa ingenious,
1625 Excellent far all mannis jugement;

1608 stentit *extended, stretched out*   1610 Waittit *watched* amendis *satisfaction*
1611 hurt *an injury* wrytis *write, engrave* marbill stane *marble stone*
1612 as now *for now* lett allane *leave, forbear*   1613 wit *know*
1614 Figure *image, example* heirof *of this*

1616 beseik *beseech*   1617 tressoun *treason* exyld *exiled*
1618 regne *reign* fay *faith*   1620 vanist *vanished*
1621 *then through the wood my journey homeward took*

1622 hie *high, lofty* prudence *wisdom, prudence* wirking *actions, works*
1623 wit *wisdom*   1624 sa perfyte *so perfect* ingenious *intelligent, discerning*
1625 Excellent *excelling* mannis jugement *man's power of judgement*

Forquhy to him all thing is ay present,
Rycht as it is or ony tyme sall be,
Befoir the sicht off his divinitie.

Thairfoir our saull with sensualitie
1630   So fetterit is in presoun corporall,
We may not cleirlie understand nor se
God as he is, nor thingis celestiall.
Our mirk and deidlie corps materiale
Blindis the spirituall operatioun,
1635   Lyke as ane man wer bundin in presoun.

In *Metaphisik* Aristotell sayis
That mannis saull is lyke ane bakkis ee,
Quhilk lurkis still, als lang as licht off day is,
And in the gloming cummis furth to fle;
1640   Hir ene ar waik, the sone scho may not se:
Sa is our saull with fantasie opprest,
To knaw the thingis in nature manifest.

1626 Forquhy *because* ay *eternally*   **1627** Rycht *just* ony *any* sall *shall*
1628 Befoir *before* sicht *sight, eye*

1629 Thairfoir *therefore* saull *soul*   **1630** fetterit *fettered, chained*
presoun corporall (the) prison of our body   **1631** cleirlie *clearly*
1633 mirk and deidlie corps materiale *dark and mortal material body*
1634 *blinds the spiritual activity*   **1635** Lyke as *as if* bundin *bound*

1636 Metaphisik *Metaphysics* Aristotell *Aristotle*
1637 ane bakkis ee *the eye of a bat*
1638 *which hides silently, as long as there is daylight*
1639 gloming *gloaming* cummis furth to fle *comes out to fly*
1640 ene ar waik *eyes are weak*
the sone scho may not se *she cannot look at the sun*
1641 with fantasie opprest *oppressed by fantasy, delusion*
1642 knaw *perceive* manifest *(which are) manifest*

For God is in his power infinite,
And mannis saull is febill and over-small,
1645 Off understanding waik and unperfite
To comprehend him that contenis all;
Nane suld presume be ressoun naturall
To seirche the secreitis off the Trinitie,
Bot trow fermelie and lat all ressoun be.

1650 Yyt nevertheles we may haif knawlegeing
Off God almychtie be his creatouris,
That he is gude, fair, wyis, and bening.
Exempill tak be thir jolie flouris,
Rycht sweit off smell and plesant off colouris,
1655 Sum grene, sum blew, sum purpour, quhyte, and reid,
Thus distribute be gift off his godheid.

The firmament payntit with sternis cleir
From eist to west rolland in cirkill round,
And everilk planet in his proper spheir,
1660 In moving makand harmonie and sound;
The fyre, the air, the watter and the ground –
Till understand it is aneuch, iwis,
That God in all his werkis wittie is.

1644 febill *feeble* over-small *too small*
1645 waik and unperfite *weak and imperfect*   1646 contenis *contains*
1647 Nane suld *none should* be ressoun naturall *by natural reason*
1648 seirche *explore* secreitis *secrets*   1649 Bot trow fermelie *but believe firmly*

1650 Yyt *yet* haif knawlegeing *have knowledge*   1651 be *by, through*
creatouris *creatures*   1652 gude *good* wyis *wise* bening *benign, benevolent*
1653 *take the example of these beautiful flowers*   1654 Rycht sweit *very sweet*
1655 Sum grene *some green* blew *blue* purpour *purple* quhyte *white* reid *red*
1656 distribute *distributed*

1657 payntit *painted, adorned* sternis cleir *bright stars*   1658 eist *east*
rolland *rolling* cirkill *circle*   1659 everilk *every*
proper spheir *particular sphere*   1660 makand *making*   1661 ground *earth*
1662 *it is enough, in truth, to enable us to understand*   1663 wittie *wise*

Luke weill the fische that swimmis in the se;
1665   Luke weill in eirth all kynd off bestyall;
The foulis fair, sa forcelie thay fle,
Scheddand the air with pennis grit and small;
Syne luke to man, that he maid last off all,
Lyke to his image and his similitude:
1670   Be thir we knaw that God is fair and gude.

All creature he maid for the behufe
Off man, and to his supportatioun
Into this eirth, baith under and abufe,
In number, wecht, and dew proportioun,
1675   The difference off tyme, and ilk seasoun
Concorddand till our opurtunitie,
As daylie be experience we may se.

The Somer with his jolie mantill grene,
With flouris fair furrit on everilk fent,
1680   Quhilk Flora, goddes off the flouris, quene,
Hes to that lord as for his seasoun lent,
And Phebus with his goldin bemis gent
Hes purfellit and payntit plesandly,
With heit and moysture stilland from the sky.

1664 Luke weill *consider well*   1665 eirth *earth* bestyall *animals*
1666 foulis *birds* forcelie *strongly* fle *fly*   1667 Scheddand *cleaving*
pennis *wings* grit *great*   1668 Syne *then*   1669 *after his image and likeness*
1670 thir *these (things)*

1671 behufe *benefit*   1672 supportatioun *support, sustenance*   1673 Into *in*
abufe *above*   1674 wecht *weight* dew *due, fitting*
1675 difference off tyme *diversity of seasons* ilk *each*
1676 *corresponding to our time and need*

1678 Somer *summer* jolie mantill grene *fine green mantle*
1679 furrit *trimmed as if with fur* fent *opening*
1680 Quhilk *which* quene *queen*   1682 Phebus *Phoebus, the sun*
goldin bemis gent *fair golden beams*
1683 Hes purfellit *has edged, decorated with a border*
1684 heit *heat* stilland *distilling, trickling*

1685 Syne Harvest hait, quhen Ceres that goddes
Hir barnis benit hes with abundance,
And Bachus, god off wyne, renewit hes
The tume pyipis in Italie and France,
With wynis wicht and liquour off plesance,
1690 And *Copia Temporis* to fill hir horne,
That never wes full off quheit nor uther corne.

Syne Wynter wan, quhen austerne Eolus,
God off the wynd, with blastis boreall
The grene garment off somer glorious
1695 Hes all to-rent and revin in pecis small.
Than flouris fair faidit with froist man fall,
And birdis blyith changeis thair noitis sweit
In styll murning, neir slane with snaw and sleit.

Thir dalis deip with dubbis drounit is,
1700 Baith hill and holt heillit with frostis hair,
And bewis bene ar bethit, bair off blis
Be wickit windis off the winter wair.
All wyld beistis than from the bentis bair
Drawis for dreid unto thair dennis deip,
1705 Coucheand for cauld in coifis thame to keip.

1685 Harvest hait *hot autumn* quhen *when* Ceres *Ceres, corn goddess*
1686 her barns has (?)furnished generously   1687 renewit *renewed*
1688 tume pyipis *empty casks*   1689 wicht *strong* plesance *delight*
1690 Copia Temporis *the season's plenty*   1691 quheit *wheat* uther *other*

1692 wan *(?) gloomy, (?) pale* austerne *austere, severe*   1693 boreall *northern*
1695 to-rent *rent apart* revin *torn* pecis *pieces*   1696 faidit *withered*
froist *frost* man *must*   1697 blyith *joyful, glad* noitis *notes*
1698 *in silent mourning, nearly slain by snow and sleet*

1699 *these deep valleys are drowned in pools*   1700 Baith *both* holt *wood*
heillit *covered* hair *white*   1701 bewis bene *pleasant boughs*
ar bethit *are withered* bair off blis *destitute of joy*
1702 wair *(?) onslaught, (?) worse*   1703 bentis bair *bare fields*
1704 *move for fear into their deep dens*
1705 *lying low in caves to protect themselves from the cold*

Syne cummis Ver, quhen winter is away,
The secretar off Somer with his sell,
Quhen columbie up-keikis throw the clay,
Quhilk fleit wes befoir with froistes fell.
1710 The mavis and the merle beginnis to mell;
The lark on loft with uther birdis smale
Than drawis furth fra derne, over doun and daill.

That samin seasoun, into ane soft morning,
Rycht blyth that bitter blastis wer ago,
1715 Unto the wod, to se the flouris spring,
And heir the mavis sing and birdis mo,
I passit furth, syne lukit to and fro
To se the soill, that wes richt sessonabill,
Sappie, and to resave all seidis abill.

1720 Moving thusgait, grit myrth I tuke in mynd,
Off lauboraris to se the besines,
Sum makand dyke, and sum the pleuch can wynd,
Sum sawand seidis fast frome place to place,
The harrowis hoppand in the saweris trace;
1725 It wes grit joy to him that luifit corne
To se thame laubour, baith at evin and morne.

1706 Ver *spring*   1707 secretar *secretary* sell *seal*
1708 columbie up-keikis *the columbine peeps up*
1709 fleit *put to flight, frightened* fell *(?)fierce, (?) many*
1710 mavis *thrush* merle *blackbird* mell *give voice*   1711 on loft *on high*
1712 drawis furth fra derne *come out from their secret hiding-place*
doun and daill *hill and valley*

1713 samin *same* into *in*   1714 ago *gone*   1715 wod *wood*   1716 heir *hear*
birdis mo *other birds*   1717 lukit *looked*   1718 soill *soil*
richt sessonabill *right for the season*   1719 *moist, and ready to receive all seeds*

1720 thusgait *in this way* myrth *delight*
1721 *to see the activity of the labourers in the fields*   1722 makand *making*
dyke *(?) ditches (?) walls* the pleuch can wynd *guided the plough*
1723 sawand seidis fast *sowing seeds constantly*
1724 harrowis *harrows (implements for breaking up the soil)* hoppand *hopping*
the saweris trace *the track of the sowers*   1725 luifit *loved*   1726 evin *evening*

And as I baid under ane bank full bene,
In hart gritlie rejosit off that sicht,
Unto ane hedge, under ane hawthorne grene,
1730   Off small birdis thair come ane ferlie flicht,
And doun belyif can on the leifis licht
On everilk syde about me quhair I stude,
Rycht mervellous, ane mekill multitude.

Amang the quhilks, ane swallow loud couth cry,
1735   On that hawthorne hie in the croip sittand:
'O ye birdis on bewis heir me by,
Ye sall weill knaw and wyislie understand:
Quhair danger is, or perrell appeirand,
It is grit wisedome to provyde befoir
1740   It to devoyd, for dreid it hurt yow moir.'

'Schir Swallow,' quod the lark agane, and leuch,
'Quhat have ye sene that causis yow to dreid?'
'Se ye yone churll', quod scho, 'beyond yone pleuch
Fast sawand hemp – lo se! – and linget seid?
1745   Yone lint will grow in lytill tyme indeid,
And thairoff will yone churll his nettis mak,
Under the quhilk he thinkis us to tak.

1727 baid *waited* bene *pleasant*
1728 gritlie rejosit off that sicht *greatly delighted by that sight*
1729 hawthorne grene *green hawthorn*   1730 ferlie flicht *wondrous flock*
1731 *and quickly alighted on the leaves*   1732 everilk *every*
quhair I stude *where I stood*   1733 mekill *great*

1734 the quhilks *which* couth cry *cried out*
1735 hie in the croip sittand *sitting high in the tree-top*   1736 bewis *boughs*
heir me by *here beside me*   1737 sall *shall* wyislie *prudently*
1738 appeirand *likely*   1739 provyde befoir *take care beforehand*
1740 devoyd *avert* dreid *fear*

1741 Schir *sir* agane *in reply* leuch *laughed*
1743 yone churll *yon, that peasant, churl*   1744 linget seid *flax seed*
1745 lint *flax* indeid *indeed*   1746 thairoff *from it* his nettis mak *make his nets*
1747 *under which he intends to catch us*

'Thairfoir I reid we pas quhen he is gone
At evin, and with our naillis scharp and small
1750   Out off the eirth scraip we yone seid anone
And eit it up, for giff it growis we sall
Have cause to weip heirefter ane and all.
Se we remeid thairfoir furthwith, *instante*,
Nam levius laedit quicquid praevidimus ante.

1755   'For clerkis sayis it is nocht sufficient
To considder that is befoir thyne ee;
Bot prudence is ane inwart argument
That garris ane man provyde befoir and se
Quhat gude, quhat evill, is liklie for to be
1760   Off everilk thingis at the fynall end,
And swa fra perrell the better him defend.'

The lark, lauchand, the swallow thus couth scorne,
And said scho fischit lang befoir the net –
'The barne is eith to busk that is unborne;
1765   All growis nocht that in the ground is set;
The nek to stoup quhen it the straik sall get
Is sone aneuch; deith on the fayest fall.'
Thus scornit thay the swallow ane and all.

1748 reid *advise* pas *go*   1749 evin *evening* naillis *claws*   1750 scraip *scrape*
anone *at once*   1751 eit *eat* giff *if*   1752 weip heirefter *weep hereafter* ane *one*
1753 *let us make sure to find a remedy for it, instantly*
1754 *whatever we foresee does us less harm*

1755 clerkis *scholars* nocht *not*   1756 that *that which* ee *eye*
1757 inwart argument *inner process of reasoning*   1758 garris *causes*
1760 Off everilk thingis *from all things*

1762 lauchand *laughing* couth scorne *scorned*   1763 fischit *fished*
1764 *it is easy to dress an unborn child*
1765 All growis nocht *not everything grows* set *placed*
1766–7 *it is soon enough to bend the neck when it must receive the stroke; let
death fall on those most doomed*

Despysing thus hir helthsum document,
1770 The foulis ferlie tuke thair flicht anone:
Sum with ane bir thay braidit over the bent,
And sum agane ar to the grene wod gone.
Upon the land quhair I wes left allone
I tuke my club, and hamewart couth I carie,
1775 Swa ferliand as I had sene ane farie.

Thus passit furth quhill June, that jolie tyde,
And seidis that wer sawin off beforne
Wer growin hie, that hairis mycht thame hyde,
And als the quailye craikand in the corne.
1780 I movit furth betuix midday and morne
Unto the hedge under the hawthorne grene,
Quhair I befoir the said birdis had sene,

And as I stude, be aventure and cace,
The samin birdis as I haif said yow air –
1785 I hoip because it wes thair hanting-place,
Mair off succour, or yit mair solitair –
Thay lychtit doun, and quhen thay lychtit wair,
The swallow swyth put furth ane pietuous pyme,
Said, 'Wo is him can not bewar in tyme!

1769 helthsum document *wholesome instruction*   1770 foulis ferlie *birds suddenly*
1771 bir *whirring rush* braidit *flew quickly* bent *field*   1772 agane *back*
wod *wood*   1773 land *ground*   1774 hamewart couth I carie *went homewards*
1775 *marvelling as if I had seen something magic*

1776 Thus passit furth *thus (the time) passed on* quhill *until* tyde *time*
1777 sawin off beforne *sown previously*   1778 hie *high*
that hairis mycht thame hyde *so that hares could hide themselves*   1779 als *also*
quailye *(?) corncrake* craikand *croaking*

1783 be aventure and cace *by fortune and chance*   1784 samin *same*
haif said yow air *have told you of earlier*   1785 hoip *suppose*
hanting-place *usual haunt*
1786 *(because it was) more sheltered or else more secluded*
1787 lychit doun *alighted* wair *were*
1788 swyth put furth ane pietuous pyme *quickly uttered a pitiful (?) cry*

1790 'O blind birdis, and full off negligence,
Unmyndfull off your awin prosperitie,
Lift up your sicht and tak gude advertence,
Luke to the lint that growis on yone le.
Yone is the thing I bad, forsuith, that we,
1795 Quhill it wes seid, suld rute furth off the eird;
Now is it lint, now is it hie on breird.

'Go yit, quhill it is tender, young, and small,
And pull it up, let it na mair incres.
My flesche growis, my bodie quaikis all,
1800 Thinkand on it I may not sleip in peis!'
Thay cryit all, and bad the swallow ceis,
And said, 'Yone lint heirefter will do gude,
For linget is to lytill birdis fude.

'We think, quhen that yone lint bollis ar ryip,
1805 To mak us feist and fill us off the seid,
Magré yone churll, and on it sing and pyip.'
'Weill,' quod the swallow, 'freindes, hardilie beid;
Do as ye will, bot certane, sair I dreid
Heirefter ye sall find als sour as sweit,
1810 Quhen ye ar speldit on yone carlis speit.

1791 awin *own*   1792 sicht *sight, gaze* advertence *heed*
1793 lint *flax* le *meadow*   1794 bad *urged* forsuith *in truth*
1795 Quhill *while* suld rute furth off the eird *should root out of the ground*
1796 hie on breird *sprouting high*

1798 na mair *no more* incres *increase*   1799 growis *shudders*
1800 sleip in peis *sleep in peace*   1801 ceis *cease*   1802 gude *good*
1803 linget *flax seed* fude *food*

1804 lint bollis *flax seed-pods* ryip *ripe*   1805 mak us feist *feast ourselves*
1806 Magré yone churll *in spite of that churl* pyip *pipe*
1807 freindes, hardilie beid *friends, so be it*   1808 bot certane *certainly*
sair I dreid *sorely I fear*   1809 *hereafter you will find it as sour as it is sweet*
1810 speldit *spread out, split open*
on yone carlis speit *on that churl's spit (for roasting)*

'The awner off yone lint ane fouler is,
Richt cautelous and full off subteltie;
His pray full sendill-tymis will he mis
Bot giff we birdis all the warrer be.
1815   Full mony off our kin he hes gart de,
And thocht it bot ane sport to spill thair blude;
God keip me fra him, and the halie rude.'

Thir small birdis haveand bot lytill thocht
Off perrell that mycht fall be aventure
1820   The counsell off the swallow set at nocht,
Bot tuke thair flicht and furth togidder fure;
Sum to the wode, sum markit to the mure.
I tuke my staff, quhen this wes said and done,
And walkit hame, for it drew neir the none.

1825   The lynt ryipit, the carll pullit the lyne,
Rippillit the bollis, and in beitis set,
It steipit in the burne, and dryit syne,
And with ane bittill knokkit it and bet,
Syne swingillit it weill, and hekkillit in the flet;
1830   His wyfe it span, and twynit it into threid,
Off quhilk the fowlar nettis maid indeid.

1811 awner *owner* fouler *bird-catcher*   1812 cautelous *cunning*
1813 *seldom will he fail to catch his prey*   1814 Bot giff *unless*
the warrer *the more cautious*   1815 gart de *caused to die*   1816 thocht *thought*
1817 *God and the holy cross protect me from him*

1818 haveand *having*   1819 be aventure *by chance*
1820 set at nocht *set at nought, despised*   1821 flicht *flight*
furth togidder fure *went away together*   1822 markit *went* mure *moor*
1824 hame *home* neir *near* none *noon*

1825 *the flax ripened, the churl pulled up the flax*
1826 Rippillit the bollis *combed away the seed-pods* beitis *bundles*
1827 steipit *soaked* burne *burn, stream* dryit syne *dried it afterwards*
1828 *And pounded and beat it with a mallet*   1829 swingillit *scraped*
hekkillit *combed* in the flet *inside the house*   1830 span *spun*
twynit it into threid *twisted it into thread*   1831 quhilk *which*
fowlar *bird-catcher*

The wynter come, the wickit wind can blaw,
The woddis grene wer wallowit with the weit;
Baith firth and fell with froistys wer maid faw,
1835   Slonkis and slaik maid slidderie with the sleit;
The foulis fair for falt thay fell off feit –
On bewis bair it wes na bute to byde,
Bot hyit unto housis thame to hyde.

Sum in the barn, sum in the stak off corne
1840   Thair lugeing tuke and maid thair residence.
The fowlar saw, and grit aithis hes sworne,
Thay suld be tane trewlie for thair expence.
His nettis hes he set with diligence,
And in the snaw he schulit hes ane plane,
1845   And heillit it all over with calf agane.

Thir small birdis seand the calff wes glaid;
Trowand it had bene corne, thay lychtit doun,
Bot of the nettis na presume thay had,
Nor of the fowlaris fals intentioun;

1832 come *came* can blaw *blew*   1833 woddis *woods* wallowit *withered away*
weit *wet*   1834 Baith firth and fell *both wood and hill*   froistys *frosts*
faw *(?) gleaming, (?) of different colours*
1835 *hollows and valleys made slippery with the sleet*
1836 *for lack of food the beautiful birds could not keep their footing*
1837 bewis *boughs* na bute *no help* byde *remain*   1838 hyit *hurried*
thame to hyde *to hide themselves*

1839 stak *stack, pile*   1840 Thair lugeing tuke *took their shelter*
1841 grit aithis *great oaths*   1842 tane *caught* trewlie *certainly*
for thair expence *(?) because of the loss they caused*
1844 *and in the snow he has shovelled a clear space*   1845 heillit *covered*
calf *chaff* agane *again*

1846 Thir *these* seand *seeing* wes glaid *were glad*   1847 Trowand *believing*
1848 presume *anticipation, inkling*   1849 fowlaris *fowler's*

1850   To scraip and seik thair meit thay maid thame boun.
       The swallow on ane lytill branche neir by,
       Dreiddand for gyle, thus loud on thame couth cry:

       'Into that calf scraip quhill your naillis bleid –
       Thair is na corne, ye laubour all in vane.
1855   Trow ye yone churll for pietie will yow feid?
       Na, na, he hes it heir layit for ane trane.
       Remove, I reid, or ellis ye will be slane.
       His nettis he hes set full prively,
       Reddie to draw; in tyme be war forthy!

1860   'Grit fule is he that puttis in dangeir
       His lyfe, his honour, for ane thing off nocht.
       Grit fule is he that will not glaidlie heir
       Counsall in tyme, quhill it availl him nocht.
       Grit fule is he that hes na thing in thocht
1865   Bot thing present, and efter quhat may fall
       Nor off the end hes na memoriall.'

1850 seik *seek* meit *food* maid thame boun *prepared themselves, set to work*
1852 Dreiddand for gyle *fearing a trick*
loud on thame couth cry *cried loudly to them*

1853 scraip quhill your naillis bleid *scrape until your nails bleed*
1855 Trow *ye do you suppose* pietie *pity* feid *feed*
1856 heir layit for ane trane *laid it here for a trap*   1857 Remove *depart*
reid *counsel* ellis *else*   1858 prively *secretly*   1859 Reddie *ready*
war *wary* forthy *therefore*

1860 fule *fool*   1861 off nocht *of no value*
1863 quhill it availl him nocht *until it is of no avail to him*
1864 thocht *thought*   1865 efter quhat may fall *of what may happen after*
1866 memoriall *consideration, recollection*

Thir small birdis, for hunger famischit neir,
Full besie scraipand for to seik thair fude,
The counsall off the swallow wald not heir,
1870 Suppois thair laubour dyd thame lytill gude.
Quhen scho thair fulische hartis understude
Sa indurate, up in ane tre scho flew –
With that this churll over thame his nettis drew.

Allace, it wes grit hartsair for to se
1875 That bludie bowcheour beit thay birdis doun,
And for till heir, quhen thay wist weill to de,
Thair cairfull sang and lamentatioun!
Sum with ane staf he straik to eirth on swoun,
Off sum the heid he straik, off sum he brak the crag,
1880 Sum half on lyfe he stoppit in his bag.

And quhen the swallow saw that they wer deid,
'Lo,' quod scho, 'thus it happinnis mony syis
On thame that will not tak counsall nor reid
Off prudent men or clerkis that ar wyis.
1885 This grit perrell I tauld thame mair than thryis;
Now ar thay deid, and wo is me thairfoir!'
Scho tuke hir flicht, bot I hir saw no moir.

1867 famischit neir *almost starved*   1869 wald *would*
1870 Suppois *although*   1871 fulische *foolish*   1872 indurate *obdurate*

1874 hartsair *grief of heart*   1875 *that bloody butcher beat those birds down*
1876 wist weill to de *knew well they were to die*
1877 cairfull sang *sorrowful song*   1878 straik *struck*
on swoun *stunned, unconscious*   1879 heid *head* brak *broke* crag *neck*
1880 on lyfe *alive* stoppit *stuffed*

1882 syis *times*   1883 reid *advice*   1884 clerkis *clerics, scholars* wyis *wise*
1885 tauld *told, warned* thryis *thrice*

Moralitas

Lo, worthie folk, Esope, that nobill clerk,
Ane poet worthie to be lawreate,
1890   Quhen that he waikit from mair autentik werk,
With uther ma, this foirsaid fabill wrate,
Quhilk at this tyme may weill be applicate
To gude morall edificatioun,
Haifand ane sentence according to ressoun.

1895   This carll and bond, of gentrice spoliate,
Sawand this calf thir small birdis to sla,
It is the feind, quhilk fra the angelike state
Exylit is, as fals apostata,
Quhilk day and nycht weryis not for to ga,
1900   Sawand poysoun and mony wickit thocht
In mannis saull, quhilk Christ full deir hes bocht.

And quhen the saull, as seid into the eird,
Gevis consent in delectatioun,
The wickit thocht beginnis for to breird
1905   In deidlie sin, quhilk is dampnatioun;

1888 Esope *Aesop*   1889 lawreate *crowned with laurel*
1890 waikit from *was freed from* autentik *authoritative*
1891 uther ma *others beside* foirsaid *foresaid* wrate *wrote*
1892 applicate *applied*   1894 Haifand ane sentence *having a meaning*
ressoun *reason*

1895 carll *churl, peasant* bond *bondman* gentrice *nobility of spirit*
spoliate *deprived*   1896 Sawand *sowing* calf *chaff* sla *slay*
1897 feind *devil* quhilk fra *who from*   1898 Exylit *exiled* apostata *apostate*
1899 weryis not *does not grow weary* ga *go*   1900 Sawand *sowing*
1901 saull *soul* full deir *dearly, at great cost* bocht *bought, redeemed*

1902 as seid *like seed* eird *earth*   1903 Gevis *gives* delectatioun *pleasure*
1904 thocht *thought* breird *sprout*   1905 deidlie *deadly*

Ressoun is blindit with affectioun,
And carnall lust grouis full grene and gay,
Throw consuetude hantit from day to day.

Proceding furth be use and consuetude,
1910 The sin ryipis, and schame is set on syde;
The feynd plettis his nettis scharp and rude,
And under plesance previlie dois hyde.
Syne on the feild he sawis calf full wyde,
Quhilk is bot tume and verray vanitie
1915 Of fleschlie lust and vaine prosperitie.

Thir hungrie birdis wretchis we may call,
Ay scraipand in this warldis vane plesance,
Greddie to gadder gudis temporall,
Quhilk as the calf ar tume without substance,
1920 Lytill of availl and full of variance,
Lyke to the mow befoir the face of wind
Quhiskis away and makis wretchis blind.

This swallow, quhilk eschaipit is the snair,
The halie preichour weill may signifie,
1925 Exhortand folk to walk and ay be wair
Fra nettis of our wickit enemie,

1906 affectioun *passion*   1907 grouis *grows*   1908 consuetude *habit*
hantit *engaged in, practised*

1909 *continuing on through practice and habit*   1910 ryipis *ripens* on syde *aside*
1911 *the devil plaits his nets rough and strong*   1912 previlie *secretly*
dois *does*   1914 tume *empty* verray vanitie *true worthlessness*

1918 *greedy to gather worldly goods*   1920 availl *value* variance *change*
1921 mow *dust*   1922 Quhiskis *(which) whisks*

1923 eschaipit is *has escaped*   1924 halie preichour *holy preacher*
1925 to walk *to be wakeful* wair *wary*   1926 Fra *of (the)*

Quha sleipis not, bot ever is reddie,
Quhen wretchis in this warldis calf dois scraip,
To draw his net, that thay may not eschaip.

1930 Allace, quhat cair, quhat weiping is and wo,
Quhen saull and bodie partit ar in twane!
The bodie to the wormis keitching go,
The saull to fyre, to everlestand pane.
Quhat helpis than this calf, thir gudis vane,
1935 Quhen thow art put in Luceferis bag,
And brocht to hell, and hangit be the crag?

Thir hid nettis for to persave and se,
This sarie calf wyislie to understand,
Best is bewar in maist prosperitie,
1940 For in this warld thair is na thing lestand.
Is na man wait how lang his stait will stand,
His lyfe will lest, nor how that he sall end
Efter his deith, nor quhidder he sall wend.

Pray we thairfoir quhill we ar in this lyfe
1945 For four thingis: the first, fra sin remufe;
The secund is to seis all weir and stryfe;
The thrid is perfite cheritie and lufe;

1927 Quha slepis *who sleeps*

1931 twane *two*   **1932** wormis keitching *worms' kitchen (the grave)*
1933 everlestand pane *everlasting torment*   **1935** Luceferis bag *Lucifer's bag*
1936 brocht *brought*

1937 hid *hidden* persave *perceive*   **1938** sarie *sorry, vile* wyislie *wisely*
1939 maist *greatest*   **1940** lestand *lasting*   **1941** Is *(there) is*
wait *(who) knows* stait *condition*   **1943** quhidder *whither*

1944 quhill *while*   **1945** fra sin remufe *to depart from sin*   **1946** seis *cease*
weir *war*   **1947** thrid *third* perfite *perfect* lufe *love*

The feird thing is – and maist for our behufe –
That is in blis with angellis to be fallow.
1950 And thus endis the preiching of the swallow.

The Fox, the Wolf, and the Cadger

Qwhylum thair wynnit in ane wildernes,
As myne authour expreslie can declair,
Ane revand wolff, that levit upon purches
On bestiall, and maid him weill to fair;
1955 Wes nane sa big about him he wald spair
And he war hungrie, outher for favour or feid;
Bot in his breith he weryit thame to deid.

Swa happinnit him in watching as he went
To meit ane foxe in middis off the way.
1960 He him foirsaw, and fenyeit to be schent,
And with ane bek he bad the wolff gude day.
'Welcum to me,' quod he, 'thow Russell gray.'
Syne loutit doun, and tuke him be the hand:
'Ryse up, Lowrence! I leif the for to stand.

1948 feird *fourth* behufe *benefit*   1949 fallow *companion*

1951 Qwhylum thair wynnit *once upon a time there dwelt*
1952 expreslie *in precise terms*   1953 revand *thieving* levit *lived*
purches *robbery/hunting/dealings*   1954 bestiall *farm animals*
maid him weill to fair *did well for himself*
1955 Wes nane sa big *(there) was no one so strong* wald spair *would spare*
1956 And he war *if he were*
outher for favour or feid *either for goodwill or enmity, i.e. for any reason*
1957 breith *fury* weryit thame to deid *worried them to death*

1958 Swa happinnit him *it so befell him* in watching *on the look-out*
1959 meit *meet* middis *middle*   1960 He him foirsaw *(the fox) saw him first*
fenyeit *pretended* schent (?) *exhausted*   1961 bek *nod, sign*
1962 quod *said* Russell *Russell (a name for a fox)*
1963 Syne loutit doun *then bent down* tuke *took*
1964 I leif the for to stand *I give you permission to stand up*

1965   'Quhair hes thow bene this sesoun fra my sicht?
      Thow sall beir office, and my stewart be,
      For thow can knap doun caponis on the nicht,
      And lourand law thow can gar hennis de.'
      'Schir,' said the foxe, 'that ganis not for me;
1970   And I am rad, gif thay me se on far,
      That at my figure beist and bird will skar.'

      'Na,' quod the wolff, 'thow can in covert creip
      Upon thy wame and hint thame be the heid,
      And mak ane suddand schow upon ane scheip,
1975   Syne with thy wappinnis wirrie him to deid.'
      'Schir,' said the foxe, 'ye knaw my roib is reid,
      And thairfoir thair will na beist abyde me,
      Thocht I wald be sa fals as for to hyde me.'

      'Yis,' quod the wolff, 'throw buskis and throw brais
1980   Law can thow lour to come to thy intent.'
      'Schir,' said the foxe, 'ye wait weill how it gais;
      Ane lang space fra thame thay will feill my sent.

1965 Quhair hes thow bene *where have you been* sesoun *time*
fra my sicht *out of my sight*   **1966** sall beir office *shall hold office*
stewart *steward*   **1967** knap *knock* caponis *capons* nicht *night*
1968 lourand law *lurking low* gar hennis de *cause hens to die*
1969 Schir *sir* ganis not *is not suitable*   **1970** rad *afraid*
gif thay me se on far *if they see me at a distance*   **1971** figure *appearance*
beist *beast* skar *take fright*

1972 Na *no* in covert creip *creep under cover*   **1973** wame *belly* hint *seize*
be the heid *by the head*   **1974** mak ane suddand schow *make a sudden attack*
scheip *sheep*   **1975** *then with thy weapons worry him to death*   **1976** roib *robe*
reid *red*   **1977** thairfoir *therefore* abyde *wait for*   **1978** Thocht *even though*
wald *would*

1979 Yis *yes* buskis *bushes* brais *braes, hillsides*   **1980** Law *low* lour *lurk*
1981 wait weill *know well* gais *goes*
1982 Ane lang space fra thame *a long way from them*
feill my sent *perceive my scent*

Than will thay eschaip, suppois I suld be schent;
And I am schamefull for to cum behind thame,
1985   Into the feild thocht I suld sleipand find thame.'

'Na,' quod the wolff, 'thow can cum on the wind;
For everie wrink, forsuith, thow hes ane wyle.'
'Schir,' said the foxe, 'that beist ye mycht call blind
That micht not eschaip than fra me ane myle:
1990   How micht I ane off thame that wyis begyle?
My tippit twa eiris and my twa gray ene
Garris me be kend quhair I wes never sene.'

Than said the wolff, 'Lowrence, I heir the le,
And castys for perrellis thy ginnes to defend;
1995   Bot all thy sonyeis sall not availl the,
About the busk with wayis thocht thow wend.
Falset will failye ay at the latter end:
To bow at bidding and byde not quhill thow brest,
Thairfoir I giff the counsall for the best.'

1983 eschaip *escape*
suppois I suld be schent *even if I should be disgraced (by letting them get away)*
1984 schamefull *ashamed*   1985 *even if I should find them sleeping in the field*

1986 cum on the wind *approach upwind*   1987 wrink *trick* forsuith *in truth*
wyle *wile*   1988 mycht *could*   1989 than *then*
1990 ane off thame *one of them* that wyis *(in) that way* begyle *deceive*
1991 tippit twa eiris *two pointed ears* ene *eyes*
1992 *cause me to be recognized (even) where I was never seen before*

1993 I heir the le *I hear you lie*
1994 *And (you) forecast dangers in order to justify your own tricks*
1995 sonyeis *excuses*   1996 busk *bush* wayis *tricks* thocht *though*
wend *go*   1997 Falset *falsehood* failye ay *always fail*
1998 *to obey an order and not wait until you break (i.e. have to yield)*
1999 giff *give* counsall *counsel*

2000　'Schir,' said the foxe, 'it is Lentring, ye se;
　　　　I can nocht fische, for weiting off my feit,
　　　　To tak ane banestikill, thocht we baith suld de;
　　　　I have nane uther craft to win my meit.
　　　　Bot wer it Pasche, that men suld pultrie eit,
2005　As kiddis, lambis, or caponis into ply,
　　　　To beir your office than wald I not set by.'

　　　　Than said the wolff in wraith, 'Wenis thou with wylis
　　　　And with thy mony mowis me to mat?
　　　　It is ane auld dog, doutles, that thow begylis;
2010　Thow wenis to drau the stra befoir the cat!'
　　　　'Schir,' said the foxe, 'God wait, I mene not that;
　　　　For and I did, it wer weill worth that ye
　　　　In ane reid raip had tyit me till ane tre.

　　　　'Bot nou I se he is ane fule perfay
2015　That with his maister fallis in ressoning.
　　　　I did bot till assay quhat ye wald say;
　　　　God wait, my mynd wes on ane uther thing.

2000 Lentring *Lent (a period of fasting)* se *see*   2001 nocht *not*
for weiting off my feit *for fear of wetting my feet*
2002 *to catch a stickleback (a tiny fish) though we both should die*
2003 nane uther craft *no other skill* meit *food*   2004 Pasche *Easter*
pultrie eit *eat poultry*   2005 As kiddis *like kids, young goats*
into ply *in condition*   2006 than wald I not set by *then I would not refuse*

2007 wraith *anger* Wenis thou *do you expect* wylis *wiles*
2008 mony mowis me to mat *many tricks to defeat me*   2009 auld *old*
doutles *in truth* begylis *beguile*
2010 drau the stra befoir the cat *draw the straw before the cat (a young cat will
jump at it, but not an old one)*   2011 wait *knows* mene *mean*
2012 and *if* weill worth *deserving*   2013 reid *red (? with blood)* raip *rope*
tyit me till ane tre *tied me to a tree*

2014 fule perfay *fool indeed*   2015 maister *master* ressoning *argument*
2016 *I did it only to test what you would say*   2017 uther *other*

I sall fulfill in all thing your bidding,
Quhatever ye charge on nichtis or on dayis.'
2020   'Weill,' quod the wolff, 'I heir weill quhat thou sayis.

'Bot yit I will thow mak to me ane aith
For to be leill attour all levand leid.'
'Schir,' said the foxe, 'that ane word maks me wraith,
For nou I se ye have me at ane dreid:
2025   Yit sall I sweir, suppois it be nocht neid,
Be Juppiter, and on pane off my heid,
I sall be treu to you quhill I be deid.'

With that ane cadgear, with capill and with creillis,
Come carpand furth; than Lowrence culd him spy.
2030   The foxe the flewer off the fresche hering feillis,
And to the wolff he roundis prively:
'Schir, yone ar hering the cadgear caryis by;
Thairfoir I reid that we se for sum wayis
To get sum fische aganis thir fasting dayis.

2019 Quhatever *whatever* charge *command*
on nichtis or on dayis *on nights or days*

2021 will *wish* aith *oath*   2022 *to be loyal over all living creatures*
2023 ane *one* maks me wraith *makes me angry*
2024 *For now I see you are suspicious of me*   2025 sweir *swear*
suppois it be nocht neid *although it is unnecessary*
2026 on pane off my heid *on pain of (losing) my head*   2027 treu *true*
quhill *until* deid *dead*

2028 cadgear *cadger, itinerant pedlar* capill *horse* creillis *creels, wicker baskets*
2029 *Came along (?) singing (?) talking to himself; then Lawrence espied him*
2030 flewer *smell* hering *herring* feillis *perceives*
2031 roundis prively *whispers secretly*   2032 yone *those* caryis by *carries past*
2033 reid *advise* se for sum wayis *look for some devices*
2034 aganis thir *in preparation for these*

2035 'Sen I am stewart, I wald we had sum stuff,
And ye ar silver-seik, I wait richt weill.
Thocht we wald thig yone verray churlische chuff,
He will not giff us ane hering off his creill –
Befoir yone churle on kneis thocht we wald kneill.
2040 Bot yit I trou alsone that ye sall se
Giff I can craft to bleir yone carlis ee.

'Schir, ane thing is, and we get off yone pelff,
Ye man tak travell and mak us sum supplé;
For he that will not laubour and help himselff,
2045 Into thir dayis he is not worth ane fle.
I think to work als besie as ane be –
And ye sall follou ane lytill efterwart
And gadder hering, for that sall be your part.'

With that he kest ane cumpas far about,
2050 And straucht him doun in middis off the way;
As he wer deid he fenyeit him, but dout,
And than upon lenth unliklie lay.

2035 Sen *since* sum stuff *some stock of food*
2036 silver-seik *silver sick, without money*
2037 *though we would beg that truly churlish boor*   2038 giff *give*
2039 *even if we went down on our knees before that churl*
2040 *but I still believe that you will see at once*
2041 *if I have the skill to dim that fellow's eye (i.e. hoodwink him)*

2042 ane *one* and we get off yone pelff *if we are to get some of that booty*
2043 tak travell *make an effort* mak us sum supplé *provide some help*
2045 Into thir *in these* fle *fly*   2046 think *intend*
als besie as ane be *as busy as a bee*
2047 follou ane lytill efterwart *follow a little afterwards*   2048 gadder *gather*

2049 kest ane cumpas *made a circuit*   2050 straucht *stretched*
middis *the middle*   2051 fenyeit *pretended* but dout *in truth*
2052 upon lenth *at full length* unliklie *objectionable (to look at)*

The quhyte he turnit up off his ene tuay,
His toung out hang ane handbreid off his heid,
2055   And still he lay, als straucht as he wer deid.

The cadgear fand the foxe, and he wes fane,
And till himself thus softlie can he say:
'At the nixt bait, in faith, ye sall be flane,
And off your skyn I sall mak mittenis tway.'
2060   He lap full lichtlie about him quhair he lay,
And all the trace he trippit on his tais;
As he had hard ane pyper play he gais.

'Heir lyis the deuyll', quod he, 'deid in ane dyke;
Sic ane selcouth sau I not this sevin yeir.
2065   I trou ye have bene tussillit with sum tyke,
That garris you ly sa still withoutin steir.
Schir Foxe, in faith, ye ar deir welcum heir;
It is sum wyfis malisone, I trow,
For pultrie pyking, that lychtit hes on yow.

2053 quhyte *white(s)* ene tuay *two eyes*
2054 *his tongue hung out a hand's breadth from his head*
2055 als straucht *as straight (and rigid)*

2056 fand *found* fane *glad*   2057 till *to* can *did*
2058 nixt bait *next halt (for resting the horse)* flane *flayed*
2059 mittenis tway *two mittens*
2060 *he leapt nimbly around him (the fox) where he lay*   2061 trace *way*
trippit *danced* tais *toes*   2062 As he had hard *as if he had heard*
pyper *piper* gais *goes, (?) dances*

2063 lyis *lies* deid in ane dyke *dead in a ditch*
2064 Sic ane selcouth *such a marvel* sau *saw* yeir *year(s)*
2065 *I think you have been worried by some cur*   2066 garris *makes*
withoutin steir *without stirring*   2067 deir *highly*
2068 wyfis malisone *wife's curse*   2069 pultrie pyking *stealing poultry*
lychtit *alighted*

2070   'Thair sall na pedder, for purs, nor yit for glufis,
      Nor yit for poyntis, pyke your pellet fra me:
      I sall off it mak mittenis to my lufis
      Till hald my handis hait quhairever I be;
      Till Flanderis sall it never saill the se.'
2075   With that in hy he hint him be the heillis,
      And with ane swak he swang him on the creillis,

      Syne be the heid the hors in hy hes hint.
      The fraudfull foxe thairto gude tent hes tane,
      And with his teith the stoppell, or he stint,
2080   Pullit out, and syne the hering ane and ane
      Out off the creillis he swakkit doun gude wane.
      The wolff wes war, and gadderit spedilie:
      The cadgear sang, 'Huntis up, up', upon hie.

      Yit at ane burne the cadgear lukit about;
2085   With that the foxe lap quyte the creillis fray.
      The cadgear wald have raucht the foxe ane rout,
      Bot all for nocht, he wan his hoill that day.

2070 pedder *pedlar* glufis *gloves*   2071 poyntis *points, laces for garments*
pyke *steal* pellet *pelt, skin*   2072 lufis *palms (of the hand)*
2073 Till hald *to keep* hait *warm* quhairever *wherever*
2074 Flanderis *Flanders*   2075 hy *haste* hint *seized* heillis *heels*
2076 swak *whack* swang *swung, threw*

2078 fraudfull *deceitful* thairto gude tent hes tane *to this has taken good heed*
2079 teith *teeth* stoppell *stopper*
or he stint *(before he stopped =) as soon as he could*
2080 Pullit *pulled* syne *then* ane and ane *one by one*
2081 swakkit *hurled* gude wane *in good number, at a great rate*
2082 war *alert* gadderit spedilie *gathered (them) quickly*
2083 'Huntis up, up', *(a popular song)* upon hie *loudly*

2084 burne *stream* lukit about *looked around*
2085 lap quyte the creillis fray *leapt clear from the creels*
2086 raucht *struck* rout *blow*
2087 *but all for nought, he (the fox) got back to his hole that day.*

Than with ane schout thus can the cadgear say:
'Abyde, and thou ane nekhering sall haif
2090   Is worth my capill, creillis, and all the laif.'

'Now,' quod the foxe, 'I schreu me and we meit!
I hard quhat thou hecht to do with my skyn.
Thy handis sall never in thay mittinnis tak heit,
And thou wer hangit, carll, and all thy kyn!
2095   Do furth thy mercat – at me thou sall nocht wyn –
And sell thy hering thou hes thair till hie price;
Ellis thow sall wyn nocht on thy merchandice.'

The cadgear trimmillit for teyne quhair that he stude.
'It is weill worthie', quod he, 'I want yone tyke,
2100   That had nocht in my hand sa mekill gude
As staff or sting yone truker for to stryke.'
With that lychtlie he lap out over ane dyke
And snakkit doun ane staff – for he wes tene –
That hevie wes and off the holyne grene

2089 ane nekhering *blow on the neck/best quality herring*   2090 capill *horse*
laif *rest*

2091 I schreu me and we meit *I'll be damned if we meet*   2092 hard *heard*
hecht *promised, vowed*   2093 thay *those* tak heit *get warm*
2094 And thou wer hangit *(?)* *would that you were hanged, (?) even if you were
hanged* kyn *kin*   2095 *get on with your trading – from me you'll get no profit*
2096 thair *there* till hie price *at a high price*   2097 Ellis *otherwise*
wyn nocht *gain nothing*

2098 *the cadger trembled with anger where he stood*
2099 *'I well deserve', said he, 'to have lost that cur*
2100 That had nocht *since I had not* sa mekill gude *so much as*
2101 sting yone truker for to stryke *pole to strike that deceiver*
2102 lychtlie *nimbly* lap *leapt* dyke *ditch*   2103 snakkit doun *broke off*
tene *furious*   2104 hevie *heavy* holyne grene *green holly*

2105 With that the foxe unto the wolff could wend,
And fand him be the hering quhair he lyis.
'Schir,' said he than, 'maid I not fair defend?
Ane wicht man wantit never, and he wer wyis;
Ane hardie hart is hard for to suppryis.'
2110 Than said the wolff, 'Thow art ane berne full bald,
And wyse at will, in gude tyme be it tald.

'Bot quhat wes yone the carll cryit on hie,
And schuke his hand?' quod he. 'Hes thou no feill?'
'Schir,' said the foxe, 'that I can tell trewlie;
2115 He said the nekhering wes intill the creill.'
'Kennis thou that hering?' 'Ye, schir, I ken it weill,
And at the creill mouth I had it thryis but dout:
The wecht off it neir tit my tuskis out.

'Now suithlie, schir, micht we that hering fang,
2120 It wald be fische to us thir fourtie dayis.'
Than said the wolff, 'Nou God nor that I hang!
Bot to be thair I wald gif all my clays,
To se gif that my wappinnis mycht it rais.'
'Schir,' said the foxe, 'God wait, I wischit you oft,
2125 Quhen that my pith micht not beir it on loft.

2105 could *did* 2106 fand *found* be *beside* lyis *lies* 2107 defend *defence*
2108 wicht *valiant* wantit never *never lacked* and he wer wyis *if he were wise*
2109 hardie *bold, courageous* suppryis *overcome* 2110 berne *man* bald *bold*
2111 wyse at will *have wisdom at your command* tald *told*

2112 yone *that* 2113 schuke *was shaking* Hes thou no feill? *have you no idea?*
2115 intill *in* 2116 Kennis thou *do you know*
2117 creill mouth *mouth of the basket* but dout *in truth*
2118 wecht *weight* neir tit my tuskis out *nearly pulled my teeth out*

2119 suithlie *truly* micht we that hering fang *if we could get that herring*
2120 to *for* thir fourtie dayis *these forty days (of Lent))*
2121 Nou God nor that I hang! *God grant that I be hanged!*
2122 I wald gif all my clays *would give all my clothes*
2123 wappinnis *weapons* rais *raise* 2124 wischit *wished for*
2125 pith *strength* on loft *aloft, up*

'It is ane syde off salmond, as it wair,
And callour, pypand lyke ane pertrik ee:
It is worth all the hering ye have thair –
Ye, and we had it swa, is it worth sic thre.'
2130 Than said the wolff, 'Quhat counsell gevis thou me?'
'Schir,' said the foxe, 'wirk efter my devyis,
And ye sall have it, and tak you na suppryis.

'First, ye man cast ane cumpas far about,
Syne straucht you doun in middis off the way;
2135 Baith heid and feit and taill ye man streik out,
Hing furth your toung, and clois weill your ene tway,
Syne se your heid on ane hard place ye lay;
And doubt not for na perrell may appeir,
Bot hald you clois, quhen that the carll cummis neir.

2140 'And thocht ye se ane staf, have ye na dout,
Bot hald you wonder still into that steid;
And luke your ene be clois, as thay wer out,
And se that ye schrink nouther fute nor heid:
Than will the cadgear carll trou ye be deid,
2145 And intill haist will hint you be the heillis,
As he did me, and swak you on his creillis.'

2126 salmond *salmon* wair *were*   2127 callour *(?) fresh* pypand *(?) glistening*
lyke ane pertrik ee *like a partridge's eye*   2129 Ye *yes* and *if* swa *thus*
sic thre *three times as much*   2130 gevis thou *do you give*
2131 wirk efter my devyis *act according to my plan*
2132 and tak you na suppryis *if no unexpected attack catches you*

2133 man cast ane cumpas *must make a detour*   2134 straucht *stretch*
2135 streik *stretch*   2136 Hing furth *hang out* toung *tongue* clois *close*
2137 Syne se *then see that*   2138 *fear not for any danger that may appear*
2139 clois *still, motionless*

2140 thocht *though* dout *fear*   2141 into that steid *in that place*
2142 luke *see that* clois *closed* as *as if*   2143 schrink *shrink, move aside*
nouther *neither*   2144 trou *believe*   2145 intill haist *in haste* hint *seize*
2146 swak *hurl, whack*

'Now,' quod the wolff, 'I sweir the be my thrift,
I trou yone cadgear carll dow not me beir.'
'Schir,' said the foxe, 'on loft he will you lift
2150   Upon his creillis, and do him lytill deir –
Bot ane thing dar I suithlie to you sweir:
Get ye that hering sicker in sum place,
Ye sall not fair in fisching mair quhill Pasche.

'I sall say *In principio* upon yow,
2155   And crose your corps from the top to tay;
Wend quhen ye will, I dar be warrand now
That ye sall de na suddand deith this day.'
With that the wolff gird up sone and to gay,
And caist ane cumpas about the cadgear far;
2160   Syne raucht him in the gait, or he come nar.

He laid his halfheid sicker hard and sad,
Syne straucht his four feit fra him, and his heid,
And hang his toung furth as the foxe him bad;
Als styll he lay as he wer verray deid,
2165   Rakkand nathing off the carlis favour nor feid,
Bot ever upon the nekhering he thinkis,
And quyte foryettis the foxe and all his wrinkis.

2147 I sweir the be my thrift *I swear to you as I may thrive*
2148 dow not me beir *is not able to carry me*
2150 do him lytill deir *do little harm to himself*   2151 dar *dare* suithlie *truly*
2152 Get ye *if you get* sicker *safe*   2153 fair in fisching *go fishing*
mair *any more* quhill Pasche *until Easter*

2154 In principio *In the beginning (the beginning of the gospel of St John,
sometimes used as a magical charm)*
2155 *and make the sign of the cross on your body from top to toe*   2156 Wend *go*
warrand *guarantor, surety*   2157 de na suddand deith *die no sudden death*
2158 gird *sprang* to gay *(to go =) went*   2159 caist ane cumpas *made a detour*
2160 *then stretched himself in the road before he (the cadger) approached*

2161 *he laid down the side of his head very firmly and heavily*
2163 hang *hung*   2164 verray *truly*
2165 *caring not at all for either the peasant's kindness or hostility*
2167 foryettis *forgets* wrinkis *tricks*

With that the cadgear, als wraith as ony wind,
Come rydand on the laid, for it wes licht,
2170 Thinkand ay on the foxe that wes behind,
Upon quhat wyse revengit on him he micht;
And at the last of the wolff gat ane sicht,
Quhair he in lenth lay streikit in the gait –
Bot giff he lichtit doun or nocht, God wait!

2175 Softlie he said, 'I wes begylit anis;
Be I begylit twyis, I schrew us baith!
That evill bat it sall licht upon thy banis
He suld have had that hes done me the skaith.'
On hicht he hovit the staf, for he wes wraith,
2180 And hit him with sic will upon the heid
Quhill neir he swonit and swelt into that steid.

Thre battis he bure, or he his feit micht find,
Bot yit the wolff wes wicht, and wan away;
He mycht not se – he wes sa verray blind –
2185 Nor wit reddilie quhether it wes nicht or day.
The foxe beheld that service quhair he lay,
And leuch on loft quhen he the wolff sa seis,
Baith deif and dosinnit, fall swonand on his kneis.

2168 wraith *angry* ony *any*   2169 rydand *riding* laid *load* licht *light*
2170 Thinkand ay *thinking always* behind *behind him, further back on the road*
2171 *on what manner he could (be) revenged on him*
2172 gat ane sicht *caught sight*   2173 in lenth *at full length*
streikit *stretched out* gait *road*   2174 lichtit doun *alighted* wait *knows*

2175 begylit *deceived* anis *once*   2176 Be I *if I be*
schrew us baith *curse us both*   2177 bat *blow* licht *fall* banis *bones*
2178 *(which) he should have received who did me the injury*
2179 On hicht *on high* hovit *raised*
2181 *until he almost collapsed and died in that place*

2182 *three blows he endured before he could get to his feet*   2183 wicht *strong*
wan away *escaped*   2185 wit reddilie quhether *know easily whether*
2186 that service *how the wolf was served*   2187 leuch on loft *laughed loudly*
sa seis *thus sees*   2188 deif and dosinnit *deaf and dazed* swonand *swooning*

He that of ressoun can not be content,
2190   Bot covetis all, is abill all to tyne.
The foxe, quhen that he saw the wolff wes schent,
Said to himself, 'Thir hering sall be myne.'
I le, or ellis he wes a stewart fyne,
That fand sic wayis his maister for to greif.
2195   With all the fische thus Lowrence tuke his leif.

The wolff wes neir weill dungin to the deid,
That uneith with his lyfe away he wan,
For with the bastoun weill brokin wes his heid.
The foxe into his den sone drew him than,
2200   That had betraisit his maister and the man:
The ane wantit the hering off his creillis;
The utheris blude wes rynnand over his heillis.

Moralitas

This taill is myngit with moralitie,
As I sall schaw sumquhat, or that I ceis.
2205   The foxe unto the warld may likkinnit be;
The revand wolf unto ane man, but leis;

2189 of ressoun *within reason, with a reasonable amount*   2190 covetis *covets*
abill *liable* tyne *lose*   2191 schent *destroyed, humiliated*   2193 le *lie* ellis *else*
stewart fyne *fine steward*   2194 fand *found* greif *harm*
2195 tuke his leif *took his leave*

2196 neir weill dungin to the deid *almost beaten to death*
2197 uneith *scarcely* wan *escaped*   2198 bastoun *staff* brokin *broken*
2199 sone drew him than *quickly made his way then*   2200 betraisit *betrayed*
2201 wantit *lacked*   2202 utheris blude *other's blood* rynnand *running*
heillis *heels*

2203 myngit *mingled, filled*   2204 schaw *show, demonstrate*
sumquhat *in some part* or that I ceis *before I stop*   2205 warld *world*
likkinnit *likened*   2206 revand *thieving* but leis *truly*

The cadgear, deith, quhome under all man preis –
That ever tuke lyfe throw cours of kynd man dee,
As man, and beist, and fische into the see.

2210 The warld, ye wait, is stewart to the man,
Quhilk makis man to haif na mynd of deid,
Bot settis for winning all the craftis thay can.
The hering I likkin unto the gold sa reid,
Quhilk gart the wolf in perrell put his heid –
2215 Richt swa the gold garris landis and cieteis
With weir be waistit daylie, as men seis.

And as the foxe with dissimulance and gyle
Gart the wolf wene to haif worschip for ever,
Richt swa this warld with vane glore for ane quhyle
2220 Flatteris with folk as thay suld failye never;
Yit suddandlie men seis it oft dissever;
With thame that trowis oft to fill the sek,
Deith cummis behind and nippis thame be the neck.

2207 deith *(may be likened to) death*
quhome under all man preis *(?) under whom all must struggle*
2208 *all that ever received life through the course of nature must die*

2211 haif na mynd of deid *have no thought of death*
2212 *but use all the tricks they know for gaining worldly possessions*
2213 reid *red (= of high quality)*   2214 gart *caused*
in perrell put his heid *put his head in danger*   2215 Richt swa *just so*
landis and cieteis *lands and cities*
2216 weir be waistit *(with) war to be laid waste* seis *see*

2218 wene *expect* worschip *honour*   2219 vane glore *vainglory*
quhyle *short time*   2220 as *as if* failye *fail*   2221 suddandlie *suddenly*
dissever *depart*   2222 trowis *expect* sek *sack*
2223 nippis thame *grasps them suddenly*

The micht of gold makis mony men sa blind,
2225 That settis on avarice thair felicitie,
That thay foryet the cadgear cummis behind
To stryke thame, of quhat stait sa ever thay be:
Quhat is mair dirk than blind prosperitie?
Quhairfoir, I counsell mychtie men to haif mynd
2230 Of the nekhering, interpreit in this kynd.

The Fox, the Wolf, and the Husbandman

In elderis dayis, as Esope can declair,
Thair wes ane husband quhilk had ane plewch to steir.
His use wes ay in morning to ryse air:
Sa happinnit him, in streiking tyme off yeir,
2235 Airlie in the morning to follou furth his feir
Unto the pleuch, bot his gadman and he.
His stottis he straucht with 'Benedicite!';

The caller cryit, 'How! Haik!' upon hicht,
'Hald draucht, my dowis!' Syne broddit thame full sair:
2240 The oxin wes unusit, young, and licht,
And for fersnes thay couth the fur forfair.

2225 settis *place*   2226 foryet *forget*   2227 stait *state, rank*   2228 dirk *dark*
2229 Quhairfoir *wherefore* haif mynd *remember, think on*
2230 interpreit *interpreted* kynd *way*

2231 elderis dayis *days of our elders* Esope can declair *Aesop declared*
2232 husband *husbandman, farmer* quhilk *who* plewch *plough* steir *guide*
2233 use *practice* ay *always* air *early*
2234 *it so happened to him, in the time of the year at which the first furrow was
ploughed*   2235 Airlie *early*
follou furth his feir *(?) follow out his companion, (?) make the first guiding furrow*
2236 bot *only* gadman *goad-man (the 'caller' who drove the oxen)*
2237 stottis *bullocks, young castrated oxen* straucht *put to work*
'Benedicite!' *'Bless the Lord!'*

2238 *the driver called out 'ho! come on!'*   2239 Hald draucht *keep pulling*
dowis *doves* broddit *goaded* full sair *sharply*   2240 wes unusit *were untrained*
licht *frisky*   2241 *And because of their unruliness they ruined the furrow*

The husband than woxe angrie as ane hair,
Syne cryit, and caist his patill and grit stanis:
'The wolff', quod he, 'mot have you all at anis!'

2245 Bot yit the wolff wes neirar nor he wend,
For in ane busk he lay, and Lowrence baith,
In ane rouch rone wes at the furris end,
And hard the hecht; than Lowrence leuch full raith:
'To tak yone bud,' quod he, 'it wer na skaith.'
2250 'Weill,' quod the wolff, 'I hecht the, be my hand,
Yone carlis word as he wer king sall stand.'

The oxin waxit mair reulie at the last;
Syne efter thay lousit, fra that it worthit weill lait.
The husband hamewart with his cattell past.
2255 Than sone the wolff come hirpilland in his gait
Befoir the oxin, and schupe to mak debait.
The husband saw him, and worthit sumdeill agast,
And bakwart with his beistis wald haif past.

2242 woxe angrie *became angry* hair *hare*   2243 caist *threw*
patill *pattle (paddle-shaped tool for cleaning earth from the plough)*
grit stanis *big stones*   2244 quod *said*
mot have you all at anis *may have you all together, i.e. take you all*

2245 yit *yet* neirar nor he wend *nearer than he thought*
2246 busk *bush* Lowrence *Laurence, the fox* baith *as well*
2247 rouch rone *(was in a) rough thicket* furris *furrow's*
2248 hard *heard* hecht *promise, vow* leuch full raith *laughed quickly*
2249 yone bud *that bribe* skaith *harm, damage*   2250 Weill *well*
hecht the *promise you* be *by*   2251 carlis *peasant's* as he *as if he were*
sall stand *shall hold good*

2252 waxit mair reulie *grew more orderly*
2253 then afterwards they released *(them from the plough) since it had become*
very late   2254 hamewart *homewards* cattell *cattle* past *went*
2255 sone *soon, immediately* come hirpilland *came limping*
gait (?) *way*, (?) *gait*   2256 Befoir *before* schupe *planned, set about*
mak debait *make contention, trouble*
2257 worthit sumdeill agast *became somewhat frightened*
2258 *And was minded to move back with his animals*

The wolff said, 'Quhether dryvis thou this pray?
2260 I chalenge it, for nane off thame ar thyne!'
The man thairoff wes in ane felloun fray,
And soberlie to the wolff answerit syne:
'Schir, be my saull, thir oxin ar all myne:
Thairfoir I studdie quhy ye suld stop me,
2265 Sen that I faltit never to you, trewlie.'

The wolff said, 'Carll, gaif thou not me this drift
Airlie, quhen thou wes eirrand on yone bank?
And is thair oucht, sayis thou, frear than gift?
This tarying wyll tyne the all thy thank:
2270 Far better is frelie for to giff ane plank
Nor be compellit on force to giff ane mart.
Fy on the fredome that cummis not with hart!'

'Schir,' quod the husband, 'ane man may say in greif,
And syne ganesay fra he avise and se.
2275 I hecht to steill; am I thairfoir ane theif?
God forbid, schir, all hechtis suld haldin be.

2259 Quhether dryvis thou this pray *whither are you driving this prey (implying
that the cattle are stolen)*   2260 chalenge *lay claim to* nane *none*
2261 thairoff *at that* felloun fray *extreme state of alarm*
2262 soberlie *gravely, temperately*   2263 be my saull *be my soul* thir *these*
2264 studdie quhy *wonder why* suld *should*   2265 Sen that *since*
faltit never to you *never committed a fault against you*

2266 gaif *gave* drift *drove, team*   2267 eirrand *ploughing* bank *slope*
2268 oucht *anything* frear than gift *more generous than a gift*
2269 tarying *delaying* tyne the all thy thank *lose you all the gratitude you have won*
2270 is *it is* frelie for to giff ane plank *freely give a plack (small Scottish coin, of
little value)*   2271 Nor *than* on force *forcibly*
mart *ox or cow fattened for slaughter*   2272 fredome *generous act* hart *heart*

2273 in greif *in anger*   2274 syne *then* ganesay *contradict, retract*
fra he avise and se *after he takes counsel and considers*
2275 hecht to steill *promise to steal*
2276 hechtis suld haldin be *promises should be kept*

Gaif I my hand or oblissing,' quod he,
'Or have ye witnes or writ for to schau?
Schir, reif me not, bot go and seik the lau.'

2280   'Carll,' quod the wolff, 'ane lord, and he be leill,
That schrinkis for schame, or doutis to be repruvit –
His sau is ay als sickker as his seill.
Fy on the leid that is not leill and lufit!
Thy argument is fals, and eik contrufit,
2285   For it is said in proverb: "But lawté
All uther vertewis ar nocht worth ane fle." '

'Schir,' said the husband, 'remember of this thing:
Ane leill man is not tane at halff ane taill.
I may say and ganesay; I am na king.
2290   Quhair is your witnes that hard I hecht thame haill?'
Than said the wolff, 'Thairfoir it sall nocht faill.
Lowrence,' quod he, 'cum hidder of that schaw,
And say nathing bot as thow hard and saw.'

2277 Gaiff I *did I give* oblissing *binding contract*   2278 writ *document*
schau *show*   2279 reif *rob* seik the lau *seek the law*

2280 and he be leill *if he is loyal*
2281 *that shrinks from shame or fears to be reproved*
2282 *his word is always as trusty as his seal*
2283 leid *man* lufit *respected, loved*   2284 eik contrufit *also fabricated*
2285 But lawté *without loyalty*   2286 uther vertewis *other virtues* fle *fly*

2288 *a true man is not caught by half a story (a one-sided story)*
2290 Quhair *where* hard *heard* haill *wholly*   2291 Thairfoir *for that reason*
2292 hidder of that schaw *hither from that copse*
2293 nathing bot *nothing except*

Lowrence come lourand, for he lufit never licht,
2295 And sone appeirit befoir thame in that place:
The man leuch nathing quhen he saw that sicht.
'Lowrence,' quod the wolff, 'thow man declair this cace,
Quhairof we sall schaw the suith in schort space.
I callit on the leill witnes for to beir:
2300 Quhat hard thou that this man hecht me lang eir?'

'Schir,' said the tod, 'I can not hastelie
Swa sone as now gif sentence finall;
Bot wald ye baith submit yow heir to me,
To stand at my decreit perpetuall,
2305 To pleis baith I suld preif, gif it may fall.'
'Weill,' quod the wolff, 'I am content for me.'
The man said, 'Swa am I, however it be.'

Than schew thay furth thair allegeance but fabill,
And baith proponit thair pley to him compleit.
2310 Quod Lowrence, 'Now I am ane juge amycabill:
Ye sall be sworne to stand at my decreit,
Quhether heirefter ye think it soure or sweit.'
The wolff braid furth his fute, the man his hand,
And on the toddis taill sworne thay ar to stand.

2294 lourand *lurking* lufit *loved* licht *light*   2295 appeirit *appeared*
2296 leuch nathing *did not laugh at all* sicht *sight*
2297 man declair *must make clear* cace *case*
2298 *of which we shall demonstrate the truth shortly*
2299 *I called on you to bear true witness*
2300 Quhat hard thou *what did you hear* lang eir *long before*

2301 tod *fox*   2302 gif *give*   2303 Bot wald ye baith *if you both would*
2304 *To abide by my perpetual judgement (i.e. valid for all time, with no right of
appeal)*   2305 pleis *please* preif *try* gif it may fall *if it may befall*
2307 Swa *so*

2308 *then they presented their allegations truthfully*   2309 proponit *propounded*
pley *suit* compleit *completely*   2310 juge *judge* amycabill *acting in friendship*
2311 stand at my decreit *abide by my judgement*
2312 Quhether heirefter *whether afterwards* soure or sweit *sour or sweet*
2313 braid furth his fute *thrust out his foot*   2314 toddis taill *fox's tail*

2315 Than tuke the tod the man furth till ane syde,
And said him, 'Freind, thou art in blunder brocht;
The wolff will not forgif the ane oxe hyde.
Yit wald myself fane help the, and I mocht,
Bot I am laith to hurt my conscience ocht.
2320 Tyne nocht thy querrell in thy awin defence;
This will not throu but grit coist and expence.

'Seis thou not buddis beiris bernis throw,
And giftis garris crukit materis hald full evin?
Sumtymis ane hen haldis ane man in ane kow;
2325 All ar not halie that heifis thair handis to hevin.'
'Schir,' said the man, 'ye sall have sex or sevin
Richt off the fattest hennis off all the floik –
I compt not all the laif, leif me the coik.'

'I am ane juge,' quod Lowrence than, and leuch:
2330 'Thair is na buddis suld beir me by the rycht.
I may tak hennis and caponis weill aneuch,
For God is gane to sleip, as for this nycht;

2315 tuke *took* furth till ane syde *out to one side*
2316 art in blunder brocht *have been brought into a disastrous situation*
2317 forgif the *remit, allow you* ane oxe hyde *one ox hide*
2318 *Yet I myself would gladly help you if I could*
2319 laith *reluctant* ocht *to any extent*
2320 *do not spoil your claim (?) by attempting to defend it yourself*
2321 *this will not go through without considerable cost and expense*

2322 *do you not see how bribes carry men through*
2323 *and gifts cause crooked things to go straight*
2324 *sometimes a hen enables a man to keep a cow*   2325 halie *holy* heifis *raise*
hevin *heaven*   2326 sex or sevin *six or seven*   2327 floik *flock*
2328 *I do not care about all the rest, but leave me the cock*

2330 na buddis suld beir me by the rycht *no bribes should take me away from
what is just*   2331 caponis weill aneuch *capons in plenty*
2332 gane to sleip *gone to sleep* nycht *night*

Sic small thingis ar not sene into his sicht.
Thir hennis', quod he, 'sall mak thy querrell sure:
2335　With emptie hand na man suld halkis lure.'

Concordit thus, than Lowrence tuke his leiff,
And to the wolff he went into ane ling;
Syne prevelie he plukkit him be the sleiff:
'Is this in ernist', quod he, 'ye ask sic thing?
2340　Na, be my saull, I trow it be in heithing.'
Than said the wolff, 'Lowrence, quhy sayis thou sa?
Thow hard the hecht thyselff that he couth ma.'

'The hecht', quod he, 'yone man maid at the pleuch –
Is that the cause quhy ye the cattell craif?'
2345　Halff into heithing said Lowrence than, and leuch:
'Schir, be the rude, unroikit now ye raif:
The devill ane stirk taill thairfoir sall ye haif!
Wald I tak it upon my conscience
To do sa pure ane man as yone offence?

2350　'Yit haif I commonnit with the carll,' quod he.
'We ar concordit upon this cunnand:
Quyte off all clamis, swa ye will mak him fre,
Ye sall ane cabok have into your hand

2333 Sic *such* sene into his sicht *seen in his sight*   **2334** Thir *these*
thy querrell sure *your cause secure*   **2335** halkis lure *(try to) lure hawks*

2336 Concordit *agreed* tuke his leiff *took his leave*   **2337** into ane ling *forthwith*
2338 prevelie *secretly* sleiff *sleeve*   **2339** ernist *earnest*   **2340** trow *believe*
in heithing *mockery*   **2341** quhy sayis thou sa? *why do you say thus?*
2342 couth ma *made*

2344 the cattell craif *ask for the cattle*   **2346** rude *cross* unroikit *(?) excited*
raif *rave*   **2347** *not a bullock's tail shall you have for that*   **2349** pure *poor*

2350 commonnit *talked* carll *peasant*   **2351** cunnand *covenant*
2352 *if you will make him quit and free of all claims*   **2353** cabok *cheese* into *in*

That sic ane sall not be in all this land,
2355 For it is somer cheis, baith fresche and fair:
He sayis it weyis ane stane and sumdeill mair.'

'Is that thy counsell,' quod the wolff, 'I do,
That yone carll for ane cabok suld be fre?'
'Ye, be my saull, and I wer sworne yow to,
2360 Ye suld nane uther counsell have for me;
For gang ye to the maist extremitie,
It will not wyn yow worth ane widderit neip:
Schir, trow ye not I have ane saull to keip?'

'Weill,' quod the wolff, 'it is aganis my will
2365 That yone carll for ane cabok suld ga quyte.'
'Schir,' quod the tod, 'ye tak it in nane evill,
For, be my saull, yourself had all the wyte.'
Than said the wolff, 'I bid na mair to flyte,
Bot I wald se yone cabok off sic pryis.'
2370 'Schir,' said the tod, 'he tauld me quhair it lyis.'

Than hand in hand thay held unto ane hill;
The husband till his hous hes tane the way,
For he wes fane he schaippit from thair ill,
And on his feit woke the dure quhill day.

2354 sic ane *such a one*   2355 somer cheis *summer cheese*
2356 *he says it weighs a stone and somewhat more*

2357 I do *(?) that I should follow*   2359 and *if*   2360 uther *other*
for me *as far as I am concerned*   2361 For gang ye *if you go*
maist extremitie *greatest severity*
2362 *It will not gain you the value of a withered turnip*
2363 keip *protect*

2364 will *desire, will*   2365 ga quyte *go free*
2366 ye tak it in nane evill *do not take it badly*   2367 wyte *blame*
2368 bid *desire* flyte *quarrel*   2369 sic pryis *such value*
2370 tauld *told* lyis *lies*

2371 held *went on*   2372 tane *taken*   2373 fane *glad* schaippit *escaped* ill *evil*
2374 feit *feet* woke the dure quhill day *guarded the door until day*

2375 Now will we turne unto the uther tway:
Throw woddis waist thir freikis on fute can fair,
Fra busk to busk, quhill neir midnycht and mair.

Lowrence wes ever remembring upon wrinkis
And subtelteis, the wolff for to begyle;
2380 That he had hecht ane caboik he forthinkis;
Yit at the last he findis furth ane wyle,
Than at himselff softlie couth he smyle.
The wolff sayis, 'Lowrence, thou playis bellie-blind;
We seik all nycht, bot nathing can we find.'

2385 'Schir,' said the tod, 'we ar at it almaist;
Soft yow ane lytill, and ye sall se it sone.'
Than to ane manure-place thay hyit in haist;
The nycht wes lycht, and pennyfull the mone.
Than till ane draw-well thir senyeours past but hone,
2390 Quhair that twa bukkettis severall suithlie hang;
As ane come up ane uther doun wald gang.

2375 uther tway *other two*   2376 woddis waist *uninhabited woods*
freikis (?) *heroes* on fute can fair *went on foot*   2377 busk *bush*
quhill neir midnycht and mair *until nearly midnight and more*

2378 wrinkis *tricks*   2379 subtelteis *stratagems*   2380 hecht *promised*
forthinkis *regrets*   2381 findis furth ane wyle *discovers a wily trick*
2382 couth *did*   2383 bellie-blind *blindman's buff*   2384 seik *search*

2385 almaist *almost*   2386 Soft yow *calm yourself*
2387 manure-place *manor-house* hyit in haist *hastened*
2388 lycht *clear* pennyfull *round as a penny* mone *moon*
2389 draw-well *draw-well (with buckets)* senyeours *lords*
but hone *without delay*
2390 severall suithlie hang *were hanging separately in truth*
2391 come *came* doun wald gang *would go down*

The schadow off the mone schone in the well:
'Schir,' said Lowrence, 'anis ye sall find me leill;
Now se ye not the caboik weill yoursell,
2395 Quhyte as ane neip and round als as ane seill?
He hang it yonder that na man suld it steill.
Schir, traist ye weill, yone caboik ye se hing
Micht be ane present to ony lord or king.'

'Na,' quod the wolff, 'mycht I yone caboik haif
2400 On the dry land, as I it yonder se,
I wald quitclame the carll off all the laif:
His dart oxin I compt thame not ane fle;
Yone wer mair meit for sic ane man as me.
Lowrence,' quod he, 'leip in the bukket sone,
2405 And I sall hald the ane, quhill thow have done.'

Lowrence gird doun baith sone and subtellie;
The uther baid abufe and held the flaill.
'It is sa mekill', quod Lowrence, 'it maisteris me:
On all my tais it hes not left ane naill.
2410 Ye man mak help upwart, and it haill:
Leip in the uther bukket haistelie,
And cum sone doun and mak me sum supplé!'

2392 schadow off the mone schone *reflection of the moon shone*
2393 anis *for once* leill *trusty* 2394 caboik *cheese* yoursell *yourself*
2395 Quhyte *white* neip *turnip* seill *seal* 2396 hang *hung* that *so that*
steill *steal* 2397 traist *trust* hing *hang*

2399 Na (?) *well* mycht I yone caboik haif *if I could have that cheese*
2401 quitclame *discharge, release* laif *rest*
2402 dart oxin (?) *wretched (?)draught oxen* compt *count*
not ane fle *not worth a fly* 2403 mair meit *more food*
2404 leip *jump* sone *quickly* 2405 the ane *the one*
quhill thow have done *until you have finished*

2406 gird *leapt* subtellie *treacherously/dexterously*
2407 uther baid abufe *other waited above* flaill (?) *crank, well-beam*
2408 mekill *big* maisteris *defeats* 2409 tais *toes* naill *nail* 2410 man *must*
upwart *upwards* it haill *pull it* 2412 mak me sum supplé *give me some help*

Than lychtlie in the bukket lap the loun;
His wecht but weir the uther end gart ryis:
2415 The tod come hailland up, the wolff yeid doun.
Than angerlie the wolff upon him cryis:
'I cummand thus dounwart, quhy thow upwart hyis?'
'Schir,' quod the foxe, 'thus fairis it off Fortoun:
As ane cummis up, scho quheillis ane uther doun.'

2420 Than to the ground sone yeid the wolff in haist;
The tod lap on land, als blyith as ony bell,
And left the wolff in watter to the waist:
Quha haillit him out, I wait not, off the well.
Heir endis the text; thair is na mair to tell.
2425 Yyt men may find ane gude moralitie
In this sentence, thocht it ane fabill be.

Moralitas

This wolf I likkin to ane wickit man
Quhilk dois the pure oppres in everie place,
And pykis at thame all querrellis that he can,
2430 Be rigour, reif, and uther wickitnes.

2413 lychtlie *nimbly* lap *leapt* loun *rascal* 2414 wecht *weight*
but weir *without doubt* gart ryis *caused to rise*
2415 hailland up *speeding up* yeid *went* 2416 angerlie *angrily*
2417 cummand thus dounwart *coming down like this*
quhy thow upwart hyis *why are you hurrying upwards*
2418 fairis it off Fortoun *fares with Fortune*
2419 ane cummis up *one comes up* quheillis *wheels*

2420 ground *bottom* yeid *went* 2421 lap on land *jumped on the ground*
blyith as ony bell *joyful as any bell (a proverbial comparison)*
2422 watter *water* 2423 Quha haillit *who pulled* wait *know*
2424 text *text of the tale* 2425 Yyt *yet* gude *good* 2426 sentence *text*

2427 likkin *liken, compare* wickit *wicked*
2428 Quhilk dois the pure oppres *who oppresses the poor*
2429 *and picks all the quarrels he can with them* 2430 rigour *harshness*
reif *robbery*

The foxe, the feind I call into this cais,
Arctand ilk man to ryn unrychteous rinkis,
Thinkand thairthrow to lok him in his linkis.

The husband may be callit ane godlie man
2435   With quhome the feynd falt findes, as clerkis reids,
Besie to tempt him with all wayis that he can.
The hennis ar warkis that fra ferme faith proceidis:
Quhair sic sproutis spreidis, the evill spreit thair not speids,
Bot wendis unto the wickit man agane –
2440   That he hes tint his travell is full unfane.

The wodds waist, quhairin wes the wolf wyld,
Ar wickit riches, quhilk all men gaipis to get:
Quha traistis in sic trusterie ar oft begyld,
For mammon may be callit the devillis net,
2445   Quhilk Sathanas for all sinfull hes set:
With proud plesour quha settis his traist thairin,
But speciall grace lychtlie can not outwin.

2431 feind *devil* into this cais *in this case, situation*
2432 *(?) inducing each man to pursue wicked courses*
2433 *thinking through that to lock him in his chains*

2435 quhome *whom* falt *fault* reids *read*
2436 Besie *busy* wayis *means, devices*   2437 warkis *works, deeds*
fra ferme faith proceidis *proceed from firm faith*
2438 Quhair sic sproutis spreidis *where such sprouts grow* spreit *spirit*
thair not speids *does not prosper there*   2439 wendis *goes* agane *back*
2440 tint his travell *wasted his effort* full unfane *(he) is very displeased*

2441 wodds waist *uninhabited woods* quhairin *in which*
wyld *(?)* beguiled, *(?) wild*   2442 gaipis *are hungry*
2443 Quha traistis *whoever trusts* trusterie *(?) rubbish*
2445 Sathanas *Satan* set *laid*   2446 plesour *(?) self-indulgence*
2447 But speciall grace *without a particular act of God's supernatural assistance
(as against 'general grace')* lychtlie *easily* outwin *escape*

The cabok may be callit covetyce,
Quhilk blomis braid in mony mannis ee:
2450 Wa worth the well of that wickit vyce,
For it is all bot fraud and fantasie,
Dryv and ilk man to leip in the buttrie
That dounwart drawis unto the pane of hell –
Christ keip all Christianis from that wickit well!

The Wolf and the Wether

2455 Qwhylum thair wes, as Esope can report,
Ane scheipheird duelland be ane forrest neir,
Quhilk had ane hound that did him grit comfort:
Full war he wes to walk his fauld, but weir,
That nouther wolff, nor wildcat durst appeir,
2460 Nor foxe on feild, nor yit no uther beist –
Bot he thame slew, or chaissit at the leist.

Sa happinnit it – as everilk beist man de –
This hound off suddand seiknes to be deid;
Bot than, God wait, the keipar off the fe
2465 For verray wo woxe wanner nor the weid:

2448 covetyce *covetousness*   2449 blomis braid *flowers extensively* ee *eye*
2450 Wa worth *woe befall* well *well, spring*
2451 fraud and fantasie *deceit and fantasy*   2452 Dryvand *driving, forcing*
ilk *each* buttrie *buttery, storeroom*   2453 drawis *pulls* pane *torment*

2455 Qwhylum *once upon a time* can report *related*
2456 *a shepherd dwelling close to a forest*   2457 Quhilk *who*
did him grit comfort *provided great support*   2458 war *alert*
walk his fauld *watch his fold* but weir *without doubt*
2459 That nouther *so that neither* appeir *appear*
2460 nor yit no uther beist *nor any other animal*   2461 chaissit *chased away*
at the leist *at least*

2462 Sa happinnit it *it so happened* everilk *every* man de *must die*
2463 off suddand seiknes to be deid *died from a sudden sickness*
2464 wait *knows* keipar off the fe *keeper of the livestock*   2465 verray *true*
wo *sorrow* woxe wanner nor the weid *grew more faded than a weed*

'Allace,' quod he, 'now se I na remeid
To saif the selie beistis that I keip,
For with the wolff weryit beis all my scheip!'

It wald have maid ane mannis hart sair to se
2470   The selie scheiphirdis lamentatioun:
'Now is my darling deid, allace!' quod he;
'For now to beg my breid I may be boun,
With pyikstaff and with scrip to fair off toun;
For all the beistis befoir that bandonit bene
2475   Will schute upon my beistis with ire and tene.'

With that ane wedder wichtlie wan on fute:
'Maister,' quod he, 'mak merie and be blyith:
To brek your hart for baill it is na bute,
For ane deid dog ye na cair on yow kyith.
2480   Ga fetche him hither and fla his skyn off swyth;
Syne sew it on me – and luke that it be meit,
Baith heid and crag, bodie, taill, and feit.

2466 quod *said* na remeid *no remedy*
2467 saif *save, protect* selie *helpless, poor* keip *guard*
2468 *all my sheep will be worried to death by the wolf*

2469 wald *would* mannis hart *man's heart* sair to se *sorrowful to see*
2470 selie scheiphirdis *poor shepherd's*   2471 deid *dead*
2472 my breid *for my bread* boun *prepared, ready*   2473 pyikstaff *pikestaff*
scrip *(beggar's) bag* fair off toun *go from this farmstead*
2474 beistis befoir that bandonit bene *(wild) beasts that previously have been
subdued*   2475 *will rush on my animals with wrath and anger*

2476 wedder *male sheep, ram* wichtlie *valiantly, swiftly* wan on fute *got up*
2477 Maister *master* blyith *happy*   2478 brek *break* baill *misery* bute *remedy*
2479 *do not express sorrow because of a dead dog*   2480 Ga *go* fla *flay*
swyth *quickly*   2481 Syne *then* luke *see, make sure* meit *well-fitting*
2482 Baith heid and crag *both head and neck*

'Than will the wolff trow that I am he,
For I sall follow him fast quharever he fair.
2485 All haill the cure I tak it upon me
Your scheip to keip at midday, lait, and air.
And he persew, be God, I sall not spair
To follow him as fast as did your doig,
Swa that I warrand ye sall not want ane hoig.'

2490 Than said the scheipheird, 'This come of ane gude wit;
Thy counsall is baith sicker, leill and trew;
Quha sayis ane scheip is daft, thay lieit of it.'
With that in hy the doggis skyn off he flew
And on the scheip rycht softlie couth it sew.
2495 Than worth the wedder wantoun off his weid:
'Now off the wolff', quod he, 'I have na dreid.'

In all thingis he counterfait the dog,
For all the nycht he stude, and tuke na sleip, –
Swa that weill lang thair wantit not ane hog;
2500 Swa war he wes and walkryfe thame to keip,
That Lowrence durst not luke upon ane scheip –
For and he did, he followit him sa fast
That off his lyfe he maid him all agast.

2483 trow *believe*   2484 sall *shall* fast *closely, quickly*
quharever he fair *wherever he goes*   2485 *I take completely upon myself the charge*
2486 keip *guard* midday, lait, and air *(midday, late, and early =) at all times*
2486 And he persew *if he pursues* be *by* spair *refrain (from)*   2488 doig *dog*
2489 Swa *so* warrand *guarantee* want *lack* ane hoig *a single young sheep*

2490 come of *came from* gude wit *good mind, understanding*
2491 counsall *counsel* sicker, leill and trew *reliable, loyal and true*
2492 Quha *whoever* thay lieit of it *lied about it*   2493 in hy *quickly*
off he flew *flayed, stripped*   2494 rycht *very* couth it sew *sewed it*
2495 *Then the wether became insolent because of his garment*

2497 counterfeit *imitated*   2498 stude *stood* tuke na sleip *took no sleep*
2499 *so that for a very long time not a single young sheep was missing*
2500 war *alert* walkryfe *vigilant*   2501 Lowrence *Laurence (the fox)*
luke upon *look upon*   2502 For and *if*
2503 off his lyfe he maid him all agast *made him terrified for his life*

Was nowther wolff, wildcat, nor yit tod
2505   Durst cum within thay boundis all about,
Bot he wald chase thame baith throw rouch and snod;
Thay bailfull beistis had of thair lyvis sic dout,
For he wes mekill and semit to be stout,
That everilk beist thay dred him as the deid,
2510   Within that woid that nane durst hald thair heid.

Yit happinnit thair ane hungrie wolff to slyde
Outthrow his scheip, quhair thay lay on ane le:
'I sall have ane,' quod he, 'quhatever betyde –
Thocht I be werryit, for hunger or I de.'
2515   With that ane lamb intill his cluke hint he.
The laif start up, for thay wer all agast;
Bot God wait gif the wedder followit fast!

Went never hound mair haistelie fra the hand
Quhen he wes rynnand maist raklie at the ra
2520   Nor went this wedder baith over mois and strand,
And stoppit nouther at bank, busk, nor bra,

2504 nowther *neither* tod *fox*
2505 thay boundis *those boundaries (of the district)*
2506 rouch and snod *rough and smooth*
2507 Thay bailfull beistis *those destructive beasts*
of thair lyvis sic dout *such fear for their lives*   2508 mekill *big*
semit to be stout *appeared to be strong*   2509 everilk *every*
dred him as the deid *feared him like death*
2510 *so that none dared show their faces in that wood*

2511 slyde *glide, slip*   2512 Outthrow *right through* quhair *where* le *meadow*
2513 ane *one* quhatever betyde *whatever befalls*   2514 Thocht *even though*
werryit *worried, killed* de *die*   2515 intill his cluke *in his claw* hint *seized*
2516 The laif start up *the rest started up* agast *terrified*   2517 gif *if*

2518 mair haistelie fra the hand *more quickly from the (hunter's) hand*
2519 *when he was running most impetuously after the roe (deer)*   2520 Nor *than*
mois *bog* strand *stream*   2521 bank, busk, nor bra *slope, bush, nor hillside*

Bot followit ay sa ferslie on his fa
With sic ane drift, quhill dust and dirt overdraif him,
And maid ane vow to God that he suld have him.

2525   With that the wolff let out his taill on lenth,
For he wes hungrie and it drew neir the ene,
And schupe him for to ryn with all his strenth,
Fra he the wedder sa neir cummand had sene;
He dred his lyfe and he overtane had bene.
2530   Thairfoir he spairit nowther busk nor boig,
For weill he kennit the kenenes off the doig.

To mak him lycht he kest the lamb him fra,
Syne lap over leis and draif throw dub and myre.
'Na,' quod the wedder, 'in faith, we part not swa:
2535   It is not the lamb, bot the, that I desyre!
I sall cum neir, for now I se the tyre.'
The wolff ran still quhill ane strand stude behind him –
Bot ay the neirar the wedder he couth bind him.

Sone efter that he followit him sa neir
2540   Quhill that the wolff for fleidnes fylit the feild;
Syne left the gait and ran throw busk and breir,
And schupe him fra the schawis for to scheild.

2522 ay sa ferslie on his fa *always so fiercely on his foe*
2523 sic ane drift *such a rush* quhill *until* overdraif him *covered him*

2525 let out *extended* lenth *length*   2526 neir the ene *near to the evening*
2527 schupe him for to ryn *set himself to run* strenth *strength*   2528 Fra *when*
sa neir cummand *coming so close* sene *seen*   2529 dred *feared for* and *if*
overtane *overtaken*   2530 Thairfoir *therefore* spairit *avoided* boig *bog*
2531 kenenes *fierceness* doig *dog*

2532 lycht *light (in weight)* kest *threw* him fra *from him*
2533 *then sprang over meadows and rushed through pool and mire*   2534 swa *thus*
2535 the *thee*   2537 strand *brook* stude *stood*   2538 neirar *nearer*
he couth bind him *(?) he (the wether) attached himself, followed him closely*

2540 fleidnes *fright* fylit *made foul with excrement*   2541 gait *road* breir *briar*
2542 *(?) and tried to protect himself from the thickets (see n.)*

He ran restles, for he wist off na beild;
The wedder followit him baith out and in,
2545   Quhill that ane breir-busk raif rudelie off the skyn.

The wolff wes wer and blenkit him behind,
And saw the wedder come thrawand throw the breir,
Syne saw the doggis skyn hingand on his lind.
'Na,' quod he, 'is this ye that is sa neir?
2550   Richt now ane hound and now quhyte as ane freir;
I fled over-fer and I had kennit the cais:
To God I vow that ye sall rew this rais!

'Quhat wes the cause ye gaif me sic ane katche?'
With that in hy he hint him be the horne:
2555   'For all your mowis, ye met anis with your matche,
Suppois ye leuch me all this yeir to scorne.
For quhat enchessoun this doggis skyn have ye borne?'
'Maister,' quod he, 'bot to have playit with yow;
I yow requyre that ye nane uther trow.'

2543 restles *without resting* wist off na beild *knew of no refuge*
2545 breir-busk raif rudelie *briar-bush tore roughly*

2546 wer *alert* blenkit *looked*   2547 thrawand *rushing*
2548 hingand on his lind *hanging on his loins*   2549 Na *well*
2550 Richt *just* quhyte as ane freir *white as a friar*
2551 over-fer and I had kennit the cais *too far (?than I would have) if I had
known what the situation was*   2552 rew *repent, rue* rais *course, running*

2553 gaif *gave* katche *chase*   2554 in hy *quickly* hint *seized*
2555 mowis *tricks* anis *once*
2556 *even if you have laughed me to scorn all this year*
2557 quhat enchessoun *what reason*   2558 bot *but, only* playit *jested*
2559 requyre *ask* nane uther trow *believe no other*

2560 'Is this your bourding in ernist than?' quod he;
     'For I am verray effeirit and on flocht;
     Cum bak agane, and I sall let yow se.'
     Than quhar the gait wes grimmit he him brocht:
     'Quhether call ye this fair play or nocht –
2565 To set your maister in sa fell effray,
     Quhill he for feiritnes hes fylit up the way?

     'Thryis, be my saull, ye gart me schute behind, –
     Upon my hoichis the senyeis may be sene;
     For feiritnes full oft I fylit the wind.
2570 Now is this ye? Na, bot ane hound, I wene!
     Me think your teith over-schort to be sa kene.
     Blissit be the busk that reft yow your array, –
     Ellis fleand, bursin had I bene this day!'

     'Schir,' quod the wedder, 'suppois I ran in hy,
2575 My mynd wes never to do your persoun ill;
     Ane flear gettis ane follower commounly,
     In play or ernist – preif quhasaever will;

2560 bourding *jesting* ernist *earnest*   2561 verray effeirit *truly frightened*
on flocht *in a flutter*
2563 quhar the gait wes grimmit *(to) where the road was fouled* brocht *brought*
2564 Quhether call ye *(whether =) do you call* nocht *not*
2565 sa fell effray *such a terrible state of fright*   2566 feiritnes *fear* fylit *fouled*

2567 Thryis *thrice* be my saull *by my soul*
gart me schute behind *caused me to defecate*   2568 hoichis *hocks* senyeis *signs*
2570 wene *think*   2571 Me think *it seems to me* teith *teeth*
over-schort *(are) too short* kene *sharp*   2572 Blissit *blessed*
reft yow your array *robbed you of your attire*   2573 Ellis *otherwise*
fleand *fleeing* bursin *destroyed, shattered*

2574 Schir *sir* suppois I ran in hy *even if I ran quickly*   2575 mynd *intention*
do your persoun ill *harm your person*
2576 *one who flees commonly gets a follower*   2577 preif *test it*
quhasaever *whosoever*

Sen I bot playit, be gracious me till,
And I sall gar my freindis blis your banis:
2580   Ane full gude servand will crab his maister anis.'

'I have bene oftymis set in grit effray;
Bot, be the rude, sa rad yit wes I never
As thow hes maid me with thy prettie play.
I schot behind quhen thow overtuke me ever;
2585   Bot sikkerlie now sall we not dissever!'
Than be the crag-bane smertlie he him tuke
Or ever he ceissit, and it in-schunder schuke.

Moralitas

Esope that poet, first father of this fabill,
Wrait this parabole – quhilk is convenient
2590   Because the sentence wes fructuous and agreabill,
In moralitie exemplative prudent –
Quhais problemes bene verray excellent,
Throw similitude of figuris, to this day,
Gevis doctrine to the redaris of it ay.

2578 Sen *since* me till *to me*
2579 *and I shall cause my friends to bless your bones*
2580 *a very good servant will annoy his master once*

2581 oftymis *often* in grit effray *great fear*   2582 rude *cross*
rad *frightened* yit *yet*   2584 overtuke *overtook*   2585 sikkerlie *certainly*
dissever *separate, part*   2586 crag-bane *neck-bone* smertlie *sharply*
2587 Or *before* ceissit *ceased* in-schunder schuke *shook it asunder*

2589 Wrait *wrote* parabole *parable, allegory* convenient *fitting, suitable*
2590 sentence *significance* fructuous and agreabill *fruitful and apt*
2591 *(?) wise in its morality which provides an example*
2592 *whose enigmas are truly excellent*
2593 *(?) through the aptness of its symbols to this very day*
2594 *gives instruction to its readers always*

2595   Heir may thow se that riches of array
       Will cause pure men presumpteous for to be;
       Thay think thay hald of nane, be thay als gay,
       Bot counterfute ane lord in all degré.
       Out of thair cais in pryde thay clym sa hie
2600   That thay forbeir thair better in na steid,
       Quhill sum man tit thair heillis over thair heid.

       Richt swa in service uther sum exceidis,
       And thay haif withgang, welth, and cherising,
       That thay will lychtlie lordis in thair deidis,
2605   And lukis not to thair blude nor thair ofspring;
       Bot yit nane wait how lang that reull will ring;
       Bot he was wyse that bad his sone consadder:
       'Bewar in welth, for hall-benkis ar rycht slidder!'

       Thairfoir I counsell men of everilk stait
2610   To knaw thameself and quhome thay suld forbeir,
       And fall not with thair better in debait,
       Suppois thay be als galland in thair geir:

2595 Heir may thow se *here you may see*   2596 pure *poor*
2597 thay hald of nane *they have no superior*
be thay als gay *if they are as handsomely turned out*
2598 counterfute *imitate, counterfeit* degré *respects*   2599 cais *situation, place*
clym sa hie *climb so high*   2600 forbeir *show deference to* na steid *no place*
2601 tit thair heillis *tips their heels*

2602 *just so some others go too far in (their) service*   2603 And *if*
withgang *advantage* cherising *encouragement*   2604 lychtlie *make light of*
deidis *acts (?as against their lineage)*
2605 *and do not consider their blood nor their descent*
2606 nane wait *no one knows* reull will ring *rule will prevail*   2607 sone *son*
2608 welth *prosperity* hall-benkis *hall-benches* rycht slidder *very slippery*

2609 stait *estate, rank*   2610 knaw thameself *know themselves*
quhome thay suld forbeir *to whom they should show deference*
2612 Suppois *even if* als galland in thair geir *as gallant in their apparel*

It settis na servand for to uphald weir,
Nor clym sa hie quhill he fall of the ledder;
2615   Bot think upon the wolf and on the wedder.

The Wolf and the Lamb

Ane cruell wolff, richt ravenous and fell,
Upon ane tyme past to ane reveir
Descending from ane rotche unto ane well;
To slaik his thrist, drank of the watter cleir.
2620   Swa upon cace ane selie lamb come neir,
Bot of his fa the wolff nathing he wist,
And in the streme laipit to cule his thrist.

Thus drank thay baith, bot not of ane intent:
The wolfis thocht wes all on wickitnes;
2625   The selie lamb wes meik and innocent:
Upon the rever in ane uther place
Beneth the wolff he drank ane lytill space,
Quhill him thocht gude, presomyng thair nane ill.
The wolff this saw, and rampand come him till,

2613 It settis *it is proper for* uphald weir *maintain strife*
2614 quhill he fall of the ledder *until he fall from the ladder*

2616 richt *very* fell *fierce*   2617 Upon ane tyme past *once went* reveir *river*
2618 rotche *cliff* well *pool*   2619 slaik *slake* thrist *thirst* cleir *clear*
2620 Swa upon cace *so by chance* selie *innocent, helpless* come neir *came near*
2621 fa *foe* nathing he wist *he knew nothing*   2622 laipit *lapped* cule *cool*

2623 ane *one, a single*   2624 thocht *thought, intention* wickitnes *wickedness*
2625 meik *meek, gentle*   2626 uther *other*   2627 Beneth *below*
ane lytill space *for a little time*   2628 Quhill *until, for as long as*
him thocht gude, presomyng thair nane ill *seemed good to him, expecting no harm*
2629 rampand *rearing up* come him till *came to him*

2630 With girnand teith and angrie austre luke,
Said to the lamb, 'Thow cative wretchit thing,
How durst thow be sa bald to fyle this bruke
Quhar I suld drink with thy foull slavering?
It wer almous the for to draw and hing,
2635 That suld presume with thy foull lippis wyle
To glar my drink and this fair watter fyle.'

The selie lamb, quaikand for verray dreid,
On kneis fell and said, 'Schir, with your leif,
Suppois I dar not say thairoff ye leid,
2640 Bot, be my saull, I wait ye can nocht preif
That I did ony thing that suld yow greif;
Ye wait alswa that your accusatioun
Failyeis fra treuth and contrair is to ressoun.

'Thocht I can nocht, nature will me defend,
2645 And off the deid perfyte experience:
All hevie thing man off the selff discend,
Bot giff sum thing on force mak resistence;

2630 girnand teith *snarling teeth* angrie austre luke *stern look*
2631 cative *miserable*   2632 sa bald *so bold* fyle *defile* bruke *brook*
2633 Quhar *where* suld *should*   2634 wer almous *would be a mercy*
the for to draw and hing *to draw and hang you*   2635 wyle *vile*
2636 glar *make slimy* fyle *defile*

2637 quaikand *quaking* verray dreid *very terror*   2638 kneis *knees*
Schir *sir* leif *leave*   2639 *although I dare not say that you lied about this*
2640 be my saull *by my soul* wait *know* can nocht preif *cannot prove*
2641 ony *any* greif *harm*   2642 alswa *also*
2643 *is lacking in truth and contrary to reason*

2644 Thocht *though*
2645 off the deid perfyte experience *(nature and) perfect knowledge of the fact*
2646 hevie *heavy* man off the selff *must of itself*   2647 Bot giff *unless*
on force mak resistence *forcibly resists (it)*

Than may the streme on na way mak ascence
Nor ryn bakwart; I drank beneth yow far:
2650 Ergo, for me your bruke wes never the war.

'Alswa my lippis, sen that I wes ane lam,
Tuitchit na thing that wes contagious,
Bot sowkit milk from pappis off my dam,
Richt naturall, sweit, and als delitious.'
2655 'Weill,' quod the wolff, 'thy language rigorus
Cummis the off kynd; swa thy father before
Held me at bait, baith with boist and schore.

'He wraithit me, and than I culd him warne,
Within ane yeir and I brukit my heid
2660 I suld be wrokkin on him or on his barne
For his exorbetant and frawart pleid:
Thow sall doutles for his deidis be deid.'
'Schir, it is wrang that for the fatheris gilt
The saikles sone suld punist be or spilt.

2648 Than *therefore* streme *stream* on na way mak ascence *in no way ascend*
2649 ryn bakwart *run backwards*   2650 Ergo *therefore* for me *because of me*
the war *worse*

2651 sen *since*   2652 Tuitchit *touched* contagious *harmful, tainted*
2653 sowkit *sucked* pappis off my dam *my mother's breasts*   2654 sweit *sweet*
als delitious *also delicious*   2655 Weill *well* quod *said* rigorus *harsh*
2656 Cummis the off kynd *comes to you from nature* swa *so, thus*
2657 *contended with me, both with threats and menaces*

2658 wraithit *vexed* him warne *warned him*   2659 yeir *year*
and I brukit my heid *if I had the use of my head, if I was alive*
2660 wrokkin *revenged* barne *child*   2661 exorbetant *immoderate, monstrous*
frawart *perverse* pleid *disputing, arguing*   2662 doutles *without doubt*
deidis *deeds* deid *dead*   2663 wrang *wrong* gilt *guilt, offence*
2664 saikles sone suld punist be *innocent son should be punished*
spilt *injured, destroyed*

2665 'Haiff ye not hard quhat Halie Scripture sayis,
Endytit with the mouth off God almycht?
Off his awin deidis ilk man sall beir the pais,
As pane for sin, reward for werkis rycht;
For my trespas, quhy suld my sone have plycht?
2670 Quha did the mis, lat him sustene the pane.'
'Yaa!' quod the wolff. 'Yit pleyis thow agane?

'I let the wit, quhen that the father offendis,
I will cheris nane off his successioun,
And off his barnis I may weill tak amendis
2675 Unto the twentie degré descending doun.
Thy father thocht to mak ane strang poysoun,
And with his mouth into my watter spew.'
'Schir,' quod the lamb, 'thay twa ar nouther trew.

'The law sayis, and ye will understand,
2680 Thair suld na man, for wrang nor violence,
His adversar punis at his awin hand
Without proces off law and evidence,

2665 Haiff *have* hard quhat *heard what* Halie *holy*
2666 Endytit *written, dictated* almycht *almighty*   2667 awin deidis *own deeds*
ilk *each* pais *burden*   2668 pane *punishment* werkis rycht *good deeds*
2669 trespas *transgression*
quhy suld my sone have plycht *why should my son have blame*
2670 *whoever wronged you, let him undergo the punishment*
2671 Yaa! *indeed!* Yit pleyis thow agane? *are you still wrangling?*

2672 let the wit *would have you know* quhen *when*   2673 cheris *hold dear*
successioun *progeny*   2674 barnis *children* amendis *recompense*
2675 twentie *twentieth*   2676 thocht to *intended to* strang *strong*
2677 spew (?) *to spew (?) spewed*   2678 thay twa *those two (points)*
nouther *neither*

2679 and *if*   2680 wrang *wrong*   2681 adversar *adversary*
punis at *punish with*   2682 proces off law *a legal proceeding*

Quhilk suld have leif to mak lawfull defence,
And thairupon summond peremtourly
2685   For to propone, contrairie, or reply.

'Set me ane lauchfull court; I sall compeir
Befoir the lyoun, lord and leill justice,
And be my hand I oblis me rycht heir
That I sall byde ane unsuspect assyis.
2690   This is the law, this is the instant wyis;
Ye suld pretend thairfoir ane summondis mak
Aganis that day, to gif ressoun and tak.'

'Na,' quod the wolff, 'thou wald intruse ressoun
Quhair wrang and reif suld duell in propertie.
2695   That is ane poynt and part of fals tressoun,
For to gar reuth remane with crueltie.
Be Goddis woundis, fals tratour, thow sall de
For thy trespas, and for thy fatheris als.'
With that anone he hint him be the hals.

2683 Quhilk *who* leif *leave*
2684 *and for that (be) summoned peremptorily (without option)*
2685 propone *state a case* contrairie *oppose*

2686 lauchfull *lawful* compeir *appear*   **2687** lyoun *lion*
leill justice *lawful judge*   **2688** oblis me *pledge myself* heir *here*
2689 byde ane unsuspect assyis *submit to an impartial judicial body*
2690 instant wyis *present practice*   **2691** pretend *undertake*
ane summondis mak *to make a summons*   **2692** Aganis *in preparation for*
gif ressoun and tak *give an argument and receive one in return*

2693 intruse ressoun *intrude reason*   **2694** reif *robbery*
duell in propertie *remain in possession*
2695 *that is an example and instance of false treason*
2696 gar reuth remane *cause pity to abide*   **2697** woundis *wounds*
tratour *traitor* sall de *shall die*   **2698** fatheris als *father's also*
2699 anone he hint him be the hals *immediately he seized him by the neck*

2700 The selie lamb culd do nathing bot bleit:
Sone wes he deid – the wolff wald do na grace;
Syne drank his blude and off his flesche can eit
Quhill he wes full; syne went his way on pace.
Off his murther quhat sall we say, allace?
2705 Wes not this reuth, wes not this grit pietie,
To gar this selie lamb but gilt thus de?

Moralitas

The pure pepill this lamb may signifie,
As maill-men, merchandis, and all lauboureris,
Of quhome the lyfe is half ane purgatorie,
2710 To wyn with lautie leving, as efferis.
The wolf betakinnis fals extortioneris
And oppressouris of pure men, as we se,
Be violence, or craft in facultie.

Thre kynd of wolfis in this warld now rings:
2715 The first ar fals perverteris of the lawis,
Quhilk under poleit termis falset mingis,
Lettand that all wer gospell that he schawis;

2700 selie *poor* culd *could* bleit *bleat*
2701 wald do na grace *would show no mercy* 2702 Syne *then* blude *blood*
can eit *ate* 2703 Quhill *until* on pace *quickly* 2704 quhat *what*
2705 grit pietie *occasion for great compassion* 2706 but gilt *without guilt*

2707 pure pepill *poor people* 2708 maill-men *tenant farmers*
lauboureris *labourers, peasants* 2709 quhome *whom*
2710 *to make a livelihood by honest means, as is fitting* 2711 betakinnis *signifies*
2713 facultie (?) *power,* (?) *disposition*

2714 wolfis *wolves* warld *world* rings *reign* 2716 poleit termis *polished words*
falset mingis *mingle falsehood* 2717 Lettand *pretending* schawis *alleges*

Bot for ane bud the pure man he overthrawis,
Smoirand the richt, garrand the wrang proceid –
2720 Of sic wolfis hellis fyre sall be thair meid.

O man of law, let be thy subteltie,
With nice gimpis and fraudis intricait,
And think that God in his divinitie
The wrang, the richt, of all thy werkis wait.
2725 For prayer, price, for hie nor law estait,
Of fals querrellis se thow mak na defence:
Hald with the richt, hurt not thy conscience.

Ane uther kynd of wolfis ravenous
Ar mychtie men haifand full grit plentie,
2730 Quhilkis ar sa gredie and sa covetous
Thay will not thoill the pure in pece to be:
Suppois he and his houshald baith suld de
For falt of fude, thairof thay gif na rak,
Bot over his heid his mailling will thay tak.

2718 bud *bribe* overthrawis *casts down, ruins*
2719 Smoirand *smothering, suppressing* richt *right*
garrand the wrang proceid *causing wrong to advance*   2720 sic *such*
hellis fyre *hell's fire* meid *reward*

2722 nice gimpis *intricate subtle points* fraudis intricait *complicated tricks*
2724 werkis *works, deeds* wait *knows*   2725 price *money*
hie nor law *high or low* estait *estate, rank*   2726 querrellis *accusations* se *see*
2727 Hald *hold*

2728 uther *other*   2729 haifand full grit plentie *possessing plenty enough*
2730 Quhilkis *who* gredie *greedy*   2731 thoill *suffer*
2732 Suppois he *even if he (the poor man)*
2733 falt of fude *lack of food* gif na rak *give no heed*
2734 his mailling will thay tak *will deprive him of his rented land (by offering a
higher rent)*

2735 O man but mercie, quhat is in thy thocht?
      War than ane wolf, and thow culd understand!
      Thow hes aneuch; the pure husband richt nocht,
      Bot croip and caff upon ane clout of land.
      For Goddis aw, how durst thow tak on hand –
2740 And thow in barn and byre sa bene and big –
      To put him fra his tak and gar him thig?

      The thrid wolf ar men of heritage,
      As lordis that hes land be Goddis lane,
      And settis to the mailleris ane village,
2745 And for ane tyme gressome payit and tane;
      Syne vexis him, or half his terme be gane,
      With pykit querrellis for to mak him fane
      To flit or pay his gressome new agane.

      His hors, his meir, he man len to the laird,
2750 To drug and draw in cairt and cariage;
      His servand or his self may not be spaird
      To swing and sweit withoutin meit or wage:

2735 but *without* thocht *thought, mind*   2736 War *worse* and if *(only)*
2737 aneuch *enough* husband *husbandman* richt nocht *nothing at all*
2738 Bot croip and caff *except crop and calf* clout *patch*
2739 Goddis aw *fear of God* tak on hand *undertake*
2740 in barn and byre *in (respect of) barn and byre (shelter for cattle)*
sa bene and big *so (comfortable and big =) well-off*
2741 fra his tak *from his leasehold farm* gar him thig *make him beg*

2742 thrid *third* heritage *inherited property*
2743 be Goddis lane *by a loan from God*   2744 settis *leases*
mailleris *tenant-farmers*
2745 gressome payit and tane *tenant's fee (is) paid and taken*
2746 vexis *harasses* or *before* be gane *is gone*
2747 pykit querrellis *contrived quarrels, accusations* fane *glad*
2748 flit *leave* new agane *over again*

2749 meir *mare* man len *must lend* laird *lord*
2750 drug and draw *drag and pull* cairt and cariage *cart and carrying*
2751 servand *servant* his self *himself* spaird *spared*
2752 swing and sweit *labour and sweat* meit *food*

Thus how he standis in labour and bondage
That scantlie may he purches by his maill
2755   To leve upon dry breid and watter-caill.

Hes thow not reuth to gar thy tennentis sweit
Into thy laubour, with faynt and hungrie wame,
And syne hes lytill gude to drink or eit
With his menye, at evin quhen he cummis hame?
2760   Thow suld be rad for richteous Goddis blame,
For it cryis ane vengeance unto the hevinnis hie
To gar ane pure man wirk but meit or fe.

O thow grit lord, that riches hes and rent,
Be nocht ane wolf, thus to devoir the pure!
2765   Think that nathing cruell nor violent
May in this warld perpetuallie indure.
This sall thow trow and sikkerlie assure:
For till oppres thow sall haif als grit pane
As thow the pure with thy awin hand had slane.

2754 scantlie may he purches by his maill *he can scarcely contrive by (means of) his rent*   2755 leve *live* breid *bread*
watter-caill *cabbage broth made with water*

2756 gar thy tennentis sweit *make your tenants sweat*
2757 faynt *weak, sickly* wame *belly*   2759 menye *household*
at evin quhen he cummis hame *when he comes home in the evening*
2760 rad *afraid* richteous *righteous* blame *reproof*
2761 cryis ane vengeance *cries out for retribution* hevinnis hie *high heavens*
2762 wirk but meit or fe *work without food or payment*

2763 grit *great* rent *revenue*   2764 devoir *devour*   2766 indure *last*
2767 trow *believe* sikkerlie assure *certainly rely on*
2768 till oppres *(to oppress =) oppression* als grit pane *as great punishment*
2769 As thow *as if* awin *own* slane *slain*

2770 God keip the lamb, quhilk is the innocent,
From wolfis byit and fell extortioneris;
God grant that wrangous men of fals intent
Be manifestit, and punischit as effeiris,
And God, as thow all rychteous prayer heiris,
2775 Mot saif our king, and gif him hart and hand
All sic wolfis to banes out of the land.

The Paddock and the Mouse

Upon ane tyme, as Esope culd report,
Ane lytill mous come till ane rever-syde:
Scho micht not waid, hir schankis wer sa schort;
2780 Scho culd not swym; scho had na hors to ryde;
Off verray force behovit hir to byde;
And to and fra besyde that revir deip
Scho ran, cryand with mony pietuous peip.

'Help over! Help over!' this silie mous can cry,
2785 'For Goddis lufe, sum bodie, over the brym.'
With that ane paddok, in the watter by,
Put up hir heid and on the bank can clym,

2770 keip *preserve*   2771 byit *bite* fell *fierce*   2772 wrangous *unjust*
2773 manifestit *revealed* as effeiris *as is proper*   2774 as *since* heiris *hears*
2775 Mot saif *may (thou) save* gif *give*   2776 sic wolfis *such wolves*
banes *banish*

2777 Upon ane tyme *once* Esope *Aesop* culd report *related*   2778 come *came*
rever-syde *bank of a river*   2779 Scho micht not waid *she could not wade*
schankis *legs* sa schort *so short*
2781 *out of sheer necessity she had to remain there*
2782 fra *fro* revir deip *deep river*
2783 cryand with mony pietuous peip *crying with many a pitiful peep*

2784 silie *poor* can cry *cried*   2785 Goddis lufe *God's love* brym *stream*
2786 paddok *toad* by *nearby*   2787 Put up hir heid *raised her head*
can clym *climbed*

Quhilk be nature culd douk and gaylie swym.
With voce full rauk, scho said on this maneir:
2790 'Gude morne, schir Mous! Quhat is your erand heir?'

'Seis thow', quod scho, 'off corne yone jolie flat,
Off ryip aitis, off barlie, peis, and quheit?
I am hungrie, and fane wald be thairat,
Bot I am stoppit be this watter greit;
2795 And on this syde I get nathing till eit
Bot hard nuttis, quhilkis with my teith I bore:
Wer I beyond, my feist wer fer the more.

'I have no boit; heir is no maryner;
And thocht thair war, I have no fraucht to pay.'
2800 Quod scho, 'Sister, lat be your hevie cheir;
Do my counsall, and I sall find the way,
Withoutin hors, brig, boit, or yit galay,
To bring yow over saiflie, be not afeird –
And not wetand the campis off your beird.'

2788 Quhilk *which* culd douk *could duck* gaylie *merrily*
2789 voce full rauk *very hoarse voice* maneir *manner*
2790 *good morning, sir Mouse, what is your errand here?*

2791 Seis thow *do you see* off corne yone jolie flat *that pretty field of corn*
2792 ryip aitis *ripe oats* peis *peas* quheit *wheat*
2793 fane wald be thairat *would like to be over there*   2794 greit *great*
2795 till eit *to eat*   2796 Bot *except* quhilkis *which* teith *teeth*
2797 *if I were on the other side, my feast would be far greater*

2798 boit *boat* maryner *mariner, boatman*
2799 thocht thair war *if there were* fraucht to pay *passage-money to pay for it*
2800 Quod *said* lat be your hevie cheir *give up your gloomy mood*
2801 Do my counsall *act according to my counsel*   2802 brig *bridge*
yit galay *yet galley*   2803 saiflie *safely* afeird *afraid*
2804 wetand the campis off your beird *wetting the whiskers of your beard*

2805 'I haif grit wounder', quod the lytill mous,
'How can thow fleit without fedder or fin?
This rever is sa deip and dangerous,
Me think that thow suld droun to wed thairin.
Tell me, thairfoir, quhat facultie or gin
2810 Thow hes to bring the over this watter wan.'
That to declair the paddok thus began:

'With my twa feit,' quod scho, 'lukkin and braid,
Insteid off airis, I row the streme full styll,
And thocht the brym be perrillous to waid,
2815 Baith to and fra I swyme at my awin will,
I may not droun, forquhy my oppin gill
Devoidis ay the watter I resaiff:
Thairfoir to droun, forsuith, na dreid I haif.'

The mous beheld unto hir fronsit face,
2820 Hir runkillit cheikis, and hir lippis syde,
Hir hingand browis, and hir voce sa hace,
Hir loggerand leggis, and hir harsky hyde.
Scho ran abak, and on the paddok cryde:
'Giff I can ony skill off phisnomy,
2825 Thow hes sumpart off falset and invy.

2805 wounder *wonder*   2806 fleit *float* fedder *feather*
2808 Me think *it seems to me*
thow suld droun to wed thairin *you should drown if you waded in it*
2809 facultie *power* gin *craft*   2810 Thow hes *you have* wan *dark*
2811 That to declair *to explain that*

2812 twa feit *two feet* lukkin and braid *webbed and broad*
2813 Insteid off airis *instead of oars* styll *quietly*   2814 thocht *though*
brym *stream* waid *wade*   2815 awin *own*   2816 forquhy *because*
oppin gill *open gills*   2817 *constantly discharge the water I take in*
2818 forsuith *in truth* na dreid I haif *I have no fear*

2819 fronsit *wrinkled*   2820 runkillit cheikis *wrinkled cheeks* syde *large*
2821 hingand browis *hanging brows* voce sa hace *voice so hoarse*
2822 loggerand (?) *loosely hanging* harsky hyde *rough skin*   2823 abak *back*
2824 *if I have any knowledge of physiognomy*
2825 sumpart off falset and invy *a certain amount of falsehood and envy*

'For clerkis sayis the inclinatioun
Off mannis thocht proceidis commounly
Efter the corporall complexioun
To gude or evill, as nature will apply:
2830   Ane thrawart will, ane thrawin phisnomy.
The auld proverb is witnes off this *lorum*:
Distortum vultum sequitur distortio morum.'

'Na,' quod the taid, 'that proverb is not trew,
For fair thingis oftymis ar fundin faikin;
2835   The blaberyis, thocht thay be sad off hew,
Ar gadderit up quhen primeros is forsakin;
The face may faill to be the hartis takin;
Thairfoir I find this scripture in all place:
"Thow suld not juge ane man efter his face."

2840   'Thocht I unhailsum be to luke upon,
I have na wyt; quhy suld I lakkit be?
Wer I als fair as jolie Absolon,
I am no causer off that grit beutie;

2826 clerkis sayis *scholars say* inclinatioun *disposition*
2827 mannis thocht *man's thought* proceidis commounly *commonly proceeds*
2828 *according to the bodily complexion (of humours, see n.)*   2829 gude *good*
apply *have it*   2830 thrawart will *perverse will*
thrawin phisnomy *distorted face*   2831 auld *old* lorum *conclusion*
2832 *Deformed behaviour follows a distorted face*

2833 taid *toad* trew *true*   2834 oftymis *often* fundin faikin *found (to be) deceitful*
2835 *the bilberries, though they be dark in colour*
2836 *are gathered up when the primrose is abandoned*
2837 faill to be the hartis takin *fail to be the token of the heart*
2838 scripture in all place *scriptural verse everywhere*
2839 juge *judge* efter *according to*

2840 unhailsum *unwholesome* luke *look*   2841 wyt *blameworthiness*
quhy suld I lakkit be? *why should I be disparaged?*
2842 *if I were as fair as handsome Absolon (see n.)*
2843 I am no causer *I am not the causer* grit beutie *great beauty*

This difference in forme and qualitie
2845 Almychtie God hes causit dame Nature
To prent and set in everilk creature.

'Off sum the face may be full flurischand,
Off silkin toung and cheir rycht amorous,
With mynd inconstant, fals, and wariand,
2850 Full off desait and menis cautelous.'
'Let be thy preiching,' quod the hungrie mous,
'And be quhat craft, thow gar me understand,
That thow wald gyde me to yone yonder land.'

'Thow wait,' quod scho, 'ane bodie that hes neid
2855 To help thameself suld mony wayis cast.
Thairfoir ga tak ane doubill twynit threid
And bind thy leg to myne with knottis fast:
I sall the leir to swym – be not agast –
Als weill as I.' 'As thow?' than quod the mous.
2860 'To preif that play, it wer rycht perrillous!

2846 prent *imprint* everilk *every*

2847 sum *some* full flurischand *glowing, beautiful*
2848 *of silken tongue and most amorous demeanour*
2849 wariand *variable*   2850 desait *deceit* menis cautelous *cunning devices*
2851 preiching *preaching*   2852 be quhat *by what* gar me *cause me to*
2853 yone yonder land *that shore over there*

2854 Thow wait *you know* bodie *person* neid *need*
2855 suld mony wayis cast *should consider many means*
2856 ga tak *go and take* twynit threid *twisted thread*   2857 fast *firmly*
2858 leir *teach* agast *afraid*   2859 Als weill *as well*   2860 preif *try, test*
play *game* rycht *very*

'Suld I be bund and fast, quhar I am fre,
In hoip off help? Na, than I schrew us baith,
For I mycht lois baith lyfe and libertie!
Giff it wer swa, quha suld amend the skaith,
2865 Bot gif thow sweir to me the murthour-aith:
But fraud or gyle to bring me over this flude,
But hurt or harme?' 'In faith,' quod scho, 'I dude.'

Scho goikit up, and to the hevin can cry:
'How! Juppiter, off nature god and king,
2870 I mak ane aith trewlie to the, that I
This lytill mous sall over this watter bring.'
This aith wes maid; the mous, but persaving
The fals ingyne of this foull-carpand pad,
Tuke threid and band hir leg, as scho hir bad.

2875 Than fute for fute thay lap baith in the brym,
Bot in thair myndis thay wer rycht different:
The mous thocht nathing bot to fleit and swym;
The paddok for to droun set hir intent.
Quhen thay in midwart off the streme wer went,
2880 With all hir force the paddok preissit doun,
And thocht the mous without mercie to droun.

2861 bund *bound* quhar *where*   2862 hoip *hope* schrew *curse*
baith *both*   2863 lois *lose*   2864 Giff *if*
quha suld amend the skaith *who would pay damages for the injury*
2865 gif thow sweir *unless you swear*
murthour-aith *murder-oath (?swearing to keep away danger)*
2866 But *without* flude *stream*   2867 dude *do it*

2868 goikit *stared* can cry *cried*   2869 How! *ho!*   2870 aith *oath* trewlie *truly*
2872 but persaving *without perceiving*   2873 ingyne *deception*
foull-carpand pad *evil-speaking toad*   2874 Tuke *took*

2875 *then foot for foot (keeping pace together) they leapt into the stream*
2876 myndis *intentions*   2877 fleit *float*   2879 midwart *middle* went *come*
2880 preissit *pressed*   2881 thocht *thought to, intended*

Persavand this, the mous on hir can cry:
'Tratour to God, and manesworne unto me!
Thow swore the murthour-aith richt now that I
2885   But hurt or harme suld ferryit be and fre.'
And quhen scho saw thair wes bot do or de,
Scho bowtit up and forsit hir to swym,
And preissit upon the taiddis bak to clym.

The dreid of deith hir strenthis gart incres,
2890   And forcit hir defend with mycht and mane.
The mous upwart, the paddok doun can pres;
Quhyle to, quhyle fra, quhyle doukit up agane.
This selie mous, this plungit in grit pane,
Gan fecht als lang as breith wes in hir breist,
2895   Till at the last scho cryit for ane preist.

Fechtand thusgait, the gled sat on ane twist,
And to this wretchit battell tuke gude heid;
And with ane wisk or owthir off thame wist
He claucht his cluke betuix thame in the threid;

2882 Persavand *perceiving* can cry *cried*   2883 Tratour *traitor*
manesworne *perjured, forsworn*   2885 But *without* ferryit *ferried across*
2886 thair wes bot do or de *there was but to do or die*
2887 bowtit *bolted, sprang* forsit *forced*
2888 *and struggled to climb on to the toad's back*

2889 *the fear of death increased her strength*   2890 hir defend *defend herself*
2891 upwart *upwards*   2892 *now to, now fro, now dived up again*
2893 selie *poor* this plungit *thus plunged*   2894 can fecht *fought*
breith *breath* breist *breast*   2895 preist *priest*

2896 Fechtand thusgait *(while they were) fighting in this way* gled *kite*
twist *twig*   2897 battell *battle* tuke gude heid *took good heed*
2898 wisk *whisk, quick dart*
or owthir off thame wist *before either of them was aware*
2899 claucht his cluke betuix thame *caught his claw between them*

2900   Syne to the land he flew with thame gude speid,
       Fane off that fang, pyipand with mony pew,
       Syne lowsit thame, and baith but pietie slew.

       Syne bowellit thame, that boucheour with his bill,
       And bellieflaucht full fettislie thame fled,
2905   Bot all thair flesche wald scant be half ane fill,
       And guttis als, unto that gredie gled.
       Off thair debait thus quhen I hard outred,
       He tuke his flicht and over the feildis flaw.
       Giff this be trew, speir ye at thame that saw.

Moralitas

2910   My brother, gif thow will tak advertence,
       Be this fabill thow may persave and se
       It passis far all kynd of pestilence
       Ane wickit mynd with wordis fair and sle.

2900 Syne *then* gude speid *speedily*
2901 Fane off that fang *pleased with that prey*
pyipand *crying* pew *pew (the cry of a kite)*   **2902** lowsit *loosed*
baith but pietie slew *killed both of them without pity*

2903 bowellit *disembowelled* boucheour *butcher* bill *beak*
2904 *and by pulling the skin off whole over the head flayed them very neatly*
2905 wald scant *would scarcely* fill *meal, fill*
2906 And guttis als *together with their guts* gredie *greedy*
2907 thus quhen I hard outred *thus when I heard their contention settled*
2908 He *(the kite)* flicht *flight* over the feildis flaw *flew over the fields*
2909 Giff *if* speir ye at thame that saw *ask those who saw it*

2910 gif *if* advertence *heed*   **2911** Be *by* persave *perceive*
2912 passis *exceeds*   **2913** sle *subtle*

Be war thairfore with quhome thow fallowis the,
2915   For thow wer better beir of stane the barrow,
Or sueitand dig and delf quhill thow may dre,
Than to be matchit with ane wickit marrow.

Ane fals intent under ane fair pretence
Hes causit mony innocent for to de;
2920   Grit folie is to gif over-sone credence
To all that speiks fairlie unto the;
Ane silkin toung, ane hart of crueltie,
Smytis more sore than ony schot of arrow;
Brother, gif thow be wyse, I reid the fle
2925   To matche the with ane thrawart fenyeit marrow.

I warne the als, it is grit nekligence
To bind the fast quhair thow wes frank and fre:
Fra thow be bund, thow may mak na defence
To saif thy lyfe nor yit thy libertie.
2930   This simpill counsall, brother, tak at me,
And it to cun perqueir se thow not tarrow:
Better but stryfe to leif allane in le
Than to be matchit with ane wickit marrow.

2914 with quhome thow fallowis the *with whom you associate yourself*
2915 beir of stane the barrow *(to) carry a barrow-load of stones*
2916 sueitand *sweating*
dig and delf quhill thow may dre *dig and burrow while you can endure it*
2917 matchit *associated* marrow *companion*

2919 de *die*   2920 *great folly it is to give credence too quickly*   2921 speiks *speak*
2923 Smytis *strikes* sore *grievously* shot of arrow *arrow-shot*   2924 gif *if*
reid *counsel* fle *flee from*   2925 to matche the *associating yourself*
thrawart fenyeit marrow *perverse deceitful companion*

2926 als *also*   2927 frank and fre *at liberty*   2928 Fra *from the time that*
2929 saif *save*   2930 tak at *receive from*
2931 *and see that you do not delay to know it by heart*
2932 but stryfe *without strife* leif allane in le *live alone in the meadow*

This hald in mynd – rycht more I sall the tell
2935   Quhairby thir beistis may be figurate.
The paddok, usand in the fludè to duell,
Is mannis bodie, swymand air and late
Into this warld, with cairis implicate:
Now hie, now law, quhylis plungit up, quhylis doun,
2940   Ay in perrell, and reddie for to droun;

Now dolorus, now blyth as bird on breir;
Now in fredome, now wardit in distres;
Now haill and sound, now deid and brocht on beir;
Now pure as Job, now rowand in riches;
2945   Now gounis gay, now brats laid in pres;
Now full as fische, now hungrie as ane hound;
Now on the quheill, now wappit to the ground.

This lytill mous, heir knit thus be the schyn,
The saull of man betakin may indeid –
2950   Bundin, and fra the bodie may not twyn,
Quhill cruell deith cum brek of lyfe the threid –

2934 hald in mynd *keep in mind*
2935 Quhairby thir beistis *whereby these animals* figurate *made into figures*
2936 usand *being accustomed* flude *water* duell *dwell*
2937 mannis bodie *man's body* air and late *(early and late =) always*
2938 *in this world, entangled with sorrows*   2939 hie *high* law *low*
quhylis . . . quhylis *now . . . now*   2940 Ay in perrell *ever in danger*
reddie *liable*

2941 dolorus *sorrowful* blyth *joyful* breir *briar*   2942 wardit *imprisoned*
2943 haill *whole* deid *dead* brocht on beir *brought to the bier*
2944 pure as Job *poor as Job (the Old Testament figure whose tribulations
included poverty)* rowand *luxuriating*   2945 gounis gay *(with) fine gowns*
brats *ragged clothes* pres *cupboard*   2946 fische *fish*
2947 quheill *wheel (of Fortune)* wappit *knocked*

2948 knit thus be the schyn *tied by the shin*   2949 saull *soul*
betakin may indeid *may signify in truth*   2950 Bundin *bound* twyn *separate*
2951 *until cruel death comes to break the thread of life*

The quhilk to droun suld ever stand in dreid
Of carnall lust be the suggestioun,
Quhilk drawis ay the saull and druggis doun.

2955   The watter is the warld, ay welterand
With mony wall of tribulatioun,
In quhilk the saull and bodye wer steirrand,
Standand distinyt in thair opinioun:
The spreit upwart, the body precis doun;
2960   The saull rycht fane wald be brocht over, iwis,
Out of this warld into the hevinnis blis.

The gled is deith, that cummis suddandlie
As dois ane theif, and cuttis sone the battall:
Be vigilant thairfoir and ay reddie,
2965   For mannis lyfe is brukill and ay mortall.
My freind, thairfoir, mak the ane strang castell
Of gud deidis, for deith will the assay,
Thow wait not quhen – evin, morrow, or midday.

2952 *which (the soul) should always stand in fear of being drowned*
2953 *by carnal lust's incitement*
2954 drawis *pulls* druggis doun *drags (it) down*

2955 ay welterand *always surging*   2956 wall *wave*   2957 steirrand *moving*
2958 standand *standing* distinct *being separate, distinct*
in thair opinioun *in their belief, as they think*   2959 spreit *spirit* precis *presses*
2960 rycht fane *gladly* iwis *indeed, certainly*

2962 gled *kite* cummis suddandlie *comes suddenly*
2963 dois ane theif *does a thief* cuttis sone the battall *cuts short the battle*
2965 brukill *fragile, uncertain*   2966 castell *castle*
2967 gude deidis *good deeds (see n.)* assay *attack*
2968 wait *know* quhen *when*

Adew, my friend, and gif that ony speiris
2970 Of this fabill, sa schortlie I conclude,
Say thow, I left the laif unto the freiris,
To mak a sample or similitude.
Now Christ for us that deit on the rude,
Of saull and lyfe as thow art Salviour,
2975 Grant us till pas intill ane blissit hour.

2969 gif that ony speiris *if anyone asks*
2970 Of *about* sa schortlie I conclude *(which) I bring to such a short conclusion*
2971 laif *rest (? of this fable)* freiris *friars* 2972 sample *example*
2973 deit *died* rude *cross* 2974 Salviour *saviour* 2975 intill *at* blissit *blessed*

THE RESSONING BETUIX
DETH AND MAN

Deth

'O mortall man, behald, tak tent to me,
Quhilk sowld thi myrrour be baith day and nycht.
All erdly thing that evir tuke lyfe mon de:
Paip, empriour, king, barroun, and knycht,
5   Thocht thai be in thair ryell estait and hicht,
May nocht ganestand quhen I pleis schote this derte;
Waltownis, castellis, and towris nevir so wicht
May nocht resist quhill it be at his hart.'

Man

'Now quhat art thow that biddis me thus tak tent
10   And mak ane myrrour day and nycht of the,
Or with thi dert I suld rycht sair repent?
I trest trewly of that that thow sall le.
Quhat freik on fold sa bald dar manniss me,
Or with me fecht, owthir on fute or hors?
15   Is none so wicht, so stark, in this cuntré,
Bot I sall gar him bow to me on fors.

1 behald *behold* tak tent *pay attention*
2 *who should be your mirror by both day and night*   3 erdly *earthly*
tuke lyfe *received life* mon de *must die*   4 Paip *pope* empriour *emperor*
barroun *baron* knycht *knight*   5 Thocht *though* ryell estait *regal state*
hicht *exalted position*   6 *cannot resist when I am pleased to shoot this spear*
7 *walled towns, castles, towers, no matter how strong*
8 resist quhill *stop (it) until* his *(man's)*

9 quhat *what*   11 suld rycht sair repent *should most grievously feel sorrow*
12 trest *trust, believe* trewly *truly* of that thow sall le *that you will lie about that*
13 freik on fold sa bald dar manniss me *man on earth (is) so bold (that he) dare*
threaten me   14 fecht *fight* owthir on fute or hors *either on foot or horseback*
15 Is none so wicht *(there) is none so powerful* stark *strong* cuntré *country*
16 Bot I sall gar him *that I shall not make him* fors *forcibly*

Deth

'My name, forsuth, sen that thow speiris,
Tha call me Deid, suthly I the declair,
Calland all man and woman to thair beiris
20   Quhenevir I pleis, quhat tyme, quhat plais, or quhair.
Is nane sa stowt, sa fresch, nor yit sa fair,
So yung, so auld, so riche, nor yit so pure;
Quhairevir I pas, owthir lait or air,
Man put thaim heill on fors under my cure.'

Man

25   'Sen it is sua that natur can so wirk
That yung and auld with riche and pur man de,
Inn my yowtheid, allace, I wes full irk,
Culd nocht tak tent to gyd and govern me
Ay gud to do, fra evill deidis to fle,
30   Trestand ay yowtheid wald with me abyd,
Fulfilland evir my sensualitie
In deidly syn and speacialy in pryd.'

17 forsuth *in truth* sen that thow speiris *since you ask*   18 Tha *they*
Deid *Death* suthly I the declair *truly I tell you*   19 Calland *calling*
thair beiris *their biers*   20 Quhenevir I pleis *whenever I please* plais *place*
quhair *where*   21 Is nane sa stowt, sa fresch *(there) is none so bold, so vigorous*
22 yung *young* auld *old* pure *poor*
23 *wherever I go, whether it be either late or early*
24 *(but they) must of necessity place themselves in my charge*

25 Sen *since* sua *thus* can so wirk *bring it about*   26 man de *must die*
27 *(and since) in my youth, alas, I was heedless*
28 Culd nocht tak tent to gyd *did not take care to guide*
29 *always to do good, from evil deeds to flee*
30 Trestand *trusting* yowtheid *youth* wald with me abyd *would remain with me*
31 Fulfilland *satisfying*   32 deidly syn *deadly sin* pryd *pride*

Deth

'Thairfoir repent and remord thi conscience,
Think on thir wirdis I now upoun the cry:
35   O wrechit man, O full of ignorance,
All thi plesance thow sall richt deir aby;
Dispone thyself and cum with me in hy,
Edderis, askis, and wormis meit to be;
Cum quhen I call; thow may me nocht deny,
40   Thocht thow wer paip, empriour, and king al thre.'

Man

'Sen it is sua fra the I may nocht chaip,
This wrechit warld for me heir I defy,
And to the, Deid, to lurk undir thi caip,
I offir me with hairt, rycht hummilly,
45   Beseikand God, the Devill, my enemy,
Na power haif my saule till assay.
Jesus, on the with peteous voce I cry,
Mercy one me to haif on Domisday.'

33 Thairfoir *therefore* remord *examine (with) remorse*
34 thir wirdis *these words* upoun the cry *cry out to you*   36 plesance *pleasure*
sall richt deir aby *shall pay for very dearly*
37 Dispone thyself *prepare yourself* in hy *in haste*   38 Edderis *adders*
askis and wormis meit *newts, and worms' food*   39 deny *gainsay*   40 thre *three*

41 fra the I may nocht chaip *I cannot escape from you*   42 heir *here*
defy *renounce*   43 lurk *hide* caip *cloak*
44 hairt *(heart =) sincerity* hummilly *humbly*   45 Beseikand *beseeching*
46 haif *may have* my saule till assay *to attack my soul*
47 peteous voce *piteous voice*   48 Mercy one me *(to have) mercy on me*
Domisday *Doomsday*

THE ANNUNCIATION

Forcy as deith is likand lufe,
Throuch quhom al bittir suet is;
No thing is hard, as writ can pruf,
Till him in lufe that letis.
5   Luf us fra barret betis:
Quhen fra the hevinly sete abufe
In message Gabriell couth muf,
And with myld Mary metis,
And said, 'God wele the gretis!
10 In the he will tak rest and rufe,
But hurt of syn or yit reprufe;
In him sett thi decret is.'

This message mervale gert that myld,
And silence held but soundis,
15 As weill aferit a maid infild.
The angell it expoundis,
How that hir wame but woundis
Consave it suld, fra syn exild;

1 Forcy as deith *strong as death* likand lufe *delightful love*
2 Throuch quhom *through whom* suet *sweet* 3 writ *writing, scripture*
can pruf *proved* 4 *to him who remains in love*
5 fra barret betis *from distress relieves* 6 Quhen *when*
sete abufe *throne above* 7 In message *carrying a message* couth muf *came*
8 myld *humble* metis *meets* 9 wele the gretis *greets thee well*
10 will tak *wishes to take* rufe *shelter* 11 *without harm of sin or any shame*
12 sett thi decret is *is set thy (judgement =) destiny*

13 mervale gert that myld *caused that gentle creature to marvel*
14 *and (she remained) silent without a sound*
15 As weill aferit *As was well fitting for* infild *undefiled* 16 expoundis *explains*
17 wame *womb* but woundis *without wounds*
18 Consave it suld *it should conceive* exild *(=exiled) completely free from*

And quhen this carpin wes compilit,
20 Brichtnes fra bufe aboundis.
Than fell that gay to groundis,
Of Goddis grace nathing begild;
Wox in hir chaumer chaist with child,
With Crist our kyng that cround is.

25 Thir tithingis tauld, the messinger
Till hevin agane he glidis;
That princes pure withoutyn peir
Full plesandly applid is,
And blith with barne abidis.
30 O worthy wirschip singuler,
To be moder and madyn meir,
As Cristin faith confidis –
That borne was of hir sidis
Our makar, Goddis sone so deir,
35 Quhilk erd, wattir, and hevinnis cleir
Throw grace and virtu gidis!

19 *and when this declaration was ended*   20 *from above brightness abounds*
21 *then that fair maid fell to the ground*
22 nathing begild *not at all deprived/beguiled*,   23 Wox *(she) grew*
chaumer chaist *chamber chaste*   24 cround *crowned*

25 Thir tithingis tauld *these tidings told*   26 *glides back to heaven*
27 princes *princess* peir *equal*   28 *most graciously has complied*
29 *and remains joyfully with child*   30 *O worthy and unique honour*
31 moder *mother* madyn meir *maiden undefiled*   32 confidis *believes*
33 *(son?) that was born from her loins*   34 makar *maker*
Goddis sone so deir *God's son so dear*
35 *who earth, water, and bright heavens*   36 virtu *power* gidis *guides*

The miraclis ar mekle and meit
Fra luffis ryver rynnis:
The low of luf haldand the hete
40   Unbrynt full blithlie brinnis;
Quhen Gabriell beginnis
With mouth that gudely may to grete,
The wand of Aaron, dry but wete,
To burioun nocht blynnis;
45   The flesch all donk within is,
Upon the erd na drop couth fleit;
Sa was that may maid moder suete,
And sakeles of all synnis.

Hir mervalus haill madinhede
50   God in hir bosum bracis,
And his divinite fra dreid
Hir kepit in all casis.
The hie God of his gracis
Himself dispisit us to speid,
55   And dowtit nocht to dee ondeid;
He panit for our peacis,
And with his blude us bacis,
Bot quhen he ras up, as we rede,
The cherite of his Godhede
60   Was plane in every placis.

37 *the miracles (see n.) are great and fitting*
38 *(which) run from love's river*   39 *low flame* haldand *holding*
hete *heat*   40 Unbrynt *unburnt, unconsumed* blithlie brinnis *joyously burns*
42 that gudely may to grete *to greet that goodly maid*   43 wand *rod*
dry but wete *dry and without any moisture*   44 *does not cease to bud*
45 *the fleece is entirely moist inside*   46 *(but) upon the earth no drop flowed*   47 Sa *so*
may maid moder suete *maiden made a sweet mother*   48 sakeles *innocent*

49 mervalus *wonderful, miraculous* haill *whole, perfect* madinhede *virginity*
50 *embraces God in her womb*   51 dreid *fear*   52 kepit *protected*
casis *events*   53 hie *high* of his gracis *out of his grace*
54 *humbled himself in order to save us*   55 *and did not fear to die indeed*
56 panit *suffered* peacis *peace*   57 blude *blood* bacis *(?) moistens*
58 ras *rose* rede *read*   59 cherite *charity, love*   60 plane *manifest* placis *place*

O lady lele and lusumest,
Thy face moist fair and schene is!
O blosum blith and bowsumest,
Fra carnale cryme that clene is;
65 This prayer fra my splene is –
That all my werkis wikkitest
Thow put away, and mak me chaist
Fra Termigant that teyn is,
And fra his cluke that kene is,
70 And syn till hevin my saule thou haist,
Quhair thi makar, of michtis mast,
Is kyng, and thow thair quene is.

61 lele *faithful* lusumest *most lovable, sweetest*   62 moist *most*
schene *bright*   63 blosum *flower* bowsumest *most humble*
64 *who art free from bodily sin*   65 fra my splene is *is from my heart*
66 werkis wikkitest *most wicked deeds*   67 put away *remove*
chaist *pure (and therefore safe from?)*
68 Termigant *Termagant, a false god, i.e. the devil* teyn *fierce, cruel*
69 cluke *claw* kene *sharp*   70 *and then hasten my soul to heaven*
71 Quhair *where* of michtis mast *greatest of power*
72 and thow thair quene is *and thou there art queen*

WILLIAM DUNBAR

RORATE CELI DESUPER

Rorate, celi, desuper!
Hevins, distill your balmy schouris,
For now is rissin the brycht day ster
Fro the ros, Mary, flour of flouris.
5   The cleir sone quhome no clud devouris,
Surminting Phebus in the est,
Is cumin of his hevinly touris
Et nobis puer natus est.

Archangellis, angellis and dompnationis,
10   Tronis, potestatis and marteiris seir,
And all ye hevinly operationis,
Ster, planeit, firmament and speir,
Fyre, erd, air and watter cleir,
To him gife loving, most and lest,
15   That come into so meik maneir
Et nobis puer natus est.

1 *send down, you heavens, dew from above* 2 distill *let fall in drops*
balmy schouris *fragrant showers* 3 rissin *risen* brycht *bright* ster *star*
4 Fro *from* ros *rose* flour of flouris *flower of flowers* 5 cleir sone *bright sun*
quhome *whom* clud *cloud* 6 Surminting *surpassing* Phebus *Phoebus, the sun*
est *east* 7 Is cumin of *has come from* touris *towers*
8 *And unto us a child is born*

9 dompnationis *dominations (one of the orders of angels)*
10 Tronis, potestatis *thrones, powers (orders of angels)* marteiris *martyrs*
seir *various, many* 11 operationis *powers* 12 speir *sphere* 13 erd *earth*
14 gife loving *give praise* most and lest *great and small*
15 *who came in such a humble manner*

Synarris, be glaid and pennance do
And thank your makar hairtfully,
For he that ye mycht nocht cum to
20   To yow is cumin full humly,
Your saulis with his blud to by
And lous yow of the feindis arrest,
And only of his awin mercy,
Pro nobis puer natus est.

25   All clergy, do to him inclyne
And bow unto that barne benyng,
And do your observance devyne
To him that is of kingis king.
Ensence his altar, reid and sing
30   In haly kirk with mynd degest,
Him honouring attour all thing,
Qui nobis puer natus est.

Celestiall fowlis in the are,
Sing with your nottis upoun hicht,
35   In firthis and in forrestis fair
Be myrthfull now at all your mycht,

17 Synarris, be glaid *sinners rejoice*   **18** makar *maker*
hairtfully *with all your heart*   **19** ye mycht nocht cum to *you could not come to*
20 is cumin full humly *has come most humbly*   **21** saulis *souls* blud *blood*
by *buy*   **22** lous *release* of the feindis arrest *from the fiend's imprisonment*
23 awin *own*   **24** *for unto us a child is born*

25 inclyne *bow*   **26** barne benyng *gracious child*
27 observance devyne *holy homage*   **29** Ensence *burn incense before*
reid *read*   **30** haly kirk *holy church* degest *solemn*   **31** attour *above*
32 *Who is born as a child for us*

33 fowlis *birds* are *air*   **34** nottis *notes* upoun hicht *on high*   **35** firthis *woods*
36 myrthfull *joyous* at all your mycht *with all your strength*

For passit is your dully nycht;
Aurora hes the cluddis perst,
The son is rissin with glaidsum lycht
40   *Et nobis puer natus est.*

Now spring up, flouris, fra the rute,
Revert yow upwart naturaly,
In honour of the blissit frute
That rais up fro the rose, Mary:
45 Lay out your levis lustely,
Fro deid tak lyfe now at the lest,
In wirschip of that prince wirthy,
   Qui nobis puer natus est.

Syng, hevin imperiall, most of hicht,
50 Regions of air mak armony.
All fishe in flud and foull of flicht
Be myrthfull and mak melody.
All *Gloria in excelsis* cry,
Hevin, erd, se, man, bird and best:
55 He that is crownit abone the sky
   Pro nobis puer natus est!

37 passit *passed, gone* dully nycht *gloomy night*
38 *Aurora (the dawn) has pierced the clouds*   **39** glaidsum lycht *joyous light*

41 rute *root*   **42** Revert yow upwart *spring up again*
43 blissit frute *blessed fruit*   **44** rais *rose*   **45** Lay out *spread*
lustely *joyfully, beautifully*   **46** deid *death* lyfe *life* at the lest *at last*
47 wirschip *honour* wirthy *excellent*

49 imperiall *empyrean* most of hicht *highest of all*   **50** armony *harmony*
51 flud *flood, stream* of flicht *in flight*   **52** Gloria in excelsis *glory in the highest*
54 se *sea* best *beast*   **55** abone *above*

DONE IS A BATTELL ON THE DRAGON BLAK

Done is a battell on the dragon blak;
Our campioun Chryst confoundit hes his force;
The yettis of hell ar brokin with a crak,
The signe triumphall rasit of the croce.
5   The divillis trymmillis with hiddous voce,
The saulis ar borrowit and to the bliss can go,
Chryst with his blud our ransonis dois indoce:
Surrexit Dominus de sepulchro.

Dungin is the deidly dragon Lucifer,
10   The crewall serpent with the mortall stang,
The auld kene tegir with his teith on char
Quhilk in a wait hes lyne for us so lang,
Thinking to grip us in his clowis strang.
The mercifull lord wald nocht that it wer so;
15   He maid him for to felye of that fang:
Surrexit Dominus de sepulchro.

1 Done *finished* on *against*   2 campioun *champion*
confoundit hes his force *has overthrown his power*   3 yettis *gates*
4 signe *standard, symbol* rasit *raised* croce *cross*
5 divillis trymmillis *devils tremble* hiddous voce *hideous voice*
6 saulis *souls* borrowit *redeemed*   7 blud *blood* ransonis *ransoms*
indoce *endorse*   8 *The Lord is risen from the tomb*

9 Dungin *beaten down* deidly *deadly*   10 crewall *cruel* stang *sting*
11 auld kene tegir *old fierce tiger* teith on char *teeth bared*   12 Quhilk *which*
wait *ambush* lyne *lain* lang *long*   13 clowis *claws* strang *strong*
14 wald nocht *did not wish*   15 felye *fail (to capture),* lose fang *prey*

He for our saik that sufferit to be slane
And lyk a lamb in sacrifice wes dicht
Is lyk a lyone rissin up agane
20   And as gyane raxit him on hicht.
Sprungin is Aurora radius and bricht;
On loft is gone the glorius Appollo;
The blisfull day depairtit fro the nycht:
Surrexit Dominus de sepulchro.

25   The grit victour agane is rissin on hicht
That for our querrell to the deth wes woundit.
The sone that wox all paill now schynis bricht,
And, dirknes clerit, our fayth is now refoundit.
The knell of mercy fra the hevin is soundit,
30   The Cristin ar deliverit of thair wo;
The Jowis and thair errour ar confoundit:
Surrexit Dominus de sepulchro.

The fo is chasit, the battell is done ceis;
The presone brokin, the jevellouris fleit and flemit;
35   The weir is gon, confermit is the peis,
The fetteris lowsit and the dungeoun temit;

17 saik *sake* sufferit *suffered (i.e. endured and allowed himself)* slane *slain*
18 dicht *made ready*   **19** lyone *lion* rissin *risen*   **20** gyane *giant*
raxit him on hicht *stretched himself on high*
21 *risen is Aurora (goddess of the dawn), radiant and bright*
22 On loft *into the heavens* Appollo *Apollo, the sun*
23 depairtit fro the nycht *separated from the night*

25 grit *great*   **26** querrell *cause*   **27** sone *sun* wox *grew*
paill *pale, dark* schynis *shines*   **28** dirknes clerit *darkness cleared*
refoundit *established again*   **30** Cristin *Christians*   **31** Jowis *Jews*

33 chasit *put to flight, hunted down* done ceis *brought to an end*
34 presone *prison*
jevellouris fleit and flemit *gaolers frightened away and put to flight*
35 weir *war* gon *ended* confermit is the peis *peace is ratified*
36 fetteris lowsit *fetters unbound* temit *emptied*

The ransoun maid, the presoneris redemit;
The feild is win, ourcumin is the fo,
Dispulit of the tresur that he yemit:
40   *Surrexit Dominus de sepulchro.*

37 presoneris redemit *prisoners redeemed*
38 feild is win *field (of battle) is won* ourcumin *overcome*
39 Dispulit *despoiled* tresur *treasure* yemit *guarded*

HALE, STERNE SUPERNE

Hale, sterne superne, hale, in eterne,
    In Godis sicht to schyne!
Lucerne in derne for to discerne,
    Be glory and grace devyne!
5   Hodiern, modern, sempitern,
      Angelicall regyne,
Our tern inferne for to dispern,
    Helpe, rialest rosyne.
      Ave Maria, gracia plena:
10   Haile, fresche floure femynyne;
Yerne us guberne, virgin matern,
    Of reuth baith rute and ryne.

Haile, yhyng benyng fresche flurising,
    Haile, Alphais habitakle!
15   Thy dyng ofspring maid us to syng
    Befor his tabernakle.
All thing maling we doune thring
    Be sicht of his signakle,
Quhilk king us bring unto his ryng
20   Fro dethis dirk umbrakle.

---

1 Hale *hail* sterne *star* superne *supernal, on high* eterne *eternity*
2 Godis sicht *God's sight* schyne *shine* 3 Lucerne *lantern*
derne *darkness* for to discerne *by which to see* 4 Be *by* devyne *divine*
5 *for this day and this age and forever* 6 *queen of angels* 7 tern *darkness, gloom*
inferne *hellish* dispern *disperse* 8 rialest rosyne *most royal rose*
9 *Hail Mary, full of grace* 10 fresche *fresh, lovely* floure *flower*
femynyne *womanly* 11 Yerne *diligently* guberne *govern, guide*
matern *(maternal =) mother* 12 reuth *pity, compassion* baith *both*
rute and ryne *root and bark (i.e. all encompassing source)*

13 yhyng *young* benyng *gracious, gentle* fresche flurising *blossoming*
14 Alphais *of Alpha (i.e. God)* habitakle *dwelling-place* 15 dyng *worthy*
maid *made* 16 tabernakle *tabernacle, dwelling-place* 17 maling *evil*
doune thring *thrust down* 18 signakle *sign (the cross)* 19 Quhilk *which*
ryng *kingdom* 20 *from death's dark shadow*

Ave Maria, gracia plena:
Haile, moder and maide but makle;
Bricht syng, gladyng our languissing
Be micht of thi mirakle.

25   Haile, bricht be sicht in hevyn on hicht,
Haile, day-sterne orientale!
Our licht most richt in clud of nycht,
Our dirknes for to scale.
Hale, wicht in ficht, puttar to flicht
30   Of fendis in battale!
Haile, plicht but sicht, hale, mekle of mycht,
Haile, glorius virgin, hale!
Ave Maria, gracia plena:
Haile, gentill nychttingale,
35   Way stricht, cler dicht, to wilsome wicht
That irke bene in travale.

Hale, qwene serene, hale, most amene,
Haile, hevinlie hie emprys!
Haile, schene, unseyne with carnale eyne,
40   Haile, ros of paradys!

22 moder *mother* but makle *without stain*
23 *bright sign bringing joy to our sorrow*   24 micht *might, power* mirakle *miracle*

25 bricht be sicht *bright to look upon* hevyn on hicht *heaven on high*
26 day-sterne orientale *day-star of the east*   27 licht *light* richt *true*
clud *cloud* nycht *night*   28 dirknes for to scale *darkness to disperse, scatter*
29 wicht in ficht *valiant in fight* flicht *flight*
30 fendis in battale *fiends in battle*   31 plicht but sicht *anchor unseen*
mekle of mycht *great in power*   34 gentill nychttingale *gracious nightingale*
35 *straight path, clearly marked, for wandering creatures*
36 irke bene in travale *are weary in journeying*

37 amene *kindly*   38 hie emprys *high empress*   39 schene *beautiful one*
unseyne *unseen* eyne *eyes*   40 ros *rose*

Haile, clene bedene ay till conteyne,
   Haile, fair fresche floure-de-lyce,
Haile, grene daseyne, haile fro the splene,
   Of Jesu genitrice!
45   *Ave Maria, gracia plena*:
   Thow baire the prince of prys,
Our teyne to meyne and ga betweyne,
   As humile oratrice.

Haile, more decore than of before
50   And swetar be sic sevyne!
Our glore forlore for to restore
   Sen thow art quene of hevyn.
Memore of sore, stern in aurore,
   Lovit with angellis stevyne,
55   Implore, adore, thow indeflore,
   To mak our oddis evyne!
    Ave Maria, gracia plena:
   With lovingis lowde ellevyn
Quhill store and hore my youth devore,
60   Thy name I sall ay nevyne.

---

41 clene bedene *wholly pure* ay till conteyne *ever to continue*
42 floure-de lyce *lily*   **43** grene daseyne *young daisy*
fro the splene *from the heart*   **44** genitrice *begetter*   **46** baire *bore* prys *glory*
47 teyne *affliction* meyne *mediate (and bring relief)*
ga betweyne *go between, intercede*   **48** humile oratrice *humble intercessor*

49 decore *beautiful*
50 swetar be sic sevyne *sweeter by seven such (i.e. seven times)*
51 glore forlore *glory lost*   **52** Sen *since*   **53** mindful of our grief, star at dawn
54 *praised by angels' voices*   **55** undeflore *undeflowered, virgin*
56 *make our odds even (i.e. ?forgive our sins, remove the disorder of our sins;
see n.)*   **58** lovingis *praises* ellevyn *(?) eleven (see n.)*   **59** Quhill *until*
store *adversity* hore *old age* devore *devour*   **60** sall *shall* nevyne *name*

Empryce of prys, imperatrice,
   Bricht polist precious stane,
Victrice of vyce, hie genitrice
   Of Jesu lord soverayne,
65   Our wys pavys fro enemys
   Agane the feyndis trayne,
Oratrice, mediatrice, salvatrice,
   To God gret suffragane!
     Ave Maria, gracia plena:
70   Haile, sterne meridiane,
Spyce, flour-de-lice of paradys,
   That baire the gloryus grayne.

Imperiall wall, place palestrall
   Of peirles pulcritud,
75   Tryumphale hall, hie trone regall
   Of Godis celsitud!
Hospitall riall, the lord of all
   Thy closet did include,
Bricht ball cristall, ros virginall,
80   Fulfillit of angell fude.
     Ave Maria, gracia plena:
     Thy birth has with his blude
Fra fall mortall originall
   Us raunsound on the rude.

---

61 imperatrice *empress* **62** polist *polished* stane *stone* **63** Victrice *conqueror*
64 soverayne *sovereign* **65** wys *wise, skilled* pavys *shield, defence*
66 *against the fiend's deception* **67** mediatrice *mediator* salvatrice *saviour*
68 gret suffragane *great assistant* **70** sterne meridiane *star of midday*
71 Spyce *spice* **72** grayne *seed (i.e. Jesus)*

73 place palestrall *(?) magnificent palace (see n.)*
74 peirles pulcritud *peerless beauty* **75** Tryumphale *triumphal*
hie trone regall *high royal throne* **76** Godis celsitud *God's majesty*
77 Hospitall riall *royal refuge*
78 closet *chamber (the Virgin's womb)* include *enclose* **79** ball *globe, orb*
cristall *crystal* **80** *filled with the food of angels (i.e. Jesus')*
82 birth *child* blude *blood* **83** *from the first fall which brought death*
84 raunsound *ransomed* rude *cross*

MY HEID DID YAK YESTER NICHT

My heid did yak yester nicht,
This day to mak that I na micht;
    So sair the magryme dois me menyie,
    Perseing my brow as ony ganyie,
5 That scant I luik may on the licht.

And now, schir, laitlie eftir mes,
To dyt thocht I begowthe to dres,
    The sentence lay full evill till find,
    Unsleipit, in my heid behind,
10 Dullit in dulnes and distres.

Full oft at morrow I upryse
Quhen that my curage sleipeing lyis;
    For mirth, for menstrallie, and play,
    For din nor danceing nor deray,
15 It will not walkin me no wise.

---

1 heid *head* yak *ache* yester nicht *last night*
2 *so that I could not write today* 3 sair *painfully* magryme *migraine*
menyie *afflict* 4 Perseing *piercing* as ony ganyie *like any arrow*
5 scant I luik may on the licht *scarcely can I look on the light*

6 schir, laitlie eftir mes *sir, recently after Mass*
7 *though I began to prepare to compose* 8 sentence *matter, theme*
evill *hard* till *to* 9 *not having slept, in the back of my head*
10 Dullit *made dull* dulnes *sluggishness*

11 at morrow *in the morning* upryse *rise up* 12 Quhen *when*
curage *vitality, (?) creative energy* sleipeing lyis *lies sleeping*
13 menstrallie *music* play *entertainment* 14 din *noise* deray *revelry*
15 walkin *awaken* no wise *in any way*

SIR JHON SINCLAIR BEGOWTHE TO DANCE

Sir Jhon Sinclair begowthe to dance
For he was new cum owt of France.
For ony thing that he do mycht
The ane futt yeid ay onrycht
5   And to the tother wald nocht gree.
Quod ane, 'Tak up the Quenis knycht!'
    A mirrear dance mycht na man see.

Than cam in Maistir Robert Schau:
He leuket as he culd lern tham a,
10   Bot ay his ane futt did waver;
He stackeret lyk ane strummall aver
    That hopschackellt war aboin the kne.
To seik fra Sterling to Stranaver,
    A mirrear daunce mycht na man see.

1 Sir Jhon Sinclair *(on persons mentioned, see n.)* begowthe *began*
2 new *newly, recently*   3 *in spite of anything he could do*
4 ane futt yeid ay onrycht *one foot always went wrong*
5 to the tother wald nocht gree *with the other would not agree*   6 Quod *said*
Tak *take, lift* Quenis knycht *queen's knight*   7 mirrear *merrier* mycht *might*

8 cam *came* Maister *master*   9 *he looked as if he could teach them all*
11 stackeret *staggered* strummall aver *(?miserable, ?stumbling old horse)*
12 hopschackellt war *hobbled were* aboin *above*
13 *to search from Stirling to Strathnaver (in Sutherland, in the far north; i.e. in all Scotland)*

15   Than cam in the maister almaser,
     Ane hommiltye-jommeltye juffler,
     Lyk a stirk stackarand in the ry;
     His hippis gaff mony hoddous cry.
        John Bute the fule said, 'Waes me,
20   He is bedirtin – fye, fy!'
        A mirrear dance mycht na man se.

     Than cam in Dunbar the mackar;
     On all the flure thair was nane frackar,
     And thair he dancet the dirrye dantoun;
25   He hoppet lyk a pillie wanton
        For luff of Musgraeffe, men tellis me;
     He trippet quhill he tint his panton –
        A mirrear dance mycht na man see.

     Than cam in Maesteres Musgraeffe;
30   Scho mycht heff lernit all the laeffe.
     Quhen I schau hir sa trimlye dance,
     Hir guid convoy and contenance,

---

15 maister almaser *master almoner (official who distributed alms)*
16 hommiltye-jommeltye juffler *bumbling, clumsy fellow*
17 stirk *young bullock* stackarand *staggering, blundering* ry *rye*
18 hippis gaff mony hoddous *hips gave many a hideous*
19 fule *fool* Waes me *woe is me*   20 bedirtin *fouled with excrement*

22 mackar *poet*   23 flure *floor* thair was nane frackar *there was none nimbler*
24 dancet *danced* dirrye dantoun *(apparently the name of a lively dance)*
25 hoppet *hopped* pillie wanton *(?wanton colt, ?lecherous fellow)*   26 luff *love*
tellis *tell*   27 *he danced until he lost his slipper*

29 Maesteres *Mistress*   30 *she could have taught all the rest*   31 Quhen *when*
schau *saw* sa *so*   32 guid convoy *good bearing* contenance *manner*

Than for hir saek I wissitt to be
The grytast erle or duk in France:
35   A mirrear dance mycht na man see.

Than cam in dame Dounteboir –
God waett gif that schou louket sowr;
Schou maid sic morgeownis with hir hippis,
For lachtter nain mycht hald thair lippis;
40   Quhen schou was danceand bisselye,
Ane blast of wind son fra hir slippis:
      A mirrear dance mycht na man se.

Quhen thair was cum in fyve or sax
The Quenis Dog begowthe to rax,
45   And of his band he maid a bred
And to the danceing soin he him med;
      Quhou mastevlyk abowt yeid he!
He stinckett lyk a tyk, sum saed:
      A mirrear dance mycht na man see.

---

33 saek *sake* wissitt *wished*   34 grytast erle or duk *greatest earl or duke*

36 Dounteboir *'dountibour', apparently a disparaging name for a lady at court*
37 waett gif *knows if* schou louket sowr *she looked sour*
38 maid sic morgeownis *made such contortions*   39 lachtter *laughter*
nain mycht hald thair lippis *none could hold their lips*   40 bisselye *busily*
41 son *soon* slippis *slips, comes*

43 sax *six*   44 rax *stretch*   45 *and from his chain made a sudden start*
46 soin he him med *quickly set himself*   47 *how mastiff-like around he went*
48 stinckett *stank* tyk *cur* sum saed *some said*

THE WARDRAIPPER OF
VENUS BOURE

The wardraipper of Venus boure,
To giff a doublett he is als doure
As it war off an futt-syd frog:
    Madame, ye heff a dangerous dog!

5   Quhen that I schawe to him your markis,
He turnis to me again and barkis,
As he war wirriand an hog:
    Madame, ye heff a dangerous dog!

Quhen that I schawe to him your wrytin,
10 He girnis that I am red for bytin –
I wald he had ane havye clog:
    Madame, ye heff an dangerous dog!

Quhen that I speik till him freindlyk,
He barkis lyk an midding-tyk
15 War chassand cattell throu a bog:
    Madam, ye heff a dangerous dog!

1 wardraipper *officer of the wardrobe*
Venus *Venus, goddess of love (the queen)* boure *chamber*   2 giff *give*
doublett *doublet (a man's close-fitting jacket)* als doure *as unwilling*
3 *as if it were a cloak reaching to the feet*   4 heff *have*
dangerous dog *dangerous, surly dog (James Doig, the wardrobe official)*

5 Quhen *when* schawe *show* markis *signs, seal (of authenticity)*
6 barkis *barks*   7 *as if he were tearing at a young sheep*

9 Quhen *when* wrytin *document*
10 *he snarls so that I am afraid of being bitten*   11 wald *would, wish*
ane havye clog *a heavy block (to restrain him)*

13 speik till him freindlyk *speak to him in a friendly way*
14 midding-tyk *dunghill cur*   15 War chassand cattell *were chasing cattle*

He is an mastive, mekle of mycht,
To keip your wardroippe over nycht
Fra the grytt Sowdan Gog Magog:
20   Madam, ye heff a dangerous dog!

He is ower mekle to be your messan;
Madam, I red you get a less an,
His gang garris all your chalmeris schog:
    Madam, ye heff a dangerous dog!

17 mastive, mekle of mycht *mastiff (of) great might*
18 keip *guard* wardroippe *wardrobe (see n.)* nycht *night*
19 *from the great sultan Gog Magog (see n.)*

21 ower *too* mekle *big* messan *lapdog* 22 red *counsel*
less an *smaller one* 23 *his walking causes all your chambers to shake*

O GRACIOUS PRINCES,
GUID AND FAIR

O gracious Princes, guid and fair,
Do weill to James your wardraipair,
Quhais faythfull bruder, maist freind, I am:
 He is na dog, he is a lam.

5 Thocht I in ballet did with him bourde,
In malice spack I nevir ane woord,
Bot all, my dame, to do your gam:
 He is na dog, he is a lam.

Your hienes can nocht gett ane meter
10 To keip your wardrope, nor discreter
To rewle your robbis and dres the sam:
 He is na dog; he is a lam.

The wyff that he had in his innis,
That with the taingis wald braek his schinnis,
15 I wald schou drownet war in a dam:
 He is na dog, he is a lam.

---

1 Princes *princess* guid *good*   2 weill *well*
wardraipair *keeper of the wardrobe*   3 Quhais *whose* bruder *brother*
maist freind *greatest friend*   4 lam *lamb*

5 Thocht *though* in ballet *in a poem* bourde *jest*   6 spack *spoke*
nevir ane woord *never a word*   7 dame *lady* to do your gam *to amuse you*

9 hienes *highness* nocht *not* ane meter *one (who is) more fitting*
10 keip *guard* discreter *more judicious*   11 rewle *manage, look after*
robbis *robes* dres *keep in order* the sam *(the same=) them*

13 wyff *wife, woman* innis *lodgings*   14 taingis *(fire) tongs*
wald braek his schinnis *wished to break his shins*
15 *I wish she were drowned in a mill-dam*

The wyff that wald him kuckald mak,
I wald schou war, bayth syd and back,
Weill batteret with an barrou tram:
20   He is na dog, he is ane lam.

He hes sa weill doin me obey
Intill all thing, thairfoir I pray
That nevir dolour mak him dram:
    He is na dog, he is a lam.

17 kuckald *cuckold*   **18** shou war *she were* bayth *both* syd *side*
19 Weill batteret *well battered* barrou tram *shaft of a hand-barrow*

21 *he has so well obeyed me*   **22** Intill *in* thairfoir *therefore*
23 dolour *sorrow* dram *dejected*

THIS WAVERAND WARLDIS
WRETCHIDNES

This waverand warldis wretchidnes,
The failyeand and frutles bissines,
The mispent tyme, the service vane,
    For to considder is ane pane.

5   The slydand joy, the glaidnes schort,
The feynyeid luif, the fals confort,
The sweit abayd, the slichtfull trane,
    For to considder is ane pane.

The sugurit mouthis with myndis thairfra,
10   The figurit speiche with faceis tua,
The plesand toungis with hartis unplane,
    For to considder is ane pane.

The liell labour lost and liell service,
The lang availl on humill wyse,
15   And the lytill rewarde agane,
    For to considder is ane pane.

---

1 waverand warldis *wavering world's*   2 failyeand *failing*
frutles *fruitless* bissines *diligence*   4 ane pane *a pain, sorrow*

5 slydand *unstable*   6 feynyeid *feigned, false* luif *love*
7 sweit *sweet, plausible* abayd *delay* slichtfull trane *crafty deceit*

9 sugurit *sugared, sweet-sounding* thairfra *elsewhere, far away*
10 figurit speiche *elaborately rhetorical speech* faceis *faces* tua *two*
11 plesand toungis *pleasing tongues* hartis *hearts* unplane *deceitful*

13 liell *loyal*   14 lang *long* availl *assistance, ready service (deserving reward)*
humill *humble*   15 agane *return*

Nocht I say all be this cuntré,
France, Ingland, Ireland, Almanie,
Bot als be Italie and Spane,
20   Quhilk to considder is ane pane.

The change of warld fro weill to wo,
The honourable use is all ago
In hall and bour, in burgh and plane,
    For to considder is ane pane.

25 Beleif dois liep, traist dois nocht tarie;
Office dois flit and courtis dois vary;
Purpos dois change as wynd or rane;
    Quhilk to considder is ane pane.

Gud rewle is banist our the bordour,
30 And rangat ringis but ony ordour
With reird of rebaldis and of swane;
    Quhilk to considder is ane pane.

The pepill so wickit ar of feiris,
The frutles erde all witnes beiris,
35 The ayr infectit and prophane;
    Quhilk to considder is ane pane.

17 Nocht I say *I do not speak* all *entirely* be this cuntré *concerning this country*
18 Almanie *Germany* **19** als *also* **20** Quhilk *which*

21 weill *well-being, prosperity* **22** use *usage, conduct* ago *gone*
23 bour *chamber* burgh *town* plane *country*

25 Beleif *faith* dois *does* liep *leap, caper* traist *trust*
nocht tarie *not linger, remain* **26** flit *shift, pass* vary *change*
27 Purpos *purpose, intention* rane *rain*

29 Gud rewle *good rule, conduct* banist our the bordour *banished over the border*
30 and discord reigns without any order
31 reird of rebaldis and of swane *uproar of knaves and churls*

33 pepill *people* wickit *wicked* of feiris *in behaviour* **34** frutles erde *infertile earth*
beiris *bears* **35** ayr *air* infectit *infected* prophane *unclean*

The temporale stait to gryp and gather,
The sone disheris wald the father
And as ane dyvour wald him demane;
40   Quhilk to considder is ane pane.

Kirkmen so halie ar and gude
That on thair conscience, rowme and rude,
May turne aucht oxin and ane wane;
Quhilk to considder is ane pane.

45   I knaw nocht how the Kirk is gydit,
Bot beneficis ar nocht leill devydit:
Sum men hes sevin and I nocht ane;
Quhilk to considder is ane pane.

And sum unworthy to browk ane stall
50   Wald clym to be ane cardinall –
Ane bischoprik may nocht him gane;
Quhilk to considder is ane pane.

Unwourthy I amang the laif
Ane kirk dois craif and nane can have;
55   Sum with ane thraif playis passage plane;
Quhilk to considder is ane pane.

37 temporale stait *worldly estate* to gryp *in order to grasp*   38 sone *son*
disheris wald *would dispossess*   39 dyvour *bankrupt* demane *maltreat*

41 Kirkmen *churchmen* halie *holy*   42 rowme *ample* rude *large*
43 *can turn eight oxen and a wagon*

45 Kirk *church* gydit *directed*   46 leill devydit *fairly distributed*
47 hes *have* nocht ane *not one*

49 sum *some, one* browk *possess, occupy* stall *seat (of a canon, etc.)*
50 clym *climb*   51 nocht him gane *be fitting, suffice*

53 amang *among* laif *rest*   54 craif *seek, desire* nane *none*
55 thraif *thrave (two stocks of corn of twelve sheaves each=) a large number*
playis passage plane *(?plays dice openly) (?i.e. who gambles with a large number
of benefices)*

It cumis be king, it cumis be quene,
Bot ay sic space is us betwene
That nane can schut it with ane flane;
60   Quhilk to considder is ane pane.

It micht have cuming in schortar quhyll
Fra Calyecot and the new fund yle,
The partis of Transmeridiane;
     Quhilk to considder is ane pane.

65   It micht be this, had it bein kynd,
Cuming out of the desertis of Ynde
Our all the grit se oceane;
     Quhilk to considder is ane pane.

It micht have cuming out of all ayrtis –
70   Fra Paris and the Orient partis,
And fra the ylis of Aphrycane;
     Quhilk to consydder is ane pane.

57 It *it (= a benefice)* cumis *comes*   58 ay *always* sic *such*
59 schut *shoot* flane *arrow*

61 micht have cuming *could come* schortar quhyll *shorter time*
62 Calyecot *Calicut (on the geographical names in this passage, see n.)*
new fund yle *newly found island, land*   63 partis *areas, countries*
Transmeridiane *beyond the meridian*

65 be this *by this time* kynd *(?well-disposed, ?behaving according to nature, normal)*
66 Cuming *(have) come* Ynde *India*   67 Our *over*
grit se oceane *great sea of ocean*

69 ayrtis *quarters*   70 Orient partis *eastern regions*   71 ylis *lands, isles*
Aphrycane *Africa*

It is so lang in cuming me till,
I dreid that it be quyt gane will –
75   Or bakwart it is turnit agane;
    Quhilk to considder is ane pane.

Upon the heid of it is hecht
Bayth unicornis and crownis of wecht;
Quhen it dois cum all men dois frane;
80   Quhilk to considder is ane pane.

I wait it is for me provydit,
Bot sa done tyrsum it is to byd it,
It breikis my hairt and birstis my brane;
    Quhilk to considder is ane pane.

85   Greit abbais grayth I nill to gather
Bot ane kirk scant coverit with hadder,
For I of lytill wald be fane;
    Quhilk to considder is ane pane.

And for my curis in sindrie place
90   With help, Sir, of your nobill grace,
My sillie saule sall never be slane
    Na for sic syn to suffer pane.

---

73 me till *to me* 74 dreid *fear* quyt gane will *completely gone astray*
75 is turnit agan *has turned back*

77 heid *head, security* hecht *promised* 78 Bayth *both*
unicornis *gold coins with figures of unicorns* crownis *crowns (gold coins)*
wecht *weight* 79 frane *ask*

81 wait *know* provydit *arranged* 82 sa done tyrsum *so utterly wearisome*
byd *wait for* 83 breikis *breaks* birstis my brane *bursts my brain*

85 Greit abbais grayth *the wealth of great abbeys* nill *do not wish*
86 scant *scarcely* hadder *heather* 87 fane *glad*

89 curis *ecclesiastical offices* sindrie *various* 91 sillie saule *silly, helpless soul*
slane *destroyed* 92 Na *nor*

Experience dois me so inspyr,
Off this fals failyeand warld I tyre
95 That evermore flytis lyk ane phane;
    Quhilk to considder is ane pane.

The formest hoip yit that I have
In all this warld, sa God me save,
Is in your grace, bayth crop and grayne,
100   Quhilk is ane lessing of my pane.

94 failyeand *failing, declining* tyre *tire* 95 flytis *shifts, changes*
phane *weather-vane*

97 formest hoip *foremost hope* yit *still*
99 crop and grayne *(shoot and seed =) completely* 100 lessing *alleviation*

SCHIR, LAT IT NEVER IN
TOUNE BE TALD

Schir, lat it never in toune be tald
That I suld be ane Yowllis yald.

Suppois I war ane ald yaid aver,
Schott furth our clewch to squische the clever,
5   And hed the strenthis off all Strenever,
I wald at Youll be housit and stald:
    Schir, lat it never in toune be tald
    That I suld be ane Yowllis yald.

I ame ane auld hors, as ye knaw,
10 That ever in duill dois drug and draw.
Gryt court hors puttis me fra the staw,
To fang the fog be firthe and fald:
    Schir, lat it never in toune be tald
    That I suld be ane Yowllis yald.

---

1 Schir *sir* in toune *(in town =) in public* tald *said*   2 suld *should*
ane Yowllis yald *old Yule nag (see n.)*

3 Suppois *even if* ald yaid aver *old worn-out horse*
4 Schott furth *pushed out* our clewch *over the cliff (i.e. (?)unceremoniously)*
squische *crush* clever *clover*   5 hed *had* strenthis *fastnesses*
Strenever *Strathnaver (in Sutherland)*
6 housit *house, provided with a horse-cover* stald *given a stall*

9 auld *old* knaw *know*   10 duill *sorrow* drug *drag*   11 Gryt *great*
hors *horses* puttis *push* staw *stall*   12 fang *take, get*
fog *dank grass (left in the fields during winter)* firthe *wood* fald *(enclosed) field*

15   I heff run lang furth in the feild
      On pastouris that ar plane and peld.
      I mycht be now tein in for eild,
      My bekis ar spruning he and bald:
        Schir, lat it never in toune be tald
20   That I suld be ane Yowllis yald.

      My maine is turned into quhyt,
      And thairoff ye heff all the wyt.
      Quhen uthair hors hed brane to byt
      I gat bot gris, grype giff I wald:
25   Schir, lat it never in towne be tald
        That I suld be ane Yowllis yald.

      I was never dautit into stabell;
      My lyff hes bein so miserabell,
      My hyd to offer I am abell,
30   For evill schoud strae that I reiv wald:
        Schir, lat it never in towne be tald
        That I suld be ane Yowllis yald.

      And yett suppois my thrift be thyne,
      Gif that I die your aucht within,
35   Lat nevir the soutteris have my skin,

15 heff *have* furth *forth, out* feild *field*
16 pastouris *(?)pastures, (?)pasterns (lower part of horses' feet)*
plane *smooth* peld *stripped bare*　17 tein *taken* eild *old age*
18 *(?)my corner teeth are sticking our prominently*

21 maine *mane* quhyt *white*　22 thairoff *for that* wyt *blame*
23 Quhen *when* uthair *other* hed brane to byt *had bran to eat*
24 *I only got grass, if I would grab it*

27 dautit *petted* into *in*　28 lyff *life* bein *been*　29 hyd *skin* abell *ready*
30 evill *bad(ly)* schoud *(?) of low quality* strae *straw* reiv *tear at*

33 suppois *even if* thrift *wealth* thyne *thin*　34 aucht *possession*
35 soutteris *cobblers*

With uglie gumes to be gnawin:
    Schir, lat it nevir in toun be tald
    That I suld be ane Yuillis yald.

The court hes done my curage cuill
40 And maid me ane forriddin muill;
Yett to weir trapperis at the Yuill
I wald be spurrit at everie spald:
    Schir, lat it nevir in toun be tald
    That I suld be ane Yuillis yald.

45 Now lufferis cummis with larges lowd;
Quhy sould not palfrayis thane be prowd,
Quhen gillettis wil be schomd and schroud
That riddin ar baith with lord and lawd?
    Schir, lat it nevir in toun be tald
50   That I suld be ane Yuillis yald.

Quhen I was young and into ply
And wald cast gammaldis to the sky,
I had beine bocht in realmes by,
Had I consentit to be sauld:
55   Schir, lat it nevir in toun be tald
    That I suld be ane Yuillis yald.

36 uglie gumes *horrible gums* gnawin *chewed*

39 done *caused* curage *spirit, sexual desire* cuill *to cool*
40 forriddin *over-ridden, worn out* muill *mule*   **41** weir *wear*
trapperis *horse-covers, trappings*   **42** spurrit *pricked with spurs*
spald *(shoulder =) limb*

45 lufferis *lovers/liveries (clothing for courtiers, provender for horses)*
larges *largess (ceremonial giving of gifts)* lowd *loud, demonstrative*   **46** Quhy *why*
palfrayis *palfreys (riding horses (esp. for ladies), as against war-horses)*
47 gillettis *mares, girls* schomd *(?)groomed, adorned* schroud *decked out*
48 baith *both* lawd *lad, menial*

51 into ply *in good condition*   **52** gammaldis *capers, leaps*
53 *I could have been bought in realms nearby*   **54** sauld *sold*

With gentill hors quhen I wald knyp
Thane is thair laid on me ane quhip;
To colleveris than man I skip,
60　That scabbit ar, hes cruik and cald.
　　Schir, lat it nevir in toun be tald
　　That I suld be ane Yuillis yald.

Thocht in the stall I be not clappit,
As cursouris that in silk beine trappit,
65　With ane new hous I wald be happit
Aganis this Crystinmes for the cald.
　　Schir, lat it nevir in toun be tald
　　That I suld be ane Yuillis yald.

Respontio Regis

Efter our wrettingis, thesaurer,
70　Tak in this gray hors, auld Dumbar,
Quhilk in my aucht with service trew
In lyart changeit is his hew.
Gar hows him new aganis this Yuill
And busk him lyk ane bischopis muill,
75　For with my hand I have indost
To pay quhatevir his trappouris cost.

---

57 gentill *noble*　knyp *graze, eat*　58 quhip *whip*
59 colleveris *horses that carry coal*　man *must*
60 scabbit *covered in scabs*　cruik *lameness*　cald *sickness caused by cold*

63 Thocht *though*　clappit *patted*　64 cursouris *coursers, war-horses*
trappit *adorned*　65 hous *cover*　happit *wrapped up*　66 Aganis *in readiness for*

The King's Reply
69 Efter *in accordance with*　wrettingis *writings, instructions*　thesaurer *treasurer*
71 Quhilk *which*　aucht *possession*　72 lyart *grey*　hew *colour*
73 Gar hows him *cause him to be clothed*　74 busk *array*　muill *mule*
75 indost *endorsed, authorized*　76 quhatevir *whatever*　trappouris *trappings*

SCHIR, YE HAVE MONY SERVITOURIS

Schir, ye have mony servitouris
And officiaris of dyvers curis:
Kirkmen, courtmen and craftismen fyne,
Doctouris in jure and medicyne,
5   Divinouris, rethoris and philosophouris,
Astrologis, artistis and oratouris,
Men of armes and vailyeand knychtis
And mony uther gudlie wichtis,
Musicianis, menstralis and mirrie singaris,
10   Chevalouris, cawandaris and flingaris,
Cunyouris, carvouris and carpentaris,
Beildaris of barkis and ballingaris,
Masounis lyand upon the land,
And schipwrichtis hewand upone the strand,
15   Glasing wrichtis, goldsmythis and lapidaris,
Pryntouris, payntouris and potingaris –
And all of thair craft cunning,
And all at anis lawboring,
Quhilk pleisand ar and honorable
20   And to your hienes profitable,

1 Schir *sir* mony *many* servitouris *servants*   2 officiaris *officials*
dyvers curis *various responsibilities*   3 Kirkmen *churchmen* fyne *excellent*
4 jure *law*   5 Divinouris *diviners* rethoris *rhetoricians*
6 Astrologis *astrologers* artistis *practitioners of the (?alchemical) art*
7 vailyeand knychtis *valiant knights*   8 uther gudlie wichtis *other fine people*
9 menstralis *minstrels* mirrie *merry*   10 Chevalouris *(?)mounted soldiers*
cawandaris *(?)entertainers* flingaris *(?)some kind of soldiers or (?)entertainers*
11 Cunyouris *coiners* carvouris *carvers*   12 Beildaris *builders*
barkis *barques, small ships* ballingaris *sloops*   13 Masounis *masons*
lyand upon *(?)lying on the ground (?)weighing heavily (?)dwelling*
14 schipwrichtis *shipwrights* hewand *hewing wood* strand *shore*
15 Glasing wrichtis *glass-makers* lapidaris *jewellers*
16 Pryntouris *(?)printers (?)workers in the mint* payntouris *painters*
potingaris *apothecaries*   17 of *in* cunning *skilled*   18 anis *at once, together*
lawboring *labouring*   19 Quhilk *who* pleisand *pleasing*   20 hienes *highness*

And richt convenient for to be
With your hie regale majestie,
Deserving of your grace most ding
Bayth thank, rewarde and cherissing.

25   And thocht that I amang the laif
Unworthy be ane place to have
Or in thair nummer to be tald,
Als lang in mynd my work sall hald,
Als haill in everie circumstance,

30   In forme, in mater and substance,
But wering or consumptioun,
Roust, canker or corruptioun,
As ony of thair werkis all,
Suppois that my reward be small.

35   Bot ye sa gracious ar and meik
That on your hienes followis eik
Ane uthir sort, more miserabill,
Thocht thai be nocht sa profitable:
Fenyeouris, fleichouris and flatteraris,

40   Cryaris, craikaris and clatteraris,
Soukaris, groukaris, gledaris, gunnaris,
Monsouris of France (gud clarat cunnaris),

---

21 richt convenient *most fitting*   22 regale *royal*   23 ding *grace*
24 Bayth *both* cherissing *affection, support*   25 thocht *though* laif *rest*
27 nummer *number* tald *reckoned*
28 *my work will continue to be remembered for just as long*
29 Als haill *as completely* circumstance *detail*
31 *without wasting away or being consumed*   32 Roust *rust*
canker *canker, gangrene*   33 ony *any* werkis *works*
34 Suppois that *even though*   35 meik *gentle*   36 eik *also*
37 uthir sort *another company*   38 Thocht *though* nocht sa *not so*
39 Fenyeouris *feigners, dissimulators* fleichouris *cajolers, plausible talkers*
40 Cryaris *criers, shouters* craikaris *clamourers* clatteraris *chatterers*
41 Soukaris *parasites*
groukaris *(?)sly lurkers (on this and the following words, see n.)*
gledaris *(?)some kind of thieves* gunnaris *(?)gunners*
42 Monsouris *monsieurs* gud clarat cunnaris *good claret tasters*

Inopportoun askaris of Yrland kynd,
And meit-revaris, lyk out of mynd,
45 Scaffaris and scamleris in the nuke,
And hall-huntaris of draik and duik,
Thrimlaris and thristaris as thai war woid,
Kokenis, and kennis na man of gude;
Schulderaris and schovaris that hes no schame,
50 And to no cunning that can clame,
And can non uthir craft nor curis
Bot to mak thrang, schir, in your duris,
And rusche in quhair thay counsale heir
And will at na man nurtir leyr;
55 In quintiscence eik ingynouris joly,
That far can multiplie in folie,
Fantastik fulis, bayth fals and gredy,
Off toung untrew and hand evill-diedie
(Few dar of all this last additioun
60 Cum in Tolbuyth without remissioun).
      And thocht this nobill cunning sort –
Quhom of befoir I did report –

---

43 Inopportoun askaris *importunate beggars* Yrland kynd *Irish, Gaelic race*
44 meit-revaris *food-stealers* lyk out of mynd *as if out of their wits*
45 Scaffaris *scroungers, beggars* scamleris *spongers* nuke *corner*
46 *And people who hunt drake and duck in the hall (i.e. who scrounge free meals or pick up scraps of food)*   47 Thrimlaris *jostlers* thristaris *thrusters*
as thai war woid *if they were mad*   48 Kokenis *rogues*
kennis na man of gude *acknowledge no man of substance*
49 Schulderaris *shoulderers (who push their way forward)* schovaris *shovers*
hes *have*   50 cunning *skill* clame *lay claim*   51 can *know* uthir *other*
curis *duties*   52 thrang *a throng* duris *doors*   53 rusche *rush*
quhair *where* counsale *council, discussion* heir *hear*
54 at na man nurtir leyr *from no one learn courtesy*
55 quintiscence *quintessence (see n.)* eik *also* ingynouris *contrivers*
joly *lusty, bold*   56 multiplie *multiply (increase, transmute)* folie *folly*
57 fulis *fools*   58 toung *tongue* untrew *untrue* evill-diedie *evil-doing*
59 dar *dare* additioun *addition (i.e. last-mentioned group)*
60 Tolbuyth *Tolbooth (used as the meeting place of the town council and court and also as a prison)* remissioun *pardon*   61 thocht *though, if*
cunning *skilled*   62 Quhom *whom* befoir *before*

Rewardit be, it war bot ressoun;
Thairat suld no man mak enchessoun.
65 Bot quhen the uther fulis nyce
That feistit at Cokelbeis gryce
Ar all rewardit, and nocht I,
Than on this fals warld I cry, Fy!
My hart neir bristis than for teyne,
70 Quhilk may nocht suffer nor sustene
So grit abusioun for to se
Daylie in court befoir myn e.
　　And yit more panence wald I have
Had I rewarde amang the laif.
75 It wald me sumthing satisfie
And les of my malancolie,
And gar me mony falt ourse
That now is brayd befoir myn e.
My mind so fer is set to flyt
80 That of nocht ellis I can endyt;
For owther man my hart to-breik,
Or with my pen I man me wreik.
And sen the tane most nedis be –
Into malancolie to de
85 Or lat the vennim ische all out –
Be war anone, for it will spout,
Gif that the tryackill cum nocht tyt
To swage the swalme of my dispyt.

---

63 it war bot ressoun *it would be only reasonable*　**64** Thairat *at that*
suld *should*　mak enchessoun *take exception*　**65** quhen *when*　nyce *silly*
66 feistit *feasted*　Cokelbeis gryce *Cokelbie's pig (see n.)*　**68** warld *world*
69 neir bristis than for teyne *nearly bursts for vexation*　**70** Quhilk *which*
sustene *endure*　**71** grit abusioun *great wrong-doing*　se *see*　**72** e *eye*
73 panence *self-discipline*　wald *would*　**75** sumthing *somewhat*　**76** les of *alleviate*
malancolie *melancholy*　**77** gar *cause, make*　falt *fault, offence*　ourse *overlook*
78 brayd *plain, evident*　**79** fer *far, deeply*　flyt *scold, abuse*　**80** nocht ellis *nothing else*
endyt *compose, write*　**81** *for either my heart must break utterly*
82 me wreik *avenge myself*　**83** *and since one (of these) must needs happen*
84 Into *in*　de *die*　**85** vennim *venom, poison*　ische *pour*　**86** anone *quickly*
87 Gif *if*　tryackill *remedy, balm*　tyt *speedily*　**88** swage *assuage*
swalme *swelling*　dispyt *resentment, anger*

THE FLYTING OF DUNBAR
AND KENNEDY (extract)

Dunbar attacks his rival

Iersche brybour baird, vyle beggar with thy brattis,
   Cuntbittin crawdoun Kennedy, coward of kynd;
Evill-farit and dryit as Densmen on the rattis,
   Lyk as the gleddis had on thy gulesnowt dynd;
5   Mismaid monstour, ilk mone owt of thy mynd,
Renunce, rebald, thy rymyng; thow bot royis;
   Thy trechour tung hes tane ane heland strynd –
Ane lawland ers wald mak a bettir noyis.

Revin, raggit ruke, and full of rebaldrie,
10   Scarth fra scorpione, scaldit in scurrilitie,
I se the haltane in thy harlotrie
   And into uthir science no thing slie,

---

1 Iersche *(Irish =) Gaelic* brybour baird *rascally vagabond bard*
brattis *ragged garments*   2 Cuntbittin *(?)impotent, (?)bitten by a cunt*
crawdoun *(?)poxed* coward of kynd *coward by nature*
3 Evill-farit *ill-favoured* dryit as Densmen *withered like Danes*
on the rattis *on the wheels (on which criminals were executed and exposed)*
4 *as if the kites had dined on your yellow nose*
5 Mismaid monstour *misshapen monster* ilk mone *each moon*
6 *renounce, rascal, your versifying; you do nothing but talk nonsense*
7 trechour tung hes tane *treacherous tongue has taken*
heland strynd *Highland character*
8 *a lowland arse would make a better noise*

9 Revin *(?)raven, (?)torn* raggit ruke *ragged rook* rebaldrie *obscenity*
10 Scarth fra scorpione *monster (sprung) from a scorpion*
scaldit *scalded, inflamed*   11 *I see you arrogant in your rascality*
12 into uthir science *in other learning* slie *skilled*

Of every vertew void, as men may sie;
Quytclame clergie and cleik to the ane club,
15   Ane baird blasphemar in brybrie ay to be;
For wit and woisdome ane wisp fra the may rub.

Thow speiris, dastard, gif I dar with the fecht:
     Ye! dagone dowbart, thairof haif thow no dowt.
Quhairevir we meit, thairto my hand I hecht
20   To red thy rebald rymyng with a rowt.
     Throw all Bretane it sal be blawing owt
How that thow, poysonit pelour, gat thy paikis;
     With ane doig-leich I schepe to gar the schowt,
And nowther to the tak knyfe, swerd nor aix . . .

*   *   *

25   Thow callis the rethory with thy goldin lippis –
     Na, glowrand, gaipand fule, thow art begyld.
Thow art bot gluntoch, with thy giltin hippis,
     That for thy lounry mony a leisch hes fyld.

---

13 vertew *virtue* void *deprived* sie *see*
14 Quytclame clergie *renounce clerkly learning* cleik *grab*
15 blasphemar *evil-speaking* brybrie *larceny* ay *ever*   16 woisdome *wisdom*
ane wisp fra the may rub *can be rubbed from you with a bunch of straw*

17 *You ask, coward, if I dare fight with you*   18 Ye! *yes!*
dagone *misshapen villain (see n.)* dowbart *(?)fool*
thairof haif thow no dowt *of that have no fear*
19 *wherever we meet, to this I give my word* 20 red *sweep away*
rowt *one violent blow*   21 *throughout all Britain it shall be proclaimed*
22 poysonit *full of poison* pelour *robber* gat *got* paikis *thrashing*
23 doig-leich *dog-leash* schepe *intend, prepare* gar *make*
24 *and use on you neither knife, sword nor axe*

25 the *yourself* rethory *rhetorician*
26 *no, staring, gaping fool, you are deceived*   27 bot *but, only*
gluntoch *(?)a bare-kneed Highlander* giltin *gilded, yellow*   28 lounry *knavery*
mony *many* leisch *leash, lash* hes fyld *has made foul*

Wan-visaged widdefow, out of thy wit gane wyld,
30   Laithly and lowsy, als lauchtane as ane leik:
       Sen thow with wirschep wald sa fane be styld –
    Haill, soverane senyeour! Thy bawis hingis throw thy breik.

Forworthin fule, of all the warld reffuse,
       Quhat ferly is, thocht thow rejoys to flyte?
35   Sic eloquence as thay in Erschry use,
       In sic is sett thy thraward appetyte.
       Thow hes full littill feill of fair indyte:
    I tak on me ane pair of Lowthiane hippis
       Sall fairer Inglis mak, and mair parfyte,
40   Than thow can blabbar with thy Carrik lippis.

Bettir thow ganis to leid ane doig to skomer,
       Pynit pykpuris pelour, than with thy maister pingill.
    Thow lay full prydles in the peis this somer
       And fane at evin for to bring hame a single,

---

29 Wan-visaged widdefow *leaden-faced gallows-bird* gane *gone* wyld *frantic*
30 *loathsome and lousy, as livid as a leek*
31 *since you would so gladly be honourably addressed*
32 soverane senyeour *sovereign lord*
bawis hingis throw thy breik *balls hang through your breeches*

33 Forworthin *deformed* reffuse *rejected*   **34** Quhat ferly *what wonder*
thocht *though, if* rejoys *rejoice* flyte *abuse*   **35** Sic *such*
Erschry *(Irishry =) the Gaelic-speaking Highlands*
36 thraward appetyte *perverse desire*   **37** hes *has* feill *understanding*
indyte *composition*   **38** tak on me *assert, vow*
Lowthiane *Lothian (the area around Edinburgh, on the south side of the Firth of*
Forth)   **39** *shall make fairer English, and more perfect*
40 blabbar *blabber, babble*
Carrik *Carrick, southern Ayrshire (then still a Gaelic-speaking area)*

41 ganis to leid ane doig to skomer *are fitted to lead a dog to shit*
42 Pynit pykpuris pelour *emaciated pickpurse robber* pingill *strive*
43 prydles *devoid of pride* in the peis *among the peas* somer *summer*
44 fane *(were) glad* evin *evening* hame *home* single *small bunch of gleanings*

45   Syne rubb it at ane uthir auld wyfis ingle:
        Bot now in winter for purteth thow art traikit –
          Thow hes na breik to latt thy bellokis gyngill;
        Beg the ane bratt for, baird, thow sall go naikit.

        Lene larbar loungeour, lowsy in lisk and lonye;
50   Fy, skolderit skyn, thow art bot skyre and skrumple;
        For he that rostit Lawrance had thy grunye,
          And he that hid sanct Johnis ene with ane wimple,
          And he that dang sanct Augustyne with ane rumple
        Thy fowll front had, and he that Bartilmo flaid.
55   The gallowis gaipis eftir thy graceles gruntill,
        As thow wald for ane haggeis, hungry gled . . .

                          *   *   *

        Ersche katherene, with thy polk breik and rilling,
          Thow and thy quene, as gredy gleddis ye gang
        With polkis to mylne and beggis baith meill and schilling.
60   Thair is bot lys and lang nailis yow amang;

45 Syne *then* rubb it *rub (the grain from the ears of corn)*
ane uthir auld wyfis ingle *at another old wife's hearth-fire*
46 purteth *poverty* traikit *worn out*
47 latt *stop* bellokis *bollocks, balls (with pun on bells)* gyngill *jingle, dangle*
48 the ane bratt for *for yourself a ragged cloak* baird *bard* naikit *naked*

49 *skinny impotent layabout, lousy in groin and loin*
50 skolderit *scorched, tanned* skyre and skrumple *crease and wrinkle*
51 rostit *roasted* Lawrance *St Laurence (on him and following saints, see n.)*
grunye *snout*   52 Sanct Johnis ene *St John's eyes* wimple *veil*   53 dang *beat*
rumple *(fish)tail*   54 fowll front *foul forehead*
Bartilmo flaid *flayed St Bartholomew*
55 gallowis gaipis *gallows gape, are hungry for*
graceles gruntill *ill-favoured snout*   56 wald *would* haggeis *haggis* gled *kite*

57 Ersche *Gaelic* katherene *reiver* polk breik *(Highland) bag*
rilling *rough shoe made of hide*   58 quene *wench* gleddis *kites* gang *go*
59 polkis *bags* mylne *mill* meill *(oat)meal* schilling *husks of oats*
60 lys *lice* lang *long* amang *among, between*

Fowll heggirbald, for henis thus will ye hang;
Thow hes ane perrellus face to play with lambis;
   Ane thowsand kiddis, wer thay in faldis full strang,
Thy lymmerfull luke wald fle thame and thair damis.

65 Intill ane glen thow hes, owt of repair,
    Ane laithly luge that wes the lippir menis.
With the ane sowtaris wyfe off blis als bair,
   And lyk twa stalkaris steilis in cokis and henis –
   Thow plukkis the pultré and scho pullis of the penis.
70 All Karrik cryis, 'God gif this dowsy be drownd!'
    And quhen thow heiris ane guse cry in the glenis,
Thow thinkis it swetar than sacryne bell of sound.

Thow lazarus, thow laithly lene tramort,
   To all the warld thow may example be
75 To luk upoun thy gryslie peteous port;
    For hiddowis, haw and holkit is thyne ee,

61 Fowll *foul* heggirbald *(?) rascal* henis *(stealing) hens*
62 perrellus *dangerous* **63** kiddis *kids, young goats*
wer thay in faldis full strang *even if they were secure in enclosed fields*
64 lymmerfull luke *villainous look* fle *put to flight* damis *mothers*

65 Intill *in* owt of repair *away from the haunts of men*
66 laithly luge *horrible hut* lippir menis *lepers'* **67** the *thee*
sowtaris *shoemaker's* off blis als bair *just as bereft of joy, miserable*
68 stalkaris *prowlers* steilis *steal upon* cokis *cocks* **69** plukkis *pluck away*
pultré *poultry* scho *she* pullis of *plucks* penis *feathers*
70 Karrik *Carrick* gif *grant* dowsy *(?)stupid fellow, (?)wench, harlot*
71 quhen *when* heiris *hears* guse *goose* **72** swetar *sweeter*
sacryne bell *sacring bell (rung at the elevation of the Host during Mass)*

73 lazarus *(= Lazarus) corpse-like figure* laithly lene tramort *putrefying carcass*
74 warld *world* **75** luk *look* gryslie peteous port *grisly, lamentable appearance*
76 hiddowis, haw and holkit *hideous, livid and hollow* ee *eye*

Thy cheik-bane bair, and blaiknit is thy ble;
Thy choip, thy choll, garris men for to leif chest;
Thy gane it garris us think that we mon de:
80 I conjure the, thow hungert heland gaist . . .

* * *

Thow held the burch lang with ane borrowit goun
And ane cap rowsy, barkit all with sweit,
And quhen the laidis saw the sa lyk a loun,
Thay bickerit the with mony bae and bleit:
85 Now upaland thow leivis on rubbit quheit;
Oft for ane caus thy burdclaith neidis no spredding,
For thow hes nowthir for to drink nor eit,
Bot lyk ane berdles baird that had no bedding.

Strait Gibbonis air that nevir ourstred ane hors,
90 Bla berfute berne, in bair tyme wes thow borne;
Thow bringis the Carrik clay to Edinburgh cors,
Upoun thy botingis hobland, hard as horne;

77 cheik-bane bair *cheek-bone bare* blaiknit *pallid* ble *complexion*
78 choip *jaw* choll *jowl* garris *cause* leif chest *live chastely*
79 gane *ugly face* mon de *must die*
80 conjure *constrain by magical incantations*
hungert heland gaist *starved Highland ghost*

81 held *stayed in, frequented* burch *town* borrowit goun *borrowed gown*
82 cap rowsy *(?)uncouth cap* barkit *encrusted* sweit *sweat* 83 laidis *boys*
loun *useless rogue* 84 bickerit *attacked, threw things at*
mony bae and bleit *many a cry of 'baa' and bleat* 85 upaland *in the country*
leivis *live* quheit *wheat* 86 burdclaith *tablecloth* neidis *needs*
87 nowthir *neither* eit *eat* 88 berdles baird *beardless bard*

89 Strait *(?)stingy (?)skinny* Gibbonis air *Gibbon's heir* ourstred *bestrode*
90 Bla *blue (? from cold)* berfute berne *bare-foot fellow* bair *destitute*
91 cors *cross (the Market Cross in the centre of town)* 92 botingis *boots*
hobland *hobbling*

Stra wispis hingis owt quhair that the wattis ar worne.
Cum thow agane to skar us with thy strais,
95 We sall gar scale our sculis all the to scorne,
And stane the up the calsay quhair thow gais.

Off Edinburch the boyis as beis out thrawis
And cryis owt, 'Hay! heir cumis our awin queir clerk!'
Than fleis thow lyk ane howlat chest with crawis,
100 Quhill all the brachattis at thy botingis dois bark.
Than carlingis cryis, 'Keip curches in the merk –
Our gallowis gaipis – lo! quhair ane greceles gais!'
Ane uthir sayis, 'I se him want ane sark –
I reid yow, cummer, tak in your lynning clais!'

105 Than rynis thow doun the gait with gild of boyis,
And all the toun tykis hingand in thy heilis;
Of laidis and lownis thair rysis sic ane noyis
Quhill runsyis rynis away with cairt and quheilis,

93 Stra wispis hingis owt *straw wisps hang out* quhair *where* wattis *welts*
94 Cum thow *if you come* skar *frighten* strais *straws*   95 scale *disperse*
sculis *schools, scholars* the to scorne *to mock you*   96 stane *stone*
calsay *paved street* gais *go*

97 boyis *lads, menials* as beis *like bees* thrawis *throng*   98 heir cumis *here comes*
awin *own* queir (?)*odd* (?)*worthless* clerk *scholar*   99 fleis *fly away*
howlat chest with crawis *owl chased by crows* brachattis *small scent-hounds*
101 carlingis *old women* cryis *cry*
Keip curches in the merk *keep your kerchiefs in the dark (i.e. hidden)*
102 gaipis *gape* greceles gais *ill-favoured wretch*   103 want *lacks* sark *shirt*
104 reid *advise* cummer *gossip* lynning clais *linen clothes*

105 rynis *run* gait *street* gild *clamour*   106 tykis *curs* hingand *hanging*
heilis *heels*   107 laidis *boys* lownis *rogues;*   108 runsyis *horses* cairt *cart*
quheilis *wheels*

And caiger aviris castis bayth coillis and creilis,
110 For rerd of the and rattling of thy butis.
　　Fische-wyvis cryis, 'Fy!' and castis doun skillis and skeilis,
　　Sum claschis the, sum cloddis the on the cutis.

Loun lyk Mahoun, be boun me till obey,
　　Theif, or in greif mischeif sall the betyd!
115 Cry grace, tykis face, or I the chece and fley;
　　Oule, rare and yowle – I sall defowll thy pryd!
　　Peilit gled, baith fed and bred of bichis syd,
And lyk ane tyk, purspyk – quhat man settis by the?
　　Forflittin, countbittin, beschittin, barkit hyd,
120 Clym-ledder, fyle tedder, foule edder: I defy the!

Mauch muttoun, byt buttoun, peilit gluttoun, air to Hilhous,
　　Rank beggar, ostir-dregar, flay-fleggar in the flet,
Chittirlilling, ruch rilling, lik-schilling in the milhous,
　　Baird rehator, theif of nator, fals tratour, feyindis gett,

109 caiger aviris *pedlars' cart-horses* castis *throw down* coillis *coals*
creilis *creels, baskets of wicker*　110 rerd of the *uproar caused by you*
butis *boots*　111 Fische-wyvis *fishwives* skillis *baskets* skeilis *wooden tubs*
112 claschis *strike* cloddis *pelt with clods* cutis *ankles*

113 Mahoun *(Mahomet =) a devil* boun *ready* till *to*　114 Theif *thief*
greif *sorrow* betyd *befall*　115 tykis *cur's* or *before* chece *pursue*
fley *frighten away*　116 Oule *owl* rare and yowle *shriek and yowl*
defowll *trample on*　117 Peilit gled *defeathered kite*
of bichis syd *from the side of a bitch*　118 purspyk *pickpocket*
settis by *esteems*　119 Forflittin *destroyed by flyting* countbittin *(?)impotent*
beschittin *beshitten* barkit hyd *tanned hide*
120 Clym-ledder *(destined to) climb the ladder to the gallows*
fyle tedder *(destined to) make foul the hangman's rope* edder *adder*

121 Mauch muttoun *maggoty mutton* byt buttoun *(?)button-biter*
peilit *destitute*
air to Hilhous *heir to (?John Sandilands of) Hillhouse (near Edinburgh)*
122 ostir-dregar *oyster-dredger* flay fleggar *(?)flea-frightener* flet *hall*
123 Chittirlilling *(?)chitterling, pig's gut* ruch rilling *rough hide shoe*
lik-schilling *licker of husked grain* milhous *mill-house*
124 Baird rehator *knavish bard* of nator *by nature* tratour *traitor*
feyindis gett *fiend's offspring*

125   Filling of tauch, rak-sauch – cry crauch, thow art oursett!
    Muttoun-dryver, girnall-ryver, yadswyvar – fowll fell the!
        Herretyk, lunatyk, purspyk, carlingis pet,
    Rottin crok, dirtin dok – cry cok, or I sall quell the!

125 Filling of tauch *lump of tallow*
rak-sauch *gallows-bird* crauch *'beaten!'* oursett *defeated*
126 Muttoun-dryver *(?)one who drives off the sheep*
girnall-ryver *granary-plunderer* yadswyvar *mare-fucker*
fowll fell the *a foul curse strike you*   127 Herretyk *heretic*
carlingis pet *old woman's fart*   128 Rottin crok *rotten old ewe*
dirtin dok *filthy arse* cry cok *shout 'cock!'; i.e. admit defeat* quell *destroy*

WE THAT AR HEIR IN
HEVYNNIS GLORIE

We that ar heir in hevynnis glorie
To you that ar in Purgatorie
Commendis us on hartlie wys –
I mene we folk of Paradys,
In Edinburgh with all merynes,   5
To yow at Striveling in distres
Quhair nowdir plesour nor delyt is,
For pietie this epistell wrytis.
O ye heremytis and ankir-sadillis,
That takkis your pennance at your tabillis   10
And eitis no meit restorative
Nor drinkis no wyne confortative
Nor aill, bot that is thin and small,
With few coursis in your hall,
But cumpany of lordis and knychtis   15
Or ony uther gudlie wychtis,
Solitar walking your alone,
Seing no thing bot stok and stone;
Out of your panefull Purgatorie
To bring yow to the blys and glorie   20
Off Edinburcht, the myrrie town,
We sall begin ane cairfull sown,

1 heir *here* hevynnis *heaven's* 3 *send greetings in heartfelt manner*
4 mene *mean* 6 Striveling *Stirling* 7 Quhair *where* nowdir *neither*
plesour *pleasure* delyt *delight* 8 pietie *pity, compassion* wrytis *write*
9 heremytis *hermits* ankir-sadillis *anchorites* 10 takkis *take, receive*
tabillis *tables* 11 eitis *eat* meit restorative *food to revive your spirits*
12 confortative *comforting* 13 *nor ale, except that which is weak*
15 But *without* knychtis *knights* 16 *or any other goodly people*
17 Solitar *solitarily* your alone *on your own* 18 Seing *seeing* stok *stump*
20 blys *joy* 21 Off *of* myrrie *merry, cheerful* 22 sall *shall*
cairfull sown *sorrowful melody*

Ane dirige devoit and meik,
The lord of blys doing beseik
25   Yow to delyver out of your noy
And bring yow sone to Edinburgh joy,
For to be merye amangis us:
The dirige begynnis thus:

Lectio prima

The fader, the sone, the holie gaist,
30   The blissit Marie, virgen chaist,
Off angellis all the ordour nyne,
And all the hevinlie court divyne,
Sone bring yow fra the pyne and wo
Of Striveling, everie courtmans foo,
35   Agane to Edinburchtis joy and blys,
Quhair wirschip, welthe and weilfair is,
Play, plesance eik and honestie.
Say ye amen, for chirritie.
Tu autem Domine.

---

23 dirige *dirige (part of the Office for the Dead, see n.)*
devoit and meik *devout and humble*   **24** doing beseik *beseeching*
25 noy *distress*   **26** sone *quickly*

First Reading
29 fader *father* sone *son* gaist *spirit*   **30** blissit *blessed* virgen chaist *virgin chaste*
31 angellis *angels* ordour *orders*   **33** pyne *torment, suffering*
34 courtmans foo *courtier's foe*   **35** Agane *back*   **36** wirschip *honour*
weilfair *good cheer*   **37** *entertainment, delight also, and goodness*
38 chirritie *charity*   **39** *Do thou, O Lord [have mercy upon us]*

Responsio

40   Tak consolatioun in your payne,
In tribulatioun tak consolatioun,
Out of vexatioun cum hame agayne,
Tak consolatioun in your payne.
Iube Domine.

45   Out of distres of Stirling town
To Edinburgh blys God mak yow bown.

Lectio secunda

Patriarchis, prophetis, apostillis deir,
Confessouris, virgynis and martyris cleir,
And all the saitt celestiall,
50   Devoitlie we upone thame call
That sone out of your paynis fell
Ye may in hevin heir with us dwell,
To eit swan, cran, peirtrik and plever,
And everie fische that swowmis in rever,

Response
40 Tak *take, receive*

43 hame *home*
44 *Give blessing, O Lord [May the eternal Father bless us with perpetual benediction]*   **46** bown *ready to go*

Second Reading
47 deir *beloved*
48 Confessouris *confessors (those who suffered for their faith but were not martyred)*   cleir *bright, glorious*   **49** saitt *assembly*
50 Devoitlie *devoutly*   thame *them*   **51** fell *cruel*   **53** eit *eat*
cran, peirtrik and plever *crane, partridge and plover*   **54** swowmis *swims*
rever *river*

55   To drink withe us the new fresche wyne
      That grew apone the revar of Ryne,
      Fresche fragrant claretis out of France,
      Of Angeo and of Orliance,
      With mony ane cours of grit daynté.
60   Say ye amen, for chirrité.
      Tu autem Domine.

      Responsio

      God and sanct Geill heir yow convoy,
      Baythe sone and weill, God and sanct Geill,
      To sonce and seill, solace and joy,
65   God and sanct Geill heir yow convoy.
      Iube Domine.
      Out of Stirling paynis fell
      In Edinburgh joy sone mot ye dwell.

      Lectio tertia

      We pray to all the sanctis in hevin,
70   That ar abuif the sternis sevin,
      Yow to delyver out of your pennance
      That ye may sone play, sing and dance
      And into Edinburgh mak gud cheir,
      Quhair welthe and weilfair is but weir.
75   And I that dois your paynis discryve
      Thinkis for to visie yow belyve –

56 apone *upon* revar *river-bank* Ryne *Rhine*   58 Angeo *Anjou*
Orliance *Orléans*   59 grit daynté *great delicacy*

62 sanct Geill *St Giles (patron saint of Edinburgh's parish church)*
convoy *conduct*   63 Baythe *both* weill *well*   64 sonce *abundance*
seill *good fortune, prosperity*   68 mot *may*

69 sanctis *saints*   70 abuif *above* sternis sevin *seven stars, planets*
73 into *in* gud cheir *good cheer*   74 but weir *without doubt, most certainly*
75 dois *do* discryve *describe*   76 Thinkis for *intend* visie *visit* belyve *soon*

Nocht in desert with yow to dwell,
Bot as the angell Gabriell
Dois go betweyne fra hevynis glorie
80   To thame that ar in purgatorie,
And in thair tribulatioun
To gif thame consolatioun
And schaw thame quhone thair pane is past
They sall to hevin cum at the last,
85   And how nane servis to have sweitnes
That never taistit bittirnes –
And thairfoir how sould ye considdir
Of Edinburgh blys quhone ye cum hiddir,
Bot gif ye taistit had befoir
90   Off Stirling toun the paynis soir?
And thairfoir tak in patience
Your pennance and your abstinence,
And ye sall cum, or Yule begyn,
Into the blys that we are in,
95   Quhilk grant the glorious Trinité!
Say ye amen, for chirritie.
Tu autem Domine.

Responsio

Cum hame and dwell no mair in Stirling,
Fra hyddows hell cum hame and dwell,
100   Quhair fische to sell is nane bot spyrling,
Cum hame and dwell na mair in Stirling.
Iube Domine.

---

79 fra *from*   82 gif *give*   83 schaw *show* quhone *when*
85 nane servis *no one deserves* sweitnes *sweetness*   86 taistit *tasted*
87 sould ye considdir *you should consider*   88 hiddir *hither*   89 Bot gif *unless*
90 soir *sore, grievous*   93 or *before*   95 Quhilk *which*

98 mair *more*   99 hyddows *hideous*   100 spyrling *smelt (a small fish)*

     Et ne nos inducas in tentationem de Stirling,
     Sed libera nos a malo eiusdem,
105 *Requiem Edinburgi dona eis Domine,*
     Et lux ipsius luceat eis.
     A porta tristitiae de Stirling
     Erue, Domine, animas et corpora eorum.
     Credo gustare vinum Edinburgi
110 *In villa viventium.*
     Requiescant statim in Edinburgo. Amen.
     Domine exaudi orationem meam
     Et clamor meus ad te veniat.
     Oremus.
115 *Deus qui justos et corde humiles ex eorum tribulatione*
     liberare dignatus es, libera famulos tuos apud villam
     de Stirling versantes a penis et tristitiis eiusdem, et ad
     Edinburgi gaudia feliciter perducas. Amen.

103ff. *And lead us not into the temptation of Stirling, but deliver us from its evil. The peace of Edinburgh grant unto them, O Lord, and let its light shine upon them. From Stirling's gate of sorrow bring forth, O Lord, their souls and their bodies. I believe that I shall taste the wine of Edinburgh in the town of the living. May they soon rest in Edinburgh. Amen.*
Lord, hear my prayer, and let my cry come unto thee.
Let us pray.
God, who has deigned to free the just and the humble in heart from their tribulation, free your servants dwelling in the town of Stirling from its torments and miseries, and lead them in happiness to the joys of Edinburgh. Amen.

NOW LYTHIS OFF ANE
GENTILL KNYCHT

Now lythis off ane gentill knycht,
Schir Thomas Norny, wys and wycht
   And full off chevelry,
Quhais father was ane giand keyne –
His mother was ane farie queyne,
   Gottin be sossery.

Ane fairar knycht nor he was ane
On ground may nothair ryd nor gane
   Na beire buklar nor brand;
Or com he in this court, but dreid,
He did full mony valyeant deid
   In Rois and Murray land.

Full mony catherein hes he chaist
And cummerid mony helland gaist
   Amang thay dully glennis;
Off the glen Quhettane twenti scoir
He drave as oxin him befoir –
   This deid thocht na man kennis.

5

10

15

---

1 *now hear of a gentle knight* 2 Schir *Sir* wys and wycht *wise and valiant*
3 chevelry *knightly qualities* 4 Quhais *whose* giand keyne *fierce giant*
5 farie queyne *fairy queen* 6 Gottin be sossery *begotten by sorcery*

7 fairar *fairer* nor he was ane *than he was* 8 *on earth may neither ride or walk*
9 *nor bear buckler or sword* 10 Or com he *before he came*
but dreid *without doubt* 11 full mony valyeant deid *many valiant deeds*
12 Rois and Murray *Ross and Moray (both in the north of Scotland)*

13 catherein *cateran, Highland robber* hes he chaist *has he pursued*
14 cummerid *harassed* helland gaist *Highland ghost*
15 *among those gloomy glens* 16 glen Quhettane *clan Chattan* scoir *score*
17 drave as oxin *drove like oxen* 18 *although no one knows about this deed*

At feastis and brydallis upaland
20 He wan the gré and the garland –
 Dansit non so on deis.
He hes att werslingis bein ane hunder,
Yet lay his body never at under –
 He knawis giff this be leis.

25 Was never wyld Robein under bewch
Nor yet Roger off Clekniskleuch
 So bauld a berne as he;
Gy off Gysburne, na Allan Bell,
Na Simonis sonnes off Quhynfell
30 At schot war never so slie.

This anterous knycht quharever he went
At justing and at tornament
 Evermor he wan the gré;
Was never off halff so gryt renowne
35 Sir Bevis the knycht off Southe Hamptowne –
 I schrew him giff I le.

---

19 festis *feasts*   brydallis upaland *weddings in the country*   **20** wan *won*   gré *prize*
21 *no one danced like he did on the dais (raised platform at the end of the hall)*
22 *he has been at a hundred wrestling matches*
23 under *underneath (his opponent's)*   **24** knawis giff *knows if*   leis *lies*

25 wyld Robein *wild Robin (on this and the following names, see n.)*
bewch *bough (i.e. in the greenwood)*   **27** bauld *bold*   berne *man*   **28** na *nor*
29 Simonis sonnes off Quhynfell *sons of Simon of Whinfell*   **30** schot *archery*
war *were*   slie *skilled*

31 anterous *adventurous*   quharever *wherever*   **32** justing *jousting*
34 gryt *great*   **36** schrew *curse*   giff I le *if I lie*

Thairfoir Quenetyne was bot a lurdane
That callit him ane full plum jurdane,
     This wyse and worthie knycht;
40 He callit him fowlar than a full,
He said he was ane licherus bull
     That croynd baith day and nycht.

He wald heff maid him Curris kneff;
I pray God better his honour saiff
45   Na to be lychtleit sua:
Yet this farfurth I dar him prais –
He fyld never sadell in his dais,
     And Curry befyld tua.

Quhairfoir ever at Pesche and Yull
50 I cry him lord off everé full
     That in this regeone duellis
And verralie that war gryt rycht
For, off ane hy renowned knycht,
     He wanttis no thing bot bellis.

---

37 *therefore Quintin was but a rogue*   **38** callit *called*
ane full plum jurdane *a (?)full (?)foul (?)foolish plump chamber-pot*
40 fowlar *fouler* full *fool*   **41** licherus *lecherous*   **42** croynd *bellowed*
nycht *night*

43 *he would have made him Curry's servant*   **44** saiff *preserve*   **45** Na *than*
lychtleit sua *insulted so*   **46** Yet this farfurth *to this extent* dar *dare*
47 fyld *fouled* sadell *saddle* dais *days*   **48** befyld tua *befouled two*

49 Quhairfoir *wherefore* Pesche *Easter* Yull *Yule, Christmas*
50 cry *proclaim* everé full *every fool*   **51** regeone *land*
52 *and truly that would be very right and proper*
53 hy *great*   **54** wanttis *lacks* bellis *bells (of a fool)*

AS YUNG AWRORA WITH
CRISTALL HAILE

The Abbot of Tungland

As yung Awrora with cristall haile
In orient schew hir visage paile,
A swevyng swyth did me assaile
    Off sonis of Sathanis seid.
5 Me thocht a Turk of Tartary
Come throw the boundis of Barbary
And lay forloppin in Lumbardy
    Full lang in waithman weid.

Fra baptasing for till eschew,
10 Thair a religious man he slew,
And cled him in his abeit new,
    For he cowth wryte and reid.
Quhen kend was his dissimulance
And all his cursit govirnance,
15 For feir he fled and come in France
    With littill of Lumbard leid.

1 Awrora *Aurora (goddess of the dawn)* haile *(?)hail (?)dewdrops*
2 orient *east* schew *showed* 3 swevyng *dream* swyth *quickly*
4 sonis *sons* Sathanis seid *Satan's progeny* 5 Me thocht *it seemed to me*
Tartary *land of the Tartars/Tartarus, hell* 6 Come *came* boundis *boundaries*
Barbary *heathendom* 7 lay forloppin *remained (as a) runaway*
Lumbardy *Lombardy* 8 waithman weid *outlaw's dress*

9 *to avoid baptism* 10 religious *in a religious order* 11 cled him *clad himself*
abeit *habit, robe* 12 cowth *knew how to* reid *read* 13 Quhen *when*
kend *known* dissimulance *deceit* 14 govirnance *conduct* 15 feir *fear*
16 leid *language*

To be a leiche he fenyt him thair,
Quhilk mony a man micht rew evirmair,
For he left nowthir seik nor sair
20   Unslane, or he hyne yeid.
Vane organis he full clenely carvit;
Quhen of his straik so mony starvit,
Dreid he had gottin that he desarvit,
    He fled away gud speid.

25   In Scotland than the narrest way
He come his cunnyng till assay;
To sum man thair it was no play,
    The preving of his sciens.
In pottingry he wrocht grit pyne;
30   He murdreist mony into medecyne.
The Jow was of a grit engyne,
    And generit was of gyans.

In leichecraft he was homecyd;
He wald haif for a nicht to byd
35   A haiknay and the hurt manis hyd,
    So meikle he was of myance.

17 leiche *doctor* fenyt him *pretended*   18 Quhilk *which* rew *regret*
evirmair *evermore*   19 nowthir seik nor sair *neither sick nor sufferers*
20 Unslane *(unslain i.e.) alive* or he hyne yeid *before he went hence*
21 Vane organis *jugular veins* clenely *elegantly, cleanly* carvit *cut through*
22 straik *stroke* starvit *died*   23 *afraid that he would have got what he deserved*
24 gud speid *at top speed*

25 narrest *shortest*   26 his cunnyng till assay *to try out his skill*   27 play *fun*
28 preving *demonstration* sciens *knowledge*
29 pottingry *the apothecary's craft* wrocht grit pyne *caused great suffering*
30 *he murdered many through his remedies*   31 Jow *infidel*
grit engyne *great ingenuity*   32 generit *engendered* gyans *giants*

33 leichecraft *medicine* homecyd *a killer*
34 *he would receive for one night's stay*
35 *a riding horse and the sick man's skin*   36 meikle *great*
myance *means, resources*

His yrnis was rude as ony rawchtir,
Quhair he leit blude it was no lawchtir;
Full mony instrument for slawchtir
40   Was in his gardevyance.

He cowth gif cure for laxatyve
To gar a wicht hors want his lyve;
Quhaevir assay wald, man or wyve,
    Thair hippis yeid hiddy giddy.
45   His practikis nevir war put to prief,
Bot suddane deid or grit mischeif;
He had purgatioun to mak a thief
    To dee withowt a widdy.

Unto no mes pressit this prelat
50   For sound of sacring bell nor skellat;
As blaksmyth bruikit was his pallatt
    For battering at the study.

37 yrnis *surgical instruments* rude *rough* rawchtir *rafter*
38 Quhair he leit blude *where he let blood* no lawchtir *no laughing matter*
39 slawchtir *slaughter*   40 gardevyance *trunk, chest*

41 *he could give a cure for diarrhoea*   42 *to make a strong horse lose his life*
43 Quhaevir assay wald *whoever would try it* wyve *woman*
44 yeid hiddy giddy *went into a giddy whirl*
45 practikis *practices, techniques* preif *test*
46 *without sudden death or great harm*   47 purgatioun *purgatives*
48 dee *die* widdy *hangman's noose*

49 mes *Mass* pressit *hastened* prelat *ecclesiastic*
50 sacring bell *consecration bell* skellat *hand-bell*
51 bruikit *blackened, streaked with smoke (from an alchemical furnace)*
pallatt *head*   52 study *anvil*

Thocht he come hame a new maid channoun,
He had dispensit with matynnis channoun;
55   On him come nowther stole nor fannoun
For smowking of the smydy.

Me thocht seir fassonis he assailyeit
To make the quintessance, and failyeit;
And quhen he saw that nocht availyeit
60   A fedrem on he tuke,
And schupe in Turky for to fle;
And quhen that he did mont on he
All fowlis ferleit quhat he sowld be
That evir did on him luke.

65   Sum held he had bene Dedalus,
Sum the Menatair marvelus,
Sum Martis blaksmyth Vulcanus,
And sum Saturnus kuke;

53 *though he came home a newly made canon*
54 matynnis *Matins, morning service* channoun *prescribed by canon law*
55 nowther stole nor fannoun *neither stole nor maniple (liturgical vestments: a strip of cloth worn over the shoulders and a band attached to the wrist)*
56 smowking *smoking* smydy *smithy*

57 seir fassonis he assailyeit *(by) various methods he tried*
58 quintessance *quintessence, the 'fifth essence' (the substance of the heavenly bodies latent in all things and discoverable by alchemy)* failyeit *failed*
59 nocht availyeit *was of no avail*   60 *he put on a coat of feathers*
61 schupe *prepared* fle *fly*   62 mont on he *mount high*
63 *all birds marvelled what he might be*   64 evir *ever, always* luke *look*

65 Sum *some* bene Dedalus *been Daedalus (see n.)*
66 Menatair *Minotaur (a monster, half-bull, half-man)*
67 Martis blaksmyth *blacksmith of Mars (god of war)*
Vulcanus *Vulcan (fire-god and divine smith)*
68 Saturnus kuke *cook of Saturn (see n.)*

And evir the tuschettis at him tuggit,
70   The rukis him rent, the ravynis him druggit,
The hudit crawis his hair furth ruggit:
   The hevin he micht not bruke.

The myttane and Sanct Martynis fowle
Wend he had bene the hornit howle;
75   Thay set aupone him with a yowle,
   And gaif him dynt for dynt.
The golk, the gormaw, and the gled
Beft him with buffettis quhill he bled;
The sparhalk to the spring him sped,
80   Als fers as fyre of flynt.

The tarsall gaif him tug for tug,
A stanchell hang in ilka lug,
The pyot furth his pennis did rug,
   The stork straik ay but stynt;
85   The bissart, bissy but rebuik,
Scho was so cleverus of hir cluik
His bawis he micht not langar bruik,
   Scho held thame at ane hint.

---

69 tuschettis *lapwings* tuggit *pulled*   70 *the rooks tore him, the ravens dragged him*
71 hudit crawis *hooded crows* furth ruggit *pulled out*   72 bruke *enjoy (the use of)*

73 myttane *an unidentified bird of prey*
Sanct Martynis fowle *(?)a hen-harrier, (?)some diving bird*
74 Wend *believed* hornit howle *horned owl*   75 aupone *upon* yowle *screech*
76 gaif *gave* dynt *blow*   77 golk *cuckoo* gormaw *cormorant* gled *kite*
78 Beft *struck* quhill *until*   79 *the sparrowhawk hastened to attack*
80 fers as fyre of flynt *fierce as fire (which springs) from flint*

81 tarsall *male hawk*   82 *a kestrel hung on each ear*
83 *the magpie pulled out his feathers*
84 straik ay but stynt *struck continuously without pausing*
85 *the buzzard, busy without any check*
86 Scho *she* cleverus *(?)firmly gripping* cluik *claws*
87 *his testicles he could no longer use*
88 thame at ane hint *them in one grasp*

Thik was the clud of kayis and crawis,
90   Of marleyonis, mittanis, and of mawis,
That bikkrit at his berd with blawis,
    In battell him abowt.
Thay nybbillit him with noyis and cry;
The rerd of thame rais to the sky,
95   And evir he cryit on Fortoun, 'Fy!'
    His lyfe was into dowt.

The ja him skrippit with a skryke
And skornit him, as it was lyk;
The egill strong at him did stryke
100   And rawcht him mony a rowt.
For feir uncunnandly he cawkit,
Quhill all his pennis war drownd and drawkit:
He maid a hundreth nolt all hawkit
    Beneth him with a spowt.

105   He schewre his feddreme that was schene,
And slippit owt of it full clene,
And in a myre up to the ene
    Amang the glar did glyd.

89 clud *cloud* kayis *jackdaws* crawis *crows*
90 marleyonis *merlins (small falcons)* mittanis *birds of prey* mawis *gulls*
91 bikkrit *attacked* berd *beard* blawis *blows*   92 him abowt *around him*
93 nybbillit *nipped* noyis *noise*   94 rerd *uproar* rais *rose*   95 Fortoun *Fortune*
96 into dowt *in doubt, at risk*

97 ja *jay* skrippit *mocked* skryke *screech*   98 skornit *derided*
as it was lyk *as it seemed*   99 egill *eagle*   100 rawcht *gave* rowt *heavy blow*
101 feir *fear* uncunnandly *(?)unwittingly (?)without control* cawkit *defecated*
102 pennis *feathers* drawkit *drenched*
103 hundreth nolt all hawkit *hundred cattle streaked*
104 spowt *one violent discharge*

105 schewre *tore* feddreme *feather cloak* schene *fine, beautiful*
106 slippit *slipped* full clene *completely*   107 myre *mire, bog* ene *eyes*
108 glar *slime, mud* glyd *glide*

The fowlis all at the fedrem dang,
110   As at a monster thame amang,
       Quhill all the pennis of it owtsprang
            Intill the air full wyde,

       And he lay at the plunge evirmair,
       Sa lang as any ravin did rair;
115   The crawis him socht with cryis of cair
            In every schaw besyde;
       Had he reveild bene to the ruikis,
       Thay had him revin all with thair cluikis.
       Thre dayis in dub amang the dukis
120   He did with dirt him hyde.

       The air was dirkit with the fowlis
       That come with yawmeris and with yowlis,
       With skryking, skrymming, and with scowlis
            To tak him in the tyde.
125   I walknit with the noyis and schowte,
       So hiddowis beir was me abowte.
       Sensyne I curs that cankerit rowte
            Quhairevir I go or ryde.

109 fowlis *birds* dang *struck*   110 thame amang *among them*
111 owtsprang *sprang out*   112 Intill *into* full wyde *far and wide*

113 at the plunge *(?)in the pool into which he had dived* evirmair *continually*
114 Sa lang as *as long as* rair *cry out*   115 crawis *crows*
socht *searched for* cair *sorrow, foreboding*   116 schaw *(small) wood*
besyde *nearby*   117 *if he had been revealed to the rooks*
118 *they would have torn him apart with their claws*   119 dayis *days*
dub *stagnant pool* dukis *ducks*

121 dirkit *darkened*   122 yawmeris *screeches* yowlis *howls*
123 skryking *shrieking* skrymming *darting* scowlis *fierce looks*
124 tak *take, catch* in the tyde *at the time*
125 walknit *woke up* schowte *clamour*   126 hiddowis beir *hideous din*
127 Sensyne *since then* cankerit rowte *evil mob*
128 Quhairevir *wherever* go *walk*

THIS HYNDIR NYCHT IN DUMFERMLING

This hyndir nycht in Dumfermling
To me wes tauld ane wondrous thing:
That lait ane tod wes with ane lam,
And with hir plaid and maid grit gam,
5   Syn till his breist did hir imbrace,
And wald have ridin hir lyke ane ram,
And that me thocht a ferlie cace.

He brasit hir bony bodie sweit,
And halsit hir with his forder feit,
10   Syne schuke his tale with quhynge and yelp,
And todillit with hir lyke a quhelp;
Syne lowrit on growfe and askit grace,
And ay the lam cryit, 'Ladie, help!'
And that me thocht a ferlie cace.

15   The tod wes nothir leyne nor skowrie,
Bot wes ane lustie rid-harit lowrie,
Ane lang-tailyt beist, and grit withall.
The syllie lam wes all to small

---

1 *The other night in Dunfermline* 2 tauld *told* 3 lait *lately* tod *fox* lam *lamb*
4 plaid *played* maid grit gam *made great sport* 5 till *then to* breist *breast*
imbrace *embrace* 6 wald *would* ridin *ridden*
7 *and that seemed to me a marvellous event*

8 brasit *embraced* bony *pretty* sweit *sweet* 9 halsit *clasped*
forder feit *front feet* 10 schuke *shook* tale *tail* quhynge *whine*
11 todillit *played amorously* quhelp *whelp*
12 lowrit on growfe *crouched flat on the ground* 13 ay *ever, always*

15 nothir leyne nor skowrie *neither thin nor scruffy* 16 rid-harit *red-haired*
lowrie *fox* 17 lang-tailyt beist *long-tailed beast* grit withall *big as well*
18 syllie *helpless*

To sic ane trybill to hald ane bace;
20   Scho fled him not – fair mot him fall –
And that me thocht ane ferlie cace.

The tod wes reyd, the lam wes quhyt,
Scho wes ane morsall of delyte.
He luiffit na yowis, auld, tewcht and sklendir:
25   Becaus this lam wes young and tendir,
He ran apone hir with a race,
And scho preissit neir for to defend hir,
And that me thocht a ferlye cace.

He grippit hir aboute the waist
30   And handlit hir as he had haist.
This innocent that never trespast
Tuke hert that scho wes handlit fast
And leit him kys hir lustie face.
His gyrnand gammys hir not agast,
35   And that me thocht a ferlie cace.

He held hir to him be the hals
And spak rycht fair thocht he wes fals,
Syne said (and swoir to hir be God)
That he sould not twyche hir preyne-cod.

19 *to such a treble/upper position to hold a bass/lower position*   20 Scho *she*
fair mot him fall *may he prosper*

22 reyd *red* quhyt *white*   23 morsall of delyte *morsel of delight*
24 *he loved no ewes, old, tough and thin*   26 race *rush*
27 preissit neir *pressed near*

30 handlit *handled* as he had haist *as if he was in a hurry*   31 trespast *did wrong*
32 Tuke hert *took heart* fast *firmly*   33 leit *let* kys *kiss* lustie *pretty*
34 *his snarling jaws did not frighten her*

36 hals *neck*   37 spak rycht fair *spoke most sweetly* thocht *though*   38 swoir *swore*
39 sould *should* twyche *touch* preyne-cod *(pin-cushion =) genitals*

40   The sillie thing trowit him allace.
     The lam gaif credence to the tod,
     And that me thocht a ferlie cace.

     I will na lesing putt in vers,
     Lyke as thir janglaris dois rehers,
45   Bot be quhat maner thai wer mard.
     Quhone licht wes out and durris wes bard,
     I wait not, gif he gaif hir grace,
     Bot all the holis wes stoppit hard,
     And that me thocht a ferlie cace.

50   Quhone men dois fleit in joy maist fer,
     Sone cumis wo or thai be wer.
     Quhone carpand wer thir two moist crows
     The wowlfe he umbeset the hous,
     Upone the tod to mak a chace –
55   The lam than chepit lyk a mows
     And this me thocht a ferlie cace.

     Throw hiddows yowling of the wowfe
     This wylie tod plat doun a-growfe,
     And in the sillie lammes skyn
60   He crap als far as he mycht wyn

40 trowit *believed* allace *alas*   41 gaif *gave*

43 na lesing *no lie, falsehood*   44 janglaris *chatterers, story-tellers*
rehers *tell their tales*   45 be quhat maner *in what way*
mard *(?)hindered, (?)compromised*   46 Quhone *when* licht *light*
durris wes bard *doors were barred*   47 wait *know* gif *if*   48 holis *holes*
stoppit *closed up*

50 fleit *float, swim* maist fer *most extremely*   51 Sone cumis *soon comes*
or *before* wer *aware*   52 carpand *talking* moist crows *very vivaciously*
53 wowlfe *wolf* umbeset *beset, attacked*   54 mak a chace *pursue, hunt*
55 chepit *squeaked* mows *mouse*

57 hiddows yowling *hideous howling*   58 wylie *wily*
plat doun a-growfe *fell down flat*   60 crap *crept* mycht wyn *could manage*

And hid him thair a weill lang space.
The yowis besyd thai maid na dyn,
And that me thocht a ferlie cace.

Quhone of the tod wes herd no peip,
65 The wolfe went all had bene on sleip,
And quhill the tod had strikin ten
The wowlfe hes drest him to his den,
Protestand for the secund place.
And this repoirt I with my pen,
70 How at Dumfermling fell the cace.

61 a weill lang space *a very long time*   62 yowis besyd *ewes nearby* dyn *noise*
64 herd *heard* peip *squeak*   65 went *thought* on sleip *asleep*
66 quhill *by the time that* strikin *struck, copulated with*
67 drest him *made his way*   68 Protestand *making a claim*   70 fell *befell*

IN SECREIT PLACE THIS HYNDIR NYCHT

In secreit place this hyndir nycht
I hard ane beyrne say till ane bricht:
'My huny, my hart, my hoip, my heill,
I have bene lang your luifar leill
5   And can of yow get confort nane;
How lang will ye with danger deill?
Ye brek my hart, my bony ane.'

His bony beird wes kemmit and croppit,
Bot all with cale it was bedroppit,
10   And he wes townysche, peirt and gukit.
He clappit fast, he kist and chukkit,
As with the glaikis he wer ovirgane.
Yit be his feirris he wald have fukkit –
'Ye brek my hart, my bony ane.'

15   Quod he, 'My hairt, sweit as the hunye,
Sen that I borne wes of my mynnye,
I never wowit weycht bot yow.
My wambe is of your luif sa fow

---

1 hyndir *other* **2** hard *heard* beyrne *man* till ane bricht *to a fair lady*
3 huny *honey* hart *heart* hoip *hope* heill *healing, the source of my health*
4 lang *long* luifar leill *faithful lover* **5** confort nane *no consolation*
6 with danger deill *behave with disdain* **7** brek *break* bony *bonny, lovely* ane *one*

8 beird *beard* kemmit *combed* croppit *trimmed*
9 cale *broth made from cabbage* bedroppit *spattered*
10 townysche *'townish', uncourtly* peirt *impudent* gukit *foolish*
11 clappit *(?)patted, (?)embraced* kist *kissed* chukkit *fondled under the chin*
12 As *as if* glaikis *sexual desire, 'hots'* wer ovirgane *were overcome* **13** Yit *yet*
feirris *behaviour* wald *would* fukkit *fucked*

15 Quod *said* hairt *heart, darling* sweit *sweet* hunye *honey* **16** Sen *since*
mynnye *mummy* **17** wowit *wooed* weycht bot *anyone except* **18** wambe *belly*
luif *love* fow *full*

That as ane gaist I glour and grane;
20   I trymble sa, ye will not trow,
Ye brek my hart, my bony ane.'

'Tehe!' quod scho, and gaif ane gawfe:
'Be still, my tuchan and my calfe,
My new spanit howffing fra the sowk,
25   And all the blythnes of my bowk.
My sweit swanking, saif yow allane,
Na leyd I luiffit all this owk –
Full leif is me yowr graceles gane.'

Quod he, 'My claver and my curldodie,
30   My huny-soppis, my sweit possodie,
Be not oure bosteous to your billie;
Be warme-hairtit and not evill-wille.
Your hals, quhyt as quhalis bane,
Garris ryis on loft my quhillelille –
35   Ye brek my hart, my bony ane.'

19 gaist *ghost* glour *stare* grane *groan*   20 trymble sa *tremble so*
trow *believe (it)*

22 Tehe! *teehee!* gaif *gave* gawfe *guffaw*   23 still *quiet*
tuchan *(?)tulchan, a calf-skin filled with straw, used to make a cow give milk*
calfe *calf*   24 spanit *weaned* howffing *(?)clumsy lad* fra *from* sowk *suckling*
25 blythnes *merriness* bowk *body, belly*   26 sweit swanking *smart fellow*
saif *save* allane *alone*   27 Na leyd *no man* luiffit *loved* owk *week*
28 *I really like your ugly face*

29 claver *clover* curldodie *curly-head (name of plant: ribwort plantain or wild
scabious)*   30 huny-soppis *honey-sops (soaked bread)*
possodie *(?)a drink of hot milk with ale or wine (?)broth*
31 oure bosteous *too boisterous* billie *friend*   32 evill-wille *ill-disposed*
33 *your neck, white as whale's bone*   34 Garris *makes* ryis on loft *rise aloft*
quhillelille *willy, penis*

Quod scho, 'My clype, my unspaynit gyane,
With moderis mylk yit in your mychane,
My belly huddrun, my swete hurle bawsy,
My huny-gukkis, my slawsy gawsy,
40   Your musing waild perse ane harte of stane;
Tak gud confort, my grit-heidit slawsy –
Full leif is me your graceles gane.'

Quod he: 'My kid, my capirculyoun,
My bony baib with the ruch brylyoun,
45   My tendir gyrle, my wallie gowdye,
My tyrlie-myrlie, my crowdie-mowdie,
Quhone that oure mouthis dois meit at ane,
My stang dois storkyn with your towdie.
Ye brek my hairt, my bony ane.'

50   Quod scho: 'Now tak me by the hand,
Welcum, my golk of Marie land,
My chirrie and my maikles munyoun,
My sowklar, sweit as ony unyoun,

36 clype *big fellow* unspaynit gyane *unweaned giant*
37 moderis *mother's* yit *still* mychane *(?)belly*
38 belly huddrun *(?)big-bellied, (?)lovely heifer*
hurle bawsy *[obscure; (?)some term of abuse used affectionately]*
39 huny-gukkis *(= honey-fool) sweet idiot* slawsy gawsy *[obscure]*
40 musing *complaint* waild perse *would pierce* stane *stone*   41 Tak *take*
gud *good* grit-heidit *big-headed*

43 kid *kid, young goat* capirculyoun *(?)capercaillie, wood-grouse*
44 baib *baby* ruch *rough, hairy* brylyoun *[obscure, see n.]*
45 tendir gyrle *(?)little girl* wallie *handsome* gowdye *(?)goldfinch, (?)goldentop*
46 tyrlie-myrlie *(?)whirligig* crowdie-mowdie *(?)a gruel of milk and meal (as
term of affection)*
47 Quhone *when* mouthis dois meit at ane *mouths meet together*
48 stang *((?)sting, (?)pole =), prick, penis* storkyn *stiffen*
towdie *(?)buttocks, cunt*

51 Welcum *welcome* golk of Marie land *cuckoo of fairyland*   52 chirrie *cherry*
maikles munyoun *matchless darling*   53 sowklar *suckling (animal)*
unyoun *onion*

My strumill stirk, yit new to spane.
55   I am applyit to your opunyoun,
I luif rycht weill your graceles gane.'

He gaiff to hir ane apill rubye.
Quod scho, 'Gramercye, my sweit cowhubye!'
And thai tway to ane play began,
60   Quhilk men dois call the derydan,
Quhill that thair myrthis met baythe in ane.
'Wo is me,' quod scho, 'Quhair will ye, man?
Best now I luif that graceles gane.'

54 strumill stirk *(?)stumbling (?)ungainly bullock* spane *wean*
55 applyit *inclined* opunyoun *proposal*

57 apill rubye *ruby apple*   58 Gramercye *thank you* cowhubye *(?)booby*
59 thai tway *they two* play *sport*   60 Quhilk *which*
derydan *(?)perhaps name of a dance (i.e. copulation)*
61 *until both their pleasures united*   62 Quhair *where* man *lover*

APON THE MIDSUMMER EVIN,
MIRRIEST OF NICHTIS

The Tretis of the Twa Mariit Wemen and the Wedo

Apon the midsummer evin, mirriest of nichtis,
I muvit furth till ane meid as midnicht wes past,
Besyd ane gudlie grein garth, full of gay flouris,
Hegeit of ane huge hicht with hawthorne treis,

5   Quhairon ane bird on ane bransche so birst out hir notis
That never ane blythfullar bird was on the beuche hard.
Quhat throw the sugarat sound of hir sang glaid
And throw the savour sanative of the sueit flouris,
I drew in derne to the dyk to dirkin efter mirthis.

10   The dew donkit the daill, and dynnit the feulis.
I hard, under ane holyn hevinlie grein hewit,
Ane hie speiche at my hand with hautand wourdis.

---

1 Apon *upon* evin *eve* mirriest of nichtis *merriest of nights*
2 muvit furth till ane meid *walked out to a meadow* midnicht *midnight*
3 Besyd *beside* gudlie grein garth *lovely green (enclosed) garden*
gay flouris *beautiful flowers*   4 Hegeit of ane huge hicht *hedged to a great height*
treis *trees*   5 Quhairon *on which* bransche *branch* birst *poured* notis *notes*
6 blythfullar *more joyful* beuche *bough* hard *heard*
7 Quhat throw the sugarat *what with the mellifluous* sang glaid *glad song*
8 throw the savour sanative *health-bringing smell* sueit *sweet*
9 drew in derne *moved secretly* dyk *wall* dirkin *lurk hidden*
efter mirthis *(?)after the revelries*
10 donkit the daill *moistened the valley* dynnit the feulis *birds sang loudly*
11 holyn *holly-tree* hevinlie grein hewit *of hue of heavenly green*
12 hie speiche *loud speech* at my hand *close by me*
hautand wourdis *(?)loudly resounding (?)haughty words*

With that in haist to the hege so hard I inthrang
That I was heildit with hawthorne and with heynd leveis.
15 Throw pykis of the plet thorne I presandlie luikit,
Gif ony persoun wald approche within that plesand garding.

I saw thre gay ladeis sit in ane grein arbeir
All grathit into garlandis of fresche gudlie flouris:
So glitterit as the gold wer thair glorius gilt tressis,
20 Quhill all the gressis did gleme of the glaid hewis.
Kemmit war thair clier hair and curiouslie sched
Attour thair schulderis doun schyre, schyning full bricht,
With curches cassin thairabone of kirsp cleir and thin.
Their mantillis grein war as the gress that grew in May
    sessoun,
25 Fetrit with thair quhyt fingaris about thair fair sydis.
Off ferlifull fyne favour war thair faceis meik,
All full of flurist fairheid as flouris in June –
Quhyt, seimlie and soft as the sweit lillies,
Now upspred upon spray as new spynist rose;
30 Arrayit ryallie about with mony riche vardour,

13 haist *haste* hege *hedge* in thrang *pushed in*
14 That I was heildit *so that I was concealed* heynd leveis *pleasant leaves*
15 pykis *prickles* plet *intertwined* presandlie *presently* luikit *looked*
16 *(to see) if any person would approach that pleasant garden*

17 ladeis *ladies* arbeir *arbour* 18 grathit into *arrayed in*
fresche *beautiful* 19 glitterit *glittering* thair *their* gilt tressis *golden tresses*
20 Quhill *until* gressis *plants* gleme *gleam* hewis *hues*
21 Kemmit *(well-)combed* war *was* clier *glowing*
curiouslie sched *artfully parted* 22 Attour *over* schulderis *shoulders*
doun schyre *(falling) down*, (?)*brightly* (?)*straight*
schyning full bricht *shining brightly*
23 curches cassin thairabone *kerchiefs, head-coverings thrown over it*
kirsp *fine fabric* 24 mantillis *mantles* gress *grass* sessoun *time*
25 Fetrit *fastened* quhyt fingaris *white fingers* sydis *sides*
26 Off ferlifull fyne favour *of wondrously beautiful appearance*
faceis meik *gentle faces* 27 flurist fairheid *blossoming fairness*
28 seimlie *seemly* 29 upspred upon spray *spreading up on their stalk*
as new spynist *like a newly opened*
30 *magnificently adorned on all sides with many a splendid green shoot*

That Nature full nobillie annamalit with flouris
Off alkin hewis under hevin that ony heynd knew,
Fragrant, all full of fresche odour, fynest of smell.
Ane cumlie tabil coverit wes befoir tha cleir ladeis
35 With ryalle cowpis apon rawis full of ryche wynis;
And of thir wlonkes wycht, tua weddit war with lordis,
Ane was ane wedow, iwis, wantoun of laitis.
And as thai talk at the tabill of mony taill sindry
They wauchtit at the wicht wyne and waris out wourdis;
40 And syn thai spak more spedelie and sparit no matiris.

Aude viduam iam cum interrogatione sua

   'Bewrie,' said the wedo, 'ye woddit wemen ying,
Quhat mirth ye fand in maryage sen ye war menis wyffis.
Reveill gif ye rewit that rakles conditioun,
Or gif that ever ye luffit leyd upone lyf mair

---

31 nobillie annamalit *nobly enamelled*

32 alkin hewis under hevin *every kind of colour known on earth*
ony heynd *any gentle person*
34 *a comely table covered was set before those fair ladies*
35 ryalle cowpis apon rawis *noble goblets in rows*
36 And of thir wlonkes wycht, tua weddit war *of these doughty beauties two were wedded*   37 *one was a widow, in truth, merry, wanton in behaviour*
38 taill sindry *various topics*   39 wauchtit at *drank deeply of* wicht *strong*
waris out wourdis *utter words*   40 syn thai spak *then they spoke*
more spedelie *(?)more pointedly, with greater emphasis*
sparit no matiris *spared no subjects*

Hear now the widow, with her question
41 Bewrie *reveal* woddit wemen ying *young wedded women*
42 *what joy you have found in marriage since you were men's wives*
43 Reveill gif *reveal if* rewit *regretted*
rakles conditioun *state imprudent(ly) entered upon)*
44 luffit leyd upone lyf mair *loved living man more*

45   Nor thame that ye your fayth hes festinit for ever,
        Or gif ye think, had ye chois, that ye wald cheis better.
        Think ye it nocht ane blist band that bindis so fast,
        That none undo it a deill may bot the deith ane?'

Responsio prime uxoris ad viduam

        Than spak ane lusty belyf with lustie effeiris:
50   'It that ye call the blist band that bindis so fast
        Is bair of blis and bailfull, and greit barrat wirkis.
        Ye speir, had I fre chois, gif I wald cheis bettir:
        Chenyeis ay ar to eschew, and changeis ar sueit.
        Sic cursit chance till eschew, had I my chois anis,
55   Out of the cheinyeis of ane churle I chaip suld for evir.
        God gif matrimony wer made to mell for ane yeir!
        It war bot merrens to be mair bot gif our myndis pleisit.
        It is agane the law of luf, of kynd, and of nature,
        Togidder hartis to strene that stryveis with uther.
60   Birdis hes ane better law na bernis be meikill,
        That ilk yeir, with new joy, joyis ane maik,
        And fangis thame ane fresche feyr unfulyeit and constant,

45 *Than those to whom you have bound your pledge forever*
46 had ye chois *if you had a choice* cheis *choose*
47 nocht *not* blist band *blessed bond*
48 *so that no one can undo it even a little except death alone*

The answer of the first wife to the widow
49 *Then spoke one merry lady at once in a merry manner*
51 bair of blis *empty of joy* bailfull *wretched*
greit barrat wirkis *causes great strife* 52 speir *ask*
53 *chains always are to be avoided, and changes are sweet*
54 Sic cursit chance *such cursed fortune* anis *for once* 55 churle *churl, boor*
chaip suld *should escape* 56 gif *grant* mell *copulate* ane yeir *one year*
57 merrens *vexation* mair *longer* bot gif *unless* pleisit *were pleased to*
58 agane *against* luf *love* kynd *kind, nature* 59 Togidder *together*
hartis *hearts* strene *force* stryveis with uther *are at strife with each other*
60 Birdis hes *birds have* na bernis be meikill *than men by far*
61 ilk *each* joyis *enjoy* maik *mate*
62 fangis thame *get for themselves* feyr *companion* unfulyeit *untired*

And lattis thair fulyeit feiris flie quhair thai pleis.
Cryst gif sic ane consuetude war in this kith haldin!
65 Than weill war us wemen that evir we war born.
We suld have feiris as fresche to fang quhen us likit,
And gif all larbaris thair leveis quhen thai lak curage.
Myself suld be full semlie in silkis arrayit,
Gymp, jolie, and gent, richt joyus and gent.
70 I suld at fairis be found, new faceis to se,
At playis and at preichingis and pilgrimages greit,
To schaw my renone royaly quhair preis was of folk,
To manifest my makdome to multitude of pepill
And blaw my bewtie on breid quhair bernis war mony,
75 That I micht cheis and be chosin, and change quhen me lykit.
Than suld I waill ane full weill our all the wyd realme
That suld my womanheid weild the lang winter nicht;
And quhen I gottin had ane grome, ganest of uther,
Yaip and ying, in the yok ane yeir for to draw,
80 Fra I had preveit his pith the first plesand moneth,
Than suld I cast me to keik in kirk and in markat,
And all the cuntré about kyngis court and uther,
Quhair I ane galland micht get aganis the nixt yeir
For to perfurneis furth the werk quhen failyeit the tother:

63 lattis *let* fulyeit feiris *tired companions*
flie quhair thai pleis *fly where they please*   64 Cryst gif *Christ grant*
consuetude war in this kith haldin *custom were observed in this country*
65 Than weill war us wemen *then it would be well for us women*
66 suld *should* fang quhen us likit *take when it pleased us*
67 Gif all larbaris thair leveis *dismiss all impotent men* lak curage *lack sexual vigour*
69 Gymp, jolie and gent *dainty, merry and elegant* richt joyus *very joyful*
70 fairis *fairs* se *see* 71 playis *plays* preichingis *sermons* 72 schaw *show*
renone *distinction* preis *crowd* 73 makdome *comeliness* pepill *people*
74 blaw *display* bewtie *beauty* on breid *publicly*
76 waill ane full weill *choose one, (?)very well, (?)of good quality* our *over*
wyd *wide* 77 weild *possess* lang *long* 78 grome *man*
ganest of uther *more suitable than any other* 79 Yaip *active, keen* yok *yoke*
80 Fra *after* preveit *tested* pith *vigour* moneth *month* 81 cast me *apply myself*
keik *look about* kirk *church* markat *market* 82 cuntré *country* uther *other places*
83 galland *fine lover* aganis *in readiness for* nixt *next*
84 perfurneis furth *keep on performing* werk *work*
failyeit the tother *the other weakened*

85   A forky fure, ay furthwart and forsy in draucht,
      Nother febill nor fant, nor fulyeit in labour,
      Bot als fresche of his forme as flouris in May;
      For all the fruit suld I fang, thocht he the flour burgeoun.'

Aude ut dicet de viro suo

         'I have ane wallidrag, ane worme, ane auld wobat carle,
90   A waistit wolroun na worth bot wourdis to clatter,
      Ane bumbart, ane dron-bee, ane bag full of flewme,
      Ane scabbit skarth, ane scorpioun, ane scutarde behind.
      To se him scart his awin skyn grit scunner I think.
      Quhen kissis me that carybald, than kyndillis all my sorow.
95   As birs of ane brym bair his berd is als stif,
      Bot soft and soupill as the silk is his sary lume.
      He may weill to the syn assent, bot sakles is his deidis.
      With goris his tua grym ene ar gladderit all about
      And gorgeit lyk tua gutaris that war with glar stoppit;

---

85 forky fure *(?)lusty fellow* ay furthwart *to the fore*
forsy in draucht *strong at drawing (the plough)*
86 Nother febill nor fant *neither weak nor faint* fulyeit *worn out*   87 als *as*
forme *body*   88 fang *get* thocht *though* flour *flower* burgeoun *cause to bud*

Hear how she speaks about her husband
89 wallidrag *worthless fellow* auld *old* wobat *hairy caterpillar* carle *churl*
90 waistit *exhausted* wolroun *(?)wretched creature*
na worth bot *no good except* clatter *chatter*   91 bumbart *lazy fellow*
dron-bee *drone* flewme *phlegm*
92 scabbit skarth *scabby(?) scabbed monster* scorpioun *scorpion*
ane scutarde behind *(?) with a behind like a hare, (?)fellow who shoots (= shits, farts) behind*
93 scart *scratch* awin *own* grit scunner *utterly disgusting*
94 carybald *(?)monster* kyndillis *is aroused*   95 birs *bristles* brym bair *fierce boar*
berd *beard*   96 soupill *supple* sary lume *wretched tool, penis*
97 sakles is his deidis *innocent are his deeds*   98 goris *clots of slime* tua *two*
gladderit *smeared*   99 gorgeit *blocked up* lyk *like* gutaris *gutters*
glar *mud, filth* stoppit *choked*

100   Bot quhen that glowrand gaist grippis me about,
       Than think I hiddowus Mahowne hes me in armes.
       Thair ma na sanyne me save fra that auld Sathane,
       For thocht I croce me all cleine fra the croun doun,
       He wil my corse all beclip and clap to his breist.
105   Quhen schaiffyn is that ald schaik with a scharp rasour
       He schowis on me his schewill mouth and schendis my lippis,
       And with his hard hurcheone scyn sa heklis he my chekis
       That as a glemand gleyd glowis my chaftis.
       I schrenk for the scharp stound bot schout dar I nought,
110   For schore of that auld schrew – schame him betide!
       The luf-blenkis of that bogill fra his blerde ene
       As Belzebub had on me blent, abasit my spreit.
       And quhen the smy on me smyrkis with his smake smolet
       He fepillis like a farcy aver that flyrit on a gillot.
115   Quhen that the sound of his saw sinkis in my eris,
       Than ay renewis my noy or he be neir cumand.
       Quhen I heir nemmyt his name than mak I nyne crocis
       To keip me fra the cummerans of that carll mangit,
       That full of eldnyng is and anger and all evill thewis.

100 glowrand gaist *staring ghost*   101 hiddowus *hideous*
Mahown *(Mahomet =) the devil* hes *has*   102 Thair ma *there may*
sanyne *making the sign of the cross* Sathane *Satan*
103 croce me all cleine *cross myself completely* croun *crown (of the head)*
104 corse *body* beclip *embrace* clap *clutch* breist *breast*   105 schaiffyn *shaved*
ald schaik *old disreputable wretch*   106 schowis *thrusts* schewill *twisted*
schendis *ruins*   107 hurcheone scyn *hedgehog skin* sa *so*
heklis *scratches (like a flax-comb)* chekis *cheeks*
108 *that my jaws glow like a live coal*   109 schrenk *shrink* stound *pain*
schout *cry out*   110 schore *threatening* schrew *rascal* schame *shame* betide *befall*
111 luf-blenkis *love-glances* bogill *goblin* blerde *bleary*
112 As Belzebub *as if Beelzebub (the devil)* blent *looked*
abasit my spreit *dismayed my spirit*   113 smy *churl* smyrkis *simpers*
with his smake smolet(?) *with his rascally mouth (?)[showing] his wretched little
penis*   114 fepillis *(?)puts out his lower lip (?)slavers*
Like a diseased old horse leering at a mare   115 saw *speech*
sinkis in my eris *enters my ears*
116 *then my disgust is always renewed before he approaches*   117 heir *hear*
nemmyt *mentioned* mak I nyne crocis *I make nine signs of the cross*
118 *to guard me from the harassing of that crazed old churl*
119 eldnyng *jealousy* thewis *qualities*

120   I dar nought luke to my luf for that lene gib;
       He is sa full of jelusy and engyne fals,
       Ever ymagynyng in mynd materis of evill,
       Compasand and castand cacis a thousand,
       How he sall tak me with a trawe, at trist of ane othir.
125   I dar nought keik to the knaip that the cop fillis
       For eldnyng of that ald schrew that evir on evill thynkis,
       For he is waistit and worne fra Venus werkis,
       And may nought beit worth a bene in bed of my mystirs.
       He trowis that young folk I yerne, yeild for he gane is,
130   Bot I may yuke all this yer or his yerd help.
       Ay quhen that caribald carll wald clym one my wambe,
       Than am I dangerus and daine and dour of my will;
       Yit leit I nevir that larbar my leggis ga betuene
       To fyle my flesche na fummyll me without a fee gret,
135   And thoght his pen purly me payis in bed,
       His purse pays richely in recompense efter;
       For or he clyme on my corse, that carybald forlane,
       I have conditioun of a curche of kersp allther fynest,
       A goun of engranyt claith right gaily furrit,
140   A ring with a ryall stane or other riche jowell,

120 nought luke *not look* luf *lover* for that lene gib *for fear of that gaunt tom-cat*
121 jelusy *jealousy* engyne fals *false ingenuity*   122 materis *matters*
123 castand cacis *contriving tricks*   124 sall tak *shall catch* trawe *(?)trick*
trist of ane othir *tryst with another*   125 keik *to peep (at)* knaip *lad* cop *cup*
126 For eldnyng *because of the jealousy* schrew *villain*
127 waistit *exhausted* Venus werkis *Venus's works, acts of love*
128 beit *relieve* worth a bene *to the value of a bean* mystirs *(sexual) needs*
129 trowis *believes* yerne *long for*
yeild for he gane is *(?)because he has become sterile*   130 yuke *itch (with desire)*
yer *year* or *before* yerd *penis*   131 caribald *(?)monstrous* wald clym *would climb*
wambe *belly*   132 dangerus *haughty* daine *disdainful* dour *sullen*   133 Yit *yet*
leit *allow* larbar *impotent man* my leggis ga betuene *go between my legs*
134 fyle *defile* flesche *flesh* na fummyll *nor fumble* gret *great*
135 pen *pen, penis* purly me payis *poorly gratifies me*   136 efter *afterwards*
137 or *before* that carybald forlane *that horrible worthless fellow*
138 *I make it a condition (to have a) kerchief of rich fabric, finest of all*
139 goun of engranyt claith *gown of dyed scarlet cloth*
furrit *trimmed with fur*   140 ryall stane *costly gem* jowell *jewel*

Or rest of his rousty raid, thoght he wer rede-wod.
For all the buddis of Johne Blunt, quhen he abone clymis
Me think the baid deir aboucht, sa bawch ar his werkis –
And thus I sell him solace thoght I it sour think –
145   Fra sic a syre God yow saif, my sueit sisteris deir!'

Quhen that the semely had said hir sentence to end,
Than all thai leuch apon loft with latis full mery,
And raucht the cop round about, full of riche wynis,
And ralyeit lang or thai wald rest, with ryatus speche.

Hic bibent et inde vidua interrogat alteram mulierem et illa
respondet ut sequitur

150   The wedo to the tothir wlonk warpit thir wordis:
'Now, fair sister, fallis yow but fenying to tell;
Sen man ferst with matrimony yow menskit in kirk,
How haif ye farne, be your faith, confese us the treuth,
That band to blise or to ban, quhilk yow best thinkis,
155   Or how ye like lif to leid into lell spousage?
And syne myself ye exem on the samyn wise,
And I sall say furth the suth, dissymyland no word.'

141 rest of *(he must) cease from* rousty raid *clumsy inroad* wer *were*
rede-wod *crazed* 142 buddis *bribes*
Johne Blunt *stupid John (apparently proverbial name)* abone clymis *climbs on top*
143 Me think *it seems to me* baid *delay* deir aboucht *dearly paid for*
bawch *feeble* werkis *deeds* 145 syre *lord, man* saif *save*

146 semely *fair lady* sentence *discourse* 147 leuch apon loft *laughed loudly*
latis *demeanour* 148 raucht *handed* 149 ralyeit lang *jested for a long time*
ryatus *noisy, riotous*

Here they drink, and the widow questions the other wife, and she replies as follows:
150 wlonk *beautiful lady* warpit *addressed* thir *these* 151 fallis yow *it falls to you*
but *(without)* fenying *deceit* 152 Sen *since* ferst *first* menskit *honoured*
153 farne *fared* confese *confess* treuth *truth* 154 blise *bless* ban *curse*
quhilk yow best thinkis *which seems best to you* 155 lif *life* leid *lead*
into lell spousage *in lawful marriage* 156 syne *then* exem *examine*
samyn wise *same manner* 157 say furth *declare* suth *truth*
dissymyland *dissembling*

The plesand said, 'I protest, the treuth gif I schaw,
That of your toungis ye be traist.' The tothir twa grantit.
160 With that sprang up hir spreit be a span hechar.
'To speik,' quod scho, 'I sall nought spar; ther is no spy neir.
I sall a ragment reveil fra rute of my hert,
A roust that is sa rankild quhill risis my stomok.
Now sall the byle all out brist that beild has so lang.
165 For it to beir on my breist wes berdin our hevy;
I sall the venome devoid with a vent large,
And me assuage of the swalme that suellit wes gret.
    'My husband wes a hur-maister, the hugeast in erd;
Tharfor I hait him with my hert, sa help me our Lord.
170 He is a young man, ryght yaip, bot nought in youth flouris,
For he is fadit full far and feblit of strenth.
He wes as flurising fresche within this few yeris,
Bot he is falyeid full far and fulyeid in labour.
He has bene lychour so lang quhill lost is his natur,
175 His lume is waxit larbar, and lyis into swoune.
Wes never sugeorne wer set na on that snaill tyrit,
For eftir sevin oulkis rest it will nought rap anys.
He has bene waistit apone wemen or he me wif chesit,
And in adultré in my tyme I haif him tane oft.

158 plesand *pleasant lady* gif *if* schaw *reveal*   159 toungis *tongues*
traist *trustworthy* grantit *agreed*   160 spreit *spirit* span *span (nine inches)*
hechar *higher*   161 speik *speak* spar *hold back* neir *near*
162 ragment *catalogue* rute *depths* hert *heart*   163 roust *rancour*
rankild *rankled* quhill risis my stomok *until my stomach rises*   164 byle *boil*
brist *burst* beild *festered*   165 beir *bear* breist *breast* berdin *burden*
our hevy *over-heavy*   166 devoid *cast out* vent *discharge*
167 swalme *swelling* suellit *swollen*
168 hur-maister *frequenter of whores* hugeast in erd *biggest on earth*
169 Tharfor *therefore* hait *hate*   170 ryght yaip *very lively*
nought in youth flouris *not in the first flourishing of youth*   171 fadit *faded*
feblit *enfeebled*   172 flurising *flower* this *these* yeris *years*
173 falyeid *weakened* fulyeid *exhausted*   174 lychour *a lecher*
natur *sexual power*   175 lume *tool, penis* waxit larbar *become impotent*
lyis into swone *lies in a swoon*
176 *never was abstinence worse expended than on that tired snail*
177 sevin oulkis *seven weeks* rap *drive* anys *once*   178 apone *upon*
or he me wif chesit *before he chose me as a wife*   179 adultré *adultery* tane *caught*

180 And yit he is als brankand with bonet on syde,
And blenkand to the brichtest that in the burgh duellis,
Alse curtly of his clething and kemmyng of his hairis,
As he that is mare valyeand in Venus chalmer.
He semys to be sumthing worth, that syphyr in bour,
185 He lukis as he wald luffit be, thoght he be litill of valour;
He dois as dotit dog that damys on all bussis,
And liftis his leg apon loft thoght he nought list pische.
He has a luke without lust and lif without curage;
He has a forme without force and fessoun but vertu,
190 And fair wordis but effect, all fruster of dedis.
He is for ladyis in luf a right lusty schadow,
Bot into derne, at the deid, he sal be drup fundin.
He ralis and makis repet with ryatus wordis,
Ay rusing him of his radis and rageing in chalmer;
195 Bot God wait quhat I think, quhen he so thra spekis
And how it settis him so syde, to segis of sic materis –
Bot gif himself of sum evin myght ane say amang thaim;
Bot he nought ane is, bot nane of naturis possessoris.

180 brankand *proudly strutting* bonet *bonnet* on syde *at a rakish angle*
181 *and eyeing the prettiest girls that live in the town*
182 Alse curtly of his clething *as courtly in dress*
kemmyng of his hairis *combing of his hair*
183 *like one that is more doughty in Venus's chamber*
184 sumthing worth *of some worth* syphyr *cypher, useless wretch*
bour *chamber, bedroom*   185 lukis *looks* valour *worth*
186 dois as dotit dog *acts like a silly dog* damys *pisses* bussis *bushes*
187 apon loft *up* thoght he nought list pische *even though he does not want to piss*
188 lust *desire*   189 forme without force *shape without strength*
fessoun but vertu *appearance without power*
190 effect *efficacy* fruster of dedis *useless in deeds*
191 schadow *(?)phantom, unreal appearance (?)reflection (of themselves)*
192 into derne *in private* deid *act* drup fundin *found feeble*
193 ralis *jests* repet *uproar* ryatus *wanton*
194 rusing him of his radis *boasting of his sexual exploits* rageing *passion*
195 wait *knows* thra spekis *wildly speaks*
196 settis *befits* syde *(?)boastfully, (?)widely* segis *men*
197 *(?)unless, (?)but if he some evening might assay (i.e. have a go at) one of them*
198 *(?) but he is not such a one, but a nobody among those who possess natural sexual powers*

Scho that has ane auld man nought all is begylit;
200 He is at Venus werkis na war na he semys.
I wend I josit a gem and I haif geit gottin;
He had the glemyng of gold and wes bot glase fundin.
Thought men be ferse, wele I fynd – fra falye ther curage –
Thar is bot eldnyng and anger ther hertis within.
205 Ye speik of berdis on bewch – of blise may thai sing,
That on sanct Valentynis day ar vacandis ilk yer.
Hed I that plesand prevelege, to part quhen me likit,
To change and ay to cheise agane – than chastité adew!
Than suld I haif a fresch feir to fang in myn armys –
210 To hald a freke quhill he faynt may foly be calit.
Apone sic materis I mus at mydnyght full oft
And murnys so in my mynd I murdris myselfin.
Than ly I walkand for wa and walteris about,
Wariand oft my wekit kyn that me away cast,
215 To sic a craudoune but curage that knyt my cler bewté,
And ther so mony kene knyghtis this kenrik within.
Than think I on a semelyar, the suth for to tell,
Na is our syre be sic sevin – with that I syth oft.
Than he ful tendirly dois turne to me his tume person,

199 nought all is begylit *is not entirely deceived*
200 na war na he semys *no worse than he seems* 201 wend *thought*
josit *possessed* geit *jet (black ignite)* gottin *got* 202 glemyng *shining colour*
glase *glass* fundin *found, proved* 203 ferse *aggressive* wele *well*
fra falye ther curage *after their sexual vigour declines* 204 Thar *there*
eldnyng *jealousy* 205 berdis on bewch *birds on the bough* blise *happiness*
206 sanct Valentynis day *St Valentine's Day (14 February, when, traditionally,
the birds chose their mates)* ar vacandis ilk yer *are free to take mates each year*
207 prevelege *privilege* part quhen me likit *depart when it pleased me*
208 cheise *choose* adew *farewell* 209 feir *consort* fang *embrace*
210 *to keep a man till he grows exhausted may be called folly* 211 mus *muse*
212 murnys *grieve* murdris myselfin *destroy myself* 213 walkand *waking*
wa *sorrow* walteris *toss* 214 Wariand *cursing* wekit kyn *wicked kin*
215 *That bound my radiant beauty to such a feeble coward* 216 ther *there (being)*
kene *bold* kenrik *kingdom* 217 semelyar *seemlier man* suth *truth*
218 Na is our syre be sic sevin *seven times more so than my husband* syth *sigh*
219 tume person *empty, feeble body*

220 And with a yoldin yerd dois yolk me in armys,
    And sais, "My soverane sueit thing, quhy sleip ye no betir?
    Me think ther haldis yow a hete, as ye sum harme alyt."
    Quoth I, "My hony, hald abak and handill me nought sair;
    A hache is happinit hastely at my hert-rut."
225 With that I seme for to swoune, thought I na swerf tak –
    And thus beswik I that swane with my sueit wordis.
    I cast on him a crabit e quhen cleir day is cummyn,
    And lettis it is a luf-blenk quhen he about glemys;
    I turne it in a tendir luke that I in tene warit,
230 And him behaldis hamely with hertly smyling.
    I wald a tendir peronall that myght na put thole,
    That hatit men with hard geir for hurting of flesch,
    Had my gudman to hir gest, for I dar God suer,
    Scho suld not stert for his straik a stray-breid of erd.
235 And syne I wald that ilk band that ye so blist call
    Had bund him so to that bryght quhill his bak werkit,
    And I wer in a beid broght with berne that me likit –
    I trow that bird of my blis suld a bourd want.'

220 yoldin yerd *exhausted penis* dois yolk *clasps*
221 soverane *peerless* quhy *why* sleip *sleep* betir *better*
222 haldis *grips* hete *fever* as ye sum harme alyt *as if you suffered some sickness*
223 hony *honey* abak *back* handill me nought sair *do not handle me roughly*
224 hache *ache, pain* happinit *come* hastely *suddenly* hert-rut *heart-root*
225 na swerf tak *do not faint*   226 beswik *deceive* swane *man*
227 crabit e *angry look* cummyn *come*   228 lettis *pretend*
luf-blenk *love-glance* glemys *looks*   229 tene *anger* warit *used*
230 him behaldis hamely *look at him in a loving way* hertly *heartfelt*
231 *I wish a young wanton girl that could not endure any thrusting*
232 hatit *hated* geir *(sexual) equipment*
233 gudman *husband* gest *lover* suer *swear*
234 stert for his straik a stray-breid of erd *flinch at his thrust a straw's breadth
of ground*   235 band *bond* blist *blessed*   236 bund *bound*
bryght *pretty girl* werkit *ached*   237 in a beid broght *brought to a bed*
berne *man*   238 trow *believe* bird *girl*
of my blis suld a bourd want *(?)would not be able to joke about (?)lack a share
of the sport*

Onone quhen this amyable had endit hir speche,
240 Ludly lauchand, the laif allowit hir mekle.
Thir gay wiffis maid gam amang the grene leiffis:
Thai drank and did away dule undir derne bewis;
Thai swapit of the sueit wyne, thai swan-quhit of hewis,
Bot all the pertlyar, in plane, thai put out ther vocis.

*Nunc bibent et inde prima due interrogant viduam et de sua
responsione et quomodo erat*

245 Than said the weido, 'Iwis ther is no way othir:
Now tydis me for to talk, my taill it is nixt.
God my spreit now inspir and my speche quykkin,
And send me sentence to say substantious and noble,
Sa that my preching may pers your perverst hertis
250 And mak yow mekar to men in maneris and conditiounis.
I schaw yow, sisteris, in schrift, I wes a schrew evir,
Bot I wes schene in my schrowd and schew me innocent;
And thought I dour wes and dane, dispitois and bald,
I wes dissymblit suttelly in a sanctis liknes;

239 Onone *forthwith* amyable *pleasant creature*
240 Ludly lauchand *loudly laughing*
laif allowit hir mekle *others praised her greatly*   241 gam *sport* leiffis *leaves*
242 did away dule undir derne bewis *put away sorrow under the shady boughs*
243 swapit of *tossed off* thai swan-quhit of hewis *those ladies swan-white in hue*
244 all the pertlyar *more impudently* in plane *plainly*
put out ther vocis *uttered their speeches*

*Now they drink, and the first two question the widow, and her response and its
manner*
245 Iwis *indeed*   246 tydis *befalls* taill *tale* nixt *next*   247 spreit *spirit*
quykkin *enliven*   248 sentence *matter* substantious *weighty*
249 preching *preaching* pers *pierce* perverst hertis *perverse hearts*
250 mekar *more gentle* maneris *behaviour* conditiounis *dispositions*
251 schaw *reveal* in schrift *in confession* a schrew evir *always a wicked creature*
252 schene *beautiful* schrowd *gown* schew me *appeared*   253 thought *though*
dour *sullen* dane *haughty* dispitois *without mercy* bald *bold*
254 dissymblit suttelly in a sanctis liknes *disguised cunningly in a saint's likeness*

255 I semyt sober and sueit and sempill without fraud,
Bot I couth sexty dissaif that suttillar wer haldin.
Unto my lesson ye lyth, and leir at me wit,
Gif you nought list be forleit with losingeris untrew:
Be constant in your governance and counterfeit gud maneris
260 Thought ye be kene, inconstant and cruell of mynd;
Thought ye as tygris be terne, be tretable in luf,
And be as turtoris in your talk, thought ye haif talis brukill.
Be dragonis baith and dowis ay in double forme,
And quhen it nedis yow, onone note baith ther stranthis;
265 Be amyable with humble face as angellis apperand,
And with a terrebill tail be stangand as edderis;
Be of your luke like innocentis, thoght ye haif evill myndis;
Be courtly ay in clething and costly arrayit –
That hurtis yow nought worth a hen; yowr husband pays for
　　　all.

270 　　　Twa husbandis haif I had, thai held me baith deir;
Thought I dispytit thaim agane, thai spyit it na thing.
Ane wes ane hair hogeart that hostit out flewme.
I hatit him like a hund, thought I it hid prevé;
With kissing and with clapping I gert the carill fon.

255 semyt *seemed* sober *meek* sempill *simple*
256 couth sexty dissaif that suttillar wer haldin *could deceive sixty that were
held to be more clever* 257 lyth *listen* leir at me wit *learn wisdom from me*
258 *if you do not wish to be abandoned by faithless deceivers*
259 governance *behaviour* 260 kene *fierce* 261 tygris *tigers*
terne *savage* tretable *compliant*
262 turtoris *turtle doves (thought to be examples of gentle devoted constancy)*
talis *tails, sexual organs* brukill *frail, quick to yield*
263 dragonis baith and dowis ay *both dragons and doves always*
264 nedis yow *is necessary for you*
onone note baith ther stranthis *straightway use both their strengths*
265 as angellis apperand *seeming like angels*
266 stangand as edderis *stinging like adders*

271 dispytit *despised* agane *in return* spyit *noticed*
272 *one was a grey-haired old man that coughed out phlegm*
273 hund *dog* prevé *secretly* 274 clapping *fondling*
gert the carill fon *made the churl become besotted*

275 Weil couth I krych his cruke bak and kemm his kewt noddill,
     And with a bukky in my cheik bo on him behind,
     And with a bek gang about and bler his ald e,
     And with a kyind contynance kys his crynd chekis,
     Into my mynd makand mokis at that mad fader,
280 Trouand me with trew lufe to treit him so fair.
     This cought I do without dule and na dises tak,
     Bot ay be mery in my mynd and myrthfull of cher.
     I had a lufsummar leid my lust for to slokyn,
     That couth be secrete and sure and ay saif my honour,
285 And sew bot at certane tymes and in sicir placis.
     Ay quhen the ald did me anger with akword wordis,
     Apon the galland for to goif it gladit me agane.
     I had sic wit that for wo weipit I litill,
     Bot leit the sueit ay the sour to gud sesone bring.
290 Quhen that the chuf wald me chid with girnand chaftis,
     I wald him chuk, cheik and chyn, and cheris him so mekill
     That his cheif chymys he had chevist to my sone,
     Suppos the churll wes gane chaist or the child wes gottin.
     As wis woman ay I wrought, and not as wod fule,
295 For mar with wylis I wan na wichtnes of handis.

275 krych *scratch* cruke *crooked* kemm his kewt noddill *comb his cropped head*
276 bukky *swelling (?with the tongue)* cheik *cheek* bo *make a face*
277 bek *respectful sign* gang *go* bler his ald e *deceive his old eye, hoodwink him*
278 kyind contynance kys his crynd chekis *affectionate manner kiss his shrivelled cheeks*   279 makand mokis *making mocking expressions*
mad fader *crazy old man*   280 Trouand *believing* treit *treat*
281 cought *could* dule *sorrow* dises *distress*   282 cher *demeanour*
283 lufsummar leid *more lovable man* slokyn *satisfy*
284 couth be *knew how to be* sure *reliable* saif *preserve*
285 sew *attend (on me)* sicir *secure*   286 ald *old fellow* akword *bad-tempered*
287 galland *young lover* goif *gaze* gladit *gladdened*   288 wit *skill* weipit *wept*
litill *little*   289 *But let the sweet always bring the sour to a good flavour*
290 chuf *churl* chid *chide* girnand chaftis *snarling jaws*
291 chuk *fondle* cheris *show affection to* mekill *much*
292 cheif chymys *main manor house* chevist *assigned* sone *son*
293 Suppos *although* gane *gone, become* chaist *continent* or *before*
gottin *begotten*   294 wrought *acted* wod fule *mad fool*
295 mar *more* wylis *wiles* wan *won* na *than* wichtnes *strength*

Syne maryt I a merchand, myghti of gudis.
He wes a man of myd eld and of mene statur;
Bot we na fallowis wer in frendschip or blud,
In fredome na furth-bering, na fairnes of persoune –
300 Quhilk ay the fule did foryet for febilnes of knawlege.
Bot I sa oft thoght him on, quhill angrit his hert,
And quhilum I put furth my voce and peddir him callit.
I wald ryght tuichandly talk, be I wes tuyse maryit,
For endit wes my innocence with my ald husband.
305 I wes apperand to be pert within perfit eild –
Sa sais the curat of our kirk, that knew me full ying.
He is our famous to be fals, that fair worthy prelot;
I sal be laith to lat him le quhill I may luke furth.
I gert the buthman obey – ther wes no bute ellis –
310 He maid me ryght hie reverens fra he my rycht knew,
For thocht I say it myself, the severance wes mekle
Betuix his bastard blude and my birth noble.
That page wes nevir of sic price for to presome anys
Unto my persone to be peir, had peté nought grantit.
315 Bot mercy into womanheid is a mekle vertu,
For nevir bot in a gentill hert is generit ony ruth.
I held ay grene into his mynd that I of grace tuk him,

296 maryt *married* merchand *merchant* myghti of gudis *of great wealth*
297 myd eld *middle age* mene *moderate*
298 fallowis *equals* frendschip *kindred* blud *blood*
299 fredome na furth-bering *generosity nor behaviour* persoune *body*
300 foryet *forget* knawlege *understanding*
301 sa oft thoght him on *made him think of it* quhill angrit *grew angry*
302 quhilum *sometimes* put furth *raised* voce *voice* peddir *pedlar*
303 tuichandly *affectingly, stingingly* be *after* tuyse *twice*
305 apperand to be pert *likely to be forward*
within perfit eild *on reaching maturity*   306 curat *priest*
307 our famous *too reputable* prelot *ecclesiastic*   308 laith *reluctant* lat *allow*
le quhill I may luke furth *tell lies while I can look around*
309 gert *made* buthman *shopkeeper* bute ellis *remedy otherwise*
310 reverens *deep respect* fra *when* rycht *due*   311 severance *difference*
mekle *great*   313 page *churl* price *worth* presome *presume*   314 peir *equal*
peté *pity*   315 womanheid *womanhood*   316 gentill *noble, gracious*
generit ony ruth *engendered any truth*   317 held *kept* grene *fresh*

And for he couth ken himself I curtasly him lerit.
He durst not sit anys my summondis, for or the secund charge
320 He wes ay redy for to ryn, so rad he wes for blame.
Bot ay my will wes the war of womanly natur:
The mair he loutit for my luf the les of him I rakit,
And eik – this is a ferly thing – or I him faith gaif,
I had sic favour to that freke, and feid syne for evir.
325 Quhen I the cure had all clene and him ourcummyn haill,
I crew abone that craudone as cok that wer victour.
Quhen I him saw subjeit and sett at myn bydding,
Than I him lichtlyit as a lowne and lathit his maneris.
Than woxe I sa unmerciable, to martir him I thought,
330 For as a best I broddit him to all boyis laubour –
I wald haif ridden him to Rome with raip in his heid,
Wer not ruffill of my renoune and rumour of pepill.
And yit hatrent I hid within my hert all;
Bot quhilis it hepit so huge quhill it behud out.
335 Yit tuk I nevir the wosp clene out of my wyde throte,
Quhill I oucht wantit of my will or quhat I wald desir.
Bot quhen I severit had that syre of substance in erd,
And gottin his biggingis to my barne and hie burrow landis,

318 couth ken *could come to know* curtasly him lerit *graciously instructed him*
319 sit anys my summondis *disregard my summons*
or the secund charge *before the second command*   320 redy *ready* ryn *run*
rad *afraid*   321 the war *the worse* of womanly nature *out of female nature*
322 loutit *humbled himself* rakit *esteemed*   323 eik *also* ferly *strange*
324 favour *good will* freke *man* feid syne for evir *hatred for ever afterwards*
325 cure *control* all clene *completely* ourcummyn haill *wholly overcome*
326 *I crowed above that coward like a victorious cock*
327 subjeit *(made) subject* sett at *ready to do*   328 lichtlyit *despised*
lowne *boor* lathit *loathed*   329 woxe *became* unmerciable *pitiless*
martir *torment*   330 as a best *like a beast* broddit *goaded*
all boyis laubour *every kind of servants' work*   331 raip *rope, halter* heid *head*
332 Wer not ruffill of my renoune *were it not for the damage to my reputation*
rumour *gossip*   333 hatrent *hatred*   334 quhilis *sometimes*
hepit *piled up* quhill it behud out *of necessity it had to burst out*
335 tuk *took* wosp *(wisp of straw used as) stopper*
336 Quhill I oucht wantit *while I lacked anything*   337 severit *deprived*
substance *wealth, property* erd *earth*   338 gottin *obtained*
biggingis *buildings* barne *child* hie burrow landis *high town tenements*

Than with a stew stert out the stoppell of my hals,
340 That he all stunyst throu the stound as of a stele wappin.
Than wald I eftir lang first sa fane haif bene wrokin
That I to flyte wes als fers as a fell dragoun.
I had for flattering of that fule fenyeit so lang,
Mi evidentis of heritagis or thai wer all selit,
345 My breist that wes gret beild bowdyn wes sa huge,
That neir my baret out birst or the band makin.
Bot quhen my billis and my bauchles wes all braid selit,
I wald na langar beir on bridill, bot braid up my heid;
Thar mycht na molet mak me moy na hald my mouth in,
350 I gert the renyeis rak and rif into sondir;
I maid that wif carll to werk all womenis werkis,
And laid all manly materis and mensk in this eird.
Than said I to my cummaris in counsall about:
"Se how I cabeld yone cout with a kene brydill.
355 The cappill that the crelis kest in the caf-mydding
Sa curtasly the cart drawis and kennis na plungeing.

339 stew *(?)stink* stert out *burst* stoppell *stopper* hals *throat*
340 all stunyst *was stunned* stound *sharp pain, shock* stele wappin *steel weapon*
341 lang first *long delay* fane *gladly* wrokin *avenged*
342 flyte *scold* fers *fierce* fell *cruel*   343 fenyeit *feigned*
344 evidentis of heritagis *legal documents for the inheritance* selit *sealed*
345 gret beild *greatly inflamed* bowdyn *swollen*   346 neir *almost*
baret *anger* birst *burst* or the band makin *before the contract was made*
347 billis *legal documents (for transfer of property)*
bauchles *(?)some kind of legal deeds or formal reproaches for breach of faith*
wes all braid selit *were plainly sealed*   348 langar *longer*
beir on bridill *bear a bridle* braid up *tossed up*   349 molet *bit (of a bridle)*
moy *quiet, submissive*   350 *I caused the reins to strain and break asunder*
351 wif carll *womanish man* werk *do* womenis werkis *women's tasks*
352 laid *laid aside* mensk *dignity*   353 cummaris *women friends, gossips*
counsall *discussion*   354 cabeld yone cout *tied up yon colt* kene *sharp*
355 cappill *horse* crelis *creels (wicker baskets)* kest *threw*
caf-mydding *dung-heap*   356 Sa curtasly *so gently* kennis *shows (no sign of)*
plungeing *violent plunging forward*

He is nought skeich na yit sker na scippis nought on syd."
And thus the scorne and the scaith scapit he nothir.
He wes no glaidsum gest for a gay lady;
360 Tharfor I gat him a game that ganyt him bettir.
He wes a gret goldit man and of gudis riche;
I leit him be my lumbart to lous me all misteris,
And he wes fane for to fang fra me that fair office
And thoght my favoris to fynd through his feill giftis.
365 He grathit me in a gay silk and gudly arrayis,
In gownis of engranyt claicht and gret goldin chenyeis,
In ringis ryally set with riche ruby stonis,
Quhill hely raise my renoune amang the rude peple.
Bot I full craftely did keip thai courtly wedis
370 Quhill eftir dede of that drupe that docht nought in chalmir.
Thought he of all my clathis maid cost and expense,
Ane othir sall the worschip haif that weildis me eftir;
And thoght I likit him bot litill, yit for luf of othris
I wald me prunya plesandly in precius wedis,
375 That luffaris myght apon me luke and ying lusty gallandis
That I held more in daynté and derer be ful mekill
Ne him that dressit me so dink – full dotit wes his heyd!
Quhen he wes heryit out of hand to hie up my honoris,

357 skeich *spirited, inclined to shy* sker *restive* scippis *skips, jumps*
on syd *to the side* 358 scaith *humiliation* scapit *escaped* nothir *neither*
359 glaidsum *entertaining* gest *lover* 360 gat *obtained* game *sport*
ganyt *suited* 361 gret goldit *greatly endowed with gold* gudis *goods*
362 lumbart *(Lombard =) banker* lous me all misteris *free me from business*
363 fane *glad* fang *receive* 364 feill *many* 365 grathit *arrayed*
gay silk *fine silk robe* arrayis *clothing* 366 engranyt claicht *dyed scarlet cloth*
chenyeis *chains* 367 ryally *nobly* 368 hely *greatly* raise *rose*
renoune *reputation* rude *common* 369 thai *those* wedis *garments*
370 dede *death* drupe *feeble fellow*
docht nought in chalmir *was of no use in the bed-chamber*
371 clathis *clothes* maid cost and expense *met the expense*
372 worschip *honour* weildis *possesses* 373 othris *others*
374 me prunya *adorn myself* 375 luffaris *lovers* gallandis *gallants*
376 daynté *regard* derer *more dearly* be ful mekill *by much*
377 Ne *than* dink *finely* dotit *stupid* heyd *head* 378 heryit *plundered*
out of hand *beyond control* hie up my honoris *increase the signs of my honour*

And payntit me as pako, proudest of fedderis,
380 I him miskennyt, be Crist, and cukkald him maid.
I him forleit as a lad and lathlyit him mekle.
I thoght myself a papingay and him a plukit herle.
All thus enforsit he his fa and fortifyit in strenth,
And maid a stalwart staff to strik himselfe doune.
385 Bot of ane bowrd into bed I sall yow breif yit:
Quhen he ane hal year wes hanyt, and him behuffit rage,
And I wes laith to be loppin with sic a lob avoir,
Alse lang as he wes on loft I lukit on him nevir,
Na leit nevir enter in my thoght that he my thing persit;
390 Bot ay in mynd ane othir man ymagynit that I haid,
Or ellis had I nevir mery bene at that myrthles raid.
Quhen I that grome geldit had of gudis and of natur,
Me thoght him gracelese on to goif, sa me God help.
Quhen he had warit all on me his welth and his substance,
395 Me thoght his wit wes all went away with the laif.
And so I did him dispise; I spittit quhen I saw
That superspendit evill spreit spulyeit of all vertu.
For weill ye wait, wiffis, that he that wantis riches
And valyeandnes in Venus play is ful vile haldin;
400 Full fruster is his fresch array and fairnes of persoune,
All is bot frutlese his effeir and falyeis at the upwith.

379 payntit me as pako *adorned me like a peacock* fedderis *feathers*
380 miskennyt *disregarded* cukkald *cuckold*   381 forleit *rejected*
lad *menial* lathlyit *loathed*   382 papingay *parrot* plukit herle *plucked heron*
383 enforsit *gave strength to* fa *foe* fortifyit *supported*   384 stalwart *strong*
strik *strike* 385 bowrd *jest* breif *tell*   386 hal *whole*
hanyt *restrained* him behuffit rage *had to have sexual pleasure*
387 *and I was unwilling to be mounted by such a clumsy old horse*
388 Alse *as* on loft *on top*   389 thing *sexual organ* persit *pierced*
391 ellis *else* myrthles *joyless* raid *inroad*   392 grome *man* geldit *gelded*
natur *sexual vigour* 393 gracelese on to goif *unattractive to look on*
394 warit *expended*   395 laif *rest* 397 superspendit *bankrupt* spreit *spirit*
spulyeit *deprived* vertu *power*   398 weill *well* wantis *lacks*
399 valyeandnes *strength* play *sport* haldin *considered*   400 fruster *useless*
401 frutlese *fruitless* effeir *bearing* falyeis *fails* upwith *(?)sexual climax*

I buskit up my barnis like baronis sonnis,
And maid bot fulis of the fry of his first wif.
I banyst fra my boundis his brethir ilkane;
405   His frendis as my fais I heid at feid evir.
Be this ye beleif may I luffit nought himself,
For nevir I likit a leid that langit till his blude;
And yit thir wismen, thai wait that all wiffis evill
Ar kend with ther conditionis and knawin with the samin.

410   Deid is now that dyour and dollin in erd;
With him deit all my dule and my drery thoghtis;
Now done is my dolly nyght, my day is upsprungin;
Adew, dolour, adew! my daynté now begynis!
Now am I a wedow, iwise, and weill am at ese!
415   I weip as I wer woful, bot wel is me for evir.
I busk as I wer bailfull, bot blith is my hert;
My mouth it makis murnyng, and my mynd lauchis;
My clokis thai ar caerfull in colour of sabill,
Bot courtly and ryght curyus my corse is therundir.
420   I drup with a ded luke in my dulé habit,
As with manis daill I had done for dayis of my lif.

---

402 buskit up *arrayed* barnis *children* baronis sonnis *barons' sons*
403 fry *offsping*   **404** banyst *banished* boundis *lands* brethir *brothers*
ilkane *each one*   **405** fais *foes* heid at feid *had in enmity, despised*
406 beleif *believe*   **407** leid *man* langit *belonged*
408 thir wismen *these wise men* wiffis evill *wicked wives*
409 kend with ther conditionis *recognized by their dispositions, behaviour*
knawin with the samin *known by the same*

410 Deid *dead* dyour *debtor, bankrupt* dollin *buried*   **411** deit *died*
drery *gloomy*   **412** done *over, done with* dolly *dismal* upsprungin *risen up*
413 dolour *misery, sorrow* daynté *pleasure, delight*   **414** iwise *indeed*
weill am at ese *am well at ease, happy*   **415** weip *weep* as *as if*
416 busk *dress* bailfull *sorrowful*   **417** murnyng *mourning* lauchis *laughs*
418 clokis *cloaks* caerfull *melancholy*
419 courtly *elegant* curyus *exquisite* corse *body* therundir *underneath them*
420 drup *droop* ded *deathly* dulé habit *mourning garment*
421 As with manis daill *as if with intercourse with man*

Quhen that I go to the kirk cled in cair-weid,
As foxe in a lambis fleise fenye I my cheir.
Than lay I furght my bright buke on breid on my kne,

425   With mony lusty letter ellummynit with gold,
And drawis my clok forthwart our my face quhit
That I may spy unaspyit a space me beside:
Full oft I blenk by my buke and blynis of devotioun
To se quhat berne is best brand or bredest in schulderis,

430   Or forgeit is maist forcely to furnyse a bancat
In Venus chalmir valyeandly withoutin vane ruse.
And as the new mone all pale oppressit with change
Kythis quhilis her cleir face through cluddis of sable,
So keik I through my clokis and castis kynd lukis

435   To knychtis and to cleirkis, and cortly personis.
Quhen frendis of my husbandis behaldis me on fer
I haif a wattir spunge for wa within my wyde clokis;
Than wring I it full wylély and wetis my chekis.
With that watteris myn ene and welteris doune teris.

440   Than say thai all that sittis about, "Se ye nought, allace,
Yone lustlese led, so lelely scho luffit hir husband.
Yone is a peté to enprent in a princis hert,

422 cled *clad* cair-weid *mourning clothes*   423 lambis fleise *lamb's fleece*
fenye *feign* cheir *behaviour*   424 furght *out* buke *book*
on breid *wide open* kne *knee*   425 lusty *fine* ellummynit *illuminated*
426 clok *cloak* forthwart *forward* quhit *white, pale*
427 unaspyit *unnoticed* a space *for a time* beside *around, nearby*
428 blenk by *glance away from* blynis of *cease from*
429 berne *man* brand *muscled, brawny* bredest *broadest* schulderis *shoulders*
430 forgeit *built* forcely *strongly* furnyse a bancat *furnish a banquet*
431 valyeandly *vigorously* vane ruse *vain boast*   432 mone *moon*
oppressit *oppressed, afflicted*   433 Kythis *reveals*
quhilis *from time to time* cleir *bright* cluddis *clouds*   434 keik *peep* kynd *fond*
435 knychtis *knights* cleirkis *clerks, clerics* cortly *courtly, elegant*
436 behaldis *behold* on fer *from afar*
437 haif a wattir spunge for wa *have a water-sponge to produce signs of grief*
438 wylély *cunningly* wetis *wet* chekis *cheeks*
439 With that watteris myn ene *at that my eyes water*
welteris doune teris *tears roll down*   440 nought *not* allace *alas*
441 lustlese led *joyless creature* lelely *faithfully* luffit *loved*
442 peté *piteous sight* enprent *imprint*

That sic a perle of plesance suld yone pane dre!"
I sane me as I war ane sanct, and semys ane angell;
445   At langage of lichory I leit as I war crabit:
I sith without sair hert or seiknes in body;
According to my sable weid I mon haif sad maneris
Or thai will se all the suth – for certis we wemen
We set us all for the syght to syle men of treuth.
450   We dule for na evill deid, sa it be derne haldin.
Wise wemen has wayis and wondirfull gydingis
With gret engyne to bejaip ther jolyus husbandis,
And quyetly with sic craft convoyis our materis
That undir Crist no creatur kennis of our doingis.
455   Bot folk a cury may miscuke that knawlege wantis,
And has na colouris for to cover ther awne kindly fautis;
As dois thir damysellis for derne dotit lufe,
That dogonis haldis in dainté and delis with thaim so lang,
Quhill al the cuntré knaw ther kyndnes and faith.
460   Faith has a fair name, bot falsheid faris beittir;
Fy on hir that can nought feyne, her fame for to saif!

443 perle *pearl* plesance *delight* suld yone pane dre *should suffer that grief*
444 sane me *cross myself* sanct *saint* semys *seem, look like*
445 langage *speech, talk* lichory *lechery* leit *behave, act* crabit *offended*
446 sith *sigh* sair *unhappy* seiknes *sickness*
447 According to *in accordance with* weid *garments* mon *must*
sad maneris *serious demeanour* 448 for certis *certainly*
449 for the syght *(?)for show (?)to avoid being seen* syle *deceive*
450 dule *grieve* derne *secret* haldin *kept* 451 wayis *ways of behaving*
452 engyne *ingenuity, cunning* bejaip *deceive* jolyus *jealous* 453 craft *skill, craft*
convoyis our materis *conduct our affairs* 454 undir *apart from* kennis *knows*
455 cury *(cooked) dish* miscuke *spoil in the cooking*
that knawlege wantis *who lack skill*
456 colouris *(colours =) disguises, deceptions*
awne kindly fautis *own natural defects*
457 dois thir damysellis *do these girls* derne dotit lufe *secret foolish love*
458 dogonis *rascals* haldis in dainté *hold in favour*
delis with *associate with, make love to* 459 cuntré *country, district*
knaw *knows* kyndnes *affection* 460 falsheid faris beittir *falsehood fares better*
461 feyne *feign* her fame for to saif *in order to save her reputation*

Yit am I wise in sic werk and wes all my tyme;
Thoght I want wit in warldlynes, I wylis haif in luf,
As ony happy woman has that is of hie blude:
465   Hutit be the halok lase a hundir yeir of eild!
I have ane secrete servand, rycht sovir of his toung
That me supportis of sic nedis quhen I a syne mak:
Thoght he be sympill to the sicht, he has a tong sickir;
Full mony semelyar sege wer service dois mak.
470   Thoght I haif cair undir cloke the cleir day quhill nyght,
Yit haif I solace undir serk quhill the sone ryse.
Yit am I haldin a haly wif our all the haill schyre:
I am sa peteouse to the pur, quhen ther is person is mony;
In passing of pilgrymage I pride me full mekle,
475   Mair for the prese of peple na ony perdoun wynyng.
Bot yit me think the best bourd, quhen baronis and knychtis
And othir bachilleris blith, blumyng in youth,
And all my luffaris lele my lugeing persewis,
And fyllis me wyne wantonly with weilfair and joy:
480   Sum rownis and sum ralyeis, and sum redis ballatis,

462 werk *business*   463 want wit *lack wisdom*
in warldlynes *in worldly matters* wylis *wiles*
464 happy *fortunate* hie *high, noble*
465 Hutit be *may (she) be hooted at, mocked* the halok lase *(who is a) giddy girl*
a hundir yeir of eild *(at) the age of a hundred*
466 servand *servant* sovir *trustworthy* toung *tongue*
467 me supportis of *helps me with* nedis *needs* syne *sign*
468 sympill *simple, innocent* to the sicht *in appearance* tong *tongue* sickir *trusty*
469 mony semelyar sege *more handsome man* wer *worse*   470 cair *misery*
quhill *until*   471 solace *consolation* serk *shift, undergarment* sone *sun*
472 haldin *considered* haly *holy* haill schyre *whole district*
473 peteouse *compassionate* pur *poor*
ther is person is mony *there are many people about*   474 passing of *going on*
475 prese *crowd* peple *people* na ony perdoun wynyng *than gaining any pardon*
476 me think *seems to me* bourd *sport*
477 bachilleris *young knights* blith *joyous* blumyng *blooming*
478 luffaris lele *trusty lovers* my lugeing persewis *keep visiting my dwelling*
479 fyllis me *pour out for me* wantonly *merrily* weilfair *good cheer*
480 Sum rownis *one whispers* sum ralyeis *another jests*
redis ballatis *reads poems*

Sum raiffis furght rudly with riatus speche;
Sum plenis and sum prayis, sum prasis mi bewté;
Sum kissis me, sum clappis me, sum kyndnes me proferis;
Sum kerffis to me curtasli, sum me the cop giffis;
485   Sum stalwardly steppis ben with a stout curage,
And a stif standand thing staiffis in mi neiff;
And mony blenkis ben our, that but full fer sittis,
That mai for the thik thrang nought thrif as thai wald.
Bot with my fair calling I comfort thaim all:
490   For he that sittis me nixt I nip on his finger;
I serf him on the tothir syde on the samin fasson;
And he that behind me sittis, I hard on him lene;
And him befor, with my fut fast on his I stramp;
And to the bernis far but sueit blenkis I cast:
495   To every man in speciall speke I sum wordis,
So wisly and so womanly quhill warmys ther hertis.
Thar is no liffand leid so law of degré
That sall me luf unluffit, I am so loik-hertit;
And gif his lust so be lent into my lyre quhit
500   That he be lost or with me lak, his lif sall not danger.
I am so mercifull in mynd, and menys all wichtis,
My sely saull sal be saif quhen Sabot all jugis.

481 Sum raiffis furght rudly *one shouts out roughly* riatus *wanton*
482 plenis *laments* prayis *prays* prasis mi bewté *praises my beauty*
483 clappis *embraces* kyndnes *affection* proferis *offers*
484 kerffis to me curtasli *carves for me in a courteous way* giffis *gives*
485 stalwardly steppis ben *boldly steps inside* stout curage *fierce desire*
486 standand *standing* staiffis *thrusts* neiff *fist*
487 *and many look into the inner room who sit outside far away*
488 thrang *throng* thrif *prosper* 489 fair calling *kindly welcome*
490 nixt *nearest* 491 serf *serve* samin fasson *same way* 492 lene *lean*
493 fut *foot* fast *firmly, persistently* stramp *tread*
494 far but *far outside* sueit blenkis *sweet glances* 495 in speciall *individually*
496 warmys *become warm* 497 liffand leid *living man* law *low* degré *rank*
498 unluffit *unloved, without being loved in return* loik-hertit *warm-hearted*
499 lent *inclined* lyre *face, complexion* 500 lak *play* danger *be endangered*
501 menys all wichtis *take pity on all creatures*
502 sely saull *innocent soul* saif *safe* Sabot *(?)Lord God of Sabaoth* jugis *judges*

Ladyis, leir thir lessonis and be no lassis fundin:
This is the legeand of my lif, thought Latyne it be nane.'

505   Quhen endit had hir ornat speche this eloquent wedow,
Lowd thai lewch all the laif and loffit hir mekle,
And said thai sald exampill tak of her soverane teching
And wirk eftir hir wordis, that woman wes so prudent.
Than culit thai ther mouthis with confortable drinkis,
510 And carpit full cummerlik with cop going round.
Thus draif thai our that deir nyght with danceis full noble,
Quhill that the day did up-daw, and dew donkit flouris.
The morow myld wes and meik the mavis did sing,
And all remuffit the myst, and the meid smellit.
515 Silver schouris doune schuke as the schene cristall,
And berdis shoutit in schaw with ther schill notis.
The goldin glitterand gleme so gladit ther hertis,
Thai maid a glorius gle amang the grene bewis.
The soft sowch of the swyr and soune of the stremys,
520 The sueit savour of the sward, singing of foulis,
Myght confort ony creatur of the kyn of Adam,
And kindill agane his curage thoght it wer cald sloknyt.

503 leir thir lessonis *learn these lessons* lassis *(?)little girls, (?)ignorant girls*
fundin *found*   504 legeand *legend*
thought Latyne it be nane *though it is not in Latin*

505 ornat *ornate, elaborate*
506 Lowd thai lewch all the laif *the others laughed loudly* loffit *praised*
507 sald *should* exampill *example* soverane teching *peerless teaching*
508 wirk eftir *act according to* 509 culit *cooled, refreshed*
confortable *comforting* 510 carpit *talked* cummerlik *intimately*
511 draif thai *they passed* deir *glorious, festive* danceis *dances*
512 Quhill *until* up-daw *dawn* donkit *moistened*   513 myld *soft*
meik *gently* mavis *thrush* 514 remuffit *vanished* myst *mist*
meid smellit *meadow gave off scent* 515 schouris *showers* schuke *fell as like*
schene *shining* 516 berdis shoutit *birds sang out* schaw *wood* schill *shrill*
517 glitterand gleme *glittering light* gladit *gladdened* 518 gle *music*
bewis *boughs* 519 sowch *murmuring* swyr *valley* soune *sound* stremys *streams*
520 savour *scent* foulis *birds* 521 kyn *kin*
522 kindill *rouse* curage *spirits* cald *cold* sloknyt *extinguished, quenched*

Than rais thir ryall rosis in ther riche wedis,
And rakit hame to ther rest throgh the rise blumys;
525 And I all prevély past to a plesand arber,
And with my pen did report ther pastance most mery.

Ye auditoris most honorable that eris has gevin
Onto this uncouth aventur quhilk airly me happinnit,
Of thir thre wanton wiffis that I haif writtin heir,
530 Quhilk wald ye waill to your wif gif ye suld wed one?

523 rais thir ryall rosis *arose these noble roses*   524 rakit hame *went home*
rise blumys *blossoms of the spray*   525 prevély *secretly*
526 pastance *pastime, entertainment*

527 auditoris *listeners* eris has gevin *have given ear*
528 Onto *to* uncouth aventur *strange event*
quhilk airly me happinnit *which befell me early in the day*
529 thir thre wanton wiffis *these three merry wives* heir *here*
530 Quhilk wald ye waill *which would you choose* suld *had to, were to*

QUHY WILL YE, MERCHANTIS
OF RENOUN

Quhy will ye, merchantis of renoun,
Lat Edinburgh, your nobill toun,
For laik of reformatioun
The commone proffeitt tyine, and fame?
5   Think ye not schame
That onie uther regioun
Sall with dishonour hurt your name?

May nane pas throw your principall gaittis
For stink of haddockis and of scattis,
10 For cryis of carlingis and debaittis,
For feusum flyttingis of defame.
    Think ye not schame
Befoir strangeris of all estaittis,
That sic dishonour hurt your name?

15 Your Stinkand Stull that standis dirk,
Haldis the lycht fra your parroche kirk;
Your foirstairis makis your housis mirk,
Lyk na cuntray bot heir at hame.

---

1 Quhy *why* renoun *repute*   2 Lat *let*   3 laik *lack*
4 *damage the general good and reputation*   5 schame *shameful*
6 onie uther regioun *any other country*   7 Sall *shall*

8 nane *none* pas throw *go through* gaittis *streets*   9 haddockis *haddocks*
scattis *skates, rays*   10 cryis of carlingis *cries of old women* debaittis *quarrels*
11 feusum *foul* flyttingis *flytings, exchanges of abuse* defame *defamation*
13 Befoir *before* estaittis *ranks*   14 sic *such*

15 Stinkand Stull *Stinking Style (a passage in a tenement; see n.)*
standis dirk *stands dark*   16 *keeps the light from your parish church*
17 *your outside stairs make your houses dark*
18 Lyk na cuntray *like no (other) country* heir at hame *here at home*

        Think ye not schame
20 Sa litill polesie to wirk,
    In hurt and sklander of your name?

    At your hie Croce quhar gold and silk
    Sould be, thair is bot crudis and milk;
    And at your Trone bot cokill and wilk,
25 Pansches, pudingis of Jok and Jame.
        Think ye not schame
    Sen as the world sayis that ilk,
    In hurt and sclander of your name?

    Your commone menstrallis hes no tone
30 Bot 'Now the day dawis,' and 'Into Joun';
    Cunningar men man serve Sanct Cloun,
    And nevir to uther craftis clame.
        Think ye not schame
    To hald sic mowaris on the moyne,
35 In hurt and sclander of your name?

    Tailyouris, soutteris, and craftis vyll
    The fairest of your streittis dois fyll,
    And merchandis at the Stinkand Styll
    Ar hamperit in ane hony-came.

20 Sa litill polesie *so little improvement* wirk *bring about*   21 sklander *slander*

22 hie Croce *high Cross (see n.)* quhar *where*   23 Sould *should*
thair is bot crudis *there is nothing but curds*
24 Trone *Tron, public weighing beam* cokill *cockles* wilk *whelks*
25 Pansches *tripes* pudingis *'puddings' (sausages stuffed with oatmeal, meat)*
Jok *Jock* Jame *Jamie*   27 Sen *since* that ilk *that same (thing)*

29 menstrallis hes no tone *minstrels have no tune*   30 dawis *dawns*
'Into Joun' *in June*   31 Cunningar *more skilled* man *must*
Sanct Cloun *(?)St Cluan (see n.)*   32 uther craftis *other skills, occupations*
clame *lay claim*   33 hald *keep, support* mowaris on the moyne *(?)gallows-birds*

36 Tailyouris *tailors* soutteris *cobblers* vyll *vile, base*   37 streittis *streets*
fyll *defile*   39 hamperit *cramped* hony-came *honeycomb*

40   Think ye not schame
        That ye have nether witt nor wyll
        To win yourselff ane bettir name?

        Your burgh of beggeris is ane nest,
        To schout thai swentyouris will not rest;
45   All honest folk they do molest,
        Sa piteuslie thai cry and rame.
            Think ye not schame
        That for the poore hes nothing drest;
        In hurt and sclander of your name?

50   Your proffeit daylie dois incres,
        Your godlie workis les and les;
        Through streittis nane may mak progres
        For cry of cruikit, blind, and lame.
            Think ye not schame
55   That ye sic substance dois posses
        And will not win ane bettir name?

        Sen for the court and the Sessioun,
        The great repair of this regioun
        Is in your burgh, thairfoir be boun
60   To mend all faultis that ar to blame

41 nether *neither* witt *intelligence* wyll *subtlety, device*

43 burgh *town* beggeris *beggars*   44 schout *cry out, clamour*
thai *those* swentyouris *vagabonds, rascals*   46 piteuslie *piteously*
rame *clamour*   48 drest *arranged, made provision*

50 incres *increase*   51 les and les *(are) fewer and fewer*   52 nane *no one*
53 cruikit *crooked, deformed*   55 substance *wealth*

57 Sen for *because of* court *(royal) court* Sessioun *Session, court of justice*
58 repair *gathering place, haunt*   59 thairfoir *therefore* boun *ready, prepared*
60 mend *amend*

And eschew schame.
Gif thai pas to ane uther toun,
Ye will decay, and your great name.

Thairfoir strangeris and leigis treit;
65   Tak not over mekill for thair meit,
And gar your merchandis be discreit;
That na extortiounes be, proclame
    All fraud and schame,
Keip ordour and poore nighbouris beit,
70   That ye may gett ane bettir name.

Singular proffeit so dois yow blind,
The common proffeit gois behind.
I pray that Lord remeid to fynd
That deit into Jerusalem,
75   And gar yow schame;
That sumtyme ressoun may yow bind
For to [recover] yow guid name.

61 eschew *avoid*   62 Gif thai *if they (i.e. the court and the Session)* pas *move*

64 strangeris *strangers* leigis *(the king's) subjects* treit *show favour to, welcome*
65 Tak not over mekill *take not too much* meit *food*
66 gar *cause* discreit *discreet, judicious*
67 That na extortiounes be *so that there be no extortion* proclame *denounce*
69 Keip ordour *keep order* poore nighbouris beit *help poor neighbours, citizens*

71 Singular proffeit *private profit* yow blind *blinds you*
72 gois behind *is neglected*   73 remeid *remedy* fynd *find*
74 deit *died* into *in*   75 *and make you feel ashamed*   76 ressoun *reason*
77 yow *for yourselves*

SWEIT ROIS OF VERTEW
AND OF GENTILNES

Sweit rois of vertew and of gentilnes,
Delytsum lyllie of everie lustynes,
   Richest in bontie and in bewtie cleir
   And everie vertew that is deir,
5   Except onlie that ye ar mercyles.

Into your garthe this day I did persew;
Thair saw I flowris that fresche wer of hew,
   Baithe quhyte and rid, moist lusty wer to seyne,
   And halsum herbis upone stalkis grene –
10   Yit leif nor flour fynd could I nane of rew.

I dout that Merche with his caild blastis keyne
Hes slane this gentill herbe that I of mene,
   Quhois petewous deithe dois to my hart sic pane
   That I wald mak to plant his rute agane,
15   So confortand his levis unto me bene.

---

1 Sweit rois *sweet rose* vertew *virtue, goodness* gentilnes *nobility, grace*
2 Delytsum lyllie *delightful lily* lustynes *loveliness, charm*   3 bontie *goodness*
bewtie *beauty* cleir *fair, shining*   4 deir *precious*
5 onlie *only* mercyles *without mercy*

6 garthe *(enclosed) garden* persew *enter*
7 Thair *there* flowris *flowers* fresche *fresh, beautiful* hew *colour*
8 *both white and red were most delightful to see*
9 halsum herbis *health-giving herbs* stalkis grene *green stalks*
10 Yit *yet* leif *leaf* flour *flower* nane *none* rew *rue (the herb), pity*

11 dout *fear* Merche *March* caild blastis *cold blasts* keyne *sharp, fierce*
12 Hes slane *has slain* gentill *gracious, noble* of mene *speak of*
13 *whose piteous death causes such suffering to my heart*
14 wald mak *would cause, attempt* rute *root*
15 confortand *comforting* levis *leaves* bene *are*

RYGHT AS THE STERN OF DAY
BEGOUTH TO SCHYNE

The Goldyn Targe

Ryght as the stern of day begouth to schyne
Quhen gone to bed war Vesper and Lucyne,
   I raise and by a rosere did me rest;
Up sprang the goldyn candill matutyne
5   With clere depurit bemes cristallyne,
     Glading the mery foulis in thair nest;
     Or Phebus was in purpur cape revest
Up raise the lark, the hevyns menstrale fyne,
   In May intill a morow myrthfullest.

10   Full angellike thir birdis sang thair houris
Within thair courtyns grene into thair bouris,
   Apparalit quhite and rede wyth blomes suete;
Anamalit was the felde wyth all colouris,
The perly droppis schake in silvir schouris,

---

1 Ryght *just* stern *star* begouth *began* 2 Quhen *when* war *were*
Vesper *Vesper (the evening star)* Lucyne *Lucina (the moon)* 3 raise *arose*
rosere *rosebush* 4 candill matutyne *candle of the morning (the sun)*
5 clere *clear, bright* depurit *pure* bemes *beams* cristallyne *crystal-clear*
6 Glading *gladdening* foulis *birds* 7 Or *before*
Phebus *Phoebus, the sun* purpur *crimson, shining* revest *arrayed*
8 hevyns menstrale fyne *heaven's exquisite minstrel*
9 intill a morow *in morning* myrthfullest *most joyous*

10 angellike *like angels* thir birdis *these birds*
houris *(liturgical) hours, services sung at fixed times during the day*
11 courtyns grene *curtains green* into *in* bouris *bowers*
12 Apparalit *arrayed* quhite *white* rede *red* blomes *blooms* suete *sweet*
13 Anamalit *enamelled* felde *field* 14 schake *shook, scattered* schouris *showers*

15   Quhill all in balme did branch and levis flete;
        To part fra Phebus did Aurora grete –
        Hir cristall teris I saw hyng on the flouris
            Quhilk he for lufe all drank up wyth his hete.

        For mirth of May wyth skippis and wyth hoppis
20   The birdis sang upon the tender croppis
            With curiouse note, as Venus chapell clerkis;
        The rosis yong, new spreding of thair knopis,
        War powdirit brycht with hevinly beriall droppis
            Throu bemes rede birnyng as ruby-sperkis;
25   The skyes rang for schoutyng of the larkis;
        The purpur hevyn, ourscailit in silvir sloppis,
            Ourgilt the treis, branchis, lef and barkis.

        Doun throu the ryce a ryvir ran wyth stremys,
        So lustily agayn thai lykand lemys
30   That all the lake as lamp did leme of licht,
        Quhilk schadowit all about wyth twynkling glemis,
        That bewis bathit war in secund bemys

15 Quhill *while* balme *balm (an aromatic substance which exudes from various
trees)* levis *leaves* flete *flow*   16 fra *from* Aurora *Aurora, the dawn* grete *weep*
17 teris *tears* hyng *hang* flouris *flowers*   18 Quhilk *which* lufe *love*
hete *heat*

19 mirth *joy* skippis *skips*   20 croppis *topmost shoots*   21 curiouse *intricate*
as Venus chapell clerkis *like the chapel clerks (choristers) of Venus*
22 rosis yong *young roses* knopis *buds*   23 powdirit *powdered, sprinkled*
brycht *brightly* hevinly *heavenly*
beriall *beryl (a transparent precious stone =), gleaming*
24 *through the red beams of the sun blazing like small rubies*   25 skyes *skies*
rang *resounded* schoutyng *clamour*   26 ourscailit *dappled (as if with scales)*
sloppis *(?)patches (of sky), (?)small clouds*
27 Ourgilt *covered with a golden colour* treis *trees* lef *leaves, foliage* barkis *barks*

28 ryce *bushes* ryvir *river* stremys *currents*   29 lustily *pleasantly*
agayn *against, facing* thai lykand lemys *those delightful rays of light*
30 lake *water* leme of licht *shine with light*
31 Quhilk schadowit *which was reflected* glemis *gleams*   32 bewis *boughs*
bathit *bathed* secund *second, further*

Throu the reflex of Phebus visage brycht.
On every syde the hegies raise on hicht,
35   The bank was grene, the bruke was full of bremys,
The stanneris clere as stern in frosty nycht.

The cristall air, the sapher firmament,
The ruby skyes of the orient,
Kest beriall bemes on emerant bewis grene;
40   The rosy garth depaynt and redolent
With purpur, azure, gold and goulis gent
Arayed was by dame Flora the quene
So nobily that joy was for to sene;
The roch agayn the rivir resplendent
45   As low enlumynit all the leves schene.

Quhat throu the mery foulys armony
And throu the ryveris soun, rycht ran me by
On Florais mantill I slepit as I lay;
Quhare sone into my dremes fantasy
50   I saw approch agayn the orient sky
A saill als quhite as blossum upon spray,
Wyth merse of gold brycht as the stern of day,
Quhilk tendit to the land full lustily
Als falcoun swift desyrouse of hir pray:

33 reflex *reflection* brycht *bright*   34 hegies raise on hicht *hedges rose aloft*
35 bruke *brook* bremys *bream (carp, bream)*   36 stanneris *pebbles* stern *star*
nycht *night*

37 sapher *sapphire*   38 orient *east*   39 Kest *cast* beriall *gleaming*
emerant bewis *emerald boughs*   40 garth *garden* depaynt *coloured*
redolent *fragrant*   41 goulis *(gules, heraldic term =) red* gent *elegant*
42 Flora *Flora (goddess of flowers)* quene *queen*   43 sene *see, look on*   44 roch *rock*
45 As low *like a flame* enlumynit *illuminated, shed light on* schene *beautiful*

46 Quhat throu *what with, as a result of* foulys armony *birds' harmony*
47 ryveris soun *river's sound* rycht ran me by *(which) ran closely by me*
48 Florais mantill *Flora's mantle* slepit *slept*
49 *where soon in my dream's fancy*   50 approch *approach* agayn *against*
51 saill *sail* als quhite *as white* spray *twig*   52 merse *top-castle (of a ship)*
53 tendit *moved*   54 falcoun *falcon* pray *prey*

55   And hard on burd unto the blomyt medis
      Amang the grene rispis and the redis
         Arrivit sche; quharfro anon thare landis
      Ane hundreth ladyes, lusty into wedis,
      Als fresch as flouris that in May up spredis,
60   In kirtillis grene withoutyn kell or bandis.
       Thair brycht hairis hang gleting on the strandis
      In tressis clere, wyppit wyth goldyn thredis,
         With pappis quhite and mydlis small as wandis.

      Discrive I wald, bot quho coud wele endyte
65   How all the feldis wyth thai lilies quhite
         Depaynt war brycht, quhilk to the hevyn did glete?
      Noucht thou, Omer, als fair as thou coud wryte,
      For all thine ornate stilis so perfyte;
         Nor yit thou, Tullius, quhois lippis suete
70   Off rethorike did into termes flete.
      Your aureate tongis both bene all to lyte
       For to compile that paradise complete.

55 hard on burd *close at hand* blomyt medis *blossoming meadows*
56 Amang *among* rispis *sedge* redis *reeds*
57 sche *she* quharfro *from which* anon *forthwith* landis *disembarks*
58 hundreth *hundred* lusty into wedis *beautiful in (their) garments*
59 fresch *fresh* up spredis *unfold* 60 kirtillis *kirtles, dresses*
kell *caul, cap* bandis *headbands* 61 hang *hung* gleting *gleaming, shining*
strandis *shores* 62 tressis *tresses* wyppit *bound round* thredis *threads*
63 pappis *breasts* mydlis *waists* small *slender* wandis *wands, young branches*

64 Discrive *describe* wald *would*
quho coud wele endyte *who could write eloquently* 65 feldis *fields* thai *those*
66 Depaynt *coloured* glete *gleam* 67 Noucht *not* Omer *Homer*
68 stilis *compositions* perfyte *perfect*
69 yit *yet* Tullius *Cicero* quhois lippis suete *whose sweet lips*
70 rethorike *rhetoric* termes *figures (of rhetoric)* flete *flow, abound*
71 aureate tongis *golden tongues* bene all to lyte *are all too inadequate*
72 compile *describe* complete *perfect*

Thare saw I Nature and Venus, quene and quene,
The fresch Aurora, and lady Flora schene,
75   Juno appellour, and Proserpyna,
Dyane the goddesse chaste of woddis grene,
My lady Cleo that help of makaris bene,
    Thetes, Pallas and prudent Minerva,
    Fair feynit Fortune and lemand Lucina –
80   Thir mychti quenis in crounis mycht be sene
    With bemys blith, bricht as Lucifera.

Thare saw I May, of myrthfull monethis quene,
Betuix Aprile and June hir sistir schene,
    Within the gardyng walking up and doun,
85   Quham of the foulis gladdith all bedene.
Scho was full tendir in hir yeris grene.
Thare saw I Nature present hir a goun,
    Rich to behald and nobil of renoun,
Off eviry hew undir the hevin that bene,
90   Depaynt and broud be gude proporcioun.

75 Juno *Juno, wife of Jupiter* appellour *(the) accuser (see n.)*
Proserpyna *Proserpina, daughter of Jupiter and Ceres, carried off to the
underworld by Pluto*   76 Dyane *Diana, virgin goddess of hunting*
woddis *woods*   77 Cleo *Clio, muse of history* makaris *poets* bene *is*
78 Thetes *Thetis, goddess of the sea* Pallas *Pallas, the goddess Pallas Athena*
Minerva *Minerva, Roman goddess of wisdom*   79 feynit *deceitful*
lemand *shining*   80 Thir mychti quenis *these mighty queens*
crounis *crowns*   81 blith *glad* Lucifera *Lucifera, the planet Venus*

82 monethis *months*   83 sistir *sisters* schene *beautiful*   84 gardyng *garden*
85 Quham of *of whom* gladdith *rejoice* bedene *together*   86 Scho *she*
yeris *years* grene *young*   88 behald *behold*   89 hew *colour*
90 Depaynt *brightly coloured* broud *embroidered*
be gude proporcioun *in a well-proportioned way*

Full lustily thir ladyes all in fere
Enterit within this park of most plesere
   Quhare that I lay, ourhelit wyth levis ronk.
The mery foulis blissfullest of chere
95 Salust Nature, me thoucht, on thair manere,
     And eviry blome on branch and eke on bonk
     Opnyt and spred thair balmy levis donk,
Full low enclynyng to thair quene so clere
   Quham of thair noble norising thay thonk.

100 Syne to dame Flora on the samyn wyse
Thay saluse and thay thank a thousand syse;
   And to dame Venus lufis mychti quene
Thay sang ballettis in lufe, as was the gyse,
With amourouse notis lusty to devise,
105   As thay that had lufe in thair hertis grene;
     Thair hony throtis opnyt fro the splene
With werblis suete did perse the hevinly skyes,
   Quhill loud resownyt the firmament serene.

Ane othir court thare saw I consequent –
110 Cupide the king wyth bow in hand ybent
   And dredefull arowis grundyn scharp and square.
Thare saw I Mars the god armypotent,
Aufull and sterne, strong and corpolent.

---

91 in fere *together*   92 Enterit *entered* of most plesere *of the greatest delight*
93 ourhelit *covered* ronk *dense*   94 chere *mood, demeanour*   95 Salust *saluted*
me thoucht *it seemed to me* manere *manner* 96 eke *also* bonk *bank*
97 Opnyt *opened* donk *moist* 98 enclynyng *bowing* clere *bright*
99 Quham *whom* norising *nourishment* thonk *thank*

100 Syne *then* samyn wyse *same manner*   101 Saluse *greet* syse *times*
102 lufis *love's*   103 ballettis *songs* gyse *fashion*   104 notis *notes*
lusty *lovely* devise *describe* 106 hony *sweet as honey* throtis *throats*
fro the splene *from the heart*   107 werblis suete *melodious songs*
perse *pierce* 108 Quhill *till* resownyt *resounded* serene *clear, calm*

109 consequent *following*   110 ybent *bent, drawn*
111 dredefull arowis *fearful arrows* grundyn *sharpened* square *strong*
112 armypotent *mighty in arms* 113 Aufull *terrible* sterne *grim* corpolent *bulky*

Thare saw I crabbit Saturn ald and haire,
His luke was lyke for to perturb the aire.
Thare was Mercurius, wise and eloquent,
    Of rethorike that fand the flouris faire;

Thare was the god of gardingis, Priapus,
Thare was the god of wildernes, Phanus,
    And Janus, god of entree delytable.
Thare was the god of fludis, Neptunus,
Thare was the god of wyndis, Eolus,
    With variand luke rycht lyke a lord unstable.
    Thare was Bacus, the gladder of the table,
Thare was Pluto, the elrich incubus,
    In cloke of grene – his court usit no sable.

And eviry one of thir in grene arayit
On harp or lute full merily thai playit,
    And sang ballettis with michty notis clere.
Ladyes to dance full sobirly assayit,
Endlang the lusty ryvir so thai mayit,
    Thair observance rycht hevynly was to here.
    Than crap I throu the levis and drew nere,
Quhare that I was rycht sudaynly affrayt,
    All throu a luke, quhilk I have boucht full dere.

---

114 crabbit *ill-natured* ald *old* haire *grey*   115 luke *look, aspect*
lyke *likely* perturb *trouble*   116 Mercurius *Mercury*
117 rethorike *rhetoric* fand *devised* flouris *flowers, ornaments*

118 gardingis *gardens*   119 Phanus *Faunus*   120 entree *entry*
delytable *delightful*   121 fludis *seas, waters*   122 wyndis *winds*
123 variand *changeable* rycht *just*   124 Bacus *Bacchus*
the gladder *he who makes glad*   125 elrich *supernatural, weird* incubus *demon*
126 cloke *cloak* sable *sable, black*

130 sobirly assayit *solemnly proceeded*   131 Endlang *along*
mayit *celebrated May*   132 observance *ritual* here *hear*
133 crap *crept*   134 affrayt *frightened*   135 boucht *paid for* dere *dearly*

And schortly for to speke, be lufis quene
I was aspyit. Scho bad hir archearis kene
   Go me arrest, and thay no tyme delayit.
Than ladyes fair lete fall thair mantillis gren;
140 With bowis big, in tressit hairis schene
   All sudaynly thay had a felde arayit –
   And yit rycht gretly was I noucht affrayit,
The party was so plesand for to sene –
   A wonder lusty bikkir me assayit.

145 And first of all with bow in hand ybent
Come dame Beautee, rycht as scho wald me schent;
   Syne folowit all hir dameselis yfere,
With mony diverse aufull instrument.
Unto the pres Fair Having wyth hir went,
150   Fyne Portrature, Plesance, and Lusty Chere.
   Than come Resoun with schelde of gold so clere,
In plate and maille, as Mars armypotent:
   Defendit me that nobil chevallere.

---

136 be *by*   **137** aspyit *espied* archearis kene *fierce archers*   **139** lete *let*
mantillis *mantles*   **140** bowis *bows* tressit hairis *braided hair* schene *beautiful*
141 felde *field of battle, armed force* arayit *drawn up*   **142** gretly *greatly*
143 party *company, troop* plesand *delightful*   **144** bikkir *assault*
assayit *attacked*

146 dame Beautee *lady Beauty* rycht as *just as if*
wald me schent *would have me destroyed*   **147** dameselis *damsels, attendants*
yfere *together*   **149** pres *melée, thick of the fight* Fair Having *Fair Demeanour*
150 Fyne Portrature *Fine Appearance* Plesance *Joy, Delight*
Lusty Chere *Pleasing Countenance*   **151** come *came* Resoun *Reason*
schelde *shield*   **152** plate *armour* maille *chain-mail*   **153** chevallere *knight*

Syne tender Youth come wyth hir virgyns ying,
155 Grene Innocence, and schamefull Abaising,
    And quaking Drede wyth humble Obedience.
The goldyn targe harmyt thay no thing.
Curage in thame was noucht begonne to spring;
    Full sore thay dred to done a violence.
160   Suete Womanhede I saw cum in presence –
Of artilye a warld sche did in bring,
    Servit wyth ladyes full of reverence.

Sche led wyth hir Nurture and Lawlynes,
Contenence, Pacience, Gude Fame and Stedfastnes,
165   Discrecioun, Gentrise and Considerance,
Levefull Company and Honest Besynes,
Benigne Luke, Mylde Chere and Sobirnes.
    All thir bure ganyeis to do me grevance,
    Bot Resoun bure the targe wyth sik constance,
170 Thair scharp assayes mycht do no dures
    To me, for all thair aufull ordynance.

154 ying *young*   155 schamefull Abaising *modest Bashfulness*
156 Drede *Fear*   158 Curage *desire, spirit* was noucht begonne *had not begun*
159 dred *feared* done *do*   160 Womanhede *Womanliness*
161 artilye *artillery* warld *great quantity*   162 reverence *respect*

163 Nurture *Courtesy, Good Breeding* Lawlynes *Humility*
164 Contenence *Continence*   165 Discrecioun *Discernment*
Gentrise *Nobility* Considerance *Consideration*
166 Levefull Company *(lawful =) Proper Companionship* Besynes *Diligence*
167 Sobirnes *Gravity*   168 bure *bore* ganyeis *arrows* grevance *harm*
169 sik *such*   170 assayes *attacks* dures *injury*
171 ordynance *order of battle*

Unto the pres persewit Hie Degree;
Hir followit ay Estate and Dignitee,
   Comparisoun, Honour, and noble Array,
175 Will, Wantonnes, Renoun and Libertee,
Richesse, Fredome and eke Nobilitee.
   Wit ye thay did thair baner hye display;
   A cloud of arowis as hayle-schour lousit thay,
And schot quhill wastit was thair artilye,
180   Syne went abak reboytit of thair pray.

Quhen Venus had persavit this rebute
Dissymilance scho bad go mak persute
   At all powere to perse the goldyn targe;
And scho that was of doubilnes the rute
185 Askit hir choise of archeris in refute.
   Venus the best bad hir go wale at large.
   Scho tuke Presence, plicht anker of the barge,
And Fair Callyng, that wele a flayn coud schute,
   And Cherising for to complete hir charge.

---

172 persewit *advanced* Hie Degree *High Rank*   173 Estate *Estate, Class*
Dignitee *High Standing*   174 Comparisoun *(?)Assessment*
175 Wantonnes *Amorous Delight* Libertee *Liberty (from restraint)*
176 Richesse *Wealth* Fredome *Generosity*   177 Wit *know* hye *high*
178 hayle-schour *shower of hail* lousit *loosed*   179 quhill *until*
wastit *exhausted*   180 went abak *retreated* reboytit *foiled, deprived*

181 persavit *become aware of* rebute *repulse*   182 Dissymilance *Dissimulation*
persute *pursuit*   183 At all powere *in full force*   184 of doubilnes *deceitfulness*
rute *root*   185 choise of *most excellent* in refute *for defence*
186 wale at large *choose unhindered*   187 Presence *(physical) Presence*
plicht anker *main anchor*   188 Fair Callyng *Fair Greeting*
wele *well* flayn *arrow* schute *shoot*   189 Cherising *Affection* charge *task*

190   Dame Hamelynes scho tuke in company,
That hardy was and hende in archery,
   And broucht dame Beautee to the felde agayn
With all the choise of Venus chevalry;
Thay come and bikkerit unabaisitly.
195   The schour of arowis rappit on as rayn.
   Perilouse Presence that mony syre has slayn,
The bataill broucht on bordour hard us by;
   The salt was all the sarar, suth to sayn.

Thik was the schote of grundyn dartis kene,
200   Bot Resoun with the scheld of gold so schene
   Warly defendit, quhoso evir assayit.
The aufull stoure he manly did sustene
Quhill Presence kest a pulder in his ene,
   And than as drunkyn man he all forvayit.
205   Quhen he was blynd, the fule wyth hym they playit,
And banyst hym amang the bewis grene:
   That sory sicht me sudaynly affrayit.

190 Hamelynes *Familiarity, Intimacy*   191 hardy *bold* hende *skilful*
192 broucht *brought*   193 choise *most excellent* chevalry *troop*
194 bikkerit *attacked* unabaisitly *fearlessly*   195 rappit *drove*
196 mony *many* syre *man*   197 bordour *edge of the field*
198 salt *assault* sarar *more grievous* suth to sayn *to say the truth*

199 schote *discharge* grundyn *sharpened* kene *fierce, piercing*   200 schene *fair*
201 Warly *(?)prudently; (?)in a warlike manner* quhoso evir *whoever*
assayit *assailed*   202 stoure *combat* sustene *endure*   203 kest *cast*
pulder *powder* ene *eyes*   204 forvayit *went astray*   205 fule *fool*
playit *played*   206 banyst *banished* bewis *boughs*
207 sicht *sight* affrayit *alarmed*

Than was I woundit to the deth wele nere,
And yoldyn as a wofull prisonnere
210   To lady Beautee in a moment space,
Me thoucht scho semyt lustiar of chere
Efter that Resoun tynt had his eyne clere
     Than of before, and lufliare of face:
     Quhy was thou blyndit, Resoun, quhi, allace?
215   And gert ane hell my paradise appere,
     And mercy seme quhare that I fand no grace?

Dissymulance was besy me to sile,
And Fair Calling did oft apon me smyle,
     And Cherising me fed wyth wordis fair;
220   New Acquyntance enbracit me a quhile
And favouryt me, quhill men mycht go a myle,
     Syne tuke hir leve: I saw hir nevir mare.
     Than saw I Dangere toward me repair –
I coud eschew hir presence be no wyle.
225   On syde scho lukit wyth ane fremyt fare.

And at the last Departing coud hir dresse,
And me delyverit unto Hevynesse
     For to remayne, and scho in cure me tuke.
Be this the lord of wyndis wyth wodenes
230   God Eolus his bugill blew I gesse,

209 yoldyn *surrendered*   211 semyt *seemed* lustiar *more pleasant*
chere *demeanour*   212 tynt *lost* eyne *eyes*   213 before *before*
lufliare *more lovely*   214 Quhy *why*   215 gert *caused*
appere *appear*   216 seme *appear to be* fand *found*

217 Dissymulance *Dissimulation* besy *busy* sile *deceive*   218 apon *upon*
220 Acquyntance *Acquaintance* enbracit *embraced*   222 mare *more*
223 Dangere *Disdain*   224 eschew *avoid* wyle *strategem*
225 syde *aside, away* lukit *looked* fremyt fare *distant expression*

226 Departing *Separation* hir dresse *prepare herself*   227 Hevynesse *Sorrow*
228 remayne *remain* cure *charge* tuke *took*   229 wodenes *madness*
230 bugill *horn* gesse *think*

That with the blast the levis all toschuke;
And sudaynly in the space of a luke
All was hyne went: thare was bot wildernes,
Thare was no more bot birdis, bank and bruke.

235   In twynklyng of ane eye to ship thai went,
And swyth up saile unto the top thai stent,
      And with swift course atour the flude thai frak.
Thai fyrit gunnis wyth powder violent,
Till that the reke raise to the firmament;
240   The rochis all resownyt wyth the rak,
      For rede it semyt that the raynbow brak.
Wyth spirit affrayde apon my fete I sprent
      Amang the clewis, so carefull was the crak.

And as I did awake of my sueving
245   The joyfull birdis merily did syng
      For myrth of Phebus tendir bemes schene,
Suete war the vapouris, soft the morowing,
Halesum the vale depaynt wyth flouris ying,
      The air attemperit, sobir and amene,
250   In quhite and rede was all the felde besene,
Throu Naturis nobil fresch anamalyng
      In mirthfull May, of eviry moneth quene.

---

231 toschuke *shook violently*   **233** hyne *hence* went *gone*   **234** bruke *brook*

236 swyth *at once* top *top, platform at the mast-head* stent *stretched, set*
237 atour *over* flude *water* frak *sped*   **238** fyrit *fired*   **239** reke *smoke*
raise *rose*   **240** rochis *rocks* rak *crash*   **241** rede *din* brak *broke*
242 sprent *sprang*   **243** clewis *cliffs* carefull *terrible, distressing* crak *explosion*

244 sueving *dream*   **247** vapouris *mists* morowing *morning*
248 Halesum *wholesome, health-giving* depaynt *coloured*
249 attemperit *temperate* sobir *mild* amene *pleasant*   **250** besene *arrayed*
251 anamalyng *enamelling*

O reverend Chaucere, rose of rethoris all,
As in oure tong ane flour imperiall
255   That raise in Britane evir, quho redis rycht,
Thou beris of makaris the tryumph riall;
Thy fresch anamalit termes celicall
    This mater coud illumynit have full brycht.
    Was thou noucht of oure Inglisch all the lycht,
260   Surmounting eviry tong terrestriall,
     Alls fer as Mayes morow dois mydnycht?

O morall Gower and Ludgate laureate,
Your sugurit lippis and tongis aureate
    Bene to oure eris cause of grete delyte.
265   Your angel mouthis most mellifluate
Oure rude langage has clere illumynate,
    And fair ourgilt oure spech, that imperfyte
    Stude or your goldyn pennis schupe to write;
This ile before was bare and desolate
270   Off rethorike, or lusty fresch endyte.

Thou lytill quair, be evir obedient,
Humble, subject, and symple of entent
    Before the face of eviry connyng wicht.
I knaw quhat thou of rethorike hes spent:
275   Off all hir lusty rosis redolent

---

253 rethoris *poets, rhetoricians*   **254** tong *tongue, language*
imperiall *pre-eminent*   **255** raise *rose, flourished* quho *whoever, if anyone*
redis *reads, understands* rycht *correctly*   **256** beris *bear* makaris *poets*
tryumph riall *regal glory*   **257** termes *figures* celicall *heavenly*
258 mater *matter, subject* illumynit *illuminated, treated gloriously*
260 terrestriall *earthly*   **261** fer as *as far* dois *does* mydnycht *midnight*

263 sugurit *(sugared =) eloquent*   **264** eris *ears*   **265** mellifluate *sweet*
266 illumynate *illuminated, made glorious*   **267** ourgilt *covered with gold*
spech *speech* imperfyte *imperfect*   **268** Stude *stood, was before* schupe *prepared*
269 ile *island*   **270** endyte *poetry*

271 quair *small book, poem*   **273** connyng wicht *learned person*
274 spent *expended*   **275** redolent *fragrant*

Is none into thy gerland sett on hicht.
Eschame tharof and draw the out of sicht.
Rude is thy wede, disteynit, bare and rent;
Wele aucht thou be aferit of the licht.

276 gerland *garland* on hicht *on high*   277 Eschame *be ashamed*
278 Rude *rough, coarse* wede *garment* disteynit *stained*
279 aucht *ought* aferit *afraid*

QUHEN MERCHE WES WITH
VARIAND WINDIS PAST

The Thrissill and the Rois

Quhen Merche wes with variand windis past,
And Appryll had with hir silver schouris
Tane leif at Nature with ane orient blast;
And lusty May, that muddir is of flouris,
Had maid the birdis to begyn thair houris
Amang the tendir odouris reid and quhyt,
Quhois armony to heir it wes delyt:

In bed at morrow, sleiping as I lay,
Me thocht Aurora with hir cristall ene
In at the window lukit by the day
And halsit me, with visage paill and grene;
On quhois hand a lark sang fro the splene:
'Awalk, luvaris, out of your slomering!
Se how the lusty morrow dois up spring.'

1 Quhen *when* Merche *March* variand *changing*   2 schouris *showers*
3 Tane leif at *taken leave of* orient blast *east wind*
4 lusty *joyous, delightful* muddir *mother* flouris *flowers*   5 birdis *birds*
houris *(liturgical) hours (services sung at fixed times during the day)*
6 Amang *among* odouris *(odours =) fragrant flowers* reid *red* quhyt *white*
7 Quhois armony *whose harmony* heir *hear* delyt *delight, pleasure*

8 morrow *morning* sleiping *sleeping*   9 Me thocht *it seemed to me*
Aurora *Aurora, goddess of the dawn* cristall ene *eyes as clear as crystal*
10 lukit *looked* by the day *at daybreak*   11 halsit *greeted* paill *pale* grene *wan*
12 quhois *whose* splene *heart*   13 Awalk *awake* luvaris *lovers*
slomering *slumber*   14 Se *see* dois *does*

15   Me thocht fresche May befoir my bed upstude
     In weid depaynt of mony divers hew,
     Sobir, benyng, and full of mansuetude,
     In brycht atteir of flouris forgit new,
     Hevinly of color, quhyt, reid, broun and blew,
20   Balmit in dew and gilt with Phebus bemys
     Quhill all the hous illumynit of hir lemys.

     'Slugird,' scho said, 'Awalk annone for schame,
     And in my honour sum thing thow go wryt.
     The lark hes done the mirry day proclame
25   To rais up luvaris with confort and delyt,
     Yit nocht incresis thy curage to indyt,
     Quhois hairt sum tyme hes glaid and blisfull bene,
     Sangis to mak undir the levis grene.'

     'Quhairto,' quod I, 'Sall I uprys at morrow?
30   For in this May few birdis herd I sing.
     Thai haif moir caus to weip and plane thair sorrow,
     Thy air it is nocht holsum nor benyng;
     Lord Eolus dois in thy sessone ring –
     So busteous ar the blastis of his horne,
35   Amang thy bewis to walk I haif forborne.'

---

15 befoir *before* upstude *stood erect*   16 weid *garment* depaynt *coloured*
hew *hue*   17 Sobir *grave* benyng *gracious* mansuetude *gentleness*
18 brycht atteir *bright attire* forgit *formed*   19 Hevinly *heavenly*
broun *dusky, dark*   20 Balmit *anointed*
gilt with Phebus bemys *made gold by the beams of Phoebus (the sun)*
21 Quhill *until* illumynit *grew bright* lemys *rays*

22 Slugird *sluggard* scho *she* annone *at once*   23 sum *some* wryt *write*
24 done proclame *proclaimed*   25 rais up *call up* confort *consolation*
26 *yet your desire to compose does not increase*   27 hairt *heart*
28 Sangis *songs* mak *make* levis grene *green leaves*

29 Quhairto *why* quod *said* Sall *shall* uprys *rise up*   30 herd *heard*   31 haif *have*
moir *more* weip and plane *weep and lament*   32 holsum *wholesome, healthy*
benyng *gentle*   33 Eolus *Aeolus, god of the winds* sessone *season*
ring *reign*   34 busteous *violent, rough*
35 bewis *boughs, branches* forborne *ceased*

With that this lady sobirly did smyll,
And said, 'Uprys and do thy observance.
Thow did promyt in Mayis lusty quhyle
For to discryve the ros of most plesance.
40 Go se the birdis how thay sing and dance,
Illumynit our with orient skyis brycht,
Annamyllit richely with new asur lycht.'

Quhen this wes said, depairtit scho, this quene,
And enterit in a lusty gairding gent;
45 And than me thocht full festely besene,
In serk and mantill full haistely I went
Into this garth, most dulce and redolent
Off herb and flour and tendir plantis sueit,
And grene levis doing of dew doun fleit.

50 The purpour sone with tendir bemys reid
In orient bricht as angell did appeir,
Throw goldin skyis putting up his heid,
Quhois gilt tressis schone so wondir cleir
That all the world tuke confort fer and neir
55 To luke upone his fresche and blisfull face,
Doing all sable fro the hevynnis chace.

36 sobirly *gravely, calmly* smyll *smile*   38 promyt *promise*
quhyle *time, season*   39 discryve *describe* ros *rose*
41 Illumynit our *covered with light*   42 Annamyllit *enamelled, coloured*
asur *azure, deep blue*

43 depairtit *departed*   44 enterit *entered* gairding *garden*
45 festely *(?)festively (see n.)* besene *arrayed*   46 serk *shirt* mantill *mantle*
full haistely *quickly*   47 garth *garden* dulce *sweet* redolent *fragrant*
48 sueit *sweet*   49 doing of dew doun fleit *flowing down with dew*

50 purpour sone *crimson sun*   52 Throw *through* heid *head*
53 tressis *tresses* schone *shone* wondir *wondrously* cleir *bright*
54 tuke *took* fer and neir *far and near*
55 luke *look*   56 *driving away all darkness from the heavens*

And as the blisfull soune of cherarchy
The fowlis song throw confort of the licht,
The birdis did with oppin vocis cry:
60   'O luvaris fo, away thow dully nycht,
And welcum day that confortis every wicht;
Haill May, haill Flora, haill Aurora schene!
Haill princes Natur, haill Venus luvis quene!

Dame Nature gaif ane inhibitioun thair
65   To fers Neptunus and Eolus the bawld
Nocht to perturb the wattir nor the air;
And that no schouris nor no blastis cawld
Effray suld flouris nor fowlis on the fold;
Scho bad eik Juno, goddas of the sky,
70   That scho the hevin suld keip amene and dry.

Scho ordand eik that every bird and beist
Befoir hir hienes suld annone compeir,
And every flour of vertew, most and leist,
And every herb be feild, fer and neir,
75   As thay had wont in May fro yeir to yeir
To hir thair makar to mak obediens,
Full law inclynnand with all dew reverens.

57 as *like* soune *sound* cherarchy *(the angelic) hierarchies*
58 fowlis *birds* song *sang*   59 oppin vocis *open (voices =) mouths*
60 luvaris fo *enemy of lovers* dully nycht *dismal night*   61 wicht *creature*
62 Flora *Flora, goddess of flowers* schene *lovely*   63 luvis quene *queen of love*

64 gaif *gave* inhibitioun *prohibition* thair *there*
65 fers *fierce* Neptunus *Neptune, god of the sea* bawld *bold*   66 Nocht *not*
wattir *water*   67 cawld *cold*   68 Effray suld *should frighten* fold *earth*
69 bad *commanded* eik *also* goddas *goddess*   70 keip *keep* amene *pleasant*

71 ordand eik *ordained also* beist *beast*   72 hienes *highness*
compeir *appear*   73 vertew *power (see n.)* most and leist *greatest and humblest*
74 be feild *in field*   75 yeir *year*   76 hir *her* makar *maker* obediens *homage*
77 Full law inclynnand *bowing very deeply* dew reverens *due veneration*

With that annone scho send the swyft ro
To bring in beistis of all conditioun.
80   The restles suallow commandit scho also
To feche all fowll of small and greit renown;
And to gar flouris compeir of all fassoun
Full craftely conjurit scho the yarrow,
Quhilk did furth swirk als swift as ony arrow.

85   All present wer in twynkling of ane e –
Baith beist and bird and flour – befoir the quene.
And first the Lyone, gretast of degré,
Was callit thair, and he most fair to sene
With a full hardy contenance and kene
90   Befoir dame Natur come, and did inclyne,
With visage bawld and curage leonyne.

This awfull beist full terrible wes of cheir,
Persing of luke and stout of countenance,
Rycht strong of corpis, of fassoun fair but feir,
95   Lusty of schaip, lycht of deliverance,
Reid of his cullour as is the ruby glance.
On feild of gold he stude full mychtely
With flour-de-lycis sirculit lustely.

78 send *sent* ro *roe, small deer* 79 conditioun *state* 80 suallow *swallow*
81 feche *fetch* fowll *birds* 82 gar *cause* compeir *appear* fassoun *kind*
83 conjurit *commanded, caused to appear* yarrow *milfoil (a herb)*
84 Quhilk *which* did furth swirk *(?) spring forth*

85 e *eye* 86 Baith *both* 87 gretast of degré *greatest of rank* 88 sene *see*
89 hardy *bold* kene *fierce* 90 come *came*
91 and curage leonyne *and a lion's spirit*

92 awfull *fearsome* cheir *demeanour, look* 93 Persing *piercing*
stout of countenance *bold in bearing* 94 corpis *body* fassoun *build*
but feir *without equal* 95 schaip *shape* lycht of deliverance *agile in movement*
96 cullour *colour* ruby glance *glint from a ruby* 97 feild *field (see n.)*
stude *stood* 98 flour-de-lycis *lilies* sirculit *encircled*

This lady liftit up his cluvis cleir,
100 And leit him listly lene upone hir kne,
And crownit him with dyademe full deir
Off radyous stonis most ryall for to se,
Saying, 'The king of beistis mak I the,
And the chief protector in woddis and schawis:
105 Onto thi leigis go furth, and keip the lawis.'

'Exerce justice with mercy and conscience,
And lat no small beist suffir skaith na skornis
Of greit beistis that bene of moir piscence;
Do law elyk to aipis and unicornis,
110 And lat no bowgle with his busteous hornis
The meik pluch-ox oppress for all his pryd,
Bot in the yok go peciable him besyd.'

Quhen this was said, with noyis and soun of joy
All kynd of beistis into thair degré
115 At onis cryit lawd, '*Vive le roy!*'
And till his feit fell with humilité;
And all thay maid him homege and fewté,
And he did thame ressaif with princely laitis,
Quhois noble yre is *parcere prostratis*.

99 cluvis *claws* cleir *bright*   100 leit *let* listly *elegantly* lene *lean*
kne *knee*   101 deir *precious*   102 radyous *radiant* ryall *royal, magnificent*
104 woddis and schawis *woods and groves*   105 leigis *liegemen, subjects*
furth *forth*

106 Exerce *exercise*   107 skaith na skornis *harm nor insults*
108 Of *from* bene of moir piscence *are of greater strength*
109 Do law elyk *enforce the law equally* aipis *apes*   110 lat *let* bowgle *wild ox*
busteous *rough, violent*   111 meik pluch-ox *meek plough-ox*
oppress *crush* for *in spite of* pryd *pride*   112 yok *yoke* peciable *peaceably*
him besyd *beside him*

113 noyis *noise*   114 into *in*   115 onis *once* lawd *praise*
'Vive le roy!' *long live the king!*   116 till *to* feit *feet*
117 homege and fewté *homage and fealty*
118 thame ressaif *receive them* laitis *demeanour*
119 yre *wrath* parcere prostratis *to spare those prostrate (see n.)*

120   Syne crownit scho the Egle king of fowlis,
And as steill dertis scherpit scho his pennis,
And bawd him be als just to awppis and owlis
As unto pacokkis, papingais or crennis,
And mak a law for wycht fowlis and for wrennis,
125   And lat no fowll of ravyne do efferay
Nor devoir birdis bot his awin pray.

Than callit scho all flouris that grew on feild,
Discirnyng all thair fassionis and effeiris.
Upone the awfull Thrissill scho beheld
130   And saw him kepit with a busche of speiris;
Concedring him so able for the weiris,
A radius croun of rubeis scho him gaif
And said, 'In feild go furth and fend the laif!'

'And sen thow art a king, thow be discreit.
135   Herb without vertew thow hald nocht of sic pryce
As herb of vertew and of odor sueit;
And lat no nettill vyle and full of vyce
Hir fallow to the gudly flour-de-lyce,
Nor latt no wyld weid full of churlichenes
140   Compair hir till the lilleis nobilnes.

120 Syne *then* Egle *eagle*   **121** as steill dertis *like steel spears*
scherpit *sharpened* pennis *feathers* **122** bawd *ordered* als *as*
awppis *(?)curlews (see n.)* owlis *owls* **123** pacokkis *peacocks*
papingais *parrots* crennis *cranes* **124** a law *a single law*
wycht fowlis *strong birds* wrennis *wrens (i.e. weaker birds)*   **125** ravyne *prey*
do *cause* efferay *affray, terror* **126** devoir *devour*
bot his awin pray *except his own prey*

128 Discirnyng *examining* fassionis *shapes* effeiris *habits*
129 awfull *dreadful, inspiring awe* Thrissill *thistle* **130** kepit *guarded*
busche *bush* speiris *spears* **131** Concedring *considering* able *fitted* weiris *wars*
132 rubeis *rubies* **133** fend *defend* laif *rest, others*

134 sen *since* discreit *prudent*
135 hald nocht of sic pryce *do not consider of such value*
138 Hir fallow *associate herself with* gudly *goodly* flour-de-lyce *lily*
139 weid *weed* **140** Compair hir *compare herself* till *to*

'Nor hald non udir flour in sic denty
As the fresche Ros of cullour reid and quhyt,
For gife thow dois, hurt is thyne honesty,
Conciddering that no flour is so perfyt,
145 So full of vertew, plesans and delyt,
So full of blisfull angilik bewty,
Imperiall birth, honour and dignité.

Than to the Ros scho turnyt hir visage,
And said, 'O lusty dochtir most benyng,
150 Aboif the lilly illustare of lynnage,
Fro the stok ryell rysing fresche and ying,
But ony spot or macull doing spring,
Cum, blowme of joy, with jemis to be cround,
For our the laif thy bewty is renownd.'

155 A coistly croun with clarefeid stonis brycht
This cumly quene did on hir heid inclois,
Quhill all the land illumynit of the licht:
Quhairfoir me thocht all flouris did rejos,
Crying attonis, 'Haill be thow richest Ros,
160 Haill hairbis empryce, haill, freschest quene of flouris!
To the be glory and honour at all houris!'

141 udir *other* sic denty *such esteem*   143 gife *if* honesty *honour*
144 perfyt *perfect*   145 delyt *joy*   146 angeilik *angelic*   147 Imperiall *noblest*

148 turnyt *turned*   149 dochtir *daughter* benyng *gentle, gracious*
150 Aboif *above* illustare *illustrious* lynnage *lineage, family*   151 Fro *from*
stok ryell *royal stock* ying *young*   152 But *without* macull *blemish*
153 blowme *flower* jemis *gems*   154 our the laif *above the rest*

155 coistly *rich* clarefeid *polished*   156 inclois *encircle*   157 Quhill *until*
158 Quhairfoir *wherefore* rejos *rejoice*   159 attonis *together*
160 hairbis empryce *empress of plants*

Than all the birdis song with voce on hicht,
Quhois mirthfull soun wes mervelus to heir.
The mavys song, 'Haill, Rois most riche and richt
165   That dois up flureis undir Phebus speir!
Haill, plant of yowth, haill, princes dochtir deir,
Haill, blosome breking out of the blud royall,
Quhois pretius vertew is imperiall!'

The merle scho sang, 'Haill, Rois of most delyt,
170   Haill, of all flouris quene and soverane!'
The lark scho song, 'Haill, Rois both reid and quhyt,
Most plesand flour of michty cullouris twane!'
The nychtingaill song, 'Haill, Naturis suffragene,
In bewty, nurtour and every nobilnes,
175   In riche array, renown and gentilnes.'

The commoun voce uprais of birdis small
Apone this wys: 'O blissit be the hour
That thow wes chosin to be our principall.
Welcome to be our princes of honour,
180   Our perle, our plesans and our paramour,
Our peax, our play, our plane felicité:
Chryst the conserf frome all adversité!'

162 song *sang* voce *voice* on hicht *on high*   164 mavys *thrush* richt *true*
165 flureis *flourish* speir *sphere*   166 yowth *youth* princes *of a prince*
167 breking out *springing* blud *blood, race*   168 pretius *precious*

169 merle *blackbird*   172 michty *mighty* cullouris *colours, hues* twane *two*
173 nychtingaill *nightingale* Naturis suffragene *Nature's deputy*
174 nurtour *courtesy*   175 gentilnes *nobility, graciousness*

176 uprais *rose up*   177 Apone *upon, in* wys *manner* blissit *blessed*
178 principall *ruler*   179 princes *princess*   180 perle *pearl* paramour *beloved*
181 peax *peace* play *delight* plane *full, complete*   182 conserf *protect*

Than all the birdis song with sic a schout
That I annone awoilk quhair that I lay,
185   And with a braid I turnyt me about
To se this court, bot all wer went away.
Than up I lenyt, halflingis in affrey,
And thus I wret, as ye haif hard toforrow,
Off lusty May upone the nynte morrow.

184 awoilk *awoke*   185 braid *start*   186 went *gone*
187 lenyt *rose* halflingis in affrey *half in fear*   188 wret *wrote*
haif hard toforrow *heard before*   189 nynte *ninth*

ILLUSTER LODOVICK, OF FRANCE
MOST CRISTIN KING

Lament for Lord Bernard Stewart

Illuster Lodovick, of France most Cristin king,
   Thow may complain with sighis lamentable
The death of Bernard Stewart, nobill and ding,
   In deid of armes most anterous and abill,
5   Most mychti, wyse, worthie, and confortable
Thy men of weir to governe and to gy:
   For him, allace, now may thow weir the sabill
Sen he is gon, the flour of chevelrie.

Complaine sould everie noble valiant knycht
10   The death of him that douchtie was in deid,
That many ane fo in feild hes put to flight,
   In weris wicht, be wisdome and manheid.
   To the Turk sey all land did his name dreid,
Quhois force all France in fame did magnifie:
15   Of so hie price sall nane his place posseid,
For he is gon, the flour of chevelrie.

---

1 Illuster *illustrious* Lodovick *Louis* Cristin *Christian*   2 complain *lament*
3 nobill and ding *noble and worthy*   4 deid *deed(s)*
anterous *bold, adventurous* abill *capable, skilled*
5 mychti *mighty* confortable *providing support and encouragement*
6 weir *war* governe *command* gy *guide*
7 allace *alas* weir *wear* sabill *sable, mourning black*
8 Sen *since* gon *gone* flour of chevelrie *flower of chivalry*

9 Complaine *lament* sould *should* knycht *knight*   10 douchtie *valiant*
11 ane fo *a foe* feild *battlefield*
12 In weris wicht *valiant in war* manheid *fortitude, manliness*
13 Turk sey *(Turkish sea =) Black Sea* dreid *fear*
14 Quhois *whose* force *strength*
15 hie price *high renown* sall nane his place posseid *none shall take his place*

O duilfull death, O dragon dolorous!
Quhy hes thow done so dulfullie devoir
The prince of knychtheid, nobill and chevilrous,
20   The witt of weiris, of armes and honour,
    The crop of curage, the strenth of armes in stoir,
The fame of France, the fame of Lumbardy,
    The chois of chiftanes, most awfull in airmour,
The charbuckell cheif of every chevelrie?

25 Pray now for him all that him loveit heir,
    And for his saull mak intercessioun
Unto the Lord that hes him bocht so deir
    To gif him mercie and remissioun,
    And namelie we of Scottis natioun,
30 Intill his lyff quhom most he did affy,
    Foryett we nevir into our orisoun
To pray for him, the flour of chevelrie.

17 duilfull *sorrowful* dolorous *grievous*
18 *why hast thou so lamentably devoured*
19 knychtheid *knighthood* chevilrous *chivalrous*
20 witt of weiris *wisest man in wars*
21 crop of curage *highest pinnacle* strenth *strength* stoir *combat*
22 Lumbardy *Lombardy*   23 chois *(choice =) most excellent*
chiftanes *commanders* awfull in airmour *terrible in armour*
24 charbuckell *ruby, carbuncle* cheif *noblest* chevelrie *chivalrous deeds*

25 loveit *praised* heir *here*   26 saull *soul*   27 bocht *bought, redeemed*
so deir *at such great cost*   28 gif *give* remissioun *pardon*
29 namelie *especially*   30 Intill *during* lyff *life*
quhom *whom* did affy *put his trust in*   31 Foryett *forget* into *in* orisoun *prayer*

QUHAT IS THIS LYFE BOT ANE
STRAUCHT WAY TO DEID?

Quhat is this lyfe bot ane straucht way to deid?
　　Quhilk hes a tyme to pas and nane to duell;
A slyding quheill us lent to seik remeid,
　　A fre chois gevin to paradice or hell,
5　　　A pray to deid, quhome vane is to repell;
A schoirt torment for infineit glaidnes –
Als schort ane joy for lestand hevynes.

1 Quhat *what* straucht *straight, direct* deid *death*
2 Quhilk *which* duell *linger*
3 quheill *wheel* lent *lent, granted* seik remeid *seek salvation*
4 fre chois *free choice* gevin *given*
5 pray *prey* quhome *whom* vane *useless* repell *drive back*
6 schoirt *short* for *in return for* infineit *infinite*
7 Als *as* lestand hevynes *everlasting sorrow*

QUHOM TO SALL I COMPLEINE MY WO

Quhom to sall I compleine my wo
And kythe my cairis, ane or mo?
I knaw not amang riche or pure,
Quha is my freind, quha is my fo,
5   For in this warld may none assure.

Lord, how sall I my dayis dispone?
For lang service rewarde is none,
And schort my lyfe may heir indure,
And losit is my tyme bigone:
10   Into this warld may none assure.

Oft Falsatt rydis with a rowtt,
Quhone Treuthe gois on his fute about,
And laik of spending dois him spure.
Thus quhat to do I am in doutt:
15   Into this warld may none assure.

1 Quhom *whom* sall *shall* compleine *complain*
2 kythe *make known* cairis *sorrows* ane or mo *one or more*
3 knaw *know* pure *poor*   4 Quha *who* freind *friend* fo *foe*
5 warld *world* assure *trust, have confidence*

6 dispone *order, dispose*   8 schort *for a short time* heir indure *last here*
9 losit *perished, wasted* bigone *past*   10 Into *in*

11 Falsatt *falsehood* rowtt *retinue*
12 Quhone *when* Treuthe *truth, loyalty* gois on his fute *goes on foot*
13 laik of spending *lack of money to spend* spure *spur*
14 quhat *what* doutt *doubt, uncertainty*

Nane heir bot rich men hes renown,
And pure men ar plukit doun,
And nane bot just men tholis injure;
Swa Wit is blyndit and Ressoun,
20   For in this warld may none assure.

Vertew the court hes done dispys –
A rebald to renoun dois rys,
And carlis of nobillis hes the cure,
And bumbardis brukis benefys:
25   So in this warld may none assure.

All gentrice and nobilité
Ar passit out of hie degré;
On fredome is led foirfalture,
In princis is thair no petie:
30   So in this warld may none assure.

Is none so armit into plait
That can fra trouble him debait.
May no man lang in welthe indure,
For wo that lyis ever at the wait:
35   So in this warld may none assure.

16 Nane *none* bot *except*   17 plukit doun *pulled down*   18 tholis *suffer*
injure *injustice*   19 Swa *so* Wit *wisdom, understanding* Ressoun *reason*

21 *the court has brought virtue into disrepute*   22 rebald *rascal* rys *rise*
23 carlis *peasants, churls* nobillis *nobles* cure *office*
24 *and lazy fellows get benefices*

26 gentrice *nobleness, graciousness*   27 *are gone from (those of) high rank*
28 *on generosity is laid forfeiture (of lands)*   29 petie *pity*

31 armit into plait *armed in plate armour*   32 fra trouble *from affliction*
debait *defend*   33 welthe *well-being, prosperity*
34 For *because of* lyis ever at the wait *lies in ambush*

Flattrie weiris ane furrit goun,
And Falsate with the lordis dois roun,
And Trewthe standis barrit at the dure,
Exylit is Honour of the toun:
40 So in this warld may none assure.

Fra everie mouthe fair wordis procedis;
In everie harte deceptioun bredis,
Fra everie e gois lukis demure,
Bot fra the handis gois few gud deidis:
45 Sa in this warld may none assure.

Towngis now ar maid of quhite quhale-bone,
And hartis ar maid of hard flynt stone,
And eyn ar maid of blew asure,
And handis of adamant, laithe to dispone:
50 So in this warld may none assure.

Yit hart and handis and body all
Mon anser Dethe quhone he dois call
To compt befoir the juge future:
Sen all ar deid or than de sall,
55 Quha sould into this warld assure?

36 weiris *wears* furrit *furred*   37 roun *whisper*   38 barrit *shut out* dure *door*
39 Exylit *exiled (from)*

41 everie *every* wordis procedis *words proceed*   42 harte *heart* bredis *breeds*
43 e *eye* gois *come* lukis *looks*   44 gud deidis *good deeds*

46 Towngis *tongues* quhite quhale-bone *white whalebone*
48 eyn *eyes* blew *blue* asure *lapis lazuli (a hard, deep blue stone)*
49 adamant *(hard) diamond* laithe to dispone *reluctant to hand out*

52 Mon anser *must answer* quhone *when*
53 *to reckoning before the future judge*   54 Sen *since* deid *dead*
or than de sall *or shall then (i.e. at the last day) die*   55 sould *should*

No thing both deithe this schortlie cravis,
Quhair Fortoun ever as fo dissavis,
Withe freyndlie smylingis lyk ane hure,
Quhais fals behechtis as wind hyne wavis:
60 So in this warld may none assure.

O quho sall weild the wrang possessioun,
Or the gold gatherit with oppressioun,
Quhone the angell blawis his bugill sture,
Quhilk onrestorit, helpis no confessioun?
65 Into this warld may none assure.

Quhat help is thair in lordschips sevin,
Quhone na hous is bot hell and hevin,
Palice of lycht or pit obscure,
Quhair yowlis ar with horrible stevin?
70 Into this warld may none assure.

Ubi ardentes anime
Semper dicentes sunt, Ve Ve!
Sall cry allace, that women thame bure:
O quante sunt iste tenebre!
75 Into this warld may none assure.

56 cravis *(?)demands (?)begs (see n.)*   **57** Fortoun *Fortune*
dissavis *deceives*   **58** freyndlie *friendly*   hure *whore*   **59** Quhais *whose*
behechtis *promises*   hyne wavis *pass hence*

61 quho *who*   weild *keep*   wrang possessioun *unjust(ly acquired) property*
62 gatherit *gathered*   oppressioun *extortion*   **63** blawis *blows*
bugill *trumpet*   sture *loud*   **64** Quhilk *which*   onrestorit *if it has not been restored*

66 lordschips *estates*   sevin *seven*   **67** na hous is *there is no house*
68 lycht *light*   obscure *dark*   **69** yowlis *howls*   stevin *voice*

71-2 *where the burning souls are always saying, 'Woe, woe!'*
73 thame bure *bore them*   **74** *O how great is this darkness!*

Than quho sall wirk for warldis wrak,
Quhone flude and fyre sall our it frak
And frelie frustir feild and fure,
With tempest keyne and thundir crak?
80   Into this warld may none assure.

Lord, sen in tyme sa sone to cum
De terra surrecturus sum,
Rewarde me with na erthlie cure;
Bot me ressave *in regnum tuum*,
85   Sen in this warld may none assure.

76 wirk *work* warldis wrak *the world's wretched possessions*
77 flude *flood* fyre *fire* our it frak *rush swiftly over it*
78 *without restraint destroy field and furrow*
79 keyne *fierce* crak *crack*

81 sa sone to cum *so soon to come*
82 *I shall be resurrected from the earth*
83 na erthlie cure *no earthly office*
84 *but receive me into thy kingdom*

INTO THIR DIRK AND
DRUBLIE DAYIS

Into thir dirk and drublie dayis
Quhone sabill all the hevin arrayis
   With mystie vapouris, cluddis, and skyis,
   Nature all curage me denyis
5   Off sangis, ballattis, and of playis.

Quhone that the nycht dois lenthin houris,
With wind, with haill, and havy schouris,
   My dulé spreit dois lurk for schoir;
   My hairt for langour dois forloir
10   For laik of Symmer with his flouris.

I walk, I turne, sleip may I nocht;
I vexit am with havie thocht.
   This warld all ovir I cast about,
   And ay the mair I am in dout
15   The mair that I remeid have socht.

1 *in these dark and gloomy days*
2 Quhone *when* sabill *black* hevin *heaven* arrayis *cloaks*
3 vapouris *exhalations, fogs* cluddis *clouds* skyis *skies*
4 curage *desire, delight* denyis *denies, deprives of*
5 Off sangis, ballattis *for songs, poems* playis *entertainments, plays*

6 nycht *night* lenthin *lengthen*   7 havy schouris *heavy showers*
8 dulé spreit *mournful spirit* dois lurk for schoir *cowers at the menace*
9 hairt *heart* langour *wretchedness* forloir *become desolate*
10 laik *lack* Symmer *Summer* flouris *flowers*

11 walk *lie awake* sleip may I nocht *I cannot sleep*
12 havie thocht *heavy melancholy*
13 warld *world* ovir *over* cast about *consider, reflect on*
14 ay *always* mair *more* dout *perplexity, apprehension*
15 remeid *remedy* socht *sought*

I am assayit on everie syde:
Despair sayis ay, 'In tyme provyde
   And get sum thing quhairon to leif,
   Or with grit trouble and mischeif
20 Thow sall into this court abyd.'

Than Patience sayis, 'Be not agast;
Hald Hoip and Treuthe within the fast,
   And lat Fortoun wirk furthe hir rage,
   Quhone that no rasoun may assuage,
25 Quhill that hir glas be run and past.'

And Prudence in my eir sayis ay,
'Quhy wald thow hald that will away,
   Or craif that thow may have no space,
   Thow tending to ane uther place,
30 A journay going everie day?'

And than sayis Age, 'My freind, cum neir,
And be not strange, I the requeir:
   Cum, brodir, by the hand me tak.
   Remember thow hes compt to mak
35 Off all thi tyme thow spendit heir.'

16 assayit *assailed*   17 ay *ever*   18 quhairon *whereon* leif *live*
19 grit *great* mischeif *harm*   20 sall *shall* into *in* abyd *remain, dwell*

21 agast *afraid*   22 Hald *hold* Hoip *Hope* Treuthe *Truth* the *thee* fast *firmly*
23 lat *let* Fortoun *Fortune* wirk furthe *work out*   24 Quhone *when, since*
that no rasoun may assuage *no reason can assuage that (Fortune's rage)*
25 Quhill *until* glass *hour-glass*

26 eir *ear*   27 Quhy *why* wald *would* that will away *that which wishes to go*
28 *or crave what you may possess for no time at all*
29 tending to *moving towards* uther *other*   30 journay *journey*

31 freind *friend* cum neir *come near*   32 strange *aloof* requeir *request*
33 Cum *come* brodir *brother* tak *take*   34 hes *has*
compt *account* mak *make*   35 spendit heir *spent here*

Syne Deid castis upe his yettis wyd,
Saying, 'Thir oppin sall the abyd;
   Albeid that thow wer never sa stout,
   Undir this lyntall sall thow lowt:
40 Thair is nane uther way besyde.'

For feir of this all day I drowp;
No gold in kist, nor wyne in cowp,
   No ladeis bewtie, nor luiffis blys
   May lat me to remember this,
45 How glaid that ever I dyne or sowp.

Yit quhone the nycht begynnis to schort
It dois my spreit sumpairt confort,
   Off thocht oppressit with the schowris.
   Cum, lustie Symmer, with thi flowris,
50 That I may leif in sum disport.

36 Syne *then* Deid *death* castis upe *throws open* yettis *gates* wyd *wide*
37 Thir oppin *These open* sall the abyd *shall await you*
38 Albeid *albeit, even though* sa *so* stout *bold*   39 lyntall *lintel*
lowt *stoop, bend*   40 Thair *there* nane *no* besyde *at hand*

41 feir *fear* drowp *droop, am cast down*   42 kist *chest* cowp *cup*
43 ladeis *lady's* bewtie *beauty* luiffis blys *love's joy*   44 lat *prevent*
45 How *however* glaid *glad, joyful* dyne *dine* sowp *sup*

46 Yit *yet* schort *shorten*   47 dois *does* spreit *spirit*
sumpairt *somewhat, to some extent* confort *comfort*   48 thocht *melancholy*
oppressit *oppressed* schowris *storms*   49 lustie *cheerful, lively*
flowris *flowers*   50 leif *live* disport *delight, merriment*

I THAT IN HEILL WES
AND GLADNES

The Lament for the Makars

I that in heill wes and gladnes
Am trublit now with gret seiknes
And feblit with infermité:
Timor mortis conturbat me.

5   Our plesance heir is all vane glory;
This fals warld is bot transitory,
The flesch is brukle, the fend is sle:
Timor mortis conturbat me.

The stait of man dois change and vary;
10   Now sound, now seik, now blith, now sary,
Now dansand mery, now like to dee:
Timor mortis conturbat me.

No stait in erd heir standis sickir;
As with the wynd wavis the wickir
15   Wavis this warldis vanité:
Timor mortis conturbat me.

---

1 heill *health* wes *was* 2 trublit *troubled* gret seiknes *sickness*
3 feblit *enfeebled* infermité *illness* 4 *the fear of death disturbs me*

5 plesance *pleasure* heir *here* 6 warld *world* bot *but* 7 brukle *frail*
fend *fiend, devil* sle *cunning*

9 stait *state, condition* dois *does* 10 sound *healthy* seik *sick*
blith *happy* sary *sorrowful* 11 dansand *dancing*
like to dee *likely to die*

13 stait *estate* erd *earth* standis sickir *stands secure*
14 wavis *waves, moves to and fro* wickir *willow* 15 warldis *world's*

Onto the ded gois all estatis,
Princis, prelotis and potestatis,
Baith riche and pur of al degré:
20   *Timor mortis conturbat me.*

He takis the knychtis into feild,
Anarmyt undir helme and scheild;
Victour he is at all mellé:
Timor mortis conturbat me.

25   That strang unmercifull tyrand
Takis on the moderis breist sowkand
The bab full of benignité:
Timor mortis conturbat me.

He takis the campion in the stour,
30   The capitane closit in the tour,
The lady in bour full of bewté:
Timor mortis conturbat me.

He sparis no lord for his piscence,
Na clerk for his intelligence;
35   His awfull strak may no man fle:
Timor mortis conturbat me.

17 Onto the ded *unto death* gois *go*   **18** prelotis *prelates*
potestatis *rulers*   **19** Baith *both* pur *poor* degré *rank*

21 *he takes the knights on the battlefield*   **22** Anarmyt *armed* helme *helm*
scheild *shield*   **23** Victour *victor* mellé *combat*

25 strang *strong* tyrand *tyrant*
26 on the moderis breist sowkand *sucking on the mother's breast*
27 bab *babe* benignité *goodness, innocence*

29 campion *champion* stour *battle*   **30** capitane *captain* closit *enclosed*
tour *tower*   **31** bour *chamber* bewté *beauty*

33 piscence *power*   **34** Na clerk *no scholar, cleric*
35 awfull strak *fearful stroke* may *can* fle *flee, escape*

Art-magicianis and astrologgis,
Rethoris, logicianis, and theologgis –
Thame helpis no conclusionis sle:
40   *Timor mortis conturbat me.*

In medicyne the most practicianis,
Lechis, surrigianis, and phisicianis,
Thameself fra ded may not supplé:
Timor mortis conturbat me.

45   I se that makaris amang the laif
Playis heir ther pageant, syne gois to graif;
Sparit is nought ther faculté:
Timor mortis conturbat me.

He has done petuously devour
50   The noble Chaucer of makaris flour,
The monk of Bery, and Gower, all thre:
Timor mortis conturbat me.

The gud Syr Hew of Eglintoun,
And eik Heryot, and Wyntoun
55   He has tane out of this cuntré:
Timor mortis conturbat me.

37 Art-magicianis *practitioners of the magic art* astrologgis *astrologers*
38 Rethoris *rhetoricians* logicianis *logicians* theologgis *theologians*
39 *no subtle arguments, conclusions can help them*

41 most practicianis *greatest practitioners*   42 Lechis *doctors*
surrigianis *surgeons*   43 *cannot deliver themselves from death*

45 se *see* makaris *poets* laif *rest*
46 *play here their scenes, then go to the grave*
47 Sparit *spared* nought *not* faculté *(?)profession, (?)skill*

49 petuously *wretchedly, pitiably*
50 of makaris flour *flower of poets [for the following list of poets, see n.]*

53 gud *good*   54 eik *also*   55 tane *taken* this cuntré *this land*

That scorpion fell has done infek
Maister Johne Clerk and James Afflek
Fra balat-making and trigidé:
60   *Timor mortis conturbat me.*

Holland and Barbour he has berevit;
Allace that he nought with us levit
Schir Mungo Lokert of the Le:
  Timor mortis conturbat me.

65 Clerk of Tranent eik he has tane
That maid the anteris of Gawane;
Schir Gilbert Hay endit has he:
  Timor mortis conturbat me.

He has Blind Hary and Sandy Traill
70 Slane with his schour of mortall haill,
Quhilk Patrik Johnestoun myght nought fle:
  Timor mortis conturbat me.

He has reft Merseir his endite,
That did in luf so lifly write,
75 So schort, so quyk, of sentence hie:
  Timor mortis conturbat me.

---

57 fell *cruel* done infek *poisoned*   **59** Fra *from*
balat-making *composition of poems* trigidé *tragedy*

61 berevit *snatched away*   **62** Allace *alas* levit *left*   **63** Schir *sir*

66 anteris *adventures*   **67** endit *brought to an end*

70 schour of mortall haill *shower of deadly hail*   **71** Quhilk *which*
myght nought fle *could not escape*

73 reft Merseir his endite *snatched away Merseir's (powers of) writing*
74 luf *love* lifly *freshly, vividly*   **75** schort *concise* quyk *lively*
of sentence hie *of noble, weighty significance*

He has tane Roull of Aberdene,
And gentill Roull of Corstorphin –
Two bettir fallowis did no man se:
80   *Timor mortis conturbat me.*

In Dunfermelyne he has done roune
With Maister Robert Henrisoun;
Schir Johne the Ros enbrast has he:
Timor mortis conturbat me.

85   And he has now tane last of aw,
Gud gentill Stobo and Quintyne Schaw
Of quham all wichtis has peté:
Timor mortis conturbat me.

Gud Maister Walter Kennedy
90   In poynt of dede lyis veraly –
Gret reuth it wer that he suld de:
Timor mortis conturbat me.

Sen he has all my brether tane,
He will naught lat me lif alane;
95   On forse I man his nyxt pray be:
Timor mortis conturbat me.

78 gentill *gracious, noble*   79 fallowis *friends, fellows*

81 done roune *whispered*   83 enbrast *embraced*

85 aw *all*   86 gentill *gracious*   87 quham *whom*
wichtis *persons, people* has peté *have pity*

90 *lies at the point of death, in truth*   91 reuth *pity* suld *should*

93 Sen *since* brether *brothers*   94 lat *allow* lif *live* alane *alone, only*
95 *of necessity I must be his next victim*

Sen for the ded remeid is none
Best is that we for dede dispone,
Eftir our deid that lif may we:
100 *Timor mortis conturbat me.*

97 remeid *remedy* **98** dispone *make ready*
99 *that we may live after our death*

FULL OFT I MUS AND HES
IN THOCHT

Full oft I mus and hes in thocht
How this fals warld is ay on flocht,
Quhair no thing ferme is nor degest;
And quhen I haif my mynd all socht
5 For to be blyth me think it best.

This warld evir dois flicht and vary;
Fortoun sa fast hir quheill dois cary
Na tyme bot turne can it tak rest,
For quhois fals change suld none be sary;
10 For to be blyth me thynk it best.

Wald man considdir in mynd rycht weill
Or Fortoun on him turn hir quheill
That erdly honour may nocht lest,
His fall less panefull he suld feill;
15 For to be blyth me think it best.

1 mus *ponder* hes in thocht *meditate*
2 warld *world* ay on flocht *always in perturbation*
3 Quhair *where* ferme *constant* degest *stable*
4 quhen *when* haif *have* socht *searched*
5 blyth *merry, cheerful* me think it best *it seems best to me*

6 flicht *flutter* vary *change*   7 *Fortune so quickly drives the wheel*
8 Na tyme bot turne *no time without turning*
9 quhois *whose* suld *should* sary *sorrowful*

11 Wald man *if man would* rycht weill *right well*   12 Or *before*
13 erdly *earthly* nocht lest *not last*   14 suld feill *should feel*

Quha with this warld dois warsill and stryfe,
And dois his dayis in dolour dryfe,
Thocht he in lordschip be possest
He levis bot ane wrechit lyfe;
20   For to be blyth me think it best.

Off warldis gud and grit riches
Quhat fruct hes man but mirines?
Thocht he this warld had eist and west
All wer povertie but glaidnes;
25   For to be blyth me thynk it best.

Quho suld for tynsall drowp or de,
For thyng that is bot vanitie,
Sen to the lyfe that evir dois lest
Heir is bot twynklyng of ane e?
30   For to be blyth me think it best.

Had I for warldis unkyndnes
In hairt tane ony havines,
Or fro my plesans bene opprest,
I had bene deid lang syne, dowtles –
35   For to be blyth me think it best.

16 Quha *whoever* warsill *wrestle* stryfe *strive*   17 dolour *sorrow* dryfe *pass*
18 Thocht *though* lordschip *landed property*   19 levis *lives*

21 warldis gud *world's goods* grit riches *great wealth*
22 Quhat fruct *what fruit* but mirines *without merriness*   23 eist *east*
24 wer *would be* but glaidnes *without joy*

26 Quho *who* tynsall *loss* drowp *be miserable* de *die*
28 Sen to *since compared to* lest *last*   29 Heir *here, this life*
twynklyng *blink* e *eye*

31 Had I *if I had* unkyndnes *cruelty*   32 *in heart felt any grief*
33 *Or from my joy been forced by affliction*
34 *I would have been dead long since without doubt*

How evir this warld do change and vary,
Lat us in hairt nevirmoir be sary,
Bot evir be reddy and addrest
To pas out of this frawdfull fary –
40   For to be blyth me think it best.

37 nevirmoir *nevermore*   **38** addrest *prepared*   **39** frawdfull *deceitful*
fary *illusion*

TEXTUAL SOURCES AND ABBREVIATIONS

(In the textual notes only substantive changes are recorded: fuller information on variants can be found in the editions of Fox, Bawcutt, and Kinsley, see Further Reading).

An   Anderson, *The Testament of Cresseid* (Edinburgh, 1663).

A   Asloan MS (1513–*c.*1530), National Library of Scotland.

B   Bannatyne MS (written by George Bannatyne in the 1560s), N.L.S.

Bd   that part of the Bannatyne MS known as the 'Draft'.

Bs   Bassandyne, *The Morall Fabillis of Esope the Phrygian* (Edinburgh, 1571).

C   Charteris, *The Morall Fabillis of Esope the Phrygian* (Edinburgh, 1569–70).

Ch   Charteris, *The Testament of Cresseid* (Edinburgh, 1593).

CM   Chepman and Myllar prints, made in Edinburgh *c.*1508 (Henryson's *Orpheus*, Dunbar's *The Goldyn Targe* and *The Flyting of Dunbar and Kennedie*).

G   Gray MS (partly compiled by James Gray, 1503/4–1532), N.L.S.

H   MS Harley 3865, British Library (dated 1571, and probably copied from a printed book).

Ht   Hart, *The Morall Fabl(es) of Esope, the Phrygian* (Edinburgh, 1621).

MF   Maitland Folio MS, Pepsyian Library, Magdalene College, Cambridge (*c.*1570–86).

Mk   Makculloch MS, Edinburgh University Library (1477, containing some vernacular poems written *c.*1500).

P   a 'Rouen' print of *c.*1507–8, perhaps made abroad or by foreign workmen in Scotland (Dunbar's *Lament for the Makars* and part of *The Tretis of the Twa Mariit Wemen and the Wedo*).

R   Reidpeth MS (an early seventeenth-century copy of part of the Maitland Folio MS made when that was more complete than at present), Cambridge University Library.

S   Smith, *The Fabulous Tales of Esope the Phrygian* (London, 1577).
Th   Thynne, *The Workes of Geffray Chaucer* (London, 1532).

Other Abbreviations

attr.   attributed to
em.   emended
L.   Latin
OED   *Oxford English Dictionary*
om.   omitted
STS   Scottish Text Society

NOTES

ROBERT HENRYSON

ROBENE AND MAKYNE

Robene and Makyne is a witty and individual poem. It has sometimes been called a *pastourelle*, and it has some of the features of that French genre – the rustic setting (with characters sometimes called Robin and Marion), a central debate, and the subject of love, but not other features. The French *pastourelle* often begins with a *chanson d'aventure* formula ('as I rode out . . .'), and often has a shepherdess being wooed by a knight. Henryson's poem is thoroughly rustic, and although it playfully puts some of the language and the topics of noble love ('courtas', 'denger'; secrecy, love's doctrines, etc.) into Makyne's mouth, treats the characters without condescension. It may be compared with Dunbar's 'In secreit place this hyndir nycht' (p. 278). The narrative and dramatic possibilities of the story are developed so that it sometimes sounds more like a ballad. In one important aspect, however, it is a true pastoral, assuming that 'you can say everything about complex people by a complete consideration of simple people' (William Empson, *Some Versions of Pastoral*, p. 137). Appropriately, Makyne's clinching proverb on 'opportunity' (91–2) is elsewhere found in both homely and learned contexts.

The title comes from Allan Ramsay's *The Ever Green* (1724), a publication which made it into a favourite with eighteenth-century readers.
Text B (attr. 'maister Robert Henrysone').   **39** In] I B

THE TESTAMENT OF CRESSEID

The date of Henryson's most complex, original, and difficult poem cannot be fixed with certainty. It has been suggested that there is an allusion to it in *The Spektakle of Luf* (1492), a Scottish prose text (which claims to be translated from Latin), but this is not certain. As its opening indicates, it was in some sense inspired by Chaucer's *Troilus and Criseyde*, to which it is a kind of continuation (though its action takes place before the death of Chaucer's hero), and with which it is associated in the 1532 edition of Chaucer's works by Thynne and in later editions (an association which made it widely available to English readers). However, the nature of the relationship between the two poems has been much debated. Henryson was a perceptive and intelligent reader of *Troilus*, and his poem is filled with echoes of it (some ironic). His *Testament* is at the same time a fully independent and autonomous work of art. But is it the work of a humane disciple of Chaucer sympathetic to the heroine, or is it a severe 'anti-*Troilus*' castigating her lust? Other more general problems have emerged. It raises questions of fate and free will, and of divine justice, but does it offer answers to them? Is there a specifically Christian moral pattern in it leading to Cresseid's 'redemption', or is there no hint of this at all? It is usually assumed that Henryson invented the story of Cresseid's wretched end as a leper, but the 'other book' to which the narrator refers may have existed.

The title, which goes back to the earliest surviving texts, is clearly suggested by Cresseid's final action, but the narrative form of the poem distinguishes it from such well-known examples of the 'poetic testament' as that of his near-contemporary, François Villon. Henryson calls his work a 'tragedy' – often taken in the Middle Ages to be a poem with a disastrous end, rather than specifically a play (though it is likely that Seneca's tragedies influenced the concept, and sometimes perhaps the technique, of medieval tragedy). There is an expectation of scenes of pathos and horror, of violently strained emotions, of eloquent rhetorical laments, and urgent moral 'sentence'. Dante says that tragedy 'is in its beginning admirable and tranquil, but in its end fetid and horrible'. The 'doolie sessoun' – a strange 'winterly spring' – at the beginning of the poem is an appropriate setting for this 'cairful dyte'. After the scene in which the narrator presents himself as an 'ane man of age' concerned with the fading of love and the coldness of age (Chaucerian in its delicate balance of tones), the stages of Cresseid's tragedy are set forth in narrative sections punctuated by a series of formal laments (the central one of which is marked off by a different stanza form). The narrative voice sometimes simply presents the scenes (with brutal abruptness in some cases), sometimes comments on them, expressing horror and pity in the manner of an ancient chorus: 'O cruell Saturne . . . Hard is thy dome and to malitious!' After this exclamation it does not 'speak out' until the final stanza. Cresseid's voice, however, continues to be heard in a series of laments (rather like the arias in early opera) until her final written testament ends on the words 'trew lufe'. The poem is remarkable for the way in which it allows her voice to be heard almost to the end. Other voices are also heard more briefly – those of the child, of Calchas, the leper woman, the band of lepers, and, finally, the comments of Troilus, and his epitaph for Cresseid.

The action, which begins with the rejection and despairing isolation of Cresseid, culminates in the 'terrible deed' of her blasphemy against Cupid and Venus and the sudden and cruel nemesis that is enacted in the eerie dream of the assembly and judgement of the gods. Cresseid's 'passion' continues in her life as a leper until the strange meeting with Troilus (a 'recognition scene' in which neither recognizes the other but which has a powerful emotional and spiritual effect on them both) and her death. Cresseid is neither totally innocent nor totally guilty, but her punishment seems far greater than deserved. The leprosy with which she is afflicted (often regarded with revulsion as a venereal disease and a source of corruption and pollution) marks the final stage in her isolation. It is very difficult to find a 'salvation according to the Christian scheme' in the final movement – Henryson keeps the action firmly in the ancient world – but there may be a gradual growth of self-knowledge, from the first recognition of her physical change revealed by the mirror (347–50) to the outpouring of remorse occasioned by the 'retrospective epiphany' of the meeting with Troilus.

A reading of this kind suggests that we have here the work of a learned 'humanist' poet. Certainly the poet is not a 'humanist' in the modern sense of one opposed to religion, and probably not one in the tradition of the philological 'new learning' which was beginning to flourish in Italy in his day, but a poet who, like Chaucer, belongs to an older and wider tradition of 'medieval humanism', which prizes the works of the ancient writers and delights in their *sentence* and *humanitas*. Like Chaucer, and other writers who retell the old stories of Troy, Henryson makes no attempt to recreate the outward appearance of the ancient world in detail (Greek and Trojan warriors were normally depicted wearing medieval dress), but suggests that the story is taking place in a different time, with its ceremonies ('efter the law was tho') and temples and gods, and yet that it is directly relevant and related to his own time. The temple is almost immediately called a 'kirk', and Calchas, the priest of Venus, has an 'oratory' like the poet's. The Greek 'camp' has become a 'town' with his 'mansion' and a leper-house on the outskirts. (This sometimes happened in medieval warfare: Froissart describes how Edward III in preparation for a long siege at Calais (1346) built a town with streets and shops and markets.) In this world, remote yet near, a figure from the ancient, pre-Christian era acts out her fate in an eternal present.

Henryson's learning is evident, and he occasionally enjoys displaying it, as in the description of the horses of the Sun (208–17), which he seems to have expanded from a reference in a school-text, the *Graecismus* of Eberhard of Béthune, or in the aside (505–11) explaining the working of memory in Aristotelian terms. Like Chaucer, he is interested in mythography and astrology, which he combines in a brilliant and original way in his extended description of the planetary gods (cf. Chaucer's descriptions of the temples in *The Knight's*

Tale and the medieval depictions in J. Seznec, *The Survival of the Ancient Gods*, trans. B. F. Sessions, New York, 1953). The elaborate and highly visual portraits are completely integrated in the dramatic structure. In these portraits traditional astrological and mythological attributes are woven together to form symbolic images expressing the essence of each planet's power, for good or evil. Thus, the distant and slow-moving planet Saturn had long been identified with the aged god of ancient myth, and associated with cold, melancholy, and pestilence, and the metal lead. Henryson presents him in his entirely malevolent aspect, a horrifyingly ugly image of winter and old age, who seems himself to have some of the symptoms of leprosy. The other planets range from the benevolent and beautiful Phoebus to those who are potentially untrustworthy (like Mercury) or malevolent (like Venus, who shares the fickleness of Fortune and her 'double face', with one eye weeping and the other laughing) or sinister (like Cynthia, where, beside an allusion to the folk-legend of the man in the moon as a thief carrying a bundle of thorns, less homely attributes that suggest leprosy are singled out – she is pale as lead and her cloak is full of black spots). The widespread medieval view that the planets rule 'all thing generabill' and the weather, and influence the human body, lies behind the 'disastrous' symbolic narrative enacted in Cresseid's dream.

Readers are likely to continue to differ in their interpretation of the poem. Many perhaps will favour a less severe verdict than that of a seventeenth-century reader who said that it shows 'the punishment and end due to a false unconstant whore'. Henryson, although his imagination has a grimmer and more macabre side than Chaucer's, like him avoids the earlier misogynistic readings of Cresseid as an example of the fickleness of women. His account of her fate emphasizes its horror and pathos. Words of sorrowful censure ('to change in filth all thy feminitie', etc.) co-exist with an intense pity.

Text Ch. Also found in Th and An. Individual stanzas appear in The Book of the Dean of Lismore (an early sixteenth-century MS collection of Gaelic poetry), the MS of the Chronicle of Fortingall, and in the Ruthven MS (?*c.* 1560). It is listed in the contents of A, but that portion of the MS has been lost. See the Fox edition (see Further Reading) for a full discussion of the variants (which usually present small but often vexing problems to an editor).
6 gart] *Ruthven MS* can Ch **7** scant me fra the cauld I micht defend] *em.* E. G. Stanley scantlie fra the cauld I micht defend Ch (Th me defende)   **48** esperane] An Esperus Ch **94** or refute Th on fute Ch   **164** gyte] gate Th gyis Ch   **178** gyte] Th gyis Ch gay] Th *om.* Ch   **205** unricht] Th upricht Ch   **216** and] An *om.* Ch Philogie] An Philogie Ch   **275** or] Th in Ch   **286** retorte] Th returne Ch   **363** beedes] Th prayers Ch   **382** spitall] hospitall Ch   **432** ray] Th array Ch   **479** Go] Th to Ch   **480** leif] leir Ch   **523** he] Th*om.* Ch

ORPHEUS AND EURYDICE

This extract consists of lines 243–414 of the whole poem (633 lines in all). The first part of the poem tells the story of the love of Orpheus, the son of Phoebus and the muse Calliope, for Eurydice, the queen of Thrace, their marriage, her abduction to the underworld, Orpheus's grief and his quest for her through the heavenly spheres. The story is completed in this extract, and is followed by a long *moralitas*. The narrative is an imaginative expansion of the poem (58 lines) which ends Book III of Boethius's *The Consolation of Philosophy* (trans. V. E. Watts, Penguin Books, 1969, pp. 113–15); the *moralitas* is based on the fourteenth-century commentary on the *Consolation* by Nicholas Trivet. The *moralitas* suggests that Orpheus represents the 'intellective' part of man's soul and Eurydice the 'affective' part ('our affectioun'), and gives allegorical significances to nearly all the figures mentioned (e.g. Tantalus 'betakenis men gredy and covatouse'). Henryson's poem is not as well known as it deserves to be: it is one of the more ambitious examples of the many medieval retellings of the Orpheus legend. It does not combine narrative and morality as successfully as the best of *The Fables*, but its treatment of the story itself is humane and sympathetic. As in Boethius's lyric there is a Platonic opposition of the 'shining fount of good' which man was once able to see, and 'the chains of earth' which draw him downwards. The 'chains of earth' are the source of the emotional tensions in the poem. Love both inspires Orpheus's heroic quest, so nearly successful (in Boethius the 'monarch of the dead' says 'in tearful voice', ' "We yield . . . Let him take with him his wife . . ." '), and is the cause of its failure. The strange paradoxes of love (159–65) and the pathos of the final movement remind us of *The Testament of Cresseid*. 'The tale of Orpheus', as Henryson calls it in the last line of the poem, is a good example of his narrative skill. He sometimes echoes the style of popular romance (like the English *Sir Orfeo* or the Scottish *King Orphius*) or ballad ('fer and full fer, and ferther than I can tell'), and his underworld has a moor with thorns and a 'brig o' dread' similar to 'The Lykewake Dirge'. But the poem is also learned and rhetorical (cf. 68–74, 159–70). Characteristically, Henryson combines the registers: the two proverbs at the end of Orpheus's lament (166–8) are homely and Scottish in form (though their European equivalents are found in tales of noble love from the high literary culture – *Roman d'Eneas*, 9,885–90, and Gottfried's *Tristan*, 16,477ff.) and his final line has a wonderful simplicity – 'bot for a luke my lady is forlore'.

The underworld (a blending of the ancient realm of the dead with medieval images of hell) appropriately contains its classical inhabitants – from Boethius come the three-headed dog Cerberus (10), the Furies (20), Ixion (who murdered his father-in-law) bound to his wheel (23–5), Tantalus (who had offended the gods) (33–46), and Tityus (a giant who had attacked the goddess Leto) (52–60). The lords of the underworld – Rhadamanthus, judge of the dead (66), and Pluto (god of the underworld) and his queen Proserpina (whom he had abducted) are joined by other classical figures – Priam, king of Troy, and Hector his son (no doubt because they are examples of mighty fallen princes) (79), Alexander the Great (356–323 BC, ruler of Macedon and a great conqueror, here a 'wrangous' overreacher) (80) and Julius Caesar (100–44 BC, Roman general and dictator, here a cruel tyrant) (82). The emperor Nero (84) (AD 27–68) is renowned especially in Christian literature for his iniquities. 'Cresus the king' (87–8) is probably the wealthy Roman triumvir Crassus (115–53 BC), murdered by the Parthians who, according to legend, poured molten gold into his mouth after his head had been cut off (or, alternatively, was killed by being made to drink molten gold). He may have been confused with Croesus, the last king of Lydia (c.560–546 BC) renowned for his wealth. Antiochus (81) may be the king of Antioch in the popular story of Apollonius of Tyre who took his daughter's maidenhood (possibly fused with or derived from Antiochus Epiphanes, king of Syria 176–164 BC). Biblical figures include Herod (83), the Herod Antipas of Mark 6:17–18, who had an incestuous union with Herodias (the Herod of line 120 is Herod the Great, but the two were often confused), Pilate (85), the procurator of Judaea, taken to be the type of a corrupt judge, Pharaoh (89) the persecutor of the Israelites in the book of Exodus (1–12), Saul, the first king of Israel, who 'rejected the word of the Lord' at various times (e.g. I Samuel 15), Jezebel, who brought about the death of Naboth because her husband Ahab coveted his vineyard (I Kings 21). The unnamed Christian inhabitants (96–102) are general types of ecclesiastical corruption. However, if we were to accept Fox's emendation in line 98 to 'archbishoppis' (on the basis of a later poem by Sir David Lindsay, the *Dreme*, which uses some lines from this section, and has 'archebischopis in thare pontificall') there could be a topical reference to Patrick Graham, Archbishop of St Andrews from 1472 until his deposition in 1478. But all three texts of Henryson agree on 'bishops'.

The world of the dead, far removed from light, where every creature is 'ay deyand and newirmore may dee' (74; an echo of Chaucer's *Troilus* 4.280?), has transformed the appearance of Eurydice (106–14), now 'dedelike, pitouse and pale of hewe'. Perhaps Henryson may be thinking of Claudian's *The Rape of Proserpina*, a well-known text in the Middle Ages, where Ceres dreams and sees the image of the abducted Proserpina: 'The hair which had been more beautiful than drawn gold / was fouled; the darkness of night had dimmed both her eyes / and the frost had driven the roses from her cheeks. / The beautiful hue of her skin and those arms, white / as morning frost, had become the colour of hell' (trans. H. Isbell, *The Last Poets of Imperial Rome*, Penguin

Books, 1971, p. 97). The recognition scene, in an eerie and terrible setting, is reminiscent of that in *The Testament of Cresseid*.

Orpheus was not only famous as a lover, but as a poet-musician. Ideas of musical harmony run through the poem. He hears the music of the spheres (of which celestial music the soul on earth was thought to carry a memory), and from that learns the art of music. The Boethian theory distinguished three types of music: *musica mundana*, the music of the universe, harmony expressed in numerical ratios, *musica humana*, within the microcosm of man, the harmony and concord of temperament, senses, and reason, and *musica instrumentalis*, the music made by man, which imitates the harmony of the spheres. Orpheus's harp is the model of harmonious proportion, and in this section briefly restores the harmony of man. His performance (125–130) is described with some technical detail, and offer 'a precise musical image, that of the choral polyphony familiar to the educated city-dweller of the period' (J. Caldwell 'Robert Henryson's Harp of Eloquence', in *The Well Enchanting Skill. Music, Poetry and Drama in the Culture of the Renaissance* ed J. Caldwell, E. Olleson, and S. Wollenberg, Oxford, 1990, p. 149). The hypodorian is the deepest of the modes (hence 'base tonys'); 'gemilling' or twin song, popular in England, in the late fifteenth-century is (Caldwell) 'the division of a voice part (usually the treble or mean) into two lines in the context of elaborate choral polyphony.' The combination of a gimel in either treble or mean parts with a single low part was not uncommon, so that probably we have here a reference to the hyperlydian mode which represents the highest *tonus*, and to 'high-pitched gemilling as opposed to the deep tones that underpin it'.

Text CM (an incomplete copy). Also found in A (incomplete) and B (attr. 'maister R. H.'). Henryson's authorship is confirmed by a side note in Douglas's *Aeneid* which refers to 'Maistir Robert Hendirson in New Orpheus'. The poem is given a number of titles: CM 'the traitie of Orpheus kyng and how he yeid to hewyn & to hel to seik his quene'; A 'the tale of Orpheus and Erudices his quene,' 'the buke of Orpheus,' and 'the buke of Schir Orpheus & Erudices'.
6 full fer and] B full CM   53 (and 60) Ticius] B Theseus CM   60 fled] A filed CM   78 Conqerouris] B conquerour CM and] B of CM   99 and] B for CM intrusioun] B ministration CM   128 gemilling] B gemynyng CM yperlydica *em.* Caldwell] ypolerica CM

THE FABLES

Henryson's fables are highly sophisticated examples of this literary kind. The animal fable was immensely popular in the Middle Ages. It was used by preachers and moralists, and by schoolmasters. Although it was a humble form, associated with children and popular lore, it was also respected as a vehicle of wisdom, and attracted the attention of a number of learned writers. It was usually associated with Aesop, though only some of the vast mass of material can be traced back through Roman authors like Phaedrus and Avianus to Greek and to the rather shadowy figure of 'Aesop' himself, who may have been, as legend has it, a clever slave of the sixth century BC, renowned for his wit and wisdom. A very much later 'Life' describing his adventures was translated into Latin in the fifteenth century, and found its way into Caxton's English Aesop of 1484. Here he is described as an ugly hunch-backed and deformed man, a striking contrast with Henryson's Aesop (see 'The Lion and the Mouse'), who is a handsome Roman, of noble blood, and a grave scholar and 'poet lawriate'.

A number of Henryson's fables are drawn from the Latin Aesopic tradition. His main source is a twelfth-century collection of fables in Latin verse attributed to Walter the Englishman. This was well known and commonly used in schools. A number of his moralities show the influence of the 'moralized Aesops', in which the text of Walter is accompanied by a commentary and allegorical interpretations. He also knew *The Nun's Priest's Tale*, and probably other collections of moral stories such as those of Odo of Cheriton. But because Aesopic fables were so numerous and well known, and circulated in oral as well as in written form, it is often difficult to specify a particular 'source'. He also used other animal tales associated with the beast-epic of Reynard the Fox. The French *Roman de Renart* is a collection of stories begun *c.* 1175 which was developed and added to for a century or more. The world of Aesop is not short of crafty animals and double-dealing, but these are surpassed by the cynical trickery of Reynard demonstrated in a series of brilliantly cunning and totally destructive exploits. The stories were known throughout Europe, and the amoral anti-hero seems to have aroused a mixture of delight and disapproval.

If the addition of the Reynard material complicates the already complex moral patterns of *The Fables* still further, it also increases the variety of the narrative patterns, by providing stories with more elaborate plots (as in 'The Trial of the Fox'; 'The Fox, the Wolf, and the Cadger'; 'The Fox, the Wolf, and the Husbandman'). But even the simple, more emblematic scenes of the Aesopic fables are expanded by Henryson. His description of his work as 'ane maner of translatioun' (32) is an understatement. Walter's brief fables are transformed into short tales in verse which still retain the traditional elegant concision. Direct speech and dialogue bring the tales alive: Walter's equivalent for 'The Paddock and the Mouse', for instance, has no direct speech at all; in 'The Lion and the Mouse', when the lion releases its captive, in Walter the mouse 'departs and gives thanks', but in Henryson falls down on her knees and lifts both her hands up to heaven. A constant interest in the psychology of the animals produces moments of self-revelation. Unusually among early fables the voice and the role of the narrator are prominent. He acts as a presenter, as a commentator, as an observer, and in a rather Chaucerian way creates an intimate relationship both with his characters and with his audience. Henryson – like Chaucer – enjoys the co-existence of 'earnest' and 'game', and makes the most of the opportunity presented by a genre which allows animals to speak, understand, and argue like humans in a poetic world in which fantasy and realism are mingled and where the boundary between animal and human is an uncertain and shifting one. He uses this, in the traditional way, to underline human vice and folly, but at the same time as a source of comedy throughout, in larger scenes and in small details, as when the town mouse 'hevilie . . . kest hir browis doun' (241) at the sight of her rural sister's food.

The medieval fable, like its ancient predecessors, was a didactic form, and usually made its point in a formal *moralitas*; Henryson asks Aesop for 'ane prettie fabill / Concludand with ane gude moralitie'. In his own practice the two are separate but not detached, both delivered by the same 'voice' – and sometimes linked by the narrator's own 'I'. Some of the moralities arise quite naturally from the tales, others are allegorical. Henryson's habit of saying that an animal *may* represent such and such, and the fact that he provides *two* distinct interpretations of his final fable suggest that he knew that differing interpretations of a fable were possible. The moralities complement the fables, and the two together are used to build up what is in effect a 'mirror of human life' in which ideals of social order and justice are more often than not ignored or cynically flouted. Henryson powerfully condemns legal injustice (see especially 'The Sheep and the Dog' and 'The Wolf and the Lamb') and the oppression of the 'poor commons'. A number of moral themes – the need for wisdom, prudence, self-knowledge – run throughout the collection, but in this deceptive and dangerous world some protagonists find intelligence and cunning the most effective defence.

The date of the composition of *The Fables* is not certain, and there have been disagreements on a variety of matters – the possibility of revisions, or the order of the fables (although that in the Bassandyne print, which is followed here, seems coherent and carefully structured). The name of the 'lord' who is said (34–5) to have requested the translation is not known, and he may never have existed.

Text Bs (with a number of readings from B, and occasionally from other witnesses: the choice of readings is often difficult). *The Fables* are found in full or in part in: A (which now has only 'The Two Mice', but in its table of contents lists six other fables; the Makculloch MS (1477, with later additions) has in another (?early sixteenth-century) hand the 'Prologue' and 'The Cock and the Jasp'; B (which has all the fables except three); H; C, Ht, and S.

Prologue

This is based on that of Walter, with additions and some changes. The opening remarks on 'feigned fables', though traditional, amount to a defence of poetic fiction (regarded with suspicion by some reformers and moralists). The image of the unbent bow (22ff.) was a proverbial one for man's need for relaxation and refreshment. The argument that fables offer instruction as well as pleasure (43ff.) is also traditional. Under the conventional modesty of lines 36–42 lies a serious and self-conscious concern with style.

Text   **40** ocht that] B it Bs   **47** Putting] B put in Bs   **55** the mynd] thair myndis Bs   **56** he . . . beist is] B thay . . . beistis ar Bs   **58** facound and purperat] B as poete lawriate Bs   **60** tak] B lak Bs

The Cock and the Jasp

This is based on the opening fable ('De gallo et jaspide') of Walter, which can be traced back to Phaedrus (where the jewel is a pearl). Precious stones were thought to possess magical or spiritual powers. Henryson has expanded Walter's version, making the scenes more detailed and the cock's monologue longer. The allegorical interpretation (found in Walter and in other fable collections) comes as a surprise to most modern readers, and in spite of attempts to find clear premonitions of it in the fable, it is probably meant to be a surprise. Perhaps it is significant that we, the readers, are no better at recognizing wisdom than the cock is. The fable is also an appropriate opening for a collection which often stresses the need for wisdom and how difficult it often is to recognize it.

Text   **74** quhat be thairin] B thay cair nathing Bs   **83** and] B on Bs **92** skraip] B scrapit Bs   **111** fen] Mk midding Bs   **118** fabill] B *om.* Bs **126** Of . . . fallis] B or . . . water Bs   **131** ay] B for Bs

The Two Mice

Based on Walter, but several differences suggest that Henryson knew other versions, whether written or oral. Ancient versions of the fable are found in Babrius and Horace (*Satires* ii.6); a later one is in Wyatt's 'My mothers maydes'. Henryson's fable is notable for its narrative control, the contrasting characters of the two mice (intensified by the fact that in this version they are sisters), and the way it has been thoroughly localized in late medieval Scotland. The *moralitas*, in a different stanza form of eight lines, is a lyrical praise of 'sickernes with small possessioun'.

Text **178** sair] sar A for Bs   **185** fra balk to balk] B quhill scho come to a balk Bs   **190** Lord God] B God Bs   **198** misterlyk] A maisterlig B febilie Bs   **199** erdfast] BA steidfast Bs   **205** hyid] BA glyde Bs   **206** peis] BA candill Bs   **216** syre levand in] A leving into Bs   **221** Forquhy] BA for quhylis Bs   **224** usit wes before] based on BA wes before usit Bs   **235** visage] BA curage Bs   **253** skugry ay] B in stubbill array Bs   **254** cowert] A buskis Bs   **285** mane full] CH manfully Bs   **336** dosor] A burde Bs   **347** ma] BA may na Bs   **357** eftirwart] BA weill thairefter Bs   **383** Luke] BA lieke Bs

The Cock and the Fox

This is not an ancient fable: the various medieval versions come ultimately from the *Roman de Renart*. Henryson's immediate source is Chaucer's *The Nun's Priest's Tale*, and his version has some of that work's rhetorical exuberance. The comic interlude in which the wives give varying estimates of the qualities of their abducted husband may well be his own invention. The hens' names differ in the various texts: B has (483) Sprowtok, Toppok and Coppok, (495) Partlot, (523) Sprowtok, (530) Coppok; the -*ok* is a Scottish diminutive. There are also some variations in the names of the dogs (546–7). A list of the dogs' names is also found in Chaucer: the idea goes back to the *Roman de Renart*, where it is probably making fun of the lists of names of knights' chargers in the *chansons de geste*. Here Curtes is the dog Courtois of the *Roman de Renart*; the others sound Scottish. Henryson regularly uses the Scottish Lowrence (429, etc.) or Lowrie as the name of a fox instead of Reynard, and enjoys linking it with *lour* or *lurk*.

Text **399** kyndis] B kynd Bs   **407** it excedis] B is excludit Bs   **466** is] B wes Bs   **474** inflate] B infect Bs   **477** walkit] B wawland Bs   **486** reylok] B hay Bs   **494** of] B in Bs   **546** Birkye] B berk Bs   **570** unto a] B out off the Bs   **581** coud nocht be] B to be sa Bs   **582** Bot spake] B quhairthrowbs **609** fell] B *om.* Bs

The Fox and the Wolf

Sometimes known as 'The Confession of the Fox' (because of the title in Bs 'The Taill how this foirsaid Tod maid his confessioun to Freir Volf Vaitskaith'): in the table of contents in A it is called 'of the tod and the wolf'. No exact source for Henryson's fable has been discovered, although there are analogues both to the confession and the baptism of the kid. The first enables Henryson both to reveal the hypocrisy of Lourence and to indulge in some satire at the expense of the mendicant friars (the Wolf is a grey friar or Franciscan), notorious for their easy confessions. The latter is a folk-motif found in saints' lives and surviving as a modern merry tale told about recent converts.

Text [Lines 776, 778–9 and 794 in Bs may show Protestant revision. See the note to 'The Trial of the Fox'. Here too it might be argued that some of the Bs readings are not necessarily unHenrysonian (with line 794, for instance, cf. *The Abbey Walk*'s refrain, 'Obey and thank thi God of all').]

621 Thetes] B *om.* Bs   **649** watt] B ken Bs   **651** fait] B men Bs   **653** Deid . . . and] B it . . . ane Bs   **697** Bot to . . . mele] B unto . . . kneill Bs   **729** falt of] C fall no Bs into] CB unto Bs   **741** net, nor bait] nor net bait Bs   **776** contritioun] B provisioun Bs   **778** conclusioun] B confusioun Bs   **779** gois now to confessioun] B now hes gude professioun Bs   **780** repentis for] repentis nor for Bs   **794** do wilfull pennance here] B obey unto your God Bs

The Trial of the Fox

The closest parallel to this fable which has been discovered is a fable added to the collection of Odo of Cheriton, which has the assembly of beasts summoned by the lion – the absent animal is an ass, and it is the fox not the wolf that receives the kick. The idea of the trial of the fox goes back to the *Roman de Renart*, though there he is not executed. This fable is the longest in Henryson's collection, and has a splendid diversity of scenes, and demonstrates his narrative skill and control of irony. The summoning of the parliament is a spectacular affair, mingling earnest with game (as when in 873ff. the three heraldic leopards of England are made to pitch the tent of the lion of Scotland). In the list of animals that attend are blended heraldry, bestiary lore, mythology, and fantasy. It is an enthusiastic rhetorical tour de force delighting in the flow of sound – and at the same time a celebration of the rich diversity of nature. Some of the strange names may have defeated early copyists as well as modern editors. The parliament is, as it was in fifteenth-century Scotland, a court of law, and its proceedings are described with precise terminology (948–9, etc.).

Text [Parts of the Bassandyne version of this fable may show later Protestant revisions. I have followed Fox in preferring the Bannatyne lines in these cases, but with some hesitation, since the matter does not seem to me to be absolutely straightforward. In 836–7, for instance, where Bs reads 'To execute, to do, to satisfie / Thy letter will, thy det and legacie' we may have a Protestant removal of a reference to prayers for the dead, but the wickedness of executors was a prominent theme in medieval moral verse. In the *moralitas*, lines 1111–14 ('men

of gude conditioun, / As pilgrymes walkand in this wildernes, / Approvand that
for richt religioun, / Thair God onlie to pleis'), 1134–5 ('Assaultand men
with sweit perswasionis, / Ay reddie for to trap tham in ane trayne'), and
1139–41 ('O Mediatour mercifull and meik, / Thow soveraigne Lord and
King celestiall, / Thy celsitude maist humilie we beseik') may be Protestant
changes, but it must be said that they do not sound clearly unHenrysonian. It
could be argued that the alternatives to the 'men of religion' passages fit quite
well with the more general theme of 'our leving' (1102) and of man in general
(1126) – though it would have to be admitted that in other moralities Henryson
sometimes does single out specific offices and officials. And though the author
of 'The Annunciation' could certainly write fervent Marian verse, it is curious
that this is the only case in *The Fables* where the Virgin is invoked, as against
God or Christ. It is difficult to choose between a number of possible alternatives:
Protestant revision (or revision in order to secure publication in a Protestant
city), alternative textual versions which perhaps go back to Henryson, or even
perhaps a 'Catholic' revision of Bannatyne. (Cf. also lines 776ff., 1345, 1616,
2437, 2967.) On the background, see Theo van Heijnsbergen, 'The Interaction
between Literature and History in Queen Mary's Edinburgh' in *The Renaissance
in Scotland* ed. A. A. MacDonald, M. Lynch, and I. B. Cowan, Leiden, 1994.]
798 That to his airschip] B Till airschip Bs micht of law] B be law that micht
Bs   **799** lemanrye] lenanrye B adulterie Bs   **806** get] B geir Bs   **832** wrangwis
guidis] B wardlie gude and Bs   **836–7** from B; see above   **841–2** these lines
transposed in Bs   **843** buste] B bill Bs   **848** Oyas! Oyas!] B on this wyis
Bs   **851** Govand] B gritlie Bs   **852** his] B ane Bs   **855** We] B the Bs   **872**
trippand] B creippand Bs   **873** Thre] B the Bs a] B with Bs   **877** pollis] B
powis C towis Bs   **881** fut, all beistis in the] B all fourfuttit beistis in Bs   **910**
globard] globert B glebard Bs   **949** call] B callit Bs   **993** My lord] B now see
Bs   **1023** hattrell] CB hattell Bs   **1060** hir] CB his Bs   **1095** basare] B
bowcher Bs   **1100** fyne] fyn B syne Bs   **1111–14, 1134–5** from B; see
above   **1137** with ithand] B draw neir with panis sore Bs   **1139–41** from B
(in **1139** Mary . . . mercy has been cancelled and lord eternall medeator for
ws mast written above it); see n. above

The Sheep and the Dog

Based on Walter's fable, which can be traced back to Phaedrus. This is a bitter
satire on the ecclesiastical consistory courts (which dealt with many matters
not connected with morality or ecclesiastical discipline), and is widened in the
moralitas into a more general attack on contemporary injustice. The language
and description of procedures are precise – thus in 1156ff. the reference is to
the three ecclesiastical punishments of *suspensio totalis*, *excommunicatio major*,
and *interdictio*; a peremptory summons (1164) would render a defendant

contumax if he did not appear; courts were not (1199–1200) to transact business on some holidays, nor to be held after dark. There was much anti-legal satire in the Middle Ages, but Henryson's has a particular power and commitment. His *moralitas* raises the whole question of injustice in the world, and the sheep's overheard lament (which seems to continue to the end of the *moralitas*) is a passionate statement of the great load of suffering desperately endured by the 'pure commounis'.

Text 1194 as juge] B juge as Bs   1216 mony volum] B law volumis full mony Bs   1218 Contra and pro] based on B contrait prostrait Bs   1273 porteous] B portioun Bs   1278 swa] CB tak Bs skat] B tat Bs   1301 Exylit] B loist Bs and law] B and eik law Bs   1306 meid] B micht Bs

The Lion and the Mouse

This is based on Walter's fable, which can be traced back to Babrius. The dream-vision framework and the meeting with Aesop are almost certainly Henryson's invention. The fable's central position in the collection and the fact that it is told by Aesop himself give it a special importance. It is a political fable, stressing the need for mutual dependence and for a ruler to enforce justice but also to show mercy. Such advice was traditionally given to princes, and Scottish kings were adjured to rule firmly and justly. After his more general 'Figure heirof oftymis hes bene sene' (1614), Aesop refers pointedly to 'this cuntré' (1617). But that Henryson had a particular event in mind (like the rebellion of 1482), as some have suggested, is far from certain. There are other moral themes in the fable – like the value and the power of true nobility and of pity – and the high ideal of social interdependence is expressed in homely proverbial form: 'Cum help to quyte ane gude turne for ane uther'. The fable blends 'earnest' with 'game'.

Text 1345 cled my heid] Bs B maid a cors   1350 chemeris] chymmeris B chemeis Bs   1386 dedene] B not disdayne Bs   1398 yit] B yis Bs   1405 wery] B verray 1405 wery B verray C war Bs   1460 Onto] B upon Bs   1562 abone] B about Bs   1616 I the beseik . . . for to pray] Bs B Perswaid the kirkmen ythandly to pray

The Preaching of the Swallow

This is a much expanded version of Walter's brief fable, which like other medieval versions goes back to the prose paraphrases of Phaedrus. In striking contrast to its predecessor it is a grim tragedy shot through with irony, but the voice of the narrator (who is here the observer), though it records the folly of the birds, is filled with pity at their terrible end. The fable has a grandly philosophical and learned opening which announces the supreme wisdom of God, and introduces the central moral theme of prudence and foresight. At the very same time we are reminded of man's weakness and blindness, of the great chasm between his powers and those of God. The acknowledgement of the limits of man's reason (1647–9) is not unusual in the later Middle Ages ('The more we trace the Trinité, / The more we falle in fantasye', Thomas G. Duncan, *Medieval English Lyrics 1200–1400* Penguin Books, 1995, p. 85). The thought that man may achieve some comprehension of God's qualities through his creation leads on to a celebration of the order and harmony of the universe – the firmament with its fixed stars enclosing within it the seven planetary spheres which as they move produce musical sounds (1660) no longer audible to humans. The ordered variety of nature is shown in the succession of the seasons, an almost masque-like procession, in which ancient deities are placed in Scottish weather. The 'business' of the workers which so delights the poet is the final part of the introduction. The tale unfolds under his eyes as he stands under a hawthorn (a 'fairy' tree). Its progress is grim and inexorable, and the warning voice of the swallow becomes increasingly urgent. The changing of the seasons (1776, 1832) and the echo of the earlier 'business' of the workers in the precise description of the making of flaxen nets (1825–31) form a sinister background to the final scene of horror.

Text **1633** materiale] B naturall Bs   **1697** changeis] B changit Bs   **1701** ar bethit] B laifit Bs   **1744** lo se and] B and gude Bs   **1758** befoir and se] B provyde and foirse Bs   **1760** thingis at] B thing behald Bs   **1873** this] C thus Bs   **1928** warldis] B warld Bs   **1946** to seis] B fra Bs

The Fox, the Wolf, and the Cadger

No exact source for this fable has been found, though there is a similar episode in the *Roman de Renart*. It is likely that versions of the story circulated in oral form. Henryson's tale shows the clever trickster Reynard (alias Russell, Lowrence) at his most ruthless, and there is not much sympathy for the more dull-witted wolf or for the vividly realized cadger (pedlar).

Text **1957** breith] C wraith Bs   **1995** sonyeis] C senyes Bs   **2103** snakkit] C hakkit Bs   **2148** dow not] C he will Bs   **2168** als . . . ony] C wavering as the Bs   **2177** bat] *em.* Fox bot Bs   **2193** a stewart] *em.* Bawcutt–Riddy efterwart Bs   fyne] Ht syne Bs

The Fox, the Wolf, and the Husbandman

A version of this fable is found in the *Disciplina clericalis*, a collection of moral tales made by Petrus Alphonsi in the early twelfth century, and this is probably the source (whether direct or not). The various motifs of the story appear separately elsewhere. Henryson elaborates it with comic gusto, and with his sharp observation of legal malpractice – at which the fox is most adept as a 'juge amycabill' (in 2316ff. his cynical advice to the husbandman is delivered with familiar and cajoling 'thou's').

Text [Protestant revision has been suspected in 2437, but it may simply be a piece of allegorical 'merie sport']   2372 hous] Ht hors Bs   2432 Arctand] C actand Bs

The Wolf and the Wether

Henryson's dramatic tale of self-delusion is developed from some version of a fable which can be traced back to the twelfth century. The closest parallel is in the fifteenth-century collection of Steinhöwel, which made its way (via a French translation) into Caxton's *Aesop*, but this is probably not Henryson's source. Although the fable does not seem to be an ancient one, it is close to Aesop in spirit (cf. 'The Ass in the Lion's Skin').

Text 2468 with] wit Bs   2476 wichtlie] Ht wretchitlie Bs   2542 [as applied to the wolf, this line does not make good sense: perhaps 'fra' is an error for 'for' ('because of') or, alternatively, 'schawis' for 'schowis' ('attacks')   2548 Syne] C tyne Bs

The Wolf and the Lamb

This fable is in Walter's collection: it can be traced back to Phaedrus (who says that it was composed to 'fit those persons who invent false charges by which to oppress the innocent') and (in Greek) to Babrius. It is common in medieval collections. As usual, Henryson expands the simple text – here into a dramatic exemplum of injustice. The long and detailed *moralitas* uses traditional moral topics but is a precise and vehement attack on what were felt to be real abuses.

Text 2628 him] B he Bs presomyng] B belevand Bs   2630 austre] B awfull angrie Bs   2632 this] B and Bs   2667 pais] B prais Bs   2673 cheris] B refuse

Bs   2677 spew] B did spew Bs   2690 wyis] B gyis Bs   2697 Goddis] B his
Bs   2701 deid] Bs hedit B   2716 poleit] B poete Bs   2750 cairt] B court
Bs   2760 be rad] B dreid Bs   2769 with] had with Bs   2771 extortioneris]
B exortioneris Bs

The Paddock and the Mouse

This 'powerful and gloomy symbol for man's earthly life' (Fox) is based on
Walter's fable, which can be traced back to antiquity: it is first found in the
Greek 'Life of Aesop', probably of the first century AD, and appears in many
medieval versions. Henryson's fable has a typically grim and ironic end. (In
the early dialogue between the mouse and the paddock, 2800–10, I follow Fox
in restoring what seems to have been an intended opposition between the
mouse's familiar 'thou's' and the paddock's deceitfully polite plural pronouns.)
The argument over physiognomy (2819ff.) uses traditional lore and examples
(such as Absalom (2842) the beautiful youth of the Old Testament (see II Samuel
14:25)), but there are some submerged ironies – the Old Testament Absalom
behaved treacherously, and the proverbial wisdom quoted (2831–2, 2839) is
deliberately inconclusive (though in this case the mouse's instinct was correct).
Physical features or different types of voices, reflecting the 'complexioun'
(2828), the balance or imbalance of the humours were often taken to be
indications of personality – or, as Henryson says, carefully avoiding an outright
determinism, clerks say that they 'commounly' incline 'mannis thocht'. (There
were four bodily fluids: blood (in excess producing a sanguine person), phlegm
(phlegmatic), choler or yellow bile (choleric), melancholy or black bile.) The
opening of the *moralitas* is in eight-line stanzas with a refrain (cf. 'The Two
Mice'). Like the 'moralized Aesops', this fable has a second interpretation, and
Henryson's reference to the friars (famous or notorious for their exegetical
skills) sounds decidedly skittish (and neatly parallels the way he ended the
fable, 2909).

Text [In 2967 Protestant revision has been suspected (see n. to 'The Trial of
the Fox'): this is possible but not certain – Henryson elsewhere urges faith
(see, e.g., line 1649), and it might be thought to be at least as good material
for an allegorical castle as good deeds].
2789 rauk] rank Bs   2800 your] B thy Bs   2803 yow] B the Bs   2804 your]
B thy Bs   2808 droun to wed] B drounit be Bs   2841 wyt] B cause Bs   2869
How] B O Bs   2877 thocht nathing bot to fleit and] B thocht off nathing bot
for to Bs   2887 Scho . . . and] B with all hir mycht scho Bs   2893 this plungit]
B plungit Bs   2898 owthir] B ony Bs   2904 fettislie] fettillie Bs   2915 For
thow . . . barrow] B to the wer better beir the stane barrow Bs   2916 Or

sueitand dig and] B For all thy dayis to Bs   **2945** gounis] gouins Bs   **2946** fische] B fitche Bs   **2947** wappit] B wrappit Bs   **2958** distinyt] B rycht different Bs   **2959** spreit] B saull Bs   **2967** gud deidis] B faith in Christ Bs   **2972** a sample or] B exempill and ane Bs

THE RESSONING BETUIX DETH AND MAN

A number of late medieval poems and plays present a dramatic confrontation between Death and Man. The best known are the play of *Everyman* and the various versions of the Dance of Death. The *Ressoning* uses traditional topics and images – Death's absolute power, his spear, etc. It does not seem to be directly indebted to the Dance of Death, but perhaps contains echoes of an earlier type of poem, the *Vado mori* ('I go to die') in which a number of 'estates' are confronted by Death and overcome by him. It is less macabre than Henryson's other mortality poem, 'The Thre Deid Pollis', in which three skulls deliver a minatory *memento mori*: as in *Everyman* Man does not at first recognize his interlocutor, and Death's words have none of the jokes at the expense of his victims that are found in the Dance of Death. Here he is an awesome and mysterious figure. His speeches are solemn and forceful, and provoke a series of reactions in Man – ignorance, bold resistance, repentance, and humble submission, offering to 'lurk' under death's 'caip'. That phrase may be ambiguous (it has been suggested that it refers to the 'cope of lead', a coffin), but it seems to suggest a covering, almost protecting, cloak, an image which leads on to the final prayer.

Text B (attr. 'Hendersone'); also found in Bd.
5 ryell estait] Bd roall stait B   **6** this] Bd the B   **12** le] Bd sone lie B   **37** in hy] Bd and try B.

THE ANNUNCIATION

This poem is an imaginative expansion of a Latin devotional poem ('Fortis ut mors dilectio'). It is a remarkable metrical and rhythmical tour de force, in which each stanza has only two rhymes, and the *b*-rhyme (*-is*) is carried on throughout the poem, giving a sense of breathless excitement. Alliteration is used for emphasis. The Annunciation (a favourite topic of devotional literature and art) is here seen as a drama of love. It uses traditional paradoxes – that Mary is both mother and maiden, a humble creature who bore the creator of all things – and Old Testament prefigurations of the Virgin Birth: the three miracles (37ff.) of the bush burning but unconsumed which was seen by Moses (Exodus 3:2), the dry wand of Aaron which flowered (Numbers 17:8, and Gideon's fleece which was moist with dew although the earth around it was dry (Judges 6:37). The poem has a virtuosity which reminds us of Dunbar.

Text G (attr. 'Ro. Henrisoun').
51 his] hir G ('her' can just be made to make sense – ?'the divinity she bore' – but this is rather tortuous).

WILLIAM DUNBAR

RORATE CELI DESUPER

This poem on Christ's Nativity is full of biblical and liturgical echoes: for example, *Rorate celi . . .* (Isaiah 45:8) used in the Advent liturgy; the refrain *Et nobis puer . . .* (Isaiah 9:6) used in the introit of the Christmas Day Mass; *Gloria in excelsis* (Luke 2:14), the angels' song to the shepherds at the Nativity, was the *Gloria* sung in the Mass. Like other Nativity lyrics, it makes extensive use of the imagery of light, driving away darkness: Christ 'the cleir sone' (probably with a pun on sun/son) surpasses the natural sun (Phoebus); and he is Aurora, piercing the clouds. The rose was frequently used as an image for the Virgin Mary. Dunbar commands the whole of creation, from the nine orders of angels, the stars and the planets, the four elements (9–13) to mankind (sinners and clergy) and the birds and the flowers – heaven, earth, sea, man, bird, and beast – to celebrate the great event.

Text B (attr. 'Dumbar').   8 *puer*] power B   44 rose, Mary] rosemary B

DONE IS A BATTELL ON THE DRAGON BLAK

A lyric on the Resurrection which celebrates in triumphant style and with an extraordinary dynamic energy the victory of 'our champion' Christ over Satan. Underlying it is the legend of the Harrowing of Hell, derived from the apocryphal Gospel of Nicodemus (ultimately perhaps from the powerful ancient near eastern myth of the hero–god who descends and slays the lord of the underworld) that before Christ rose on the third day he descended into hell, breaking open its doors and raising his cross (3–4), where he destroyed the power of the devil, released the patriarchs from captivity, and made it possible for souls to go into bliss (6). This is widespread in the Middle Ages in painting, drama, and literature (an especially impressive treatment is found in Langland's *Piers Plowman*). Dunbar concentrates on the triumphant moment of Easter Day: the refrain *Surrexit Dominus de sepulchro* is a versicle from the Easter Day Mass. The poem has a dense texture of predominantly Biblical imagery (with the images often boldly juxtaposed). Lucifer (once the brightest of the angels) is identified with the great dragon of Revelations 12, that old serpent called the devil, and a fierce lurking tiger. Christ is both lamb and lion (cf. Genesis 49:9, Numbers 24:9) and a giant (Psalms 19:5), and is figured by the ancient deities Aurora and Apollo. Solar imagery is commonly used in Resurrection hymns and lyrics. The sun darkened at the hour of Christ's death (line 27; cf. *Luke* 23:45) now shines brightly, and the bells ring out (27) both in heaven and on earth (29).

Text B (attr. 'Dunbar'). 4 rasit] is B 13 clowis] clowss.

HALE, STERNE SUPERNE

This lyric in praise of the Blessed Virgin has at its root the angelic greeting *Ave Maria, gracia plena* (cf. *Luke* 1:28, 42) which is used as an internal refrain. It is an extraordinary display of poetic virtuosity, which must be read aloud if its full aural effect is to be appreciated. It is the most coruscating example of 'aureate' writing in Dunbar. The use of 'golden' terms – unusual Latinate words, sometimes of liturgical origin – had been developed by John Lydgate and other fifteenth-century poets. Henryson has one example (with internal rhymes as Dunbar has) in some lines towards the end of his 'Ane Prayer for the Pest': one line in particular (addressing God, not the Virgin) sounds very similar to Dunbar – 'Superne lucerne, guberne this pestilens'. Possibly Dunbar knew this poem. Late medieval poets normally use aureate diction with some sense of decorum: the Blessed Virgin enthroned in glory as the queen of heaven is an appropriate subject. Dunbar skilfully varies his aureate lines with the repeated Latin phrase and by interwoven phrases in ordinary Scots ('In Godis sicht to schyne', etc.). Sometimes these are formulaic ('rute and ryne', etc.), sometimes perhaps colloquial. A case in point may be the phrase 'mak our oddis evyne' (56) apparently meaning something like 'forgive our shortcomings'. This seems to be the first recorded use of 'odds', and it is not clear quite what form of (numerical) adjustment lies behind the phrase: James Kinsley (see Further Reading) thought of her intervening in the weighing of souls at the Judgement, but it may refer more generally to a numerological restoration of order (the sense of 'advantage conceded' in games is later, and does not seem to fit this context).

There are allusive phrases from the Bible ('Alphais habitakle', 14; cf. Revelation 1:8), 'angell fude' (*panis angelorum*, Psalm 78:25, interpreted as Christ), but the bulk of the poem is made up of invocations to Mary by means of her traditional titles or 'figures' in the Bible or in the universe. A number of late medieval English poems and carols use this technique. Thus she is the star (*stella celi, stella maris*), a lantern or lamp, an anchor, a nightingale, a rose, a lily, a daisy, a jewel, rich spice, a protecting wall, a royal throne, etc. The ecstatic outpouring of images has a dizzying effect. But the words are precisely used: 'rosyne' (8) is formed on the model of L. *regina*, 'queen': besides 'queenly rose' it may also suggest 'little rose'.

There are two difficult words which might justify emendation: in 58 there seems no special point to the number 'eleven'. It might be used to mean 'a large number', but this seems strange. It could be a forced rhyme. Or (Bawcutt and Riddy, see Further Reading) it might be a variant of 'all evin' ('all equally, without exception') used vaguely as a line filler. Perhaps more likely is a scribal error (perhaps helped by the apparently numerical phrase 'oddis evyne') for something more precise, such as 'ilk evyn' ('every evening'), i.e. the evening recitation of the 'Ave Maria', a medieval antecedent of the Angelus. (Identical rhymes are not always avoided in medieval poetry: see *General Prologue* to the *Canterbury Tales* ll. 17–18.) In 73 'palestrall' should mean 'to do with wrestling'. It has been suggested that Dunbar confused it with 'palatial', perhaps helped by a misunderstanding or misremembrance of the 'pleyes palestral' (wrestling matches) of Chaucer's *Troilus* (5.304). It might however be a scribal misreading of an otherwise unattested aureate word 'prelustral' invented by Dunbar (L. *praelustris*, 'magnificent'), especially if, as was often the case, *pre-* was represented in abbreviated form.

Text A (attr. 'Dunbar', and entitled, as are some other poems in the MS, 'Ane Ballat of our Lady').

MY HEID DID YAK YESTER NICHT

This early description of 'writer's block' may have been addressed to the king (cf. 'schir', l. 6), perhaps by way of apology, but nothing certain is known about its context. The 'sentence' or matter of the poem Dunbar cannot write is in the back of his head (the third cell of the brain, the home of memory), but he cannot find (or 'invent') it.

Text R (attr. 'Dumbar').

SIR JHON SINCLAIR BEGOWTHE
TO DANCE

This lively, comic, and irreverent account of a dance names members of the court. Sir John Sinclair of Dryden was there throughout the reign of James IV, and was still in the queen's service in 1513; Robert Shaw was probably a court physician; the unnamed 'maister almaser' would have been Sir Andrew McBrek; 'John Bute the fule' was a court fool; Mistress Musgrave, perhaps Agnes Musgrave, wife of Sir John Musgrave, was one of the queen's attendants; 'the Quenis Dog' is James Dog or Doig (a keeper of the queen's wardrobe, who appears also in the two following poems). Dunbar places himself exactly at the centre of the poem, and ridicules himself also – though less savagely than he does the other men. There is a sudden and teasing shift from 'Dunbar the Mackar' to the 'I' of lines 31–3 who so admires Musgraeffe. Although there is a sly reference (2) to France, probably as the home of fashionable behaviour, the absurd and Rabelaisian mishaps suggest the accounts of Scottish peasant dances or 'brawls'. That James Dog is first recorded as a servitour to the queen in 1511, and Mistress Musgrave is prominent in the records from 1511 to 1513, may suggest a date of composition about this time (Bawcutt).

Text MF (attr. 'Dunbar', 'of a dance in the quenis chalmer'). Also found in R.

THE WARDRAIPPER OF VENUS BOURE

This poem, addressed to the queen, is a witty attack on James Dog (see also previous poem), a keeper of her wardrobe (the section of the household which dealt with clothes, liveries, tapestries, and furnishings), who had previously been groom of the king's wardrobe. He is recorded as one of the queen's servitors from 1511. Dunbar complains about his reluctance to give him a doublet, a gift of clothing authorized by the queen (9). The poem plays with the different senses of 'dangerous' ('perilous', 'disdainful, reluctant', 'surly') and with different kinds of dogs and canine behaviour. Dog must be a fearsome mastiff if he can guard the wardrobe from Gog Magog, in legend the chief of the giants of Albion destroyed by Brutus and the Trojans when they came to Britain, conflated with the biblical Gog and Magog, and transformed into an exotic eastern tyrant.

Text MF (attr. 'Dunbar'). Also found in R.

O GRACIOUS PRINCES, GUID AND FAIR

This is clearly a companion poem to 'The wardraipper of Venus boure', with
the same metre and the same number of stanzas. It survives in MF and R.
The colophon in MF reads 'quod Dunbar of the said James quen he had plesit
him'. However the tone and content of the poem suggest that it is far from
being generously apologetic.

THIS WAVERAND WARLDIS
WRETCHIDNES

The verse petition is one of Dunbar's favourite forms. There had been excellent
earlier English examples – by Chaucer, Hoccleve, and Lydgate – but Dunbar's
sometimes have a touch of genius. This witty poem begins as a satirical
complaint on the wretched state of the world nowadays, gradually turns to the
woes of Scotland and in particular the abuses in the church and the granting
of benefices (the lines on ambitious clerics, 49–52, though quite general, could
well apply to contemporary figures like bishops Blacader and Forman). Finally
it turns to the unfortunate state of the unbeneficed Dunbar ('Unwourthy I',
53), whose desires are humble – just one church with a roof of heather (85–
6) would do. In a passage of fantasy (57ff.) he contemplates the tribulations
and delays of the promised benefice, which might have arrived more quickly
if it were coming from the exotic parts of the world. The lines that follow have
often been seen as a very early response to the great discoveries at the end of
the fifteenth and the beginning of the sixteenth centuries. This is not absolutely
certain, though there is a sense of excitement (which might also come partially
at least from the poetic invention of a fantastic world). Some of the places
which can be identified were known well before 1492 – like Calicut, the trading
port in southwest India, or the great 'sea of ocean' (67) encircling the world,
which derives from classical geography. The 'new fund yle' may be Newfound-
land (discovered by Cabot in 1497) or the new lands discovered by Columbus
in the Caribbean, but the phrase may be quite general and/or vague ('yle'
could mean 'land' as well as 'island'). The 'parts beyond the meridian' might
refer to the meridian in the Atlantic, but meridian is used by Scottish writers
to mean the equator: the reference then would be to the southern hemisphere.
If Paris (70) is really Paris, and not a garbled form of 'Persia', then lines 70–
71 (with the 'ylis of Aphrycane' being the Atlantic islands off the African coast)
would be a (slightly fantastic) allusion to the traditional three parts of the world
– Europe, Asia, and Africa.

Text MF (attr. 'Dumbar'). Also found in R.   81 it] R *om.* MF.

SCHIR, LAT IT NEVER IN TOUNE
BE TALD

Another petition in the form of a carol with the 'burden' (lines 1–2) repeated between the stanzas. Carols were not exclusively associated with Christmas in the Middle Ages, but this one clearly is. The phrase 'Yowllis yald' ('Yule nag') may mean someone who did not have new clothes for the celebration. It is tempting to associate the poem with the record of a payment of £5 that Dunbar received on 27 January 1506 'for caus he wantit his goun at Yule'. The way in which Dunbar imagines himself as an old, worn-out and neglected horse is developed throughout the poem. There are a number of difficult words, e.g. 'bekis' (18). The usual gloss 'corner teeth' makes sense but is not supported by strong lexical evidence (Jamieson's Dictionary, 1808, records that 'beik', the beak of a bird, is 'sometimes used for a man's mouth, by way of contempt'). There is an English dialect word 'beck' or 'beak' meaning 'a horseshoe' – and a word 'sprun' or 'spurn' meaning to add a sharp piece of iron to the front of the horse's shoe, but these do not seem to be recorded in Scotland. Similarly 'schoud' (30; ?a past participle, ?the first part of a compound noun) seems certainly to refer to straw of poor quality, but the origin of the word is obscure. An English dialect noun 'shood' meaning 'the husk of oats after threshing; a mixture for horses, consisting of chopped hay and peas' is recorded in the north, but not apparently in Scotland.

Text lines 1–32 MF (incomplete), remainder R (attr. 'Dumbar').
1 toune] R toume MF   5 Strenever] Streneverne MF, R   36 gnawid] gnawin R

SCHIR, YE HAVE MONY SERVITOURIS

A more elaborate petition to the king, which gives a vivid and satirical account of his servants both 'profitable' and less profitable. The hint of bitterness found in the previous poem is here felt much more strongly, and Dunbar is moved to a defiant statement of his pride in his writing, and at the end to an open threat that vengeance through the power of his pen is preferable to dying in melancholy. A number of the words in the lists are difficult or obscure, e.g. 'cawandaris' (10), where the context might be taken to suggest either some kind of soldier, or some kind of entertainer; even 'lyand' (13) is uncertain –

unless it is a joke, some kind of professional activity would seem appropriate. If 'Pryntouris' (16) are printers and not workers in the mint, it would suggest a date after September 1507 when Walter Chepman and Andrew Myllar were granted the first licence to print in Scotland, but it is quite likely that the word is used in its older sense. Among the miserable 'other sort' a number are unidentified: the 'groukaris' (though this word might be related to the English dialect word 'groak' (also 'grouk, growk') 'to look over with a watchful and suspicious eye'); the 'gledaris' (perhaps connected with 'gled', 'kite', which in early Modern English was used to mean 'a person who preys upon others' or 'a sharper'; or even with Scottish 'gleyar', 'one who squints'); the 'gunnaris', if they are 'gunners', seem oddly placed here (unless they had a very low reputation, perhaps because many of them were foreign) – or unless the word is a slang term for 'rogue', as it may have been later: see *OED* s.v. 'gunster'; 'monsour' (from Fr. *monsieur*) is a sarcastic term for a French nobleman or would-be nobleman (cf. later 'mounseer', 'monsewer' etc.): there is a reference in 1512 in the *Treasurer's Accounts* to 'Monsure Lamote servitouris that dansit ane moris to the King'. Traditional satire on the miserable life of courtiers often makes merry at their expense (Alexander Barclay, in his second *Egloge* (*c.*1515), describes their abominable food – cheese 'all full of magots and like to the raynebowe', etc. – and John Skelton's *Bowge of Courte* (1498) evokes their sinister scheming), but Dunbar's frantic list of fools and rogues is all his own. It resembles (Bawcutt, see Further Reading) the technique of the Scottish comic poem *Colkelbie Sow*, to which he alludes in lines 65–6, where a crowd of assorted fools is invited to feast on a small pig.

Text MF (attr. 'Dunbar').   **85** Or] and MF.

THE FLYTING OF DUNBAR AND KENNEDY

(*Dunbar attacks his rival*)

These extracts correspond to lines 49–72, 97–128, 145–68, and 201–48 of the whole piece (552 lines in all), and are intended to give some idea of Dunbar's skill in this curious satirical form. The 'flyting', a (more or less) formal exchange of insults, is found in various societies and at various social levels. This example (like the nearly contemporary English example of John Skelton's flyting against Garnesche) seems to be a kind of court entertainment. The element of 'game' and the display of rhetorical skill perhaps overshadow that of 'earnest', although there is some of that probably (and to be fully entertaining and rhetorically impressive the exchanges have to sound as if they are for real). It would be rash to believe all the scurrilous stories told by the poets, but sometimes perhaps in the manner of later caricaturists they are exaggerating an actual foible or feature for satirical effect. Perhaps the poet Walter Kennedy (of whom Dunbar elsewhere speaks warmly – see 'I that in heill wes and gladnes', 89–91) was gaunt and thin – or was he rather rotund? We shall never know. He was certainly not the wretched Highland thief that Dunbar describes, but he did come from a land-owning family in Ayrshire and Carrick, which still was a Gaelic-speaking area. In his sections Kennedy gives as good as he gets, and incidentally remarks that Gaelic 'was the gud langage of this land' before the treason of Dunbar's ancestors. Dunbar's section contains some memorable satirical scenes and rises to a crescendo of abuse and 'rough music'.

The flood of abusive taunts contains many examples of scurrilous words, some probably colloquial, some perhaps inventions. Many remain completely obscure, or have been interpreted in widely different ways. And other allusions remain obscure, like that to 'Hilhous' (121). Little is known of 'strait Gibbon' (89) except that a man of that name (perhaps an entertainer) received payments in 1503: the adjective (?skinny, ?stingy, ?strict, ?stern) sounds like a nickname, and to be 'heir' to him presumably means 'very similar to'. 'dagone' (18) is probably Dagon, the god of the Philistines (I Samuel 5), perhaps imagined as a horrible idol. Kennedy (51ff.) has the ugly features given in medieval art to the tormentors of saints: St Lawrence was roasted on a grid-iron; St John's eyes were blindfolded before he was beheaded; St Augustine of Canterbury was, according to legend, attacked with fishtails by the pagan English. Lazarus (73) was raised by Christ from the dead (John 11:1–44): in the medieval drama he appears in his grave-clothes and gives a warning to the audience that they too must die. Dunbar imagines the gaunt figure of Kennedy as similar to the horrifying corpses and skeletons which in late medieval art and literature confront the living with a *memento mori*.

There are probably a number of topical references, now uncertain, but a reference later in *The Flyting* (line 331) to 'Stobo' (d.1505; see 'I that in heill wes and gladnes', line 86) as still alive is the only clear indication of the poem's date.

Text B. Also found in MF, R, and a fragment (not this section) in a Chepman and Myllar print).
3 Densmen] MF denseman B   10 Scarth fra scorpione, scaldit] B skitterand scorpioun scauld MF   30 lauchtane] MF lathand B   48 bratt] R club B   49 lowsy] lowsie MF baith lowsy B   64 lymmerfull] B lymmair MF   72 sacryne] MF seccrind B   100 brachattis] R bichis B   121 byt] MF byle B   122 flay] MF foule B

WE THAT AR HEIR IN HEVYNNIS GLORIE

Often called 'The Dregy of Dunbar' from the beginning of the title given to it in the Bannatyne MS (in the Maitland Folio MS it is called 'Dumbaris dirige to the king / Bydand ovir lang in Stirling'): the 'dirige' (23) is the first line and title of a part of the Office for the Dead. Parodies of the liturgy are commonly found in medieval literature: in English there is a 'lovers' mass', and Skelton's mock-elegy in *Phyllyp Sparowe* also uses parts of the Office for the Dead. With a display of metrical and linguistic skill Dunbar adapts the Office to a 'prayer' for those unfortunates languishing in the austere and purgatorial town of Stirling (which was often visited by the king and the court, sometimes, but not always, for penitential reasons) by those happy souls rejoicing in the 'heavenly' delights of Edinburgh, 'the mirrie town'.

Text MF. Also found in B and R.   **49** saitt] B hevinlie court MF   **53** plever] B pluver MF   **87** sould ye] suld ye B ye sould MF

NOW LYTHIS OFF ANE GENTILL KNYCHT

Thomas Norny was a member of the king's household who appears in the records from 1503 to 1512 (he accompanied the king to the north in 1505); his name is usually listed with entertainers, and he is once called a fool – which would seem to be confirmed by Dunbar's treatment. The title 'schir' which is sometimes given to him in the records is probably derisive or the result of some festive mock-investiture. Dunbar's poem is a mock-heroic 'celebration' of 'this anterous knycht' which begins in narrative form, with echoes and parodies of the popular romance, in the manner of Chaucer's *Sir Thopas*, using the traditional phraseology and formulae (like the opening call for attention, 'Now lythis'). His supposed exploits take place, however, in the country (19) or in the north of Scotland (against the warlike clan Chattan, etc.) rather than in the faery or exotic world of romance. As in *Sir Thopas* there is a list of famous heroes to whom our hero is favourably compared, but here the largest part consists of a string of what seem to be outlaws – Robin Hood (25), Guy of Gisborne who in a ballad fought against Robin, Allan Bell, almost certainly Adam Bell, the hero of another outlaw ballad. Roger of Clekniskleuch is unknown, and Simon of Whinfell's sons are known only in the title of a song or dance in *Colkelbie Sow*: perhaps they were outlaws from Cumbria. Sir Bevis

(35), however, is a genuine knightly hero – of a very popular Middle English romance, *Bevis of Hampton*. The following stanzas seem to refer to some real or imagined episode at court. Quenetyne cannot be identified with certainty, but Curry was a court fool (recorded from 1495 until his death in 1506), married to 'daft Anne'. It is usually said that Curry's death in 1506 means that the poem must have been written before that date. This is not necessarily the case, but presumably it would have been written before Curry's memory had irrevocably faded.

Text MF (attr. 'Dumbar'). Also found in R.   10 com he in] com in MF

AS YUNG AWRORA WITH
CRISTALL HAILE

(*The Abbot of Tungland*)

The title sometimes given to this poem, 'The Fenyeit Freir of Tungland', is derived from the descriptive titles in the Bannatyne and the Asloan MSS – although the title given in Asloan's table of contents, 'a ballat of the abbot of Tungland', accords better with the poem, which calls the central figure a 'newly made canon' (53), and with a reference to him in another poem of Dunbar's as an 'abbot' whose flying above the moon is a premonition of Antichrist. He is identifiable as John Damian, who was made abbot of Tongland (a house of Premonstratensian canons) in Galloway in 1504, an Italian or French physician and alchemist who enjoyed the patronage of the king. The only other mention of his ill-fated attempt at flight comes from Bishop Leslie *c.*1570, who says that he tried to fly from the castle wall at Stirling and fell to the ground, breaking his thigh. Whatever the truth of the incident, Dunbar has made it into a fantastic dream-vision, making his 'abbot' into a murderous Eastern charlatan, and satirically describing his medical and alchemical practices and his flight with hyperbolic glee and fanciful comparisons: Daedalus (65), the creator of the Labyrinth, made wings for himself and his son Icarus in order to escape from the Minotaur, but Icarus fell and drowned; Vulcan a fire-god and smith (also hurled down from the heavens); Saturn's cook (not a mythological figure) is perhaps blackened by smoke like an alchemist – Saturn, when malevolent, is associated with pestilence and destructive melancholy, wild places, and graves. This is followed by a vivid account of his 'mobbing' by the birds who take him to be an owl (74) – a scene of satirical disorder reminiscent of Kennedy's pursuit through the streets of Edinburgh ('The Flyting of Dunbar and Kennedy', 97ff.).

The abrupt ending is a dark echo of the end of Chaucer's *Parliament of Fowls*, made by Dunbar into an unnatural and apocalyptic scene with a nightmarish quality worthy of Hitchcock's film *The Birds*.

Text B (attr. 'Dumbar'). Also found in A (lines 1–69 only).
9 till] A to B   **63** fowlis] A fowill B

THIS HYNDIR NYCHT IN DUMFERMLING

The title given to this poem in the Bannatyne MS, 'the Wowing of the King quhen he wes in Dumfermeling', is not supported by any other evidence apart from the reputation of James IV. It may be a complete invention, but possibly some actual court scandal lies behind it. The pointed reference to Dunfermline suggests an allusion to Henryson, though the 'ferlie cace' described by Dunbar is strikingly different from Henryson's fables. Its ending is not altogether clear, and has been interpreted differently. Do lines 59–61 imply that the sheep has been killed and its skin has been removed and is being used by the fox as a disguise, or are they crudely sexual – the fox has taken refuge as far as he can in the living body of the sheep?

Text MF. Also found in B (attr. 'Dumbar') and R.
20 him (2)] MF hir B   **27** preissit neir] MF schup nevir B [in 20 and 27 I have retained the MF variants because they may be taken to show a cynicism in keeping with the treatment of the fable]   **37** he] B hes MF   **38** swoir] B sweir MF   **65** went] B wont MF   **66** tod] B bell MF

IN SECREIT PLACE THIS HYNDIR NYCHT

The poet overhears a comic and often bawdy wooing scene. Similar Scottish poems are found in the Bannatyne MS. Henryson's *Robene and Makyne* is in some ways similar. Terms associated with courtly love ('luifar leill', 'danger') quickly give way to more rustic terms of endearment and naked desire. The language is full of *double entendre* and sexual *joie de vivre*: the precise meaning of many of the words remains uncertain (e.g. the obscure 'brylyoun' (44) may be a word for the female pudendum (Kinsley) or (Bawcutt) an error for 'rylyoun' the rough hide shoe of peasants).

Text MF (attr. 'Dunbar'). Also found in B and R.   33 hals] B heylis MF

APON THE MIDSUMMER EVIN, MIRRIEST OF NICHTIS

(*The Tretis of the Twa Mariit Wemen and the Wedo*)

This is Dunbar's longest poem. It is also notable as a late example of the long tradition of poetry written in unrhymed alliterative lines. It makes use of a number of literary conventions in a strikingly individual way. As in the medieval *chanson d'aventure*, the poet goes out and overhears a conversation or a lament – sometimes a *chanson de mal mariée* in which a wife or wives complain about their husbands. What he overhears in this case is table talk of an uninhibited kind as the cup passes round. It is related to the literary kind known as the 'gossips meeting', in which wives and their friends sit and drink and talk. Skelton's *The Tunnyng of Elynour Rummynge* is a particularly boisterous example. *The Tretis* is on a more intimate scale but is just as vivacious – in talk rather than in action. The recital of the inadequacies of husbands and of the 'wo that is in mariage' clearly owes much to the eloquent monologue of Chaucer's Wife of Bath. But the 'autobiographical' narrative is placed within a framework of discussion instigated by the widow's questions (lines 41–8), and the whole poem is rounded off by a question from the poet to the audience that sounds like an ironic variant of the courtly *demande d'amour*. Ironic contrasts run throughout: the three ladies are placed in a *locus amoenus*, a landscape of extraordinary beauty (which is matched by their own exquisite appearance, including the golden hair and the soft white faces and fingers conventionally attributed to ideals of feminine beauty) but the matter and the language of their discourse are far from courtly. Readers often differ in their estimate of the final effect this has. Some see the poem as a joyous endorsement of the women's views, others as satirical and deeply antifeminist. While it is true that the women do reveal those traits that medieval antifeminist writers thought were an essential part of women's nature, the treatment of the wiles of women and the folly of men seems evenhanded, or, at least, equally outrageous. Perhaps, like other poems of Dunbar's, it has some bitter and uneasy undertones, but there is a strong element of burlesque exaggeration. The setting has a hint of fairyland – the fine long midsummer night, the magic hawthorn tree, the green mantles of the ladies – forming a marvellous setting for a strange event. (Dunbar perhaps found hints for this in Chaucer: momentarily in the scene in *The Wife of Bath's Tale* when the ladies dancing 'under a forest side' suddenly vanish, leaving only the ugly old hag (who answers the question about what women most desire), or in January's garden in *The Merchant's Tale*, where the king and queen of 'fayerye' disport themselves – and discuss the nature of women.) But more important is what C. S. Lewis called the 'sheer preposterousness' of the poem, an exaggerated and exuberant display of 'misrule' appropriate to the midsummer festival with its licence and carnival spirit.

The language, a heady mixture of alliterative formulae and colloquial diction, makes this one of Dunbar's most difficult poems. A number of the abusive terms remain obscure: for instance, 'forky fure' (85), where 'fure' might mean 'man, fellow' and 'forky' 'strong, powerful' or something more like 'lusty' – or, since there is a word 'fure' meaning 'furrow', perhaps 'one who "forks" a furrow'?; 'scutarde' (92), which might be from the verb 'scout', 'shoot, spurt' with a derogatory *-ard* ending, or connected with a nickname for a hare, 'scotard' (cf. 'scut', a short erect tail); or 'smolet' (113), which, it has been suggested, may be a form of the later Scottish dialect word 'smowt', 'little fellow' used derisively of the husband's penis. The syntax too can sometimes be contorted (e.g. lines 196–8).

Text lines 1–103 MF (which contains complete text, attr. 'Maister William Dunbar') and 104–end P (incomplete). L. rubrics from MF. Parts of MF are now faded at the edges and are difficult to read.
2 till ane] *em.* Burrow allane MF   **36** thir wlonkes wycht] MF here is very faded. The STS edn (1919) recorded 'thir fair wlonkes with' [editors have normally omitted 'with']. Burrow (1977) says that there is no room for 'fair', 'thir' being apparently followed by a deletion, and emends to 'whit' ('white'). But Dunbar's form of this word is 'quhit' or 'quhyt' (as 25), which is less likely to alliterate with *w-*. The first part of the line is now virtually illegible, but 'wyt' or 'wyt' can be seen. This could be an abbreviation for 'wyth' or 'wycht'. The latter makes good sense and I suggest it as an emendation and even perhaps as a reading   **66** feiris] freiris MF   **157** suth] MF south P   **184** semys] MF sunnys P   **196** segis] MF sege P   **275** krych] keyth P claw MF   **421** I] MF *om.* P   **451** wemen] MF men P   **480** rownis] MF rowis P

QUHY WILL YE, MERCHANTIS OF RENOUN

This vehement complaint to the merchants (the term included both wealthy traders and shopkeepers) to reform and clean up the burgh gives us, as part of its satiric design to shame them into action, some vivid evocations of Edinburgh. The habit of throwing fish and meat trimmings into the street was the subject of burgh edicts – (1505) to cleanse the High Street 'of all maner of muk, filth of fische and flesche' and to forbid the furriers and skinners hanging skins on the outside stairs ('foirstairis'). Appropriately enough, the references are very local and precise: the 'Stinkand Stull' (15) or 'Styll' (38) refers (Bawcutt) to a 'style' or passage in a high tenement next to the parish church (16). The 'hie Croce' (22) is the Market Cross, northeast of the church, the central point of the town, from which proclamations were made, and the Trone (24) is the public weighing-house. These, Dunbar laments, are surrounded by common food for common folk ('Jok and Jame'). The town minstrels seem able to play only two tunes (30), apparently popular songs. The following lines are clearly critical (as in the remarks on the worthless 'servitouris' of the king in 'Schir, ye have mony servitouris'), but not easily interpreted. 'Sanct Cloun' (31) is mysterious: Kinsley suggests Cluanus, a sixth-century Irish abbot apparently associated with eating and drinking; 'St Clown' (Bawcutt) would make excellent sense (it would be the first attested record of the word).

Text R (attr. 'Dumbar').   **15** Stull] scull altered from stull R   **17** foirstairis] foirstair R   **25** Jame] James R   **37** streittis] streit R   **67** proclame] proclameid R   **77** recover] *om.* R [editorial suggestions include 'win bak to', 'restore to', 'reconquis'].

SWEIT ROIS OF VERTEW AND OF GENTILNES

An elegant courtly lyric addressed to a beautiful lady who has all the virtues except mercy. The topic and the love-allegory (the garden as the lady's heart) are traditional. This kind of lyric presents the lover's feelings in an indirect and polite manner, and offers to the lady a pleasing artefact.

Text MF (attr. 'Dumbar').

RYGHT AS THE STERN OF DAY
BEGOUTH TO SCHYNE

(*The Goldyn Targe*)

Dunbar's elaborate, ornate, and intricately fashioned allegorical dream-poem has sometimes been criticized by modern readers for its artificiality and for the thinness or insubstantiality of its central 'plot'. Both charges seem misguided. It is deliberately, and triumphantly, artificial – one of Dunbar's most brilliant displays of stylistic virtuosity, with aureate words like 'matutyne' set against the simplest diction ('The skyes rang for schoutyng of the larkis'). The opening descriptive sequence presents nature in terms of art ('Apparalit', 'Anamalit', 'Ourgilt', etc.) and creates a landscape bathed in the most extraordinary light, a setting appropriate for the arrival of the wonderful ship with its white sail and golden top-castle. What follows is not a profound exploration of the paradoxical nature of love, but a wittily told 'aventure', a mixture of courtly game and mythological masque. The hundred ladies who disembark include a number of goddesses, and are followed by another 'court' of gods, dressed in green for the Maying, and singing, playing instruments, and dancing. There is a touch of satire in the 'variand luke' of the god of winds, 'rycht lyke a lord unstable', and of the uncanny fairy world in Pluto, 'the elrich incubus' who had carried off Proserpina. Two versions of the text include among the goddesses a curious interloper 'Appollo' (75). This is surely an error, since Dunbar elsewhere associates Apollo with the sun, and presumably knew that he was the sun-god. Kinsley's suggestion that the name should be taken with Juno as an appellative, 'Juno goddess of the sky', is not convincing; Bawcutt's that it may be a mistake for a supposed goddess Apolleine is more likely. I would suggest that the Maitland Folio's reading 'appello' may represent the word 'appell*our*' with the abbreviation sign omitted. 'One who makes accusations' is a reasonable epithet for Juno as she appears in Ovid's *Metamorphoses* (see, for instance, her speeches against Callisto (Book ii) and Ino (Book iv)). When the dreamer is discovered by Venus, her attendants – personified female qualities from the world of the *Roman de la Rose* – are set upon him like a band of Amazons. This 'wonder lusty bikkir' is described with delight and wit. His doughty defender Reason with his golden targe is overcome only by rather unchivalric means, when Perilouse Presence ('that mony syre has slayn') throws a powder in his eyes which blinds him ('eyes' and 'looks' recur throughout the narrative). The suffering of the dreamer, now a 'wofull prisonnere' of Beautee, brings him to his lowest point when Departing delivers him to Hevynesse (or melancholy). At this moment suddenly and mysteriously the scene vanishes, and the ship sails off, firing its cannon (238–40) – we are really in the world of gunpowder and Mons Meg here: the earlier 'artilye' (179) of the ladies consisted of arrows. This very self-consciously literary poem, with rhetorical disclaimers (64–72) and echoes of Chaucer (e.g. 20), concludes with an elaborately modest apology and a celebration of the earlier poets Chaucer, Gower (the author of the *Confessio Amantis* – the adjective 'moral' is Chaucer's) and the early fifteenth-century monk-poet John Lydgate, whose voluminous works include an allegorical love-vision, *The Temple of Glass*. By this time the linking of the three (a kind of early 'canon') had become traditional. Dunbar appropriately singles out their rhetorical skills for special praise, before urging (very eloquently) his own poor poem to be humble and ashamed.

Text CM. Also found in B and MF (all three attribute it to Dunbar, and call it 'The Goldyn Targe').
19 hoppis] B, MF happis CM   75 appellour] appello MF Appollo CM, B   140 bowis] B, MF lowis CM   187 anker] B, MF ankers CM   201 assayit] B, MF assayes CM   203 Quhill] B, MF quhilk CM   228 tuke] B, MF take CM   231 toschuke] B, MF toschake CM   254 ane] and CM, B, MF   274 hes spent] B may spent CM may spend MF

QUHEN MERCHE WES WITH VARIAND WINDIS PAST

(*The Thrissill and the Rois*)

The title is a modern one, given by Allan Ramsay (*The Ever Green*, 1724), but it is an appropriate one, since the poem is clearly connected with a particular occasion, the marriage of the king, James IV, to Margaret Tudor, the daughter of Henry VII of England. This was celebrated with great ceremony in Edinburgh on 8 August 1503. A surviving account by the English herald John Young describes the pageants arranged along the route of the royal entry: as the royal couple passed under the last gate they could see a heraldic device – a unicorn (a badge of James IV) and a greyhound (a Tudor badge) holding a thistle and a red rose interlaced, a symbol of union and harmony. Dunbar uses similar heraldic imagery – the rose 'of cullour reid and quhyt' (perhaps an allusion to the Tudor particoloured rose) and the Lion, Eagle, and Thistle (giving the Scottish king a prominence which accords with the part he played in the entry). The central stanza of the poem (92–8) describes the royal arms of Scotland. The specific date of 9 May given in the final line may be the date of the actual composition of the poem in 1503, but it is as likely that it is the traditional May setting of love-visions, or (Bawcutt) that 9 May had particular associations (it was the feast of the Translation of St Andrew and was traditionally regarded as the beginning of summer). As in *The Goldyn Targe*, Dunbar uses traditional motifs and imagery. There are a number of deliberate echoes of Chaucer's *Parliament of Fowls* – e.g. the 'parliament' of birds, and the awakening of the dreamer by their noise. Although the *Parliament* is sometimes thought to have been written for a royal wedding or betrothal, it is much more than an 'occasional' poem, a wide-ranging philosophical work which investigates the place of love in nature and society. *The Thrissill and the Rois* is on a much smaller scale, but adapts a number of Chaucer's ideas to the royal marriage. Dame Nature, who in Chaucer presides over the birds' choosing of their mates, and is, as God's 'vicar', responsible for plenitude and the continuation of life in all its individual species, reappears here as a spokesman and a powerful spiritual presence watching over the marriage (issuing – as in an epithalamium – a command to the elements to be calm and benign). Just as Dunbar makes the language of the love-vision more ceremonious (the 'purpour' sun – with its classical and imperial resonances) or more formally heraldic (the 'feild of gold' on which the royal lion stands), so he adapts Chaucer's material: Nature here summons a threefold parliament, of 'beist and bird and flour'. With her great authority she gives the king (Lion, Eagle, and Thistle respectively) solemn advice: 'Exerce justice with mercy and conscience', quoting the same Latin motto that Henryson alluded to in his *Fables* (line 930). Justice must be dealt impartially to small as well as great, to those less beautiful as well as those with bright colours or appearance – 'be als just to awppis and owlis / As unto pacokkis, papingais or crennis' (122–3; here 'awppis' are almost certainly not 'bullfinches' (Kinsley), but 'curlews' (Bawcutt) – modern Scots dialect *awp* or *whaup*, usually recorded in older Scots as *quhap*). In the 'garden of the realm' ruled over by the Thistle king, the virtue (73) – medicinal or magical – of the planets becomes moral virtue (135), and the advice becomes direct: 'sen thow art a king, thow be discreit . . .' It is likely that the following lines allude to the king's fondness for a number of mistresses. Nature's words on the perfection of the Rose (144ff.) are both a eulogy of the new queen and a statement of medieval horticultural–symbolical opinion: an earlier encyclopedia by Bartholomew the Englishman says that 'among all the flowers of the world the flower of the rose is chief and beareth the prize'; roses 'by fairness feed the sight, and please the smell by odour, and the touch by soft handling, and by their "virtue" withstand and succour many sicknesses and evils'. The songs of praise by flowers and birds complete and celebrate Nature's blessing on the union.

Text B (attr. 'Dumbar').   **45** festely] hestely B [in 45–6 B's 'full hestely besene' and 'full haistely' sound suspiciously repetitive. Editors deal with the problem by substituting 'weill' for 'hestely' or 'eftir hir' for 'full haistely'. Perhaps 'hestely' is an error (occasioned by the 'haistely' in the following line) for 'festely' (*OED* 'feastly'), i.e. the dreamer in festive mood (or guise) hurries out]   67 nor no] nor B   119 parcere] proceir B

ILLUSTER LODOVICK, OF FRANCE MOST CRISTIN KING

(*Lament for Lord Bernard Stewart*)

Lord Bernard Stewart of Aubigny was a famous Scottish general in the service of the king of France (at the time of his death, Louis XII), who had fought with distinction in the French invasions of Italy at the end of the fifteenth and the beginning of the sixteenth centuries. He came to Scotland in May 1508 on a mission, and his visit was the occasion of a panegyric ballade by Dunbar, which was printed by Chepman and Myllar. He died in Scotland on 11 June of that year, and this poem of Dunbar's must have been composed shortly afterwards. It is an example of the formal rhetorical lament or *déploration* common in late medieval literature.

Text R (attr. 'Dumbar').

QUHAT IS THIS LYFE BOT ANE STRAUCHT WAY TO DEID?

'Vita nostra brevis est', the idea that our life is brief and is but a journey to death is an ancient one ('the whole of life is nothing but a journey to death' says Seneca), and a favourite with medieval moral poets. This poem of Dunbar's presents a series of definitions (cf. Henryson's lines on love in *Orpheus and Eurydice*). The mnemonic potential of such verses was realized by preachers, who used and expanded them in sermons. Thus, in one example, the heading 'Mors' ('Death') is followed by four images ('A lyoun raunpand wit his powe / An ape making a mowe / A scriveyn [scribe] writing on a scrowe [scroll] / An archer drawing in his bowe').

Text MF (attr. 'Dumbar'). Also found in B.

QUHOM TO SALL I COMPLEINE MY WO

This poem begins as a lament on the wicked state of the world of the kind which Dunbar elsewhere uses to introduce a petition, but the tone becomes increasingly sombre and apocalyptic, with echoes of the Bible and the liturgy, and concludes with a prayer for a heavenly reward rather than an earthly one. The language is sharp and vigorous. Occasionally the syntax is ambiguous, as in line 21, or, more seriously, in line 56, where it is not clear what 'this' refers to. It might refer back to lines 52–3, i.e. 'it is only death who makes this demand abruptly'; or, with generally similar meaning, 'thus'; or (Bawcutt) look forward to the untrustworthy world of lines 57–9, i.e. '(which) in short, demands nothing (no other end?) but death'. Perhaps the scribal 'schortlie/schortly' is an error for 'schort life/lyfe', i.e. ?'this short life (subject to hostile fortune) craves (or begs for) nothing but death'.

Text MF (attr. 'Dumbar'). Also found in B and R.
9 bigone] B bigane MF   **40** this] B the MF   **54** than] B *om.* MF   **62** the gold gatherit] B gadderit gold MF   **81** in] B the MF

INTO THIR DIRK AND DRUBLIE DAYIS

Sometimes called 'Meditatioun in Winter' or 'In Winter', this is one of Dunbar's more personal and subtle poems on the instability of life and the fear of death. The gloomy weather parallels and occasions the poet's melancholy (cf. the opening of Henryson's *Testament*): in his tormented sleeplessness he is 'assailed' by suggestions from Despair, Patience, Prudence, Age, and Death. Age speaks gently but firmly ('Cum, brodir, by the hand me tak'); Death is abrupt in action and in speech. The poem ends on a tentative and hesitant note, with melancholy only partially assuaged.

Text MF (attr. 'Dumbar'). Also found in R.

I THAT IN HEILL WES AND GLADNES

(*The Lament for the Makars*)

The poem 'I that in heill wes' (its usual title comes only from the eighteenth century) was probably written in late 1505 or early 1506, because Stobo, who was dead by 13 July 1505, is apparently only recently dead ('last of aw', line

85). Its haunting refrain '*Timor mortis conturbat me*' (a response from the Office for the Dead, which had previously been used in some fifteenth-century English poems and carols) would in fact be a better modern title, since the poem is a meditation on death, both general and personal (framed by the poet's sickness). It uses a number of themes common in medieval 'mortality' literature – the suddenness and inevitability of Death's coming, and his levelling power. It is often related to the Dance of Death, which is the best-known example of the late medieval 'macabre' tradition, but some caution is necessary. The idea that all estates are taken off by death without mercy is also found in other poems on death (such as that which begins 'Vado mori' or 'I wend to death'). And Dunbar makes no reference to the distinctive 'dance' in which Death leads his victims off. His poem has touches of the grim irony of the macabre tradition ('Thame helpis no conclusionis sle') and it ends on a note of resignation and a call to make ready for Death's coming. Yet the catalogue of the poets whom Death has taken, moving though it is, is not simply a 'lament' – although the records have forgotten many of them, Dunbar's poem has rescued them (his 'brothers') from oblivion. That the famous dead are poets is a testimony to Dunbar's sense of the importance of the poetic calling.

The list (50ff.) is headed by the three English poets invoked at the end of *The Goldyn Targe* – Chaucer (d.1400), John Lydgate (d.1449), a monk of Bury St Edmunds, and John Gower (d.1408). Of the Scottish writers a number cannot be identified. Of the following something is, or may be, known: Hew of Eglintoun (53) is perhaps Sir Hugh Eglinton of that Ilk (d.1377), though none of his writings survive; Andrew Wyntoun (54), the prior of Lochleven (d.1425), wrote a vernacular verse chronicle, *The Oryginalle Chronykill of Scotland*; Maister (i.e. a university graduate) Johne Clerk (58) is not certainly identified (some poems in the Bannatyne MS are attributed to 'Clerk', but in a later hand; an English poet 'Master John Clerk' seems an unlikely candidate for the list in 'this cuntré' of Scotland), nor has James Afflek or Auchinlek (though a James Auchinleck is recorded, d. by 1492); Richard Holland (61), the author of *The Buke of the Howlat* (?1448); John Barbour (d.1395), the author of *The Bruce*; Mungo Lokert (63), probably the knight Sir Mungo Lockhart of the Lee (d.by 1489), but no works of his survive; Clerk of Tranent, a small town near Edinburgh is unidentified, as is his work; Gilbert Hay (?d.before 1470), perhaps the author of the romance *The Buik of Alexander the Conquerour* (?1460) and the translator of *The Buke of the Law of Armys* and other treatises, spent many years in the service of the French king; Blind Hary (69) wrote *The Wallace* (c.1475–8), but little is known of his life; Patrick Johnston (d.1495), a notary and land-owner, produced court entertainments 1476–89; Merseir (73), who receives special praise, is not certainly identified – Lindsay mentions a poet of that name, and three poems in the Bannatyne MS are attributed to a 'Mersar'; neither Roull (77–8) is identifiable – *The*

Cursing of Sir Johine Rowlis in the Bannatyne MS may well be the work of one; Henryson, the poet of Dunfermline; Sir John the Ross, a friend of Dunbar's mentioned in *The Flyting*, may be Sir John Ross of Mountgrenan (d.1494) or Sir John Ross of Halkhead (d.before 1502), but neither is known as a poet; Stobo (86), the name of John Reid (who was perhaps born there), a secretary of the king's and rector of Kirkcrist; Quintyne Schaw, another of the king's servitors – a satire on court life is attributed to him in the Maitland Folio MS; Walter Kennedy (89–91), author of a number of religious and moral poems, and the opponent of Dunbar in *The Flyting*.

Text P (with minor misprints silently corrected). Also found in B and MF. Attr. 'Dumbar' in both MSS, and in the print to 'Dunbar quhen he wes sek'. **26** Takis] B; *text* tak   **71** fle] B, MF *om.* P

FULL OFT I MUS AND HES IN THOCHT

This poem with its proverbial sounding refrain counsels a (somewhat) cheerful detachment from the world's adversities.

Text B (attr. 'Dunbar'). Also found in MF and R.   **8** it] MF *om.* B   **11** man] MF men B

LIST OF SOME COMMON WORDS
AND FORMS

abak *backwards*
aboif, abone, abufe *above*
agane, aganis *again, against*
air *previously, early*
ald *old*
alkin *every kind of*
allace *alas*
allane *alone*
almaist *almost*
als *also; as*
amang, amangis *among*
and *and, if*
ane *a, an, one*
aneuch, an(n)ewch(e) *enough*
anis *once*
anone *quickly*
apon(e) *upon, on*
ar *are*
at(t)our(e), at(t)ouir *over*
auld *old*
awalk *awake*
awin *own*
ay *always, ever*

bair *bore; bare; boar*
baith, bayth *both*
be *by, when*
befoir *before*
begouth, begowthe *began*
behald *behold*
beir *bear, carry*
bene *be, is, are*
beseik *beseech*
betwene *between*

betuix, betwix *between*
bewtie, bewty *beauty*
blenk(is) *glance(s), look(s)*
blith, blyith *happy*
blud(e), bluid *blood*
bot *but, only, without*
bricht, brycht *bright*
brocht *brought*
but(e) *but, without*

cair *sorrow*
cald *cold*
can *can, did*
cauld *cold*
ce(i)s *cease*
cheir, chere *countenance, bearing,*
    mood
cleir, clere *clear, bright*
come *came*
couth, culd *could, knew how to, did*
cum, cummis *come, comes*

de(e) *die*
deid *deed*
deid, dede *death, dead*
deir, dere *dear*
deit *died*
deith *death*
dois *does, do*
doun *down*
dout *fear, dread*
dreid, drede *fear*
dule *grief, sorrow*
dure *door*

e, ee *eye*
efter, eftir *after*
eik *also*
eir, eiris *ear, ears*
eird, eirth *earth*
eirdlie *earthly*
ellis *else, besides, otherwise*
ene *eyes*
erd(e), erthe *earth*
erdly, erthly *earthly*
eris *ears*
everilk *every*
evir, ewir *ever*

fa *foe*
fane *glad, pleased; gladly*
fang *take*
feild *field*
fer *far*
fle *flee, fly*
flour(e), flouris, flowris *flower,*
         flowers
flud(e) *flood, water, river sea*
foulis, fowlis *birds*
fra *from*
fre *noble, generous, free;*
fresch(e) *fresh, lovely*
fro *from*
fude *food*
fule, fulis *fool, fools*
furth *forward, forth*
fut(e) *foot*

ga *go*
gaif *gave*
gais *goes*
gan *did*
gane *gone*
gang *go, walk*
gar *cause (to) make;* gart *caused*
gentil(l) *noble, courteous, gracious*
gentrice *nobility*

gevin *given*
gif(f) *if; give*
greit, gret(e), grit *great, large*
gud(e) *good;* gud(e)lie *goodly*

haif *have*
haill *whole, wholly*
hairt *heart*
hald, hauld *hold*
haly, halie *holy*
hame *home*
hard *heard*
hart *heart*
he, heich *high, loud*
heid *head*
heill *whole, wholly*
heir *here; hear*
hert *heart*
hes *has, have*
hevin *heaven*
hew *hue, colour*
hicht *height*
hie *high, loud*
hir *her*

ilk *same*
ilk, ilka *each, every*
into *in, within*

jolie, joly *pretty, handsome, joyful*

keip *keep*
ken *know, perceive, teach*
kest *cast*
knaw(e) *know*
knicht, knycht *knight*
kynd(e) *nature, species*

laif *rest, others*
lang *long*
lap *leapt, capered*
lat(t), let(t) *let, allow; prevent*

lauch *laugh*

law *low*

le *tell lies*

leif *leave; live*

leill *loyal, faithful, true*

leir *learn*

leit *allowed*

lele *loyal, faithful, true*

leuch, lewch *laughed*

licht *light*

list *desire, choose, please*

luf(e), luif, luve *love*

luke, luik *look, appearance; look, observe, consider*

lycht *light*

lyk(e) *like*

ma, mare *more*

maist *most*

maister, maistir *master*

mak *make*

man *must*

mair *more*

meit *meet*

mekill, meikill, mekle *much, great*

micht *might*

mo *more*

moder, modir *mother*

moir *more*

mon(e) *must*

mony *many*

mot *may*

mycht *might*

na *no, nor, than*

nan(e) *no, none*

nathing *nothing; not at all*

neid *need*

neir *near, nearly*

nicht *night*

nocht *not, nothing*

nor *nor; than*

nothair *neither*

no(u)ther, nouthir *neither*

noucht, nought *not, nothing*

nowder, nowdir, nowther, nowthir *neither*

nycht *night*

ocht *anything*

off *of*

oftymis *often*

one *in*

ony *any*

or *or; before*

o(u)thir *other*

our *over, throughout*

owther, owthir *either*

pane *pain, suffering, grief; penalty*

peté, pietie, pitee *pity, compassion, duty*

plesand, plesant *pleasing, pleasant*

price, pryce, pryis *price, value, money; honour, praise*

quha *who*

quhair *where*

quhais *whose*

quham(e) *whom, that*

quhar(e) *where*

quhat *what*

quhen *when*

quhether *whether*

quhilk *which, who, that*

quhill *until, while, as long as*

quhit(e), quhitt, quhyt(e) *white*

quhom(e) *whom*

quhow *how*

quhy *why*

quod *said*

reid, rede *counsel, advise; advice*

resso(u)n(e) *reason, statement*

riale, riall *royal*
richt *right, very*
rin *run*
ring *reign*
ryall *royal*
rycht *right, very; that which is just*
ryn *run*

sa *so*
sair *sore, grievous, sorely, grievously*
sall *shall*
sam *same*
sarie, sary *sorry, wretched, lamentable*
schaw *show; wood*
schene *beautiful, bright*
schir *sir*
scho *she*
se *see; sea*
seik *seek, search*
selie, sely *poor, hapless, innocent*
sen *since*
sic, sik *such, thus*
sicht *sight, glimpse, look; sigh*
sil(l)ie *poor, hapless, innocent*
sla *slay*
slane *slain,* soir *sore, grievous; sorely, grievously*
somer *summer*
sone *son; sun; soon*
sould *should*
speid *prosper, hasten*
spreit *spirit, soul*
stern *star*
sua *so*
sueit *sweet*
suld *should*
sum *some, one*
suppois *although*
suth *truth*
swa *so, thus*
sweit *sweet; sweat*

syn(e) *then*

ta, tak, taik *take;* tane *taken*
thai, thay *they, those;* thaim *them*
thair *their; there*
thairfoir *therefore*
thame *them*
than *then*
the *thee*
think, thinkis *seem, seems*
thir *these*
tho(u)cht *(al)though; thought; melancholy*
thow *thou*
throw *through*
till *to, till, until*
togidder *together*
tother *the other*
trew *true, faithful*
tua *two*
tuik, tuke *took*
twa, tway *two*

udir, uther, uthir *other*

verray *true, very*

wa *woe, misery*
wait *know, knows*
wald *would, wished*
walk, walkin *wake, awake*
war *were; worse*
warld *world*
weill, wele *well*
wene *expect, think*
wes *was*
wirk *work, make*
with that *thereupon, at that*
wrang *wrong*
wrocht *wrought, made*

yeid *went*

ying *young*

yit *yet*

yon(e) *yon, that*

FIRST LINES AND TITLES

Ane cok sum tyme with feddram fresch and gay, 53
Ane cruell wolff, richt ravenous and fell, 187
Ane doolie sessoun to ane cairfull dyte 10
The Annunciation 211
Apon the midsummer evin, mirriest of nichtis, 282
Apon the midsummer evin, mirriest of nichtis, 282
As yung Awrora with cristall haile (The Abbot of Tungland) 267
As yung Awrora with cristall haile 267

Cock and the Fox, The 70
Cock and the Jasp, The 53

Done is a battell on the dragon blak 220
Done is a battell on the dragon blak 220

Esope ane taill puttis in memorie 110
Esope, myne authour, makis mentioun 58

Flyting of Dunbar and Kennedy, The 249
Forcy as deith is likand lufe, 211
Fox and the Wolf, The 81
Fox, the Wolf, and the Cadger, The 151
Fox, the Wolf, and the Husbandman, The 166
Full oft I mus and hes in thocht 357
Full oft I mus and hes in thocht 357

Hale, sterne superne 223
Hale, sterne superne, hale, in eterne, 223

I that in heill wes and gladnes 351
I that in heill wes and gladnes 351
... I will tell how Orpheus tuke the way 41
Iersche brybour baird, vyle beggar with thy brattis, 249
Illuster Lodovick, of France most Cristin king 340
Illuster Lodovick, of France most Cristin king, 340

In elderis dayis, as Esope can declair, 166
In middis of June, that sweit seasoun, 119
In secreit place this hyndir nycht 278
In secreit place this hyndir nycht 278
Into thir dirk and drublie dayis 348
Into thir dirk and drublie dayis 348

Leif we this wedow glaid, I yow assure, 81
Lion and the Mouse, The 119

My heid did yak yester nicht 227
My heid did yak yester nicht, 227

Now lythis off ane gentill knycht 264
Now lythis off ane gentill knycht, 264

O gracious Princes, guid and fair 233
O gracious Princes, guid and fair, 233
'O mortall man, behald, tak tent to me, 208
Orpheus and Eurydice 41

Paddock and the Mouse, The 196
Preaching of the Swallow, The 134
Prologue, The 50

Quhat is this lyfe bot ane straucht way to deid? 342
Quhat is this lyfe bot ane straucht way to deid? 342
Quhen Merche wes with variand windis past 330
Quhen Merche wes with variand windis past, 330
Quhom to sall I compleine my wo 330
Quhom to sall I compleine my wo 330
Quhy will ye, merchantis of renoun 310
Quhy will ye, merchantis of renoun, 310
Qwhylum thair wes, as Esope can report, 178
Qwhylum thair wynnit in ane wildernes,

Ressoning Betuix Deth and Man, The 208
Robene and Makyne 3
Robene sat on gud grene hill 3
Rorate Celi Desuper 217
Rorate, celi, desuper! 217
Ryght as the stern of day begouth to schyne 315
Ryght as the stern of day begouth to schyne 315

Schir, lat it never in toune be tald 241
Schir, lat it never in toune be tald 241
Schir, ye have mony servitouris 245
Schir, ye have mony servitouris 245
Sheep and the Dog, The 110
Sir Jhon Sinclair begowthe to dance 228
Sir Jhon Sinclair begowthe to dance 228
Sweit rois of vertew and of gentilnes, 314
Sweit rois of vertew and of gentilnes, 314

Testament of Cresseid, The 10
The hie prudence and wirking mervelous, 134
The wardraipper of Venus boure, 231
This foirsaid foxe that deit for his misdeid, 91
This hyndir nycht in Dumfermling 274
This hyndir nycht in Dumfermling 274
This waverand warldis wretchidnes, 235
This waverand warldis wretchidnes, 235
Thocht brutall beistis be irrationall, 70
Thocht feinyeit fabils of ald poetré 50
Trial of the Fox, The 91
Two Mice, The 58

Upon ane tyme, as Esope culd report, 196

Wardraipper of Venus boure, The 231
We that ar heir in hevynnis glorie 258
We that ar heir in hevynnis glorie 258
Wolf and the Lamb, The 387
Wolf and the Wether, The 178

READ MORE IN PENGUIN

In every corner of the world, on every subject under the sun, Penguin represents quality and variety – the very best in publishing today.

For complete information about books available from Penguin – including Puffins, Penguin Classics and Arkana – and how to order them, write to us at the appropriate address below. Please note that for copyright reasons the selection of books varies from country to country.

In the United Kingdom: Please write to *Dept. EP, Penguin Books Ltd, Bath Road, Harmondsworth, West Drayton, Middlesex UB7 ODA*

In the United States: Please write to *Consumer Sales, Penguin Putnam Inc., P.O. Box 999, Dept. 17109, Bergenfield, New Jersey 07621-0120.* VISA and MasterCard holders call 1-800-253-6476 to order Penguin titles

In Canada: Please write to *Penguin Books Canada Ltd, 10 Alcorn Avenue, Suite 300, Toronto, Ontario M4V 3B2*

In Australia: Please write to *Penguin Books Australia Ltd, P.O. Box 257, Ringwood, Victoria 3134*

In New Zealand: Please write to *Penguin Books (NZ) Ltd, Private Bag 102902, North Shore Mail Centre, Auckland 10*

In India: Please write to *Penguin Books India Pvt Ltd, 210 Chiranjiv Tower, 43 Nehru Place, New Delhi 110 019*

In the Netherlands: Please write to *Penguin Books Netherlands bv, Postbus 3507, NL-1001 AH Amsterdam*

In Germany: Please write to *Penguin Books Deutschland GmbH, Metzlerstrasse 26, 60594 Frankfurt am Main*

In Spain: Please write to *Penguin Books S. A., Bravo Murillo 19, 1° B, 28015 Madrid*

In Italy: Please write to *Penguin Italia s.r.l., Via Benedetto Croce 2, 20094 Corsico, Milano*

In France: Please write to *Penguin France, Le Carré Wilson, 62 rue Benjamin Baillaud, 31500 Toulouse*

In Japan: Please write to *Penguin Books Japan Ltd, Kaneko Building, 2-3-25 Koraku, Bunkyo-Ku, Tokyo 112*

In South Africa: Please write to *Penguin Books South Africa (Pty) Ltd, Private Bag X14, Parkview, 2122 Johannesburg*

READ MORE IN PENGUIN

A SELECTION OF POETRY

American Verse
British Poetry since 1945
Caribbean Verse in English
Chinese Love Poetry
A Choice of Comic and Curious Verse
Contemporary American Poetry
Contemporary British Poetry
Contemporary Irish Poetry
English Poetry 1918–60
English Romantic Verse
English Verse
First World War Poetry
German Verse
Greek Verse
Homosexual Verse
Imagist Poetry
Irish Verse
Japanese Verse
The Metaphysical Poets
Modern African Poetry
New Poetry
Poetry of the Thirties
Scottish Verse
Surrealist Poetry in English
Spanish Verse
Victorian Verse
Women Poets
Zen Poetry

READ MORE IN PENGUIN

A CHOICE OF CLASSICS

Anton Chekhov	**The Duel and Other Stories**
	The Kiss and Other Stories
	The Fiancée and Other Stories
	Lady with Lapdog and Other Stories
	The Party and Other Stories
	Plays (The Cherry Orchard/Ivanov/The Seagull/Uncle Vania/The Bear/The Proposal/A Jubilee/Three Sisters)
Fyodor Dostoyevsky	**The Brothers Karamazov**
	Crime and Punishment
	The Devils
	The Gambler/Bobok/A Nasty Story
	The House of the Dead
	The Idiot
	Netochka Nezvanova
	The Village of Stepanchikovo
	Notes from Underground/The Double
Nikolai Gogol	**Dead Souls**
	Diary of a Madman and Other Stories
Mikhail Lermontov	**A Hero of Our Time**
Alexander Pushkin	**Eugene Onegin**
	The Queen of Spades and Other Stories
Leo Tolstoy	**Anna Karenin**
	Childhood, Boyhood, Youth
	How Much Land Does a Man Need?
	The Kreutzer Sonata and Other Stories
	Master and Man and Other Stories
	Resurrection
	The Sebastopol Sketches
	What is Art?
	War and Peace
Ivan Turgenev	**Fathers and Sons**
	First Love
	A Month in the Country
	On the Eve
	Rudin
	Sketches from a Hunter's Album

READ MORE IN PENGUIN

A CHOICE OF CLASSICS

Hesiod/Theognis	**Theogony/Works and Days/Elegies**
Hippocrates	**Hippocratic Writings**
Homer	**The Iliad**
	The Odyssey
Horace	**Complete Odes and Epodes**
Horace/Persius	**Satires and Epistles**
Juvenal	**The Sixteen Satires**
Livy	**The Early History of Rome**
	Rome and Italy
	Rome and the Mediterranean
	The War with Hannibal
Lucretius	**On the Nature of the Universe**
Martial	**Epigrams**
Ovid	**The Erotic Poems**
	Heroides
	Metamorphoses
	The Poems of Exile
Pausanias	**Guide to Greece** (in two volumes)
Petronius/Seneca	**The Satyricon/The Apocolocyntosis**
Pindar	**The Odes**
Plato	**Early Socratic Dialogues**
	Gorgias
	The Last Days of Socrates (Euthyphro/ The Apology/Crito/Phaedo)
	The Laws
	Phaedrus and **Letters VII and VIII**
	Philebus
	Protagoras/Meno
	The Republic
	The Symposium
	Theaetetus
	Timaeus/Critias